SUBSTATE DICTATORSHIP

NETWORKS, LOYALTY, AND

INSTITUTIONAL CHANGE

IN THE SOVIET UNION

YORAM GORLIZKI AND
OLEG KHLEVNIUK

Hoover Institution
Stanford University
Stanford, California

Yale UNIVERSITY PRESS
New Haven and London

Some material from chapter 7 first appeared in "Scandal in Riazan: Networks of Trust and the Social Dynamics of Deception," *Kritika: Explorations in Russian and Eurasian History* 14 (2): 243–78, and is published here in revised form with the permission of *Slavica* publishers.

Some material from chapter 10 first appeared in "Too Much Trust: Regional Party Leaders and Political Networks under Brezhnev," *Slavic Review* 69 (3): 676–700, © Association for Slavic, East European, and Eurasian Studies, 2010, and is published here in revised form with the permission of Cambridge University Press.

Yale University Press books may be purchased in quantity for educational, business, or promotional use. For information, please e-mail sales.press@yale.edu (U.S. office) or sales@yaleup.co.uk (U.K. office).

Set in Sabon and Berthold City Bold types by Newgen North America.
Printed in the United States of America.

Library of Congress Control Number: 2019955507
ISBN 978-0-300-23081-9 (hardcover : alk. paper)

A catalogue record for this book is available from the British Library.

This paper meets the requirements of ANSI/NISO Z39.48-1992 (Permanence of Paper).

10 9 8 7 6 5 4 3 2 1

To Vera

Contents

A Note on Usage

The Soviet Union was a multiethnic and multilingual state. For most senior party officials who managed the Soviet regions Russian was the default language of official communication. As a rule we have transliterated from Russian the spellings of names and have used contemporary Russian place-names rather than the current non-Russian ones, so, for example, Lviv appears as L'vov and Moldova as Moldavia. At the same time, some of the non-Russian republics covered in the book saw the emergence of a proto-national movement which favored the use of local languages in informal and occasionally in public communications. Here the choice of which language to transliterate names from is a matter of judgment. In two cases, Latvia in the 1950s and Lithuania in the 1960s, we have, on balance, chosen to transliterate names from their spellings in the local languages. When transliterating from the Russian we have, with the exception of well-known names such as Beria, used the Library of Congress system of transliteration. Although for most Russian words we have retained the soft sign, in order to improve readability we have dropped the final soft sign from those words, such as *Riazan* and *oblast,* which appear in the text with particular frequency.

SUBSTATE DICTATORSHIP

Introduction

WHAT IS DICTATORSHIP and how does it work? How do countries move from one form of dictatorship to another? This book addresses these questions by looking at one of the most important dictatorships of the modern era, but it does so from a new perspective. Most studies of the personal dictatorship that formed in the Soviet Union from the 1930s center on the supreme leader, Joseph Stalin, and they do so for good reason. For over twenty years Stalin enjoyed unparalleled discretion over regime policy, over the selection of cadres, and over the statewide system of surveillance and repression. As important as he was, however, Stalin was not the only dictator in the Soviet Union, for he was joined at key pressure points by scores of substate dictators. These territorial leaders differed in important respects from the dictator in chief. For one thing they were susceptible, unlike Stalin, to control from above. Moreover, they rarely enjoyed the access he had to the means of repression. However, in significant ways they were also dictators in their own right. Each headed a territory, sometimes the size of a small European country, where for a few years and sometimes longer they controlled the levers of government; while in charge they often silenced critics, destroyed fellow leaders, and terrorized ordinary citizens.

The substate dictators with whom we begin this book were nested in Stalin's statewide dictatorship. Other modern political systems have authoritarian local bosses, but what sets the substate dictator apart is that he operates within the context of a central dictatorship.[1] Substate dictators and the local party machines they headed were not an incidental feature of the overarching dictatorship but an essential part of it, on which it was reliant for the promulgation of central policies and the management of local cadres. Stalin's dictatorship at the statewide level has received the lion's share of attention, but here we redress the balance by looking at the substate level, where most state policies were realized and put into effect.[2]

The book builds on a recent development in the theory of dictatorship: the distinction between the dictator's problem of controlling threats from the masses, the problem of authoritarian control—and his problem in dealing with threats from those with whom he shares power—the problem of authoritarian power sharing.[3] We suggest that the twofold challenge facing the supreme dictator was systematically replicated at the substate level, presenting the substate leader with three problems. The first involved controlling the ruling coalition at the regional level. At the statewide level Stalin himself faced a version of this problem. But while one of the main building blocks of Stalin's power was fear, based on straightforward repression, this strategy was not a luxury afforded to most substate leaders. Instead, they often had to work hard on winning over their colleagues. Most ended up subjugating their ruling group, but the strategies they adopted were necessarily more nuanced and conditional than Stalin's. Substate leaders then had to balance this problem with a second one: How could regional leaders prevent revolts by the masses? The comparison with Stalin is instructive here too. Recent research has shown that Stalin was surprisingly sensitive to a "revolution constraint" among urban workers: whenever his policies threatened to provoke worker revolts he tended to back down.[4] By the late Stalin era most territorial leaders were socially and geographically insulated from ordinary people and desensitized to their needs, but this did not mean they were completely unresponsive to demands from below. Substate rulers did face a popular constraint in the form of activists and district-level officeholders who could express, sometimes in a quite outspoken form, grievances, frustrations, and outright hostility at public gatherings.[5] Keeping this group on board was one of the substate leader's most pressing challenges.

The typical substate ruler needed to reconcile these two challenges with a third: meeting pressures from above. In the Soviet Union the demands bearing down on territorial party leaders were unrelenting, and it was in this area more than any other that the would-be substate dictator differed from Stalin. But control from above was mitigated by two factors. First, the center's patronage system in reality penetrated only a thin upper crust of regional appointments, leaving the rest at the disposal of the regional leader. Second, the center tended to refrain from intervening in regional conflicts. In general, Moscow was extremely wary of unseating a territorial party leader before his term was up. Doing so could have undesirable knock-on effects, such as destabilizing the regional elite and forcing Moscow to find a replacement from a small pool of candidates at short notice. For a fixed term, substate leaders tended to be left to their own devices.

The typical strategy for dealing with these three challenges was to set up a trust network. In Stalin's Soviet Union this was not always easy. Soviet organizational life was penetrated by informers and police spies, and most working relationships were blighted by suspicion and mistrust. Counting on anyone was fraught with risk. One possible solution to this problem, of relying on kinship groups, was usually blocked by the formal patronage system, the *nomenklatura*.[6] Nomenklatura rules also leaned against group transfers of cadres with shared career or life trajectories. Instead, substate leaders normally had to start up networks from scratch. The strategies they chose had something in common with group formation in other low-trust environments. The trick was to make followers structurally dependent, thereby creating a platform for longer-term loyalty.

Three principal strategies are described in this book. First, substate leaders could use their control of the regional party organization to inflict various gradations of exclusion, a classic instrument of network formation. This could range from informal exclusion, such as ostracism at party meetings, to party reprimands and expulsion from the party. A second strategy involved the deployment of classified information. Substate leaders could use incriminating materials, usually held in party files, as a lever against their colleagues. In some regions systematic use of sensitive information, or *kompromat,* was converted into a regular form of governance. In fact, the stock of ambient trust was often so low that possession of incriminating materials served, paradoxically, as one of the more reliable foundations of trust: sometimes only if you had "the goods" on someone could you truly count on them.[7] A third strategy was overpromotion. The Great Purges of the 1930s had cleared the upper echelons of many organizations, opening up vast opportunities for upward mobility. After the war substate leaders were still building on this precedent by elevating junior and underqualified officials over the heads of more senior and, often, more deserving colleagues, thereby stirring up the indignation of the whole organization. Many territorial leaders had a penchant for surrounding themselves with so-called clients of this kind, people who had little basis of support or respect other than their connection to the regional leader.

Institutionally, the party and its executive arm, the regional party apparatus, were well suited to the requirements of the substate leader, offering him key resources on the two planes on which he needed them most.[8] At the level of authoritarian power sharing the party bureaucracy was the main vehicle of exclusion and of kompromat at the regional level. Regional party leaders could inflict various forms of party punishment, up to and including expulsion from the party, and they could utilize the party's vast store of personnel files to intimidate potential rivals. The party was also the key channel of authoritarian control over the masses. As the principal agency of mobilization, the party apparatus was the main attack force for cajoling the rank and file and for implementing campaigns. In addition, regular shows of party "democracy" at regional party meetings were a helpful means of addressing popular opposition. The regional party organization was on the whole well adapted to answering the three challenges that lay before most substate leaders.[9]

DICTATORSHIP AND INSTITUTIONAL CHANGE

If one goal of the book is to understand how this dictatorship worked, another is to make sense of how it changed over time. While most of the literature on institutional change in dictatorship has focused on transitions from authoritarianism to democracy, a recent vein of scholarship has turned to explaining transitions among dictatorships.[10] The Soviet Union in the period we cover here is an example of a significant within-system shift in one important dictatorship. From the 1940s to the 1970s the country moved from being a repressive autocracy to an oligarchy with low to medium levels of repression. This raises a broader question: Why does an established autocracy, marked by an acute imbalance of power between the autocrat and those around him, turn into a contested autocracy, in which there is relative parity between the two?[11]

Most scholars working on this question tend to focus on the death or removal of the statewide autocrat. In the case of the Soviet Union it was, according to this view, the death of Stalin that prompted the institutional transition from one-person to collective rule, along with other changes such as the widening of the "selectorate," the body to which policy makers are held accountable.[12] In an earlier book we argued that some of the most important institutional changes at the summit of the system occurred while Stalin was still alive. We showed that these changes were driven by an act of delegation: namely, Stalin created a sphere he could control, the Politburo, and he delegated power to an institution, the Council of Ministers, in which he had no role. This act of delegation was provisional in that Stalin reserved the right to interfere with and reorganize the Council whenever he wished. At the same time, the act of delegation was real and fully institutionalized in that it was codified in a set of rules that key actors understood and followed. Although it may not have been Stalin's intention, it was the Council of Ministers that incubated the practices of autonomous, collective decision making which came to the fore when Stalin died.[13]

In this book we observe a similar process at work at the regional level. On a provisional basis, the dictator delegated power to his regional and republican principals. This act of delegation was provisional in that regional leaders' terms of office were fixed and in that the dictator was able, when he so wished, to dislodge any regional leader and attack his network.[14] At the same time, as was true of the Council of Ministers, the act of delegation was institutionalized. Whether or not it was the dictator's intention, the resulting institutional arrangements had consequences that would outlast him.

Why did Stalin delegate? In the 1930s the Soviet leadership created what was, by any standard, a highly centralized state, one in which resources were allocated from the center, party officials down to the lowest, district level were formally appointed from Moscow, and local cadres had to contend with frequent, centrally coordinated campaigns.

But this high degree of centralization presented Stalin with a problem, one that social scientists refer to as the problem of agency.[15] Agency theorists distinguish between formal authority or organizational structures and the distribution and flow of information. Although the dictator may sit atop an enormous authority structure, accurate information on the capacity and performance of frontline officials will usually be locked up below.[16] The problem for Stalin was that much of the most important information on the economy, on the system of administration, and on the progress of his most cherished campaigns was trapped at the lowest levels of the bureaucratic hierarchy. His dilemma was that the people he could control directly—the first secretaries of the regional party committees (the *obkoms*)—were not necessarily the ones who got things done on the ground. Worse still, on appointment many of these obkom secretaries lacked the local ties, the local authority, and the local knowledge they needed in order to implement the dictator's decisions.

Stalin's way around this problem was through delegation. In fact, delegation lay behind a number of key aspects of Soviet rule under Stalin, such as the policy of indigenization—the fostering of national elites, national languages, and national cultures—and Stalin's surprising willingness (as we shall see in this book) to let regional leaders cultivate their own patronage networks. So long as he did not sense a political threat in doing so, Stalin was a surprisingly disciplined delegator. Indeed, notwithstanding his morally repugnant regime, we shall suggest that Stalin may have had a better intuitive understanding of the agency problem and may have come up with a more internally consistent solution to it than any of his successors.

Stalin's acts of delegation were hedged in by various institutional safeguards, including the rotation of regional leaders, regional elections, and an elaborate system of monitoring and control. These safeguards kick-started processes of institutional change that would unfold over decades and cut across the changes of administration in Moscow. Two such processes of institutional change stand out. The first relates to repression. Most work on repression under dictatorship focuses on how it is used to address the problem of authoritarian control. Dictators use repression to ward off threats from the masses and, once they have consolidated their rule, to achieve other societal goals that may be dear to them.[17] Recent refinements have seen progress in measuring repression, enabling it to be integrated into broader theories of dictatorship.[18] By contrast, theorists of dictatorship have far less to say about the effects of repression on the ruling coalition.[19] One reason for this may be the spread of what might be termed an economic approach to the study of dictatorship. This way of looking at the subject has contributed to a misperception that underlying key relationships between the dictator and his inner circle are "agreements" or "bargains" based on voluntary exchanges.[20] Yet in some dictatorships fear of the dictator may be so real that, even in the loosest or most metaphorical sense it is hard to speak of exchanges between the ruler and his inner circle being voluntary. Indeed, fear of repression may reach such a pitch that although personal rivalries may fleetingly well up around the dictator they are unlikely to coalesce into organized groups capable of collective action. Thus it is not always helpful to speak of factions, let alone of bargains between them.[21] From the dictator's point of view this may be one of the greatest benefits of repression.

Even scholars who recognize the general effects of repression on the ruling coalition tend to have quite crude and undifferentiated understandings of it. Milan Svolik, for example, views it as a constant, unchanging environmental factor, an "ever-present and ultimate arbiter of conflicts."[22] But levels of violence may change over time. If we consider the Soviet system from the mid-1940s to the mid-1970s the decline in repression against members of the leadership is one of the most outstanding features of the period. Senior Soviet politicians, including regional leaders, were far less likely to have been arrested or executed in the 1960s or 1970s than in the 1930s or 1940s. The book traces this decline in the use of repression against members of the ruling coalition, including regional leaders, to institutional innovations that occurred while Stalin was still alive.

A second form of institutional change concerned regional party elections. To this day elections remain one of the most mysterious and least understood of authoritarian institutions. Most studies of elections under authoritarianism focus on cases of liberal authoritarianism in which there are multiple-candidate elections and in which the ruling elite consists of clearly identifiable rival groups.[23] But what of an implacably closed and illiberal authoritarian regime such as the Soviet Union was under Stalin? What kind of elections could there be against the backdrop of ever-present fear of repression and arrest?

Whereas most research on Soviet elections analyzes state elections to the Supreme Soviet, our focus is on party elections.[24] As in state elections, voters at regional party conferences had no choice among candidates. Moreover, they had no realistic possibility of removing an incumbent party leader. One reason we need to take these elections seriously is the provision, introduced into the party rules in 1939 and elaborated in a detailed Instruction of April 1941, for a closed or secret ballot.[25] When delegates chose to reject candidates in sufficient numbers, the provisions for a secret vote could afford them a measure of anonymity. This was the case in 1948, when in party elections across the USSR voters staged electoral mutinies against regional party leaders.[26]

We suggest that the regime introduced these elections so that it could address its agency problem in an ideologically palatable form. Elections enabled Moscow to extract information from the very depths of the system about the effectiveness of regional principals and about the cohesion of regional elites and then wrap this up in the language of "Bolshevik democracy." Some contemporary observers surmised that the purpose of these sham exercises in democracy was to strengthen authoritarianism by mobilizing support, deflecting criticism of the center, and keeping regional leaders on their toes.[27] We go further to suggest that elections provided otherwise hard-to-get information on regional leaders' ability to enlist the support of local functionaries, something they needed to do in order to implement the center's decisions. We then go on to argue that although this may have been the original intention behind these elections, they came to be redeployed by regional leaders for other purposes. This was to be a second source of institutional change.

Focusing on processes of institutional change at the regional level has two merits. First, it shows that institutional change was not all about Stalin. There were some important forms of institutional development in which the statewide dictator had no role and of which he may have been unaware. Second, by examining incremental forms of institutional development we bring the study of the Soviet Union into line with recent innovations in the comparative analysis of institutions. These new approaches have tended to focus less on exogenous shocks like revolution, military defeat, or the death of a leader than on slow-moving forms of institutional development that are endogenous to the institutional environment itself.[28]

DICTATORSHIP AND SOCIAL CHANGE

Dictatorships consist not only of institutions but also of people and their lived experiences. The years after the Great Patriotic War were ones of enormous social flux. The war had claimed an estimated 26 to 27 million Soviet lives and left a bitter emotional and economic legacy for those who survived it. The early postwar years were also ones of poverty and material hardship. A terrible drought-induced famine in the autumn and winter of 1946–47 left an estimated 1.5 million people dead. One measure of social and economic upheaval was the large migration flows. Some of these, such as the demobilization of 8.5 million soldiers and former prisoners of war and the deportation of ethnic groups from the western borderlands, were organized by the state. But there were also surges of spontaneous migration, especially from the countryside, where a punitive agrarian policy and desperate living conditions led to 9 million citizens departing for towns and cities from 1950 to 1954.[29]

What were the effects of these social and economic changes on the typical substate leader? First, in the immediate aftermath of the war, bridging the gap between the often chaotic economic reality on the ground and the center's pursuit of rapid economic reconstruction led to a redoubling of demands on regional leaders, demands which heightened as the regime became enmeshed in a deepening geopolitical conflict with the West. Second, population movements, especially after Stalin's death, triggered localized flashpoints of political instability. The release of four million inmates from the Gulag, the transfer of young workers to the Virgin Lands of Kazakhstan and Western Siberia, and the massing of rural migrants and former inmates on the margins of large cities sparked a series of riots and uprisings. From the perspective of regional leaders these were experienced as a problem of authoritarian control.[30]

Yet it was a third, less immediately visible form of social change that would run deepest and have the most profound impact on leadership dynamics in the typical Soviet region. From the late 1930s most Soviet regions experienced a gradual consolidation of social and political hierarchy. In the wake of the Great Purges, Stalin had effected a wholesale replacement of an earlier generation of regional first secretaries, many veterans of the 1917 Revolution and of the Civil War, with a new, much younger cohort.[31] By the late 1940s the majority of these leaders had themselves become party veterans, older than the generation of regional party leaders they had replaced.[32] The social profile of the party membership had also changed. From 1938 to the time of Stalin's death the share of white-collar employees grew from 10.4 percent to over a half of the party membership.[33] Most significantly, the 1940s saw a growing stratification of cadres, a development reflected in two emerging forms of seniority: seniority of office, as expressed in one's place in the formal hierarchy; and seniority of person, as measured in length of party membership and tenure in line or executive positions.

The entrenchment of a class of veteran regional party leaders, a party membership dominated by white-collar workers, and new forms of seniority were translated into a more deferential value system. As officialdom became preoccupied with social status greater importance was attached to inequalities of rank, precedence, and propriety. This in turn blended in with a growing conservatism in public culture. As Katrina Clark has observed, if the typical hero of the 1930s novel was a youth, in the 1940s his counterpart was between thirty-five and forty years old, "no longer a potential member of the Soviet hierarchy but actually in it."[34]

As we move into the 1950s the consolidation of these status hierarchies would have had a major effect on the strategies of the typical substate leader. For one thing it was harder for regional leaders to resort to the classic Stalin-era tactic of overpromotion, which, by its nature, involved a violation of hierarchical norms. Moreover, a new impetus from Moscow pushed the number of expulsions from the party down, making it harder for regional party bosses to wield the threat of political exclusion with impunity.[35] While the threat was far from eliminated, the new climate of de-Stalinization reduced the available supply and changed the content of charges used in kompromat. Alongside the institutional changes implemented under Stalin, these societal changes would push substate dictators toward a new model of leadership.

This was not a smooth or linear process, however. Defying conventional chronologies, this book follows the story into the Leonid Brezhnev era. The transition from the predominantly tight, highly asymmetric networks of the late Stalin era to the broader, more finely graded networks of the 1970s was an uneven one. One of the arguments of the book is that the administration of Nikita Khrushchev was in certain respects continuous with Stalin's in that it reinforced and encouraged substate dictators at the regional level. These tendencies led to a systemic crisis at roughly the midpoint of our study, 1960–61, a crisis which, at the regional level, was more pronounced than anything that had occurred at the time of Stalin's death. Our argument is that notwithstanding the various detours and reverses the thirty-year time span from the mid-1940s to the mid-1970s encompasses a single, integrated process. Describing the inner logic of this process is the main subject of this book.

A MULTIETHNIC STATE

So far we have looked at the challenges facing substate leaders in their most abstract and rarefied form. We now add a vital layer of complexity. As was true of its tsarist predecessor, the Soviet Union embraced a highly heterogeneous assortment of ethnolinguistic and ethnoreligious communities. Soviet policy toward these ethnic groups was quite novel. Arguably its most distinctive feature was that it never elaborated a doctrine of Soviet nationhood at a statewide level. Instead, nationhood and nationality were institutionalized exclusively at the substate level, mostly through the formation of national republics.[36] This is not to say that the majority of substate units were organized along ethnic lines. Most of those which figure in this book were not.[37] But for those that were, this fact could alter the substate leader's calculus of rule.

To understand this we need to take stock of the two pillars of Soviet nationalities policy, that is, the policy adopted by the Soviet regime to manage the country's national minorities. First, in order to defuse the threat of nationalism that had wreaked havoc across Europe's land-based empires at the outbreak of the First World War, the Bolsheviks granted the Soviet Union's larger ethnic minorities national territories of their own. To lead these territories the regime promoted ethnoterritorial elites, and it encouraged the national language of the titular ethnic group as the language of primary and secondary education and, initially, of state. Collectively these policies fell under the umbrella term "indigenization" (*korenizatsiia*).[38] The second pillar of Soviet nation-alities policy concerned the classification of persons. This policy had its origins in the introduction, in 1932, of an internal passport, that included a section on nationality. While the categories overlapped with those for ethnoterritorial federalism, one's individual nationality was based on descent, not residence.[39] Like the system of territorial nation-hood, individual nationality in the Soviet Union was institutionalized exclusively at the substate level, as citizens were barred from choosing a pan-Soviet national identity.

After the Great Patriotic War the two lines of nationalities policy converged. As the bureaucratic process of assigning individual nation-ality was refined, ethnic quotas for training and promoting national cadres, based on data regarding one's individual nationality, were in-troduced. Whereas in the 1920s and early 1930s indigenization had been forced through by the center, often to the consternation of local officials, especially ethnic Russian ones, by the late 1940s indigeniza-tion found growing social support among titular nationals, who saw in it an institutional mechanism through which they might prosper. Thus "indigenization from above" came to be replaced by "indigenization from below."[40]

How did the institutionalization of territorial nationhood and per-sonal nationality at the substate level alter the calculus of the substate national leader? These policies had two consequences. First, indigeni-zation entailed not only quotas on the ethnic composition of local elites but also a growing insistence that republican first secretaries come from the titular nationality. Titular first secretaries were better placed to tap into local ethnic networks and thereby deal with the problem of authoritarian power sharing. They could also communicate with the national population in their own language and were thereby better po-sitioned to address the problem of authoritarian control. Initially this aspiration to secure the right personnel was limited by the small pool of available and, as viewed by Moscow, sufficiently loyal candidates, but by the mid-1950s enough cadres from the titular nationalities had risen through the ranks to make the policy feasible.[41] As we saw earlier, indigenization was a subset of a more general principle of delegation: without national leaders who could cohere ethnic elites and commu-nicate with titular populations in their own language, Moscow would have struggled to put its central policies in the republics into effect.

In the non-Slavic republics the appointment of a titular first secretary was supplemented by a Slavic second secretary, a practice pioneered in the late Stalin era in the Baltic republics. Appointed to monitor the assignment of cadres, to oversee the activities of the security police, and to keep an eye on the activities of the first secretary, the Slavic second secretary limited the opportunity of the first secretary to resort to the classic instruments of the substate dictator.[42]

Soviet nationalities policy also had a second effect. Like other substate leaders, the heads of the national republics had to address the dual problems of authoritarian control and authoritarian power sharing. Bolshevik policies gave republican substate leaders a head start in this regard. If traditional theories of the rise of nationalist movements in Europe have pointed to the role of the cultural intelligentsia in fomenting a national consciousness, in the USSR this role was assumed by titular party organizations.[43] Substate leaders in the national republics could finesse the problems of authoritarian control and power sharing by playing the national card and activating the party as an agent of mobilization. In order to dissuade republican leaders from such a course the center had to tread carefully. Such caution involved granting concessions, such as allowing more moderate forms of "permissible nationalism," and finding ways through which republican party organizations could have their say in the selection of republican leaders.[44]

COMPARISONS

Although the primary purpose of this book is to probe the inner workings of one twentieth-century dictatorship, its findings can also shed light on broader debates on comparative dictatorship. The Soviet Union was the prototype of the Leninist one-party state, which, alongside an institutionally related category of dictatorship, the "hegemonic" or "dominant party" regime, accounted for three-fifths of the world's nondemocratic states over the second half of the twentieth century.[45] One striking feature of these regimes has been their longevity and resilience relative to other forms of authoritarianism, such as military or monarchical dictatorships.[46] Closer examination of the Soviet case can cast light on the two competing explanations that have come to explain this resilience. The first focuses on the role of institutions.[47] Empirical analysis of one-party states shows that they are less prone to coups from inner circles or to revolts from the population at large.[48] At the level of authoritarian power sharing, the scarcity of coups is attributed to "inner sanctums" like politburos, which enable the leader to keep an eye on his or her rivals.[49] At the level of authoritarian control, the lack of popular revolts is credited to the institutional capacity of ruling parties to co-opt insiders by making rewards organizationally contingent on party service and seniority, thereby creating an enduring stake in the regime's survival.[50]

A rival set of explanations points to the historical origins of revolutionary regimes.[51] The most durable one-party regimes are those rooted in a period of sustained, violent struggle, such as a civil war or a war of liberation. It is the identities, norms, and organizational structures forged during a prolonged period of ideologically driven conflict that serve to consolidate partisan boundaries, to mobilize popular support, and to ensure elite cohesion. The deeper forms of allegiance that stem from conflict are better able to sustain a regime through subsequent moments of crisis than support earned through mere co-optation.[52] In the case of the Soviet Union there was, in fact, not one armed conflict but two: the Civil War of 1918 through the early 1920s followed by the Great Patriotic War of 1941–45, which played a crucial role in prolonging the life cycle of the Soviet regime.

Evidence presented in the book suggests ways in which both approaches might be refined. In focusing so narrowly on the formation of the revolutionary elite, the social conflict approach is quite vague about forms of governance and how these evolve over time.[53] In this book we argue that the resilience of the Soviet regime owed much to the adaptability of its institutions and their capacity for change. Against the institutional approach, our research suggests that the regional party leader's power often rested less on co-optation than on exclusion.

The ruling party in the Soviet Union effected two forms of exclusion. The first was political exclusion, which in its most extreme form amounted to expulsion from the party. Unlike liberal democracies, where party membership is voluntary, in the single-party state membership was an exclusive privilege, and this exclusivity of membership is what made expulsion possible.[54] In the first two decades of the Soviet Union's existence the mass purge, a vast periodic bureaucratic sweep of party members, was a prominent feature of party life. In 1939 the mass purge was formally abolished.[55] Nonetheless, the expulsion of individual members continued, albeit now on a case-by-case basis. As

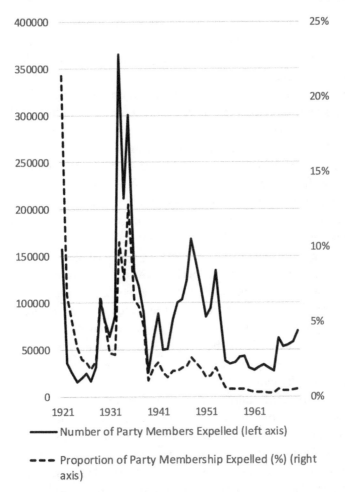

Figure o.1. Expulsion of Communist Party members, USSR, 1921–70. The numbers expelled (left axis) and the proportion of members expelled (right axis) include full members and candidates but exclude mechanical and automatic withdrawals (i.e., voluntary withdrawals or failure to attend meetings or to pay party dues). *Sources:* RGASPI f.17 op.117 d.873 l.23; RGANI f.77 op.1 d.14 ll.78 (ob), 7 (ob); d.13 ll.9 (ob), 102 (ob), 171 (ob); d.12 l.217 (ob); Cohn (2015: 38); Rigby (1968: 52–53; 1976: 322).

is apparent in figure o.1, while party members continued to be expelled in large numbers, the end of the mass purge and a surge in members— from 2.3 million in 1939 to 5.76 million in 1945 and 14 million in 1970—meant that after 1939 annual expulsions never exceeded 3 percent of the party membership.

Three aspects of the system of expulsions after 1939 are notable. First, as in the use of repression by the state, the strategic significance of expulsions lay not in the act of expulsion itself but in the credible threat of it. Expulsions were merely the tip of an iceberg that included reprimands, warnings, cautions, and a panoply of other penalties that could place any regional actor on notice that his standing in the party elite was in jeopardy. Second, the arrest and prosecution of members of the elite were made conditional on expulsion from the party, the decision on which now lay in the hands of party principals. Much as protection from prosecution is a classic function rendered by patrons in traditional patron–client societies, so now regional party leaders exercised what was, in effect, the power of protection.[56] In this regard the significance of expulsion was closely connected to the continued prevalence of state repression which, from 1939 to 1953, remained at high levels. Third, throughout the period covered in this book repression and co-optation remained central instruments of rule. The resources to carry out both were, however, in the hands of other agencies. It was here that political exclusion proved to be crucial, for it enabled party principals to intercede in the processes of co-optation and repression and to assert their primacy over the actors and institutions charged with their implementation.

In order to make sense of the second form of exclusion—informal exclusion—we move from the macro to the micro level. Earlier we noted that over the second half of his rule Stalin was a surprisingly disciplined delegator. There was, however, one occasion when he let rip. In the Great Purges of 1937–38 Stalin exterminated almost every regional leader in the USSR. In some regions the situation was so bad that Stalin liquidated not only one regional leader but, in the space of two years, up to two or three in close succession.[57] In many regions entire contingents of obkom staff were obliterated. In some cases whole networks of colleagues, friends, and relatives were exposed as spies, traitors, and enemies of the people. The Great Purges have been presented by at least one comparative theorist as "perhaps the greatest deliberate experiment in pervasive distrust."[58] The purges and the witch hunts that led up to them certainly weakened bonds of trust among officials, friends, and even relatives to an unusual degree.

What effect did this low-trust environment have on the new cohort of regional leaders who took office in the wake of the Great Purges?[59]

Most leaders needed to devise methods for achieving cooperation in an environment where trust and the institutions which support it were in short supply. To grasp their strategy, we turn to research on cooperation in other low-trust environments. One solution was to admit into one's inner circle a person with some kind of visible handicap.[60] As we have seen, under Stalin one could do this through overpromotion, thereby securing the loyalty of a junior or inexperienced official, or through the manipulation of "black spots" in their past, for example, through kompromat.[61] There was also a third source of leverage. One of the main triggers of regional network formation was the need to meet targets set by the center. To the extent that many of these targets were unfeasible, those charged with implementing them inevitably had to break rules and do so with the connivance of other rule breakers.[62] The conspiratorial bonds which resulted were the stuff of strong local networks. Normally these networks were regulated through acts of informal exclusion. Unlike its prerevolutionary forms, in the Soviet era acts of exclusion were invariably staged in party forums and choreographed by party officials.[63]

SOVIET POLITICAL HISTORY

In addition to touching on comparative themes this book intersects with a body of work in Soviet and Russian political history. This corpus embraces two discrete strands of scholarship. The first is a long-standing tradition of research on the political history of the Soviet regions. Much of this work focuses on the prewar period and, in particular, on the events leading to the Great Purges of 1937–38.[64] For the sake of brevity, we focus on one point of difference between our analysis and that offered by much of this existing literature. In a widely cited passage from February 1937 Stalin lambasted the tendency of regional leaders to form "family circles" and to "select as fellow leaders so-called acquaintances, personal friends, fellow countrymen, and personally devoted individuals," thereby "creating a certain independence . . . from the Central Committee."[65] This rebuke has been taken as a general sign of Stalin's distaste for regional political networks. We shall suggest that although Stalin repeatedly catechized about the dangers of nepotism and family circles, his use of such terms was largely a rhetorical device.[66] Following two seminal articles by Rigby (1981) and

Fairbanks (1983), we suggest not only that Stalin himself made use of clientelist norms in binding regional party organizations to the center, but that he recognized the need and prerogative of regional leaders to do the same thing.[67] This recognition on Stalin's part of the effective right of regional leaders to form their own networks was all the more evident after 1938 and the arrival of a new generation of young regional leaders who had been educated and socialized under Stalin and who owed their political careers to him.[68]

A second strand of area studies scholarship that has now become a branch of Soviet political history consists of Western social science publications on Soviet regional politics from the 1950s to the 1980s. This literature came in various forms: there were studies of individual regional party organizations,[69] of regional elite recruitment and turnover,[70] of patron–client relations, networks, and circulation chains,[71] and of regional party management of the economy.[72] In order to sharpen the distinction between our work and these we fix on two particular traditions from this corpus, the first exemplified by Jerry Hough's *The Soviet Prefects* and the second by a series of works on patron–client relations.

Reading Hough's *The Soviet Prefects* (1969) half a century after its publication, one is struck by its ambition and by the depth and subtlety of its readings of the Soviet and especially the provincial Soviet press.[73] Although ostensibly about the role of local party organs in industrial management, this work's claims are wider, extending to the nature of political power and to the source of political change in the Soviet Union. The book proposes that the behavior of obkom first secretaries was driven by their need to fulfill the plan.[74] Hough elaborated not only a structure of incentives but also a theory of change. He observed how, over time, an ever-larger share of obkom secretaries had higher technical and educational qualifications. This, he suggested, was not because they were directly selected on these criteria but because bettertrained, more highly educated cadres were more likely to possess the technical, administrative, and bargaining skills required to achieve the plan. Despite the book's insights, we depart from Hough's approach in key ways. Hough presents the party as a coordinator of disputes that are brought to it for resolution.[75] Ultimately, however, it is not clear what the source of the party's power is. The fixation on industrial issues means we get a one-sided view of what the party does and of why we should take it seriously. The activities examined in this book, especially in regard to the party's role in the processes of exclusion, repression, and ideological coordination, help to fill this gap.

A second vein of publications looked at patronage and patron–client relations.[76] These works traced how forms of mutual dependence among patrons and clients created pockets of commitment in what was a politically harsh environment. To that extent, they have much in common with the approach we employ here.[77] While these forms of dependence were expressed as personal relationships, they rested on the access to resources granted to the patron through his or her formal position in the nomenklatura. Of all the resources available to patrons the most significant was the power of appointment.[78] Since the filling of positions in the nomenklatura system was in the hands of senior *party* officials, it was they who emerged as the most important patrons in this system and the nodes of the largest networks.[79] Yet, for want of appropriate sources, scholars on patronage tended to emphasize the assignment of appointments and promotions. As important as it was, the placement of personnel captures only a small slice of the political process. The act of appointment was one step, but it was not in and of itself enough to secure ongoing loyalty and had to be reinforced by other instruments in the substate leader's toolbox.

METHOD

Our starting point for this project was to ascertain the goals of the substate leader. We have gone on to surmise that in the late Stalin era a successful substate leader's strategy rested on forging a working relationship with a small and dependent inner network and that it was his ability to do this successfully that turned him into a substate dictator. Yet the goals of politicians and their informal interactions with political networks are not easily observable. This presents us with a methodological problem: How can we recognize a substate dictatorship when we see one? Although neither the strategies of the substate dictator—exclusion, kompromat, and overpromotion—nor the outcomes—small, pliable, and heavily asymmetric power networks—were visible to the naked eye, some expressions of substate dictatorship were. The uncouth regional boss who raged and bellowed at subordinates was a mainstay of the novels and plays of the postwar era. Moreover, certain epiphenomena of substate dictatorship, such as plenipotentiaries who pressed and harangued in his name, were observable, and their activities could, in principle, be measured and quantified. But to get to the nub of substate dictatorship we need to dig deeper. How can we detect the small, informal, trust-based networks that formed around the leader and that, by their very nature, were supposed to be hidden from view?

There are no easy metrics to pick up the ebb and flow of these networks. Thus our approach rests on in-depth regional case studies framed around a clear set of theoretically informed expectations. Our task in gathering evidence was facilitated by the fact that the Soviet system was highly bureaucratized and left meticulous paper trails of all manner of complaints, allegations, and running feuds. While some disputes led only to superficial, routine inquiries, the more weighty ones could result in teams of inspectors being sent out from Moscow, interviewing participants, and compiling voluminous reports. The prompt for such visits was normally a scandal: where a regional leader had crossed a red line, he could be taken to task and have his alliances scrutinized. Even in the case of a leader who held on to his post, these moments of regional crisis could throw up information of great value. For even though politicians were ordinarily reserved and secretive about their networks and patronage groups, the lineaments of these networks could suddenly be laid bare, for example, when regional battle lines were drawn, when clients sought protection from patrons, or when higher-level investigations revealed the webs of protection and mutual assistance that ran through a region. A focus on moments of crisis and scandal thus enables us to shine a light on the dynamics of the regional power system.

The obvious danger of such an approach is that all we are illuminating are the kinds of networks that lead to scandals. To compensate, our research design included regions right across the scandal spectrum, including but not limited to regions that were completely calm and devoid of conflict. Studying these latter regions required a different method: more oblique, more piecemeal, and often more retrospective, it made use of memoirs, biographies, and interviews supplemented by intermittent low-key official reports. In general, to guard against selection bias our research design was structured around two principles. First, we opted for a comparative case study approach in which conflict-prone regions were balanced against calm ones (and a range of regions in between), large regions against smaller ones, ethnic regions against various gradations of nonethnic ones, and predominantly urban against rural ones. Second, the logic of our argument yielded a clear set of expectations, which we operationalized through the use of categories with a broader comparative resonance.

Our research design aimed to combine the benefits of in-depth regional analysis with the scope and perspective afforded by comparison. To achieve this we focused on thirty case study regions over a thirty-year period. Our selection of case studies rested on two criteria. First, we needed to settle on a unit of analysis. What were our substate territories? Our goal here was to examine the management and coordination of the Soviet state on the ground, where policies were put into effect, while at the same time picking up the activities of truly powerful actors who wielded formidable political resources in their own right and whose actions might have transregional and even statewide consequences. Our compromise was to focus on the *oblast* (regional) level, one tier below the Soviet Union's fifteen union republics.[80] Given the asymmetric nature of the Soviet federal system, however, and the importance of nationalities policy in a large share of substate territories, there were a number of cases in which we departed from this rule (see appendix B). Second, given the size of the country, the number of substate units (139 in 1947 and more later on), and the labor-intensive nature of the research, we narrowed our scope by selecting a sample. To ensure representativeness the variance in this sample was maximized on six dimensions (see appendix C). Given the emphasis on scandal as an entry point for investigating regional-level networks, we paid special attention to the circumstances under which first and second secretaries were replaced.[81]

If our only aim had been to find signs of substate dictatorship we would have ended up with a skewed picture of the pattern of leadership across the country. To reflect the distribution of regional leadership regimes more accurately, we balance substate dictatorship against two other models. In keeping with our inductive research design, these models are ideal types, each consisting of a variety of elements. While no region conformed exactly, most approximated one or the other. Our second category revolved around *contested autocrats*. The empirical difference between substate dictators and contested autocrats approximates the theoretical difference between an *established autocracy* and a *contested autocracy.* Whereas the leader in the former has amassed enough power that he no longer faces a credible threat from his inner circle, the latter represents a qualitatively distinct power-sharing arrangement in which the leader remains susceptible to some form of allied rebellion.[82] Yet there remains one key difference between a region with a contested autocrat and a statewide contested autocracy. In the latter a ruling coalition can always remove a leader. In the former, although members of the ruling coalition can hedge in a leader and fatally damage his reputation, they cannot get rid of him. To the extent that the Soviet Union remained, to the end, a centralized dictatorship that right was reserved for the Central Committee.

What were the empirical markers of a contested autocrat? Normally perceived as passive and weak-willed, such a leader often had to contend with powerful alternative networks in his region. The telltale features of a contested autocrat were that he was unable to appoint or to get rid of individuals within his own nomenklatura; district-level leaders were able to lobby him successfully for lower-plan targets; he was regularly defeated on matters of policy; he was subjected to regular criticism at party meetings; and, when he departed from the region, he rarely held on to his rank within the nomenklatura. Indeed, many contested autocrats were prematurely squeezed out by a Moscow dissatisfied that it could not achieve its targets in a region and by regional networks which, while they enjoyed greater autonomy, craved greater clout and lobbying power at the center.

Substate dictators and contested autocrats were the two central categories of territorial leader in the late Stalin era. In order to keep track of change, we introduce a third category, one which emerged under Khrushchev but fully came into its own under Brezhnev. These regions were headed by what we refer to as *party governors*. By contrast with contested autocrats, party governors controlled appointments on their own nomenklatura. While the political networks in these regions could be quite extensive, they were generally subordinated to the first secretary. Unlike substate dictators, party governors headed organizations that were held together by a system of norms. First, there were norms of seniority, so that leaders were promoted incrementally, often in accordance with the length of their nomenklatura service. Although party governors were able to get rid of individual subordinates, the entrenchment of hierarchical norms limited the substate leader's room for maneuver when it came to overpromoting clients or carrying out collective purges. Second, party governors tended not to display their power through frequent acts of willfulness, as did the substate dictator, but to comply with an emerging etiquette, for example, on politeness and courtesy, which helped to glue the regional political elite together.

Regional leaders and their clients had strong incentives to conceal a first secretary's support network from other actors in the region and from the center. Accordingly, uncovering how these networks operated and whether they even existed has not been easy. In most cases it is unlikely that we have managed to reconstruct these networks in full. Our approach has been more approximate. It is based on comparing real-life cases with the three network ideal-types as set out here (see appendix D for a full discussion).

Although our starting point in this book has been to establish the goals of the substate leader, we recognize that politicians acted under constraints. One set of constraints was the institutional environment, which, as we saw earlier, underwent considerable change after the war. A second set of constraints involved economic and coercive resources. In some regions the presence of an especially large factory or an un-usually powerful head of the secret police who took his orders from Moscow could present a major counterweight to the first secretary. A third set of constraints consisted of fixed effects, which might include a region's size, its distance from Moscow, and its demographic profile.[83] Although we do not propose or test causal hypotheses on the conse-quences of these effects on network dynamics or on the structure of the regional elite, we believe that the research we present provides a platform for others to do so.

SOURCES

One reason we can move beyond earlier scholarly concerns is our ex-panded source base. By contrast with contemporary studies that relied overwhelmingly on such official publications as newspaper articles, encyclopedias, and authorized biographies or memoirs, we gained ac-cess to a continuous run of documents on areas untouched by ear-lier scholars.[84] These include records of investigations into regional-level conflicts, uncensored transcripts of speeches at *obkom* plenums and conferences, internal correspondence between central and local departments of the party apparatus, minutes and protocols of *obkom buro* (the top decision-making body of the regional party organization) and Central Committee Secretariat meetings, and documents detailing the internal functioning of the regional and unionwide nomenklatura. These materials have enabled us to provide a clearer picture of conflicts and how they were resolved, to follow the changing mechanisms and rationales of exclusion, and to penetrate previously closed institutions such as regional party elections.

We understand that these party materials need to be handled with care. Many either reflected activities that were designed to deceive superiors or were collated and subsequently edited with the same view in mind.[85] Where possible we have tried to situate party reports in their social context and to interpret them in light of our general understanding of how the political system worked.[86] A wider danger of relying too heavily on party archives is that they might lead us to view the whole political system from the party bureaucracy's point of view. Thus, as a balance, we supplemented these sources with other archival materials, including documents from the state archives (especially the justice agencies and the council of ministers), postcommunist memoirs, biographies, regional encyclopedias, and a small number of interviews (see appendix E for precise details).

Two lacunae remain, which we should acknowledge. The first relates to materials from the state security archives, which, except for some local archives in the Baltic states and Ukraine, are off-limits and are likely to stay so for the foreseeable future. On the activity of the security police and its interactions with the party, we have tended to work obliquely by reconstructing the activities of republican and regional security police organizations from party records. While that approach may not be ideal, we feel that the patterns of behavior are sufficiently consistent to allow us to make sound, reliable inferences. A second gap relates to one of the three lines of action pursued by party leaders, the use of kompromat. A cursory examination of the literature on the use of blackmail and dirty tricks across political systems shows that systematic empirical research on this topic is thin on the ground.[87] The evidence we have for kompromat is more fragmentary than for the other tactics of the substate leader—thus we are less confident about how widespread it was and how its use changed over time—but this is so in part because such activities were the ones least likely to have been observed or recorded. Yet judging by the evidence we do have, we believe it was sufficiently important to be not only included but even elevated into a key element of our analysis.

OVERVIEW

Of the book's four parts, three (I, III, and IV) are organized sequentially to coincide with leadership administrations in Moscow, and part II is devoted to the short interregnum after Stalin's death. Chapter 1 is a discussion of the challenges facing substate leaders after the war and the party-based tools they used to forge networks. In chapter 2 we show how, despite their immense power, substate dictators did not always have things their own way. We assess institutional constraints on the plane of authoritarian power sharing (factory directors, heads of the regional state apparatus, and the secret police) and authoritarian control (electoral revolts) and trace how, in response to these constraints, substate dictators began to adapt their behavior. Chapter 3 examines the stabilization of hierarchies and the changing balance between co-optation and political exclusion after the war.

Although the primary focus of the book is on the regional level, there is one moment—after Stalin died—when attention shifts to the center. Chapter 4 looks at the succession struggle in Moscow and its effects on the environment in which substate leaders operated. Chapter 5 brings the story back to the regional level, exploring the various ways in which substate leaders responded to new impulses from above. Chapter 6 moves on to the national territories. It shows how formal recognition by the Soviet state of ethnolinguistic elites and cultures created opportunities for republican leaders to negotiate the problems of authoritarian control and authoritarian power sharing through ethnic mobilization. Chapter 7 assesses how Khrushchev's solution to the dictator's agency problem led to an epidemic of data falsification and, in turn, to the most radical purge of the post-Stalin era. The purge of 1960–61 was not only a turning point in center–regional relations but would mark a break between the high-pressure approach practiced by both Khrushchev and Stalin and the more accommodating stance of Khrushchev's successor, Brezhnev.

Chapter 9 looks at why Brezhnev extended the principles of indigenization to the Slavic republics. It also assesses the changing balance, after Khrushchev, of co-optation, repression, and political exclusion and how the latter in particular took on a more muted form as levels of repression fell. In the last chapter we see that, as in the late 1940s, regional leaders had to find solutions to the problems of authoritarian control and authoritarian power sharing. But the change in environment also elicited new tactics. By now each of the original strategies of the classic substate dictator had become harder to activate. Instead, many regional *aktivs* (politically engaged rank-and-file members of the party) now threw their weight behind a package of authority-enhancing norms that included public shows of deference, the hiding of policy differences, and a carefully calibrated system of seniority based on step-by-step promotions.

The book ends by suggesting how the framework it employs can help provide a benchmark for comparing the Soviet Union with other regimes, including that of contemporary postcommunist Russia.

I
STALIN

1 Substate Dictators

IN AUGUST 1946 the Central Committee received a complaint from a party member in Tambov, A. Bespalov, about his regional first secretary, I.A. Volkov. "Volkov has become a dictator and is turning our whole region into a dictatorship," lamented Bespalov. "Criticism from below is not only disparaged and belittled, but actively suppressed . . . in return Volkov will come up with any reason to get rid of you." "Turnover has reached frightening levels," Bespalov went on, "our people have no confidence in the future and feel themselves to be entirely expendable." Volkov's coercive approach toward the rank and file was matched by the treatment of his peers. In his drive for power Volkov had, claimed Bespalov, usurped the prerogatives of other regional leaders and masterminded the breakdown of the region's collective decision-making bodies.[1]

Bespalov's claims were largely corroborated by a Central Committee inquiry, but they did Volkov little harm. He stayed on as first secretary in Tambov for another five years before being transferred to an identical post in Orel. Bespalov could not have known it, but Volkov's behavior had become the norm in Soviet regional politics in the years after the war. In his role as territorial first secretary Volkov appeared to be the regional pivot of a fiercely coercive system of administration. Yet while Volkov's treatment of ordinary party members like Bespalov was open for all to see, many of his other tactics, especially in relation to his inner circle, were less visible. But they played an equally important part in the formation of his substate regime. In fact, most substate leaders like Volkov operated on two planes. Out in the open they steered district-level officials and the regional aktiv by wielding threats and causing high levels of cadre turnover, while behind the scenes they managed their inner circle through an assortment of covert techniques.

How did substate leaders subjugate rank-and-file officials? The centrally managed economy set strict goals for officials at all levels, tight targets they were expected to hit with inadequate resources: this meant that, in general, rules had to be broken. When a territorial leader came under pressure to fulfill the plan, he tended to pass this pressure on to his subordinates, often in magnified form. Given that rules violations were so common, it was a relatively straightforward matter for a regional leader to take out his frustration on local officials by sacking them. But treating his peers in this manner was more problematic. Most senior leaders were on the Central Committee nomenklatura, which meant they could be fired only with Moscow's express permission.[2] There were other considerations too. Highly placed provincial officials were privy to insider information on how the region was run. A defection could suddenly bring to light all manner of breaches and violations that most regional leaders would have much rather kept hidden. This meant that outright coercion of the kind they practiced against rank-and-file officials was best avoided. In the pressure cooker atmosphere of the late Stalin era an obkom leader needed colleagues who were not just competent but, in view of the rules that had to be broken, loyal too. Four mechanisms—kompromat, informal exclusion, overpromotion, and political exclusion—were deployed by regional leaders as they sought to secure this loyalty. What these mechanisms had in common was an ability to foster strange and often unexpected forms of solidarity.

The Soviet Constitution differentiated national territories, that is, the republics, from nonnational ones, which we refer to as regions. By the late 1940s there were notable differences between leaders of the two types of territory, differences which were closely bound up with the evolution of Soviet nationalities policy.[3] However, the four processes of network formation were generic and followed a logic that was common to all substate units. For that reason we draw freely from republics and regions and occasionally intersperse examples between the two.

AUTHORITARIAN CONTROL

Two contextual factors shaped territorial leaders' strategies toward local officials in the early postwar years. The first was the taut fourth five-year plan of 1946–50, whose ambitious targets touched nearly every sphere of the Soviet economy. No sooner had the plan period started than these targets were rendered even more unreachable when a major drought-induced famine claimed an estimated one and a half million lives. Initially driven by the center, economic campaigns assumed a particularly virulent form at the local level, where regional leaders bridged the gap between unfeasible goals and inadequate resources through the use of force. Nowhere was this more apparent than in agriculture, a primary responsibility of many regional first secretaries, even in nonrural areas. Squeezing farms to the maximum required procurement campaigns that took the form of what were, in effect, raids on the countryside. Such campaigns were administered along an "executive vertical" that tied the region's districts to its capital. The immediate targets were usually *raikom* (local party organization) secretaries, who were either summoned to the obkom capital for progress reports or were at the receiving end of directives, either orally or by phone, telegraph, or radio conferences.[4] When the grain campaign went badly regional leaders paid a heavy price. In Stavropol' A.L. Orlov was fired for "not following the party line on grain procurements," while in Riazan S.I. Malov was sacked for "incompetence" for having secured only 62 percent of the grain procurement plan.[5]

A second factor influencing territorial leaders was the cultural imprint of the war. Provincial first secretaries had been sucked into the Second World War in a variety of ways. Some had served as political commissars or even as military commanders at the front. Others had sat on local defense councils, where their everyday interaction with military commanders and local police bosses from the People's Commissariat of Internal Affairs (NKVD) had sharpened their own propensity to lead through "military-bureaucratic" forms of leadership. As the war progressed, regional leaders picked up the argot and mannerisms of their colleagues from the military. A good example is the first secretary of the L'vov obkom, I.S. Grushetskii, who had begun his career as a party functionary but who had joined the army during the war, rising to the rank of major general. A full three and a half years after the war the Central Committee cadres administration reported that "Comrade Grushetskii does not have an understanding of how our primary party organizations work. . . . [H]is high positions in the Red Army instilled conceit, a habit for giving orders, and an expectation of unquestioning obedience to his commands. Through some kind of inertia these qualities have carried over into his party work, and he has found it hard to adapt."[6]

Understanding the behavior of territorial first secretaries toward their rank and file requires taking into account not only the pressure of the plan or the influence of the war but also the secretaries' personal backgrounds. In May 1945 a bare majority of territorial first secretaries had been appointed to their post for the first time during the war, while all others had been appointed on the eve of the war, in the wake of the Great Purges of 1937–38.[7] Unlike the generation of provincial first secretaries whom they had replaced—the victims of the purges—many of whom had been senior Bolsheviks with experience of the Revolution and of the Civil War, the new leaders were overwhelmingly younger figures, most often in their early thirties. Having first entered the party in the mid to late 1920s, most members of this new cohort had been educated and politically socialized under Stalin.[8] Stalin valued these leaders because, in what was still a very traditional society, they were his juniors, and could not, unlike those they had replaced, present a direct political threat to him. In addition, however, these young men had largely internalized the values of Stalin's great breakthrough of the early 1930s and understood the need for force in attaining the regime's prized targets.[9]

Not every leader fit into this mold. In general, however, the cumulative effect of the use of quasi-military discipline to achieve hyperambitious targets meant that most leaders, even those at the rear, tended to gravitate toward a new norm. One local official offered the following view of her party leader in Khabarovsk: "The *kraikom* [regional party committee] secretary R.K. Nazarov arrived in the region from Moscow in 1938 and has served here for seven years. On arrival he was keen, party-minded, energetic, unaffected, and wholly attentive in his dealings with people, but over that time he has progressively lost these qualities. . . . [I]f anything he has started to take on airs, grown quite rude, and is prone to bouts of foul language and swearing."[10] Of A.I. Marfin, who became obkom first secretary in Riazan in 1943, one raikom secretary noted in 1948 that "his rudeness has become intolerable. It gets particularly bad during the sowing and harvesting campaigns. At these times it is impossible to deal with him. . . . [H]is rudeness becomes quite degrading."[11]

Through a chain reaction in many regions these traits were picked up and imitated by the district party secretaries. One report from Novosibirsk in August 1946 noted, "Threats of prison, barking out orders and shouting at the top of his voice—that is how obkom first secretary Kulagin leads the rural districts. His approach is then mimicked by the raikom secretaries, who enact it in a yet cruder form in their dealings with the rural soviets and collective farms. We hear from the chairs of the rural soviets . . . , and the chairs of the collective farms . . . that when they go to a meeting they are usually told to get their prison things ready, for they are unlikely to 'escape the nick' (*katalazkhi ne minovat'*)."[12] Another report from the same province noted that "cursing and slandering people is the common practice here. . . . [O]n any pretext [one of the raikom secretaries] addresses people as 'Hitler' or 'fascist' and threatens to shoot them on the spot; things have become so bad that certain communists have even come to refer to the raikom as the 'police zone.'"[13]

Such characteristics contributed to the two observable traits Bespalov noted in his obkom first secretary. First, the early postwar years saw extremely high levels of turnover among raikom officials, most of whom were sacked for failing to meet their plan target. It is a measure of the high degree of centralization in this system that the pressures intensified and the levels of turnover rose the further down one moved in the party hierarchy. Thus whereas turnover of cadres on the Central Committee nomenklatura as a whole (which included raikom secretaries) hovered between 20 percent and 22 percent from 1945 to 1950, the levels among raikom secretaries were invariably higher, rising, depending on the region, to 40 percent or even 50 percent per annum in some provinces.[14] Second, campaigns had the effect of eroding collective leadership structures. One of the most important carryovers from the war was the use of plenipotentiaries, direct representatives of the regional leadership who were assigned to the districts in order to carry out high-priority tasks. Plenipotentiaries were expected to goad the rank and file into action, but they also had an unintended effect on collective decision-making structures. As one report from Kostroma noted, "The dispatch of all manner of plenipotentiaries to the districts and collective farms by the Kostroma obkom has become almost the only form of leadership in an agricultural campaign. . . . Last year [in 1947] the obkom cadres secretary . . . spent three months as a plenipotentiary in [one] ward, while the deputy chair of the regional executive committee . . . and the head of the regional administration of agriculture were not allowed to leave the [farming areas] for two months. The same was true of many other leading personnel."[15] The regular dispatch of high-level plenipotentiaries made it impossible to arrange regular meetings of the full buro.[16] In Riazan, owing to the regular absence of buro members on campaign business, the second secretary, Aleksandriuk, commented, "To all intents and purposes our obkom buro does not exist."[17]

Exceptionally high levels of turnover, sometimes accompanied by threats of party punishment or even of repression were the most visible manifestations of the highly coercive approach to district party officials taken by most regional leaders after the war. Yet territorial first secretaries could not rule alone. They needed trustworthy colleagues at the regional level to run their administrations, to implement decisions, and, most seriously, to cover up when things went wrong. Here, unalloyed coercion was of limited use. Territorial leaders not only had to get the dismissal of most regional-level officials past the Central Committee but also ran the risk of alienating high-ranking figures who might be privy to information that could do them harm. To bring regional leaders on board they needed other means—beyond the threat of a sacking—of obtaining their cooperation and, ideally, of winning their loyalty.

AUTHORITARIAN POWER SHARING

Recognizing the difficulty of making a mark on a new region, Moscow gave incoming secretaries some license to sweep out sitting officials and even coined a phrase for such actions: "Creating a more healthy working environment" (*ozdorovlenie obstanovki*).[18] Demonstrative cadre transfers of this kind underlined the power of the new first secretary and the support he enjoyed from Moscow. Where a republic or region was strategically important or beset with long-running problems Moscow permitted the new incumbent to bring with him one or two selected colleagues.[19] A good example was the incoming first secretary of the Belorussian Republic in 1947, N.I. Gusarov, who was accompanied by a sizeable "tail" from his former province of Molotov, including the first secretary of the Molotov Komsomol organization, two personal assistants from Molotov, one regional economic manager, who was made head of construction at the Belorussian tractor factory, and the former head of the Molotov MGB (regional administration of the ministry of state security), who became deputy minister of state security for Belorussia.[20]

In general, however, nomenklatura norms discouraged such practices.[21] Most incoming leaders had to find other ways of making ruling coalitions at the regional level cohere. Four central mechanisms drew on the low-trust environment of regional politics after the Great Purges of 1937–38 to yield strange, unexpected forms of solidarity.

Kompromat

Like other midlevel leaders, Mir Jafar Bagirov, the first secretary of Azerbaijan, faced three core challenges. The first was to ward off the attentions of the center. For most of the early postwar years the Central Committee signaled that it would afford Bagirov considerable latitude in running his affairs.[22] To address the second challenge, that of authoritarian control, Bagirov relied heavily on coercion. This involved the normal forced mobilizations in agricultural campaigns as well as the meting out of punishments to district-level officials who failed to achieve their targets. Low-lying officials were not only dismissed from their posts but also arrested and locked up for supposedly sabotaging the regime's policies.[23] To whip up a climate of fear, Bagirov ordered criminal cases to be fabricated against local officials, including journalists, heads of party electoral commissions, and whistle-blowers. By their nature, these policies were relatively open and could be read about in the republican press.

But Bagirov also faced a third problem. How could he obtain the cooperation of those around him? Here, unalloyed repression was of limited use, as he needed people with whom he could forge ongoing working relationships, not one-off collaborations. It is germane to Bagirov's story that prior to becoming first secretary in 1933 he had served for eight years (1921–27 and 1929–30) as the head of the republic's secret police. It was here, in the murky world of informers and double agents, that he had become acquainted with the secret service's trademark practices of manipulation and blackmail. By the postwar period Bagirov had carved out his own channels of communication with the secret police and, in particular, with its long-standing head from 1939 to 1953, S.F. Emel'ianov. After Bagirov's fall, Maliutin, the secretary of the Baku city committee and himself a member of the buro of the Azerbaijan central committee, would comment on this point: "Not a single question relating to the ministry of internal affairs (MVD) or the ministry of state security was brought up for discussion by members of the [official] buro; they had no idea what was going on nor was it thought necessary to tell them. It was in this regard that Emel'ianov was [for Bagirov] an especially trusted person."[24]

Bagirov's relationship with Emel'ianov serves as an entry point for understanding his treatment of his ruling group. The two men's relationship stretched back to the late 1930s when, in the wake of the Great Terror, which had claimed many of his closest allies, Bagirov set about forging a new team. Emel'ianov likely appealed to Bagirov for two reasons. First, Emel'ianov was a newcomer. For most of the 1920s and 1930s he had served in low-level economic posts. His first big break came in May 1938 with his appointment as first secretary of a district party committee in Baku. Even by the standards of the time, his promotion within six months to lead the republican NKVD was unusual. He was now the head of a republican organization for which he had no experience or qualifications. His tentative hold on his new post rested entirely on the support of his patron.[25]

One of Emel'ianov's main functions was to build up a store of compromising material, to which end his agents tapped phones, placed listening devices in apartments, and subjected their targets to so-called honey traps.[26] Where compromising materials were not easily at hand, they were fabricated. According to one source, Bagirov "converted the ministry of internal affairs into a kind of supraparty agency, an obedient tool for implementing his dirty deeds. (Their method was always the same.) This agency converted the idea of the politically unreliable person, the 'PN' [*politicheskii neblagonadezhnyi*], into an instrument

The award of the Order of Lenin being given to First Secretary Mir Jafar Bagirov of the Azerbaijani central committee (*right*) on 26 January 1946. Courtesy of Russian State Archive of Photographic and Cinematic Documents in Krasnogorsk.

that Bagirov could use as and when he wished. Bagirov turned the ministry into a workshop for fabricating forged documents and creating false charges against all those who were not on his side."[27] A Central Committee report of December 1953 elaborated: "All those who had their own views . . . were blackmailed and openly threatened with being

'left to rot' in prison or 'being chased out of Azerbaijan.' ... Many leading functionaries were threatened with compromising materials [*kom-
prometiruiushie materialy*] and were either evicted from the republic
or, when they themselves couldn't take it any longer, they just left of
their own accord."[28]

Critical to Bagirov's hold on his ruling circle was that the use of
kompromat was not confined to his opponents but was extended to all
who came near him, including his supposed allies and friends. Trust in
the shadowy world of late 1940s Azeri politics was in such short supply
that Bagirov could not allow himself to befriend or depend on anyone
on whom he did not have the goods. In fact, virtually the entire ruling
group around Bagirov, including those who became his firm friends
and closest allies, were people on whom Emel'ianov and his team had
pinned kompromat. This was the ticket into Bagirov's ruling circle.[29]

Evidence on this is somewhat sketchy, but we do have a number of
relatively well-supported sources that surfaced at the time of Bagirov's
fall. In one such account, Bagirov's "best friend," whom Bagirov promoted to secretary of the presidium of the supreme soviet, was in fact
the former "officer of the Turkish Army, Musa Shamsadinskii." When
presented with kompromat against Mir Kasimov Asadully, "what does
Bagirov do? He promotes [Asadully] to president of the Azeri academy
of sciences, knowing full well that as a scholar (a surgeon) he is not up
to much."[30] A Central Committee report of December 1953 observed
what appeared to be a pattern. The upper reaches of the Azeri elite,
including the most senior offices in the party organization, and key
ministries, were filled with people on whom Bagirov had incriminating
material. "Over a number of years," it noted,

> Bagirov has ... elevated to top-ranking positions people of bourgeois-
> kulak origin, sons of policemen, those with close kin in emigration and
> those compromised by their past work. ... The son of the prominent
> merchant Aliev was made secretary of the Azeri central committee ...
> [while the] long-serving secretary of the Azeri central committee, com-
> rade Seidov (now head of gosplan [the Azeri state planning commit-
> tee]), had relations repressed for anti-Soviet activity and others who
> are now based abroad. ... [Moreover] Bagirov promoted as head of
> the industrial-transport department comrade Gasan-Zade, who had
> concealed from the party his social origins and the convictions of close
> relatives for anti-Soviet activity. ... All these people were necessary

to Bagirov so that, in relying on them, he was always sure to have his way.[31]

Owing to the tentative and partial nature of these sources we are not in a position to generalize about the role of secret police–sourced governance through kompromat in this period. What we can say is that Azerbaijan provides a relatively solid example of how kompromat could be used to cohere a ruling coalition.

Informal Exclusion

A second mechanism of network formation is informal exclusion, an example of which comes from the republic of Uzbekistan, where the first secretary from 1937 to 1950 was Usman Iusupov.[32] Like Bagirov's in Azerbaijan, Iusupov's dictatorship operated on two planes. The first concerned his relationship with the outer ring of district-level officials who were expected to fulfill regime policies on the ground. Iusupov's approach toward this group rested on coercion. A predominantly monocultural economy oriented to the cultivation of cotton (in the 1947 plan the republic was expected to account for 71 percent of the all-union plan), agricultural production in Uzbekistan was suited to such a method. Cotton yields depended on high labor effort and low levels of skill and technology, which the party, as a key agent of labor mobilization, was well suited to achieving. A lead role in the seasonal recruitment of a nonagricultural workforce to pick cotton was played by the low-level party *apparat*. For the 1947 season they succeeded in getting over 190,000 urban dwellers out into the countryside. For three months that autumn schoolchildren between the ages of eleven and seventeen and students at technical colleges were forced to abandon their studies. Coercion was exerted through a mix of party-based punishments and police repression. Individual collective farms could have three or four party-mandated plenipotentiaries each to micromanage the campaign at the local level. In the Namanganskii region police detained people in the bazaars, pulled them off the streets, loaded them into lorries, and sent them off, under escort, to the collective farms.[33]

Iusupov's bond with local officials and the party aktiv was also cemented through a personality cult. His articles and speeches were printed in the manner of sacred directives of the party-state and put out for discussion at party meetings. At times this was at odds with the requirements of the party's propaganda machine. In February 1947 the all-union Central Committee held one of its rare postwar plenums, devoted to agriculture. The Central Committee's resolutions were disseminated in *Pravda* and in a mass-circulation pamphlet, in the expectation that they be studied and debated at party meetings. However, in Uzbekistan it was Iusupov's latest article on agriculture, not the Central Committee resolutions, that was circulated. Another element of the Iusupov cult was the numerous portraits which adorned state institutions and loomed over public spaces such as squares, clubs, and recreational parks. Although, as a token gesture, the Uzbek buro, with Iusupov's blessing, called for some of these to be removed, most Uzbek officials knew better than to take this decree seriously and simply ignored it.[34]

But it was in the second dimension of his rule, at the level of authoritarian power sharing, that we can observe the distinctive mechanism by which Iusupov honed his ruling network. Unlike Bagirov, Iusupov had risen through the party ranks on a conventional trajectory. Of peasant stock from a small village in Ferghana, he had joined a local cotton-cleansing plant in 1918. Eight years later, at the age of twenty-six, he was admitted to the party as a "worker-communist." His ascent from that point on was swift. Within three years, in 1929, he had become secretary of the Uzbek central committee. In the 1930s his career took a sideways turn. A three-year stint as the head of the Central Asian buro of the Trade Union Council, followed by two years attending courses on Marxism-Leninism at the Central Committee, had the advantage of keeping Iusupov out of the mainstream of Uzbek politics at a time when the leadership were being wiped out in the Great Purges. In 1937 he became first secretary of the republican party.

By the second half of the 1940s, ten years of running the Uzbek republic had turned the hardened, poorly educated, but quick-witted leader into a skillful politician. A Central Committee report on Uzbekistan early in 1948 depicted a system of one-person rule with a leader surrounded by a circle of acolytes. "In pursuit of his own personal authority," noted the Central Committee report, "comrade Iusupov decides all matters himself and appears to be the initiator of all new proposals."[35] "He is extremely touchy when it comes to objections or disagreement from any member of the buro," one of the Uzbek central

Few photographs of First Secretary Usman Iusupov of the Uzbek central committee survive. This rather blurred one, from 21 December 1949, shows him giving a speech at the Bolshoi Theater as part of the celebrations to mark Stalin's seventieth birthday. Courtesy of Russian State Archive of Photographic and Cinematic Documents in Krasnogorsk.

committee secretaries later remarked.[36] The Central Committee report observed that senior leaders in the republic, and especially the party leaders, had, in effect, turned into Iusupov's clients: "The secretaries of the Uzbek central committee, comrades Lomakin, Bylbas, and others are unable to hold consistent positions of their own and in effect carry out the functions not of central committee secretaries, but of 'aides' or 'assistants' to comrade Iusupov. At one of the meetings of the buro the second secretary, Lomakin, grovelingly declared: 'Your words are golden, Usman Iusupovich, I hope I won't forget them.'"[37]

How had Iusupov managed to achieve this hold over his ruling circle? A principal strategy was to "quarantine" an individual in the leadership, so that while still technically within the ruling elite she or he was informally isolated and marginalized by the others. In Uzbekistan the individual given this treatment was the head of government, A. Abdurakhmanov. Iusupov not only decided all important economic issues that were formally under Abdurakhmanov's jurisdiction but also took charge of cadre issues in the government. "Comrade Iusupov," affirmed the Moscow inspectors, "ignores comrade Abdurakhmanov, does not give him the chance to develop policy through state channels, usurps his functions, and he tries to show that comrade Abdurakhmanov is a poor worker, that he is lazy."[38] Isolating Abdurakhmanov had various benefits. For one thing Abdurakhmanov had to take the flak for any policy failures in the republic. Iusupov could also line up his clients within the ruling group to attack Abdurakhmanov. This was precisely the kind of activity that went beyond their formal duties and could be used to test their loyalty. In this way, informal exclusion was not simply directed against an individual but was a means for the formation of group norms.

Iusupov drew on pressure from above to dramatize these norms. A good example occurred in early 1948, following a downturn in the Uzbek economy. As the disappointing results for cotton procurements in 1947 came in, the Uzbek leaders were summoned to Moscow to explain what had gone wrong. On 3 February 1948 the Politburo passed a resolution "on the mistakes of the Uzbek central committee and of the Uzbek council of ministers in managing the production of cotton." Iusupov and the chair of the council of ministers, Abdurakhmanov, were given severe reprimands, while the second secretary, N.I. Lomakin, was warned about his "uncritical attitude toward shortcomings."[39] Iusupov's visit to Moscow could have gone far worse, but his difficulties were not quite over. By convention, any leader reprimanded by Moscow was, on his return, to brief his party with a modicum of self-criticism. In principle this could have been a moment of danger for the midlevel leader and his network, as there was always a chance that the volley of criticisms might ricochet in unexpected ways. However, as was noted by the Central Committee inspector in attendance, I.I. Pozdniak, the proceedings of the plenum of the Uzbek central committee convened on 26–28 February 1948 were surprisingly muted. The plenum was unusually small, with only 168 participants, largely ex-officio personnel on the party payroll. While Iusupov conceded some mistakes, he remained tight-lipped and refused to go beyond the exact script of the Politburo resolution. Furthermore, while speaking scathingly of his adversary Abdurakhmanov and recycling the Politburo's criticism of Lomakin, he refused to rebuke any other secretary or member of the buro.[40] Meanwhile, other speakers lined up to defend Iusupov. One of the obkom secretaries, for example, explained away Iusupov's "usurpation" of the government's duties by referring to the fact that the council of ministers, headed by Abdurakhmanov, was not doing its work properly. On Podniak's insistence there was a break and a meeting of the Uzbek buro was called, at which point Iusupov was asked "to retract his mistakes."[41] Yet when the plenum reconvened, Iusupov pointedly limited himself to a formal statement, making it clear he was doing so under duress.[42]

The February plenum highlights certain norms that had formed within Iusupov's network. Where the threat from the center was not expressed in a categorical form, republican networks could suddenly tighten as members fell over themselves in defense of their territorial leader. In Uzbekistan each attack afforded Iusupov's clients an opportunity to demonstrate their solidarity. Iusupov reciprocated by showing his own loyalty and by refusing to criticize them. In between, the quarantined Abdurakhmanov and the defector Lomakin acted as lightning rods of the region's failings. The attack from Moscow thus had the odd effect of cohering Iusupov's network.

Overpromotion

In August 1947, in a character reference summarizing his first two years as first secretary of the Vinnitsa obkom, the cadres administration at the Central Committee noted characteristics that would have been broadly familiar to Bespalov in Tambov: "Comrade [Mikhail] Stakhurskii sometimes allows violations of collegiality in the work of the obkom buro and, in dealing with members of the obkom apparat and more generally with party members, he can be rude and tactless."[43] As in Tambov, a later report in April 1948 went on to note that "the turnover of cadres is exceptionally high" with no less than a third of the region's party functionaries having being replaced in the previous year.[44]

And yet, as was true in Volkov's case in Tambov, such criticisms did Stakhurskii little harm. While paying lip service to these failings the Central Committee's overall assessment of Stakhurskii was positive: "Comrade Stakhurskii is a mature party leader, who can adjust quickly to new priorities and mobilize the party organization for the successful implementation of the party and government's decisions."[45] Stakhurskii had a strong reputation for fulfilling plans and maintaining order.

After six years in Vinnitsa he was redeployed as first secretary in Poltava from 1952 to 1955 before moving on to stints in Khabarovsk
from 1955 to 1957 and Zhitomir' from 1957 to 1961.

To fulfill the plan Stakhurskii needed a viable ruling coalition. One
clue to his success was that he was himself a model *vydvezhenets*, a
man of lowly social origins who was fast-tracked into a senior leadership role. Owing to his relative youth (he was forty-two when he
became first secretary), his education (a degree from an agricultural
institute), and his long years of service in the party, which he had joined
in 1921, Stakhurskii was well placed to exploit the opportunities for
promotion opened up by the Great Purges. Within a few years he rose
from director of a machine-tractor station to deputy commissar of agriculture in the Ukraine. During the war he served at the front in a number of political posts, earning the rank of general. As the first secretary
in Vinnitsa, Stakhurskii proceeded to elevate junior cadres, sometimes
over the heads of more senior and deserving colleagues, to senior posts.
A classic mode of network formation in bureaucratic systems, overpromotion of this kind may have elicited feelings of gratitude in the
promoted official but it also had more practical foundations. The promoted cadres knew that their rise was most likely resented by the rest
of the aktiv and that should their patron lose office they too would be
vulnerable. They thus had an objective interest in doing everything in
their power to support their patron and keep him in his post.[46]

In November 1948 the Vinnitsa obkom prepared the papers for the
appointment of district functionaries. Among those nominated to key
posts were candidates with no more than three years' service in the
party.[47] In some cases poorly prepared candidates were nominated for
positions in Stakhurskii's inner circle, positions like the obkom second
secretary. Stakhurskii's tendency to cultivate clients was carefully noted
by the Central Committee inspector, who observed "the faulty practice
in Vinnitsa of transferring functionaries who have patently failed to
new leading positions."[48] This pattern of overpromotion merged with
Stakhurskii's nomination of candidates who may have been vulnerable
for other reasons, such as being opposed by the local party organization. One candidate for raikom secretary who had been blocked by the
district party conference was promoted by Stakhurskii to the apparat
of the regional executive committee. Stakhurskii also demonstratively
stood by another obkom secretary, for ideology, who had attracted the
ire of his superiors in Moscow.[49]

In Kostroma First Secretary I.S. Kuznetsov boasted to the Central Committee that "[under my tenure] dozens of local people have been promoted to leading positions."[50] The pattern of advancement was telling, for it pointed to an important facet of Kuznetsov's network-building strategy. In violation of informal understandings on the established order of precedence Kuznetsov orchestrated a series of rapid promotions of junior figures over the heads of their peers and immediate superiors. This strategy had the effect of antagonizing party "public opinion" and of thereby strengthening the loyalty of the promoted colleague. One example that would later catch the eye of the Central Committee was that of a raikom third secretary, Luk'ianov, who leapfrogged various tiers of the regional hierarchy to become head of the regional administration of agriculture. In a visit to Kostroma in September 1950 the deputy head of the Central Committee party agencies department, E.I. Gromov, censured the practice: "It may very well be that [Luk'ianov] is a fine comrade, but such a method of advancement does him little good, and instead casts a shadow on both Luk'ianov and Kuznetsov."[51]

Overpromotion was regularly practiced in the union republics. Earlier we noted the spectacular promotion of Emel'ianov from raikom party secretary to republican NKVD chief in Azerbaijan within six months, a fact that almost certainly made him beholden to Bagirov. A type of overpromotion was also practiced in Uzbekistan by Iusupov, who, himself lacking higher education, surrounded himself with cadres who were in the same boat. Of the five Uzbek central committee secretaries only one, the propaganda secretary, had a higher education, while three (including Iusupov himself) had only elementary schooling.[52] Iusupov was resolved that what they lacked in qualifications they would more than make up for in loyalty.

Political Exclusion

From 1945 to 1953, out of a membership that grew from 5.76 million to 6.89 million, 1,210,859 members were expelled from the Communist Party. Expulsion from the party meant the loss of nomenklatura benefits, benefits that were more generous and substantial the higher one moved up the pecking order. Moreover, for those party members who had devoted their life to the party and defined their personal identity in party terms, expulsion could be a deeply emotional, even traumatic, experience, one which led in some instances to suicide.[53]

The obkom and in particular the obkom buro exercised tight control over all expulsions. Although the disciplinary process ordinarily involved numerous steps, usually starting with the party cell, the final decision to expel was taken by the obkom buro, under the leadership of the first secretary.[54] It was at this moment that the expelled member had to hand in his or her party card and that they lost the right to attend party meetings; henceforth any appeals to the Commission of Party Control in Moscow came from the appellant as a former party member. Although disciplinary proceedings relating to ordinary rank-and-file members were always initiated by the party cell to which the member belonged, a separate track, normally under the control of the obkom bureaucracy, was created for members of the nomenklatura. Should he so wish, the obkom first secretary could use the threat of expulsion to discipline wayward members of the party, especially full-time party officials, as the mechanisms for initiating and deciding expulsion cases ultimately lay in his hands.[55]

Two factors gave the party's disciplinary process added weight. First, in addition to expulsion, the party's disciplinary proceedings envisaged a number of intermediary punishments, the most important of which were the numerous variants of reprimand (*vygovor*). Although, unlike the figures for expulsions, no overall data are available for the number of reprimands handed out in the late Stalin era, the nearest estimates suggest somewhere between two and three million from 1945 to 1953. Unlike expulsions, reprimands were supposed to have been temporary, with the option of having them expunged from one's party record. However, over time an elaborate eight-grade hierarchy of reprimands was created, with those at the upper end involving the stamping of a permanent mark on a member's registration card.[56] A second factor was the close connection between expulsions and criminal prosecutions. As a safeguard against a repeat of the mass arrests of party members that had occurred in the Great Purges, a rule of November 1938 stipulated that members of the party could be prosecuted only if they had been expelled from the party first. For most members of the party this rule existed in name only.[57] In the cases of more senior officials, however, the rule was observed, and the ability of a party secretary to block an expulsion from the party in effect gave him the power to stop an arrest or a prosecution. The party's disciplinary mechanism thus mutated into a system of protection.

In the early postwar years a large plurality of expulsion cases related not to political offenses, which by then accounted for a tiny fraction of the overall number of expulsions, but to various cases of abuse of office and administrative wrongdoing. These were generated by a series of campaigns, the most prominent of which concerned violations of the agricultural charter on collective farms (September 1946), theft (June 1947), and the money reforms of December 1947.[58] Each of these campaigns exposed party officials and those party members in senior economic posts to the very serious possibility of prosecution, often because it was only by taking shortcuts and violating the rules that these officials could hope to achieve the otherwise unfeasible targets mandated by the center.[59] In these circumstances the power to block a criminal case, which was attached to the office of the party secretary, could become a major source of leverage.

As in the case of kompromat and informal exclusion, the management of political exclusion was significant not so much for the control it afforded over individuals as for the ways it was used to forge group and interagency norms. One of the best examples of this concerns the relationship between the obkom and the regional administration of the security police (MGB). By the late 1940s the situation that had briefly pertained during the Great Purges, when the security police had been placed in control of party structures, was a thing of the past. One reason for this was a rule forbidding the security service from recruiting informants from territorial party structures.[60] Another was that the majority of MGB regional personnel were themselves on the nomenklatura of the obkom.[61] This gave the first secretary leverage over the regional head of the MGB, as the first secretary could have a major say in the selection of the latter's leadership team. But it was a third factor that would play a particularly important role in ensuring that security structures meshed with the overarching system of party governance. This was the party secretary's control over the system of party punishment.

In the early postwar years this would have two direct consequences. First, the MGB could not arrest a party official without the consent of the obkom party secretary. This meant that while campaigns to "raise vigilance" and to "unmask enemies" continued to be a feature of the postwar period, the security police at the regional level were often stopped in their tracks by the regional party organization. As

P.G. Drozdetskii, the exasperated head of the MGB administration in Sverdlovsk oblast complained at a city party conference in February 1950, signals from the MGB containing compromising information on leading personnel were being brushed aside by party secretaries. "There is no forward movement!" he complained. "Rather than purging the apparatus of hostile and alien elements, our efforts are constantly being knocked back."[62]

Second, regional party heads could determine what form of party punishment—up to and including exclusion—MGB leaders themselves could face in the event of wrongdoing. A good example involves the numerous MGB officials, including many regional heads, who were embroiled in the money reforms of December 1947.[63] The reforms, which involved the withdrawal of old denominations and their replacement with new ones, were confiscatory, hitting in particular those with cash holdings. Funds held on the day of the reform in the state savings bank were to be exchanged at more favorable rates. Many Soviet citizens, especially peasants, who rarely made use of the savings bank, found that their cash savings were wiped out. Given the direct threat to their personal holdings many officials with good connections found ways around the reforms. The most common ruse was to deposit the cash in the savings bank but have the transaction backdated, so that it appeared as if the funds had been in the bank before the new policy was announced. Some officials managed to have large sums broken up into smaller parcels of less than three thousand rubles, which, under the provisions of the reforms, were to retain their full value. Among those found to have broken the rules were a relatively large number of MGB officials. In February–March 1948 the head of the MGB in Sverdlovsk, T.M. Borshchev, was sacked for "discrediting himself as a communist during the money reforms." At the obkom plenum of 16 March 1948 the obkom first secretary, Nedosekin, revealed that serious violations had been committed, not only by Borshchev but also by others in the state security apparatus.[64] At the beginning of 1948 a major case in Molotov was brought against the head of the regional MGB, I.I. Zachepy and his subordinates, for rule breaking during the money reforms. Zachepy was fired and expelled from the party.[65] Such scandals underlined to MGB officials their structural dependence on regional party leaders and the benefits of insinuating themselves as loyal members of the wider regional network.

One consequence of this structural dependence was that MGB officials were often simply placed at the service of party secretaries. Their specialist expertise could be used, for example, to deanonymize letters of complaint to the center and to expose critics from the party aktiv. In Pskov at the beginning of 1949 the obkom ordered the local MGB to identify the authors of anonymous complaints.[66] Similarly, in January 1951, in the run-up to the Kytshtymskii *gorkom* (city party committee) conference in Cheliabinsk, the first secretary, Shutov, assigned the head of the town MGB, Malakhov, to "use your intelligence apparatus to discover which of the delegates to the conference is minded to criticize [me], and what sort of criticisms are likely to come up."[67] In many regions party leaders refused to ascribe a special status to MGB functionaries and simply deployed them as special agents and plenipotentiaries in economic campaigns.[68]

Most substate leaders in the postwar period operated in a high-pressure environment in which interpersonal trust was in short supply. They were generally tasked with achieving ambitious targets with limited resources. This could involve them in cutting corners, illicitly shifting resources from one use to another, and tinkering with data. To do this they needed not mere coordination or even cooperation, but loyalty. The rules of the nomenklatura leaned against securing this loyalty through friendship or kinship structures. How were they able to gain it? Their most common devices were kompromat, informal exclusion, overpromotion, and political exclusion, and it was their prolific use of these techniques that turned many substate leaders at the regional level into substate dictators.

Although we have provided evidence of what we believe to have been the ample use of each of these methods in the Soviet regions after the war, we are not in a position to quantify their use or to suggest how widely one method was used in relation to the others. The examples we have suggest that each substate leader drew on a repertoire of such practices. In thinking about the extent of these methods we should remember that each was, in its own way, a double-edged sword. The use of kompromat or overpromotion, for example, could help secure a network, but it could also open charges that the secretary was offering protection to alien elements or that he was encouraging nepotism. Informal exclusion could also elicit complaints and the unwonted intervention of the center. The overuse of any one method was risky, and in this regard most substate leaders found themselves in something of a predicament. Each method carried the risk of intervention from the center. Had they not employed these methods, however, regional leaders would have been unable to secure their networks and to consolidate their power.

CONTESTED AUTOCRATS

In February 1946 an official from the organization and instruction department of the Central Committee, Enodin, reported to Georgii Malenkov on the results of his recent trip to Rostov. Enodin's account focused almost entirely on the liberalism of the regional first secretary, P.I. Aleksandriuk, and his inability to impose his authority in the region. "Meetings of the buro are poorly organized," wrote Enodin.

> All the time obkom personnel are walking in and out and there are constant rejoinders and interruptions. Everyone smokes. Aleksandriuk is withdrawn and unable to bring order to the proceedings. He himself is often late. In fact, the buro is usually led by the second secretary, Pastushenko, while Aleksandriuk fades into the background. His speeches lack sharpness or analysis and are often quite superficial. . . . As a rule, Aleksandriuk does little more than paraphrase what has already been said, with hollow formulations such as: 'We have to do this, it must be done. We cannot go on like this. No one will thank us for it. We must implement the directives of the obkom, we have to work better . . .' and so on.

Enodin noted that Aleksandriuk often yielded to other members of the buro: "He has no problem coming up with a proposal only to withdraw it should another buro member disagree." At a buro meeting on 30 December 1945 Aleksandriuk proposed that a plenipotentiary from the commissariat of procurements be given a warning. When the second secretary proposed a harsher punishment—a reprimand—Aleksandriuk instantly gave in. "I do not insist on my position," he said. "I just raised it for discussion." On 18 January 1946 Aleksandriuk proposed sacking leading officials from a local factory. When he ran into resistance from the obkom third secretary, again the idea was dropped. "I never said that my proposal was final," he added. None of this did much to raise Aleksandriuk's prestige or authority in the eyes of his colleagues. The second secretary scathingly confided to Enodin that, in his view, "Petr Il'ich is a very feeble person."

Enodin recommended that Aleksandriuk be removed from his post, and his boss, Malenkov, duly agreed, ordering that arrangements be made for a replacement.[69] Effecting the change, however, turned out to be a drawn-out process. A further Central Committee report in 1947 concluded that "Aleksandriuk is not up to managing such a large and complex region. . . . He is amiable and easy-going but not sufficiently firm and plainspoken in his dealings with others. There is inertia and a lack of drive in resolving pressing politico-economic questions. He often skirts the difficult issues and responds only slowly to signals from the party organization."[70]

While Aleksandriuk did not lack the requisite party experience, his bearing and temperament were deemed excessively meek for a first secretary. In this regard, his educational background may have counted against him. Aleksandriuk had completed his higher education, having graduated in 1931 from the Kuban pedagogical institute as a teacher of political economy. But in the world of regional machine politics being a cultured or educated secretary was not always an asset. At the September 1946 obkom plenum Aleksandriuk came in for criticism from the rank and file for being aloof and out of touch and for presiding over a breakdown in party discipline.[71]

Aleksandriuk was released as first secretary in August 1947 with the instruction that he be "placed at the disposal of the Central Committee." Aleksandriuk reacted to his unhappy time in Rostov by resolving to be tougher. Yet once reassigned to a new post as second secretary in Riazan, he failed again to make a connection with the rank and file. At the regional party conference eight months after his arrival accusations of arrogance and haughtiness in his dealings with district-level officials came to a head at the election of the obkom, at which fifty-three votes, or 13 percent of the total, were cast against him.[72] Soon after he was dispatched to Moscow "to continue with his studies." This time, however, following a brief stint in the Central Committee apparatus, he was moved on to a succession of low-level positions.[73]

In the comparative theory of dictatorship, contested autocrats, unlike established autocrats, are vulnerable to allied rebellions by their inner circle. The parallel does not work exactly the same way at the substate level because ultimately the right to get rid of a leader rested with the center, in this case the Central Committee. The ruling circle could, however, play a major role in communicating their dissatisfaction with their regional leader to Moscow. This could be a problem for the obkom first secretary, especially when the regional ruling group acted in concert. When this happened, as was the case with Aleksandriuk, it normally did not take long for the first secretary to be sacked.

Another leader who fell into this category was the first secretary of the Smolensk obkom, D.M. Popov, who was accused of weakness by Central Committee officials at around the same time as Aleksandriuk. In October 1947 the cadres administration prepared a dossier on Popov, who had been in his post since 1940, for the Central Committee secretary, Aleksei Kuznetsov. Popov lacked determination and a talent for organization and was insufficiently assertive. Decisions of the obkom were not implemented. At buro meetings lengthy arguments and disagreements arose with obkom secretaries, and in some cases Popov had even found himself in the minority. Moreover, although a number of obkom secretaries and *ispolkom* (regional executive committee) leaders had worked poorly, they had not been fired or replaced.[74] The Popov dossier drew on firsthand accounts by Central Committee officials who had been to Smolensk and had witnessed Popov's leadership at close quarters. They commented on how Popov was "insufficiently tough and hands-on," suggested that he was "too trusting" and "insufficiently resolute." "He has too much faith," they went on, "in whether decisions are passed and not enough concern for whether they are implemented. . . . Despite the fact that Popov has been in leading party work for a while, one feels that he is more of a teacher than an organizer."[75]

As people, Aleksandriuk and Popov were temperamentally averse to conflict, indecisive, and reluctant to follow through on decisions, especially when implementation required the use of force. But they also had very specific relationships with their regional elites. It was their failure to bring together a tightly knit and obedient ruling circle and to win over the aktiv that was the source of their undoing. Although these dynamics were not always easily observed, other outcomes of this kind of leadership were. They could include the inability of a leader to appoint (or to get rid of) individuals within their nomenklatura; the capacity of district-level leaders to lobby successfully for lower plan targets; regular defeats on matters of policy; criticism of their leadership at party meetings; and, after they had departed the region, the first secretary's inability to hold on to his position on the nomenklatura. The immediate postwar period was a particularly uncongenial environment for indecisive, conflict-averse leaders, and for this reason the likes of Aleksandriuk and Popov were rare.[76] When they managed to break through the ranks, they seldom survived for long and were usually unceremoniously ejected from office. Branded as liberal, indecisive, and unassertive, they were undercut by colleagues and repelled by the aktiv.

A PERMISSIVE ENVIRONMENT

On the evening of 4 May 1946 I got a call from Poskrebyshev [Stalin's secretary]. "Come immediately to comrade Stalin's apartment at the Kremlin," he said and put the phone down. Why I was suddenly being summoned to see Stalin was unclear. I had met Stalin before, but this would be my first time in his apartment. As we got there we lingered for a while in the entrance hall. Poskrebyshev slapped me on the shoulder, urged me not to worry, and then left me on my own. Looking around, I saw a rail with one greatcoat, the one we all knew belonged to Stalin. A line from Henry Barbus's novel came to mind: "In the tiny entrance hall your attention was seized by the long army greatcoat, with the peak-cap at the top." It was one thing to read about it but quite another to see it with one's own eyes. So here I was, in the entrance hall. To say that I was extremely nervous would have been something of an understatement.[77]

A month earlier the author of these words, Nikolai Patolichev, had come to Moscow to head the party organs department.[78] Before his current posting he had been obkom first secretary in Iaroslavl' from 1939 to 1941, and afterward, from 1942 he had served as the head of the regional party organization in Cheliabinsk, one of the largest industrial regions in the country. After a while Patolichev was admitted to Stalin's rooms.

"Tell me," Stalin said, "you are the head of the party organs department at the Central Committee. How does the Central Committee manage its regional party organizations?" I couldn't quite tell what he had in mind. He repeated. "Tell me, how are party organizations operating in the regions, and how is the Central Committee leading them?" The question in itself was a simple one but answering it was not easy. "Comrade Stalin I have been in charge of the party organs department for no more than a month, and in that capacity I can't tell you much that will be useful. But I do understand the importance of your question and, if you will allow me, will address it not from the point of view of a Central Committee department, but from that of a former obkom first secretary." Stalin agreed and began to listen carefully. I began to share various episodes from Cheliabinsk . . . and then went on to explain that some of our most important questions . . . were completely unknown to the apparatus of the Central Committee. . . . Moreover, that wasn't just my view, for it was shared by other obkom [first] secretaries. . . . "We shall have to restore the power of the Central Committee over the regional party agencies," he said. "Let's think, how can we reorganize the work of the Central Committee? What new organizational forms should we introduce at the Central Committee? Let's create a new administration at the Central Committee and let's call it the administration for checking party organs." We agreed. The suggestion, it seemed, was a good one. With the matter settled, he then added: "And we shall appoint you as its head."[79]

Two aspects of this exchange are worth highlighting. The first is Patolichev's admission that many of the most important issues facing regional party organizations "were completely unknown to the apparatus of the Central Committee."[80] The second is what appears to be Stalin's deep interest in organizational matters, in trying to find an organizational solution to the center's problem of managing its regions.

Although the new administration was intended, in Stalin's words, to "restore the power of the Central Committee over the regional party agencies," the general tendency in the early years after the war was to let regional party leaders run their own affairs as they saw fit. This was reflected in two developments. First, on 21 April 1947 the plenipotentiaries of the Commission of Party Control, the KPK, were disbanded, and the institutional structures that had supported them were closed down. A continuing legacy of the war, these plenipotentiaries, who by April 1947 were stationed in fifty regions and *krais* (larger administrative units) in the Russian Soviet Federative Socialist Republic (RSFSR) as well as in four regions of the Ukraine and seven of the union republics (Azerbaijan, Belorussia, Kazakhstan, Kirgizia, Tajikistan, Turkmenia, and Uzbekistan), had long been a thorn in the side of provincial party leaderships. As a package, the dual reorganization—the establishment of the administration and the withdrawal of the KPK plenipotentiaries—suited most territorial leaders, for unlike the administration's officials, who were based in Moscow, the KPK plenipotentiaries had resided permanently in the regions and had been better placed there to intervene in the activities of local leadership networks.

Second, Moscow remained extremely accommodating of its most unruly substate leaders. To highlight this point let us consider two examples. The first concerns the inaugural head of the new Kaluga obkom, I.G. Popov, following the formation of a new Kaluga oblast (out of parts of the old Moscow and Smolensk oblasts) in July 1944. Although Kaluga fulfilled its procurement plan that autumn, Popov soon emerged as a heavy-handed boss who suppressed those around him, including his fellow obkom secretaries. Two reports, in August 1945 and April 1946, noted Popov's "incorrect style and methods of leadership" and the "unhealthy working atmosphere" he had created. The reports cited claims of data falsification in Kaluga and noted Popov's personal indulgence, crowned by his seizure of the finest mansion in the city center, formerly the gorkom building, for his own personal use.[81] As *Pravda*'s correspondent remarked in a communiqué to the Central Committee a month later, this act went down particularly badly in a town still in ruins.[82] Short of firing a regional leader, a standard Central Committee response was to clip his wings by removing a dependent or two from his inner circle, which Moscow proceeded to do. When a later Central Committee brigade, on a visit to the region, unearthed yet more abuses, the Central Committee apparatus decided to go a step further by proposing that Popov be sacked.[83] That month the chair of the Kaluga regional executive committee, Shurygin, took matters into his own hands. He traveled to Moscow and, on gaining entry to the Central Committee building, burst into the office of the Central Committee secretary, Aleksei Kuznetsov, and unloaded his grievances, reciting in detail stories of Popov's ill treatment of his colleagues.[84]

This did little to move Popov. Indeed, having seen off the region's KPK plenipotentiary, an inveterate opponent, in April 1947, he managed as well to have the obkom second secretary, who had tried to stand up to him, recalled. He went so far as to table a proposal that the chair of the regional executive committee, Shurygin, be dismissed.[85] In the summer of 1947 the increasingly sour atmosphere in the region prompted a string of communiqués from the cadres administration making the case, in even bolder terms, for Popov's removal.[86] In December 1947 a further report calling for the sacking of Popov accused him of poor leadership of agriculture and of forming "unhealthy relations" with colleagues.[87]

This latest bid to unseat Popov might well have met the same fate as earlier ones had Popov not carried out what was, even by his standards, a completely reckless act. On the eve of the currency reform of December 1947, he colluded with the head of the regional administration of the savings bank to backdate large deposits to the bank under his own name as well as those of his brother and son. His objective was to preserve the value of his assets, which, as bank deposits, could be exchanged at a rate of three old rubles to one new one whereas cash denominations were exchanged at the punitive rate of ten to one. The move was a bold one because it could easily be traced by outside auditors, as it duly was. Popov had finally crossed Moscow's red line. In an exceptionally rare move, on 13 March 1948 Popov was expelled from the party by the Politburo.[88] It thus took almost eighteen months and a major breach of the law for Popov to be fired.

The party apparatus was joined by other, more specialized supervisory central agencies whose inspectors and commissions were a common feature of life in the provinces. Yet here too we find that in clashes between agents of the center and a powerful regional party leader it was the latter, most often, who came out on top. A striking example of such an outcome involves an infamous scandal in Azerbaijan in the summer of 1948. The case began with a review in May 1948 of the financial operations of the Azerbaijan government by the USSR Ministry of State Control (*goskontrol*).[89] The review had been prompted by an unusually heavy flow of letters and complaints detailing cases of bribery and protectionism in the republic. On arriving in Azerbaijan the ministerial team soon discovered other violations, including instances of large-scale theft by senior officials and the construction of country houses at state expense. The goskontrol commission was sufficiently confident of its materials to lay the politically loaded charge that certain senior leaders in Azerbaijan "do not inspire political trust." Sensing the threat hanging over him, Bagirov launched a counteroffensive which involved setting up a honey trap. To this end his security chief arranged an orgy attended by the head and other members of the goskontrol team that was secretly filmed.[90] Bagirov forwarded the films to Stalin, who ordered an inquiry.[91]

The commission's conclusions were sufficiently one-sided to suggest that Stalin had signaled at a relatively early stage of the proceedings that he would stand by Bagirov. On 30 July 1948 the Politburo, presided over by Stalin and attended by Bagirov, condemned the goskontrol investigation for having been improperly conducted, citing "the Minister of State Control, Mekhlis, for without sufficient reason . . . broadening the scope of the inquiry" and allowing it to be carried out in a "biased and tendentious way."[92] The main thrust of the charges against the Moscow inspectors was that they had been "particularly solicitous of the concerns of the 'complainants,' taking no account of the position of the central committee of Azerbaijan, thereby prompting a surge of appeals from all manner of dubious individuals." In connection with the Azerbaijan scandal, the Politburo curtailed the powers of the ministry over regional agencies.[93] There was no attempt to fudge the issue or to present the result as some kind of compromise: Bagirov and the regional interests he represented had won a clear victory over a formidable adversary, one with long-standing and well-known ties to the statewide dictator. Emboldened by this victory, the buro of the Azeri central committee on 24 September 1948 adopted a resolution "On anonymous statements against leading party and soviet functionaries in Azerbaijan." This move, in a series of widely publicized show trials, mobilized the system of justice and law enforcement to apply " the most severe punishments" to "slanderers" and other "unscrupulous, enemy types."[94]

What accounts for the proliferation of substate dictators after the war? A number of circumstantial factors flowed from the war itself. One was the assumption by regional party leaders during the war of important decision-making powers from the center.[95] Another was the cultural imprint of quasi-military forms of decision making from the war years. The economic context also played a role. The challenges of reconstruction and the first traces of the looming Cold War fed into a hyperambitious five-year plan, inaugurated by Stalin in February 1946. As national goals were disaggregated into extremely taut branch and territorial quotas, local leaders were expected to use all available means to attain these targets. Most important of all, however, was that the obkoms had been led, since the Great Purges, by a new generation of so-called young generals who had been politically forged under Stalin and who owed their rise to him. For all the rhetoric about nepotism and family circles and for all of the efforts to improve the center's control mechanism, the dictator appears to have understood the need to grant his generals some leeway in managing their regions as best they could.

How did the substate leaders respond? In terms of the dilemma of authoritarian control—containing the rank and file—most tended to effect high levels of turnover and to resort to extremely coercive methods of rule. In terms of the dilemma of authoritarian power sharing, they turned to more oblique and indirect forms of leverage, which included informal and political exclusion, overpromotion, and the use of incriminating materials from party and security police repositories, in order to fashion small and compliant inner circles.

2 Authoritarian Checks and Balances

INSTITUTIONS ARE REGULAR, rule-like practices that shape human interaction. They can be large or small, formal or informal, political or economic, but for an institution to be effective the rules need to be clearly articulated and rooted in shared expectations. When Nikolai Patolichev was transferred as obkom first secretary from Iaroslavl' to Cheliabinsk he was, notes one commentator, "not consulted in advance but simply instructed by telephone to appear in the Kremlin the next day."[1] The appointment was grounded in an ensemble of rules on the transfer and promotion of obkom secretaries that was accepted by all the relevant actors. Stalin's difficulty was that the rules which allowed him to exert control over the obkom secretaries did not enable him to pierce into the very depths of the system, where statewide policies were put into effect.

The Soviet dictatorship got around this problem through acts of controlled delegation. The recipients of these power transfers were the midlevel leaders, the obkom first secretaries. They in turn drew on institutions for gathering information, for expelling party members, and—an informal institution—for imposing social exclusion to build their own ruling alliances. In the institutional design of the Soviet system, however, party leaders did not hold all the cards. The party apparatus was at the center of an interlocking directorate that radiated out and

encompassed a number of other organizations. Ministries and large enterprises disposed of resources, state organizations performed administrative and ceremonial functions, and the security police were charged
with various forms of surveillance and repression. In some cases even
the most skillful territorial party leader could run up against regional
actors whose institutions and resources lay beyond his control.

Echoing the depiction of party leaders as dictators, Soviet fiction of
the postwar period is awash in images of headstrong directors of all-
union economic enterprises like the head of a large car plant in the
Urals who "bullied, crushed, and stamped on everybody under him"
and the head of a steel combine, also in the Urals, who "for all practical purposes was also the boss of the city."[2] We examine these actors,
suggesting that their authority stemmed not only from the assets at
their disposal, but also from the fact that they and the territorial first
secretaries with whom they worked were assessed on the same criteria,
so that both actors had a strong incentive to cooperate. In some cases
party leaders went further than merely cooperating by acquiescing in
the emergence of alternative rule-like practices at the behest of an economic ministry or an all-union enterprise. We also assess leaders of two
other regional organizations, the state apparatus and the security police. In general these were far less powerful than the directors of large
factories. In two limiting cases, however, they too presented serious
challenges to a territorial party leader.

Obkom first secretaries, the directors of large factories, and heads
of regional state and security organizations operated at the level of authoritarian power sharing. In the second part of the chapter we move
on to the limits of authoritarian control. In order to mitigate his agency
problem the statewide dictator came up with a variety of institutional
checks to test the effectiveness of regional leaders. A key function of
elections was to convey information to the center on the ability of obkom secretaries, in the language of the day, to "lead the aktiv." Yet
when upward of six or seven hundred delegates assembled to give vent
to anger from below, some regional leaders found it hard to cope. This
could turn into a real problem, especially for some of the more forceful
substate dictators of the kind encountered in chapter 1.

The relatively lax policy of the center toward the regions that prevailed after the end of the war was ruptured with the Leningrad Affair
of 1949. This was followed by a series of dismissals of territorial party

leaders in Cheliabinsk, Perm, Ul'ianovsk, Estonia, and Georgia. For the first time in almost a decade the regime embarked on regional network purges with real casualties. But despite the potential of these purges to spread and envelop the rank and file, they were surprisingly targeted and muted in their effects. A key institutional innovation gave cadres who had run into trouble a soft landing, affording not only them but their overseers in Moscow a new degree of protection.

FACTORY DIRECTORS

In the Stalinist economy the party apparatus was often an important source of noneconomic incentives to spur growth. This was especially so in the countryside, where agricultural production often depended on coercive pressure from party officials. In the industrial sector the situation was more complex. Industrial enterprises often operated under Moscow or republican-based ministries with their own chains of command. Here, too, the party leadership could be called on to solve particular problems, especially when a party-led campaign was on and the "party's leadership of industry" was being emblazoned by the press.

Factory directors, however, often had interests of their own that sometimes were at odds with those of regional party leaders. The main goal of the director was to fulfill the plan at any cost. In many cases this entailed a predatory approach to local resources; everything was done to maximize output, even if it were to the detriment of social welfare. The goals of regional leaders were more complex. Along with plant directors, they were accountable for plan fulfillment of enterprises on their territory. Yet as heads of the regional party-state they were also responsible for the other, nonindustrial branches of the economy, such as agricultural procurement, and for the provision of public goods. Underlying the relationship between the two there was normally a tacit exchange. Territorial party leaders knew that their standing often depended on the ability of their large factories to meet the plan, and they did what they could to help them by easing production blockages, mobilizing labor, and arranging emergency transportation and the provision of food. For their part, factory directors could siphon off central ministerial investments in order to meet welfare goals, so that housing stock was maintained and the transportation, health, and educational systems in their company towns were supported. A successful relationship between a party secretary and factory directors tended to rest on cooperation based on compromises and mutual concessions.

Moscow was aware of such arrangements and, on the whole, quite comfortable with them. But there was also scope for slippage. Party leaders sometimes became so fixated on plan fulfillment that they lost sight of their own independent role as auditors and enforcers of discipline. The proliferation of gifts and financial inducements from factory and ministerial officials to party leaders was also a matter of concern, for although, when given in public, these gifts symbolized the status superiority of party leaders, they also seemed to suggest that these leaders were being bribed. Worryingly for Moscow, the spread of such practices appeared to blunt the party's wider claim to ideological leadership.[3] On 29 May 1946 the newly appointed Central Committee secretary Nikolai Patolichev (until recently the first secretary of Cheliabinsk) wrote to the new Central Committee inspector, Vasilii Andrianov (previously the first secretary of Sverdlovsk), instructing him to phone "all the obkom first secretaries and agree to put an immediate end to the awarding of bonuses and prizes [by economic managers] to party functionaries."[4] On 2 August 1946 the Politburo passed a resolution "On granting prizes and bonuses to regional leaders by USSR ministries and other economic organizations." Some of the examples given were primarily material or pecuniary in nature. The resolution cited the USSR minister of paper industries who had awarded a deputy secretary of the Molotov obkom a month's salary and a lavish gift. Other presentations were more symbolic. The USSR minister of timber industries presented gold watches to the first secretary and chair of the council of ministers of the Udmurt autonomous republic and hunting rifles to the first secretary and chair of the executive committee of the Kalinin region. But in each case what worried the Central Committee was a wider issue:

> We condemn as wrong and harmful the awarding of prizes and bonuses by economic managers to party and soviet leaders. The acceptance by party workers of sops and gratuities symbolizes an unhealthy relationship and marks, in effect, a form of bribery [podkup]. In making party leaders obliged to the economic agencies and trapping them in webs of nepotism [semeistvennosti], such practices prevent party officials from holding the economic agencies to account, so that party workers lose sight of their role and purpose and become mere playthings in the hands of economic organizations. This is a disgrace . . . and opens a path to the ruin and destruction of our party agencies.[5]

The Central Committee campaign that followed revealed how ministries and factory directors were "topping up" the salaries of party functionaries and lavishing scarce commodities on them.[6] From the point of view of senior party leaders in Moscow there was a yet more worrying development. Economic managers were not just engaged in individual acts of exchange but were introducing regular practices that appeared to encroach on the party's primary institutional role. One investigation in Ukraine, which focused on Dnepropetrovsk, Kharkov, Voroshilovgrad, and Stalinsk, scathingly criticized the understandings that had crystallized between economic and party leaders because they seemed to suggest that factory directors were actively subverting the party's nomenklatura by preparing their own rival lists of party officials that detailed side payments and entitlements by rank. In Dnepropetrovsk the list of recipients included the second secretaries of the Dnepropetrovsk obkom and gorkom and nine lower-order obkom functionaries. In Kharkov the gorkom gave factory directors a precise schedule of who among its officials was entitled to what combination of supplements, groceries, and industrial goods. The investigation was quite candid about what exactly each side was bringing to the table. For their part, party leaders were paid for suspending their statelike functions, such as the accurate auditing of exchanges and the application of punishment to offenders. In 1945 the Voroshilovgrad coal combine perpetrated a statistical fraud in order to make it seem it had met the plan. But the cheating was so blatant that it could have been achieved only with the collusion of the obkom. For turning a blind eye, obkom functionaries were given generous one-off payments, including fourteen thousand rubles to the deputy secretary of the obkom for coal industries. In addition to money and goods there were services on offer. In Kharkov airplane factory no. 135 repaired fifteen cars that obkom functionaries, including the first secretary, Churaev, had looted during the war. In return, party officials swept under the carpet a host of offenses and violations by the factory's director and chief engineer.[7]

The formal prohibition on bonuses and awards did little to disturb the underlying culture of ministerial condescension toward regional party actors. On 10 March 1948 the deputy head of the administration for checking party organs, G.A. Borkov, complained to the Central Committee secretary, Andrei Zhdanov, that "recently, certain all-union and republican ministries . . . have got into the habit of issuing . . . barefaced orders to the obkoms and kraikoms. . . . Many telegrams . . . from the ministries and chief administrations are not only unacceptable in their mode of address, but betray in their content a complete misunderstanding of the role and position of the party committee."[8] In Penza the RSFSR minister of state farms refused to recognize the obkom's appointment of a state farm director, even though the position was included on the latter's nomenklatura. The minister followed up his decision with a warning: "I refuse to recognize you as director. Your right to draw funds from the Agricultural Bank and from the State Bank has been annulled. You are warned that should you stay on the territory of the *sovkhoz* [state farm] any longer we will press criminal charges."[9]

With the backing of powerful ministries in Moscow, heads of large factories could sometimes deal with territorial party leaders on equal terms; where the factories were especially large and their directors well-known, they could even overshadow them. Probably the best-known example of this was in Cheliabinsk, home to the massive Kirov tractor plant. On 26 January 1950 the regional first secretary, A.A. Beloborodov, was dismissed by the Politburo. The accompanying resolution listed a number of faults in his work, but what stood out was the criticism that Beloborodov, along with the obkom second secretary, Leskov, had in effect suspended the obkom's leadership and supervisory duties over the Kirov plant and instead turned the obkom bureaucracy into a shield and instrument of protection for the recently departed director of the plant, I.M. Zal'tsman. The resolution read, "Not only did [Beloborodov and Leskov] fail to act on the various signals they had received on Zal'tsman's antiparty activities, but they hid these from the Central Committee and even tried to root out and punish those who had come out against Zal'tsman."[10] Rather than holding the plant and Zal'tsman to account the obkom's auditing and policing had been turned on their head and used instead to silence dissenters and to discipline Zal'tsman's critics.[11]

Six months earlier Zal'tsman, one of the best-known factory directors in the USSR, had been dismissed in the "anticosmopolitan" witch hunt that had aimed to rid the upper ranks of the party and the economic elite of persons of Jewish descent.[12] While it had an unmistakable anti-Semitic coloring, the Zal'tsman Affair also exposed a more general fault line in the Soviet system of administration. As one of the most important enterprises in the USSR, the Kirov plant is a stark example of how the director of a large factory might occupy a special position

Director Isaak Zal'tsman of the Cheliabinsk Tank Factory, 15 March 1946. Courtesy of Russian State Archive of Photographic and Cinematic Documents in Krasnogorsk.

First Secretary Aleksandr Beloborodov of the Cheliabinsk obkom in 1946. Courtesy of Russian State Archive of Photographic and Cinematic Documents in Krasnogorsk.

Director Grigorii Nosov of
the Magnitogorsk Metal-
lurgical Industrial Com-
plex in 1946. Courtesy of
Russian State Archive of
Photographic and Cinematic
Documents in Krasnogorsk.

in a regional network. This was especially true in Cheliabinsk, as the
Kirov plant was not the only enterprise of all-union significance. Two
hundred miles southwest of the city of Cheliabinsk, but still within
the province, was the famous Magnitogorsk metallurgical combine,
headed by Grigorii Nosov.[13] Although Nosov was not mentioned in
the Politburo resolution of 26 January, his role, like Zal'tsman's, was
discussed at some length at the obkom plenum convened to discuss
Beloborodov's dismissal.

How had Zal'tsman and Nosov become so powerful? Born in the
same year, both were archetypical *vydvizhentsy*, young men who, in
their early thirties, had risen to preeminence in the aftermath of the
Great Purges. Zal'tsman's ascent was the most striking. In 1938, at
the age of thirty-three, he had been put in charge of the Leningrad
Kirov plant, which, as "Krasnyi putilovets" (as it had been known until
Kirov's assassination in 1934), was one of the oldest and largest metal
and machine plants in the country. Moved at the beginning of the war
to Cheliabinsk, the factory, with Zal'tsman at the helm, adapted its
production to military use and became one of the most important

defense enterprises in the Soviet Union, supplying the front with tanks and other military equipment. Apart from its size the factory had great symbolic meaning, producing, first, tractors and then tanks, the two hallmarks of Stalinist industrialization. It was testimony to the position of the factory and of Zal'tsman's role in it that in 1941, while still director, he became deputy commissar for tank production in the USSR. The following year, from June 1942 to June 1943, Zal'tsman briefly left Cheliabinsk to become commissar of tank industry, but he resumed the directorship of the plant on stepping down from that position. Heading one of the largest enterprises in the country, Zal'tsman had independent channels to Moscow, as manifested in an office telephone with a direct line to Stalin.[14] As a mark of his achievements, Zal'tsman was awarded the most coveted prizes and medals in the Soviet system.[15] While even those sympathetic to him conceded that he could be brusque and frank to the point of rudeness, all agreed that the charismatic and energetic Zal'tsman had an unusual capacity to get things done.[16] The other factory director of note was G.I. Nosov. At the age of thirty-five, in 1940, Nosov had become the director of the largest plant in the country, the symbol of the first five-year plan, the Magnitogorsk Metallurgical Combine. Like Zal'tsman, Nosov was nominated as deputy of the Supreme Soviet in 1946 and had several decorations as well as twice being a recipient of the Stalin prize.

By contrast, the regional party secretary Beloborodov cut a pale, unprepossessing figure. Like Zal'tsman and Nosov, Beloborodov was a vydvezhenets, a man of working-class origins who quickly shot up to a position of prominence. Within two years, from 1939 to 1941, he had gone from a rank-and-file agronomist to the chair of the Cheliabinsk regional executive committee; by 1946 he had become first secretary of one of the largest and strategically most important regions in the country. But from the beginning Beloborodov's fortunes and career opportunities were almost entirely dependent on the achievements of the two directors and their factories. Much of his energy was devoted to serving their plants, whose value and import in Moscow's eyes were more or less coterminous with those of the province. Beloborodov inherited his stance toward the two directors from his predecessor, Nikolai Patolichev. We catch a glimpse of this from Patolichev's frank, unguarded reminiscences of the two, especially Zal'tsman: "Ok, the man can behave like a hooligan and he can be rude, but what can one do? He is a veritable Atlas [that is, in Greek mythology a Titan who holds up the sky], an incredible organizer, and we need such people now. We have absolutely no choice but to put up with him."[17]

Beloborodov's inability to stand up to the Cheliabinsk directors was the main theme of the obkom plenum of 3 February 1950 that ratified his dismissal. The tone was set by the Central Committee representative at the meeting who accused the obkom secretaries of "canoodling with the directors of certain large factories and removing them from the purview of our party committees."[18] This position was expressed more sharply by the secretary of the Traktorozavodskii raikom, on whose territory the Kirov plant was situated: "Beloborodov's lack of firmness comes from the fact that he cozies up to the factory directors. This puts him in a position of dependence, so that all matters of broader principle end up being settled informally [po-semeinomu]. How . . . could he have possibly punished these directors when he himself was so afraid of them?"[19] Beloborodov's error was not simply that he failed to hold the factory and its directors to account but that he converted the obkom and its apparatus into a protective buffer that could be used to "take care" of those in the party organization who dared to criticize the plant or its director.[20]

If one measure of the effective sovereignty of factory directors was their ability to nullify the auditing and supervisory functions of the party apparatus, another was the credit they took for the provision of public goods. As Nosov boasted at the plenum, "Our factory controls the town, the tram system, the water supply, the provision of electricity, the construction of public buildings and housing . . . and around 60% of the trade as well as large-scale agriculture."[21] The local authorities depended entirely on Nosov's goodwill for the distribution of resources. In some cases Nosov seemed to have gone further than he needed in order to demonstrate his power over the local administration. For example, he ignored requests from the local authority to help the city hospitals, only later to assign, at his own convenience, five doctors to a five-story building under his control so that he could start up an independent hospital for the factory. Acting in this way, it was said at the plenum, "[Nosov] deeply humiliated the city soviet and the gorkom and in doing so had underlined his own importance."[22] In Magnitogorsk Nosov did as he pleased and dealt, as did Zal'tsman, directly with regional leaders over the head of city and district structures.[23]

At the February 1950 plenum the factory directors were shown to have bragged about their powers, humiliated local party secretaries, and given the impression that the obkom leader, Beloborodov, was at their beck and call. In relation to the Central Committee, however, Zal'tsman and Nosov were no match. The factory directors were easily swatted aside by Moscow which, in addition to sacking them, expelled Zal'tsman from the party and forced Nosov publicly to recant his mistakes.[24] Neither ever recovered. While Zal'tsman was consigned to rank-and-file positions in medium-sized provincial enterprises, Nosov was completely crushed, had a breakdown, and within a year and a half, at the age of forty-six, he was dead.[25]

Given the unusual prominence of the plants in Cheliabinsk, the power of the directors there can be regarded as a limiting case. The basic model of the relationship between industrial bosses and territorial party leaders which it exposed was not unusual however. As were the directors of large enterprises, territorial party leaders were judged on the ability of large factories in their region to meet the plan, and to that extent the two had a common interest. In addition, large enterprises could have important welfare functions and use their control of economic assets to disburse financial rewards and other supplements to obkom officials. In return, the obkom could offer cover to the enterprise director who broke the rules by intercepting complaints, blocking channels of communication, and doing what it could to ease the regulatory and disciplinary burden on the factory. In some cases, by introducing their own practices—for example, on the allocation of financial supplements—factory directors threatened to undercut the prerogatives of the party. Even after the national crackdown on such practices, party secretaries and the directors of large factories knew that to achieve their own goals they had to strike compromises. This was, in general, one of the most important constraints on the power of any regional party leader.

PARTY AND STATE

Largely because they did not command resources on the same scale, it was rare for other regional-level actors to compete with a territorial party leader in the way that the director of a factory of all-union significance could. The heads of most other regional agencies could be reeled in using the techniques outlined in chapter 1. There were, however, some instances where rival coalitions could form, especially where an organizational cleavage coincided with a personality clash. The most common examples of this involved the obkom first secretary and the head of the state apparatus.

In theory the regional political system consisted of interlocking party and state directorates, with one supplementing and reinforcing the other. Although the Soviet constitutional order aimed to integrate the two, the harmony was sometimes disfigured by personal conflicts, with both sides mobilizing the resources of their office to fight bureaucratic turf wars. In the early postwar years there was one contextual factor which could add spice to such disputes. This was the regime's war-time policy of ethnic mobilization, aimed at galvanizing mass support among the country's national minorities for the Soviet war effort, usually through the publication of national histories and of popular heroic literature in the national language of the titular ethnic group. In some cases, regional heads of state who were members of the titular national group could harness these policies to build up a personal following.[26]

A good example of the head of the state apparatus capitalizing on the war-era policy of ethnic mobilization in order to drive home their own claim to lead the republic comes from the Chuvash autonomous republic (ASSR). Early tensions there between the first secretary, I.M. Charykov, and the chair of the council of ministers, A.M. Matveev, first came to light in 1943. According to the recollections of members of the obkom buro, Matveev began to avoid the first secretary and cut him out of important decisions that, while technically within the remit of the council of ministers, had broader ramifications and would normally have been regarded as being within the jurisdiction of the first secretary. One of the most flagrant cases occurred when Matveev, without consulting Charykov, unilaterally set higher rations for workers in the soviet apparat than for those in the party bureaucracy. After this, the two men's relations worsened. From 1943 to the beginning of 1944 "not a single meeting of the obkom buro passed without violent arguments between Matveev and Charykov."[27] Before long Moscow got wind of the feud, and Charykov and Matveev were summoned to the Central Committee, where they promised to mend their "unhealthy relations" (*nenormal'nye vzaimootnosheniia*).[28] Little good, however, came of this agreement.

On 25 December 1944 the KPK plenipotentiary in the Chuvash ASSR, I. Logvin, filed a detailed report to Malenkov on the deepening squabble between Charykov and Matveev. Included in the report were accounts of how Matveev failed to recognize Charykov's authority and even refused to meet with him. A matter of high concern was that the conflict had begun to fan out as each leader enlisted his supporters. In the ensuing battle it was Matveev who made the most headway, gaining the backing of the obkom second secretary, Akhazov, among others. As Logvin explained, Matveev was regarded by many members of the ruling network as the real boss of the republic, and even those who did not view themselves as his natural supporters thus began to take their lead from him.[29] In March 1945 a Central Committee commission visiting the republic confirmed the thrust of Logvin's report. As was its wont, the Central Committee lent its support to the first secretary, Charykov. At a closed meeting of the obkom buro attended by the head of the organization and instruction department of the Central Committee, M.A. Shamberg, Matveev was reprimanded. Still, however, he refused to cede ground, speaking out against Charykov and blocking decisions of the obkom buro with which he disagreed. At this point Matveev used the state-based apparatus as a tool of ethnic mobilization by painting himself as, in effect, the leader of the republic. Ahead of upcoming elections to the USSR Supreme Soviet he ordered a local Chuvash writer to compose a sketch on "Anton Matveevich Matveev— true son of our people," comparing Matveev with Lenin. The sketch was broadcast on local radio.[30]

In June 1946 Charykov went on the offensive. He attacked Matveev at the obkom plenum and at the obkom buro, accusing him of sidelining the regional party administration and of personally rebuffing him. Matveev responded that Charykov was touchy and small-minded and that he obsessed over minor issues. Some members of the buro backed Charykov, but the second secretary, Akhazov, adopted a holding position, proposing that the matter be revisited at a later date.[31] The confrontation at the buro backfired, for it demonstrated that Charykov lacked the personal authority to bring Matveev to heel. The buro was split down the middle, Charykov gaining the support of the obkom third secretary and the minister of internal affairs and Matveev that of Akhazov. "Other members of the buro," the inspector from the cadres administration reported, "are aware of this division and find it difficult to come to any decision, for they do not know which side to back."[32] The situation approximated the classical predicament of dual power as divisions at the top were replicated lower down the political order, with two chains of command, one loyal to Matveev and the other to Charykov, lining up against each other. "In various districts the chairs of district executive committees are beginning to follow Matveev's example [and to bypass] the raikoms," noted the instructor from the cadres administration.[33]

Once the feud between Charykov and Matveev began to undermine the machinery of government, the Central Committee was forced to take a stand. In March 1947, after three years of conflict, Matveev was sacked.[34] Although Matveev was gone, the ongoing saga had also eroded Charykov's credibility. A year and a half later, in November 1948, he too was removed, and, following a study break in Moscow, he permanently lost his rank on the nomenklatura.[35]

Although the Soviet constitutional order aimed to integrate the party and state apparatuses, in some cases the two divided. In a number of regions high-level conflict between obkom first secretaries and the chairs of regional executive committees appeared to grow, as in Chuvashiia, almost organically out of the two-pronged structure of the soviet party-state.[36] A second type of conflict saw the cleavage between an obkom first secretary and a regional head of state overlapping with a split between native and outside officials appointed from beyond the region. The Central Committee would normally appoint an outsider with a view to shaking up a local network, but on occasion the ensuing conflict could be quite destabilizing and go beyond what Moscow had in mind. In such instances Moscow, mindful of the need to maintain authority, could take the side of the local politician, even if he was not the first secretary.

A good example of such a conflict occurred in the Mari autonomous republic where, again, the origins of the dispute went back to the war. Incessant disagreements between the then first secretary and members of the buro had led Moscow to a clear-out of the obkom buro.[37] The new first secretary, who took office in the spring of 1945, was I.T. Kolokolkin, a sector head from the Central Committee. According to some reports Kolokolkin did not view the posting with particular enthusiasm. One local official recalls that from the beginning

Kolokolkin showed contempt toward the local cadres and insisted on new blood being brought in from the outside.[38] Certainly Kolokolkin did little to ingratiate himself with the local cadre and ethnic Mari, G.I. Kondrat'ev, who became head of the republican council of ministers. In January 1948 Kondrat'ev wrote directly to the Central Committee secretary, Aleksei Kuznetsov, to complain of Kolokolkin's behavior: "For a while now Kolokolkin has been rude and quite tactless toward our people . . . he suppresses criticism . . . and runs meetings in a tense atmosphere. [He will say] 'With one flick of the wrists I can have the whole lot of you fired.' . . . More than once he has wrapped up meetings with intimidation and insults. . . . [I]n one of our conversations this year he declared: 'Your fate hangs on me. I can just pick up the phone and [it's all over for you].'"[39] Sensing a repeat of the original debacle which had induced Moscow to send Kolokolkin in the first place, Moscow withdrew its support for him. In September 1948 he left the region to pursue his studies at the Higher Party School in Moscow, vacating the position for Kondrat'ev.

It is notable that both these cases of party–state conflict occurred in autonomous republics with ethnically diverse populations. Unlike the union republics, where the population tended to be dominated by the titular national group, autonomous republics were more ethnically divided, with the titular nationality forming no more than a bare majority or even a plurality of the population. The institutional split between party and state, each fostering its own network, was thus reinforced by an opposition between a host population and outsiders, normally ethnic Russians. In both the Chuvash and the Mari ASSRs the conflicts were given added weight by the wartime policy of accelerated indigenization by which Moscow aimed to court the titular nationalities for the war effort. The application of mass propaganda in a national idiom was used by regional heads of state who belonged to the titular national group to mobilize support for their office.

SECURITY POLICE

In the late 1930s the security police earned a fearsome reputation for unseating and disposing of regional party leaders. A decade later, as we saw in chapter 1, regional security chiefs tended to slot into their assigned place in the regional hierarchy. One reason was the adoption of new rules and safeguards, after the Great Purges, on the arrest of party functionaries; another was the prohibition on stationing spies and moles in senior party committees. Even where the secret police obtained incriminating information on members of the nomenklatura, it was rarely in a position to act on it.

Only when a regional MGB head had exceptional connections in Moscow could he be a true counterweight to the obkom first secretary. The best (and, as far as we know, only) example of this comes from Khabarovsk. The chief of the MGB there, S.A. Goglidze, was not a run-of-the-mill MGB head, as he had worked for a number of years in the Transcaucasus with Lavrentii Beria, where the two struck up a close friendship.[40] Before arriving in Khabarovsk in 1941, Goglidze's previous posting in the months leading up to the war had been as Moscow's chief plenipotentiary to the newly established Moldovian Soviet Socialist Republic, where, to all intents and purposes, he ran the republic. At the beginning of the war Goglidze was transferred to Khabarovsk, where he worked with the then first secretary, Gennady Borkov. While in Khabarovsk, Goglidze was put in charge of "the Mill," a kind of open-air stage not far from the border with China but entirely within Soviet territory. At the Mill, Goglidze, with the full complicity of his superiors in Moscow, set up a make-believe border fitted with a fake Manchurian border post and fake Japanese military mission. Soviet suspects were instructed to cross the imaginary border and hand themselves in to the supposed Japanese and volunteer themselves for spying missions. Most were then shot for treason.[41]

As the war came to an end Borkov was replaced by R.K. Nazarov. While the precise circumstances that triggered their clash are not known, it was perhaps only a matter of time before the headstrong Goglidze collided with the new first secretary, who, according to a Central Committee reference, was constantly on edge and "often goes around shouting at people . . . is touchy, hot-tempered and, in terms of his personality, a little unbalanced [*neuravnoveshennyi*]."[42] The conflict between Goglidze and Nazarov took a sharp turn for the worse at the beginning of 1948, when Goglidze filed a report to the Central Committee on failures in the regional party committee's agricultural work. On 1 April the Central Committee sent a brigade to the region, and it came to the view that there were indeed shortcomings in the work of the kraikom and that these could be traced to the first secretary.[43] Goglidze himself gave

The head of the administration of state security in Khabarovsk, Sergei Goglidze, in 1950. Courtesy of Russian State Archive of Photographic and Cinematic Documents in Krasnogorsk.

a no-holds-barred account of Nazarov to the brigade: "Nazarov has no authority with the broader ranks of the party leadership. They don't believe he can lift the region from the doldrums. He is frightened of really shaking things up, for this might undermine his own prospects . . . he comes to buro meetings unprepared, his speeches are long and tedious, his speech coarse and unrefined. He constantly bears grudges."[44] On 13 December 1948 the Orgburo (the Organizational Bureau of the Central Committee) considered the brigade's report and ordered that measures be taken.[45] For over a year the Central Committee cadres department had prevaricated on Nazarov's suitability for the job, but the Orgburo resolution appears to have been the last straw.[46] On 22 April 1949 the Politburo dismissed Nazarov with a recommendation that he go to Moscow to continue his studies. His place as first secretary was taken by the outgoing first secretary from Irkutsk, A.P. Efimov.[47]

As the new first secretary, Efimov immediately set about making his mark on the region. While still savoring his triumph over Nazarov, Goglidze gradually found himself sucked into a new conflict with

Nazarov's successor. In this case what kick-started the clash between the two regional heavyweights was quite clear. One of Efimov's first moves as first secretary was to order a kraikom inquiry into cadre work at the regional security police. This seemingly innocuous check on cadres was in fact a typical flexing of the muscles by a regional party leader. Rather than dismissing or reprimanding the odd individual, trawls of this kind tended to net large flows of information that could be used to put a whole organization under pressure. Inevitably, the inquiry highlighted the presence of dubious cadres in the ranks of the MGB and the occasional lack of zeal in prosecuting enemies. Goglidze hotly contested the findings, but Efimov was able to marshal support on the kraikom buro, on which Goglidze was quickly outflanked. On 25 July 1949 Efimov sent Malenkov a report about what had happened. He gave special weight to the fact that some of the MGB's district agencies in Khabarovsk were "trying to evade party control and sometimes even to counterpose themselves against the party committees. . . . Within the leadership of the administration there has grown an unhealthy sense of overimportance and smugness at their 'successes' and, worse still, they are trying to pull themselves out from under the control of the party." Efimov put in a request that the MGB leadership "be strengthened," which was in effect code for having Goglidze fired.[48]

Malenkov ordered that Efimov's report be circulated to the Central Committee secretaries and to the minister of state security, V.S. Abakumov. He also wanted it discussed with Abakumov at a meeting of the Secretariat in Moscow. The ensuing reports and inquiries dragged on for nine months before Efimov and Goglidze were eventually summoned to Moscow for a meeting of the Secretariat on 28 April 1950. The Secretariat's position bore the hallmarks of a compromise thrashed out at the very highest levels. Goglidze was alerted to certain shortcomings in his work with cadres, while the "Khabarovsk kraikom"—in effect Efimov—was warned of certain mistakes in the kraikom's assessment of the regional MGB: it all boiled down to an admonishment to Goglidze and Efimov that they should learn to get along with each other.[49]

The Central Committee aimed to foster harmonious relations between regional first secretaries and MGB leaders in which the latter slotted into the wider regional power structure under the leadership of the first secretary. The fact that in this case Goglidze came out on even terms with Efimov was due almost entirely to Goglidze's support from a member of the Politburo, Beria. Having spent ten years in Khabarovsk, the following year Goglidze was transferred to the central apparatus of the MGB, where, with Beria's support, he rose to become first deputy minister.[50]

The balanced outcome of this conflict between an unusually influential head of a regional MGB, Goglidze, who benefited from a hugely powerful patron in Moscow, and a typical kraikom secretary such as Efimov gives some indication of the general preeminence of regional party structures over their state security counterparts after the war. Unless an MGB head had a patron of Beria's standing in Moscow it was unlikely he could act as a real check on a territorial first secretary. More often than not the services of the regional MGB were, within limits, put at the disposal of the obkom leader.

In chapter 1 we saw that territorial party leaders resorted to four mechanisms in order to forge what were normally small, obedient ruling coalitions. Here, we have described some limits to these strategies. In some cases other regional actors commanded considerable resources of their own. In others, organizational divisions might be reinforced by ethnic cleavages or cross-cutting ties to powerful patrons in Moscow. But there was also another reason why the overbearing substate dictator had to be wary of his peers. Regional leaders not only worked but also lived side by side, often picking up tidbits on each other's lives. Leaks of derogatory information from regime insiders could sap a first secretary's authority, making him vulnerable to new intrigues. While any ordinary citizen could lodge a complaint, the most damaging defections came from those within the regional elite. By contrast with signals from ordinary citizens, which often consisted of mere rumor or supposition, statements from high-level regional functionaries usually contained hard facts. Substate dictators came to learn that needless or gratuitous clashes were best avoided, for they always ran the risk of triggering credible and factually substantiated allegations that might cast them in an unflattering light.

REVOLTS FROM BELOW

A second type of constraint derived not from within the ruling coalition but from ordinary members of the party's rank and file. One factor that served as a check on substate dictators was the various mechanisms for "inner-party democracy" at the lower tiers of the party. According to the party rules, regional party organizations were supposed to hold conferences once every eighteen months at which the regional party committee (the obkom), the obkom's officers, and an auditing commission were elected.[51] Because of the sheer numbers of delegates involved—sometimes up to six or seven hundred in the larger regions—and the fact that some were willing to stand up to the obkom secretaries and to give vent to vociferous criticism from below, the obkom party conferences shed light on the regional leader's problem of authoritarian control.

As much as regional leaders tried to stage-manage the elections, their integrity was protected by various safeguards. The first was the presence of a representative from a higher agency, as a rule the Central Committee, assisted by a multimember vote-counting commission, to supervise the proceedings. Second, the elections were carried out via closed ballots.[52] Whether the ballots were actually closed was a moot point. Any delegate who wanted to vote against a candidate had to detach him- or herself from the broad contingent of voters and walk into a booth or to a table in order to cross out the name on the ballot paper. To the extent that this action was quite visible it could hardly be regarded as closed. At the same time—and this was very much part of their design—the procedures for closed ballots were quite different from those for open ballots. Whereas open ballots consisted of a show of hands or of shouts of "approve" or of "yes" or "no" from the auditorium, closed ballots involved the allocation of an individual voting paper to each delegate who would then place it (unmarked or not) in a sealed box. In many regions the number of votes cast against at least one candidate was so large and distributed in such complex combinations that it offered those delegates who decided to cast one or more "no" votes a certain measure of anonymity, as it was not clear whom they were voting against.

The results of the elections could have real consequences. Communicated from the dais by the counting officers, a poor showing could sap the leader's authority. Moscow followed the results carefully and viewed them as an indicator of the ability of a leader to "win over the aktiv." Party conferences gave substate leaders a headache, which helps explain why they were generally quite averse to holding them, even if that meant violating the time frames laid out in the party rules. According to the rules adopted at the XVIII Party Congress in 1939, regional conferences were supposed to have been held once every eighteen months. The war and the challenges of early postwar reconstruction had given regional party leaders a convenient pretext for delaying them. However, by July 1947, over two years after the end of the war, figures collected by the Central Committee showed that of the 157 territorial party organizations only 24 had held party conferences over the previous eighteen months;[53] moreover, in 105 of them a conference had not been held in over six years.[54] In the autumn of 1947 the party leadership in Moscow decided to put matters right by launching a broad campaign for regional inner-party democracy. From October 1947 to May 1948 conferences were held in 107 regions, including 55 territorial party organizations in the RSFSR and in 25 organizations in Ukraine, 16 in Kazakhstan, 6 in Kirgizia, 3 in Tajikistan, and 2 in Turkmenia.[55]

The campaign, carefully monitored in Moscow, proved to be a test for many secretaries and their networks. At 46 of the 107 elections the protest vote was sufficiently large to trigger follow-up investigations.[56] The protest votes were not geographically concentrated but were distributed quite evenly across the country, with 25 in the Russian Federation (45 percent of all conferences there), 8 in Ukraine (32 percent), 8 in Kazakhstan (50 percent), 4 in Kirgizia (67 percent), and 1 in Tajikistan (33 percent). Protest votes varied from region to region, but they tended to be directed at two targets. The first were the obkom first secretaries (see table 2.1).

Among the list of first secretaries who attracted strong protest votes were classic substate dictators like M.V. Kulagin from Novosibirsk, I.S. Grushetskii from L'vov, and R.K. Nazarov from Khabarovsk. Delegates, especially raikom leaders, accused these three first secretaries of repressing criticism, of rudeness, of slighting subordinates, of being cut off from the district party committees, and of wholesale assaults on cadres.[57] In some regions, for example, Omsk, L'vov, and Khabarovsk, protest votes were not confined to the first secretaries but extended also to other members of the leadership, especially cadres secretaries, who were perceived as belonging to the first secretary's inner circle. In all these regions the voting pattern suggests a real revolt of members of the aktiv against the obkom leader and those closest to him. These votes

Table 2.1. Obkom party conferences from October 1947 to May 1948 at which 8 percent or more of delegates voted against the obkom first secretary (percent and, in parentheses, absolute number)

Region	First secretary	Chair of regional executive committee	Second secretary	Third secretary	Cadres secretary	Propaganda secretary
Omsk	26.0 (102)	8.1 (32)	4.5 (18)	4.5 (18)	8.1 (32)	1.8 (7)
Khabarovsk	15.2 (70)	12.6 (59)	2.2 (10)	0.8 (4)	0.0 (0)	0.0 (1)
L'vov	14.0 (44)	0.9 (3)	0.0 (1)	4.4 (14)	14.1 (45)	1.9 (6)
Astrakhan	14.7 (62)	2.6 (11)	4.3 (19)	1.7 (7)	3.3 (14)	24.5 (103)
Penza	13.0 (48)	35.5 (132)	0.0 (0)	6.0 (20)	3.2 (12)	0.5 (2)
Stalingrad	10.5 (46)	23.7 (104)	0.5 (2)	8.2 (36)	7.3 (32)	3.6 (16)
Chita	9.4 (34)	2.0 (8)	0.5 (2)	0.3 (1)	1.5 (5)	23.2 (84)
Saratov	9.0 (57)	4.0 (24)	4.0 (25)	2.5 (16)	2.4 (15)	8.2 (51)
Novosibirsk	9.0 (42)	2.0 (10)	12.0 (57)	17.0 (80)	4.0 (19)	3.0 (14)

Source: RGASPI f.17 op.88 d.901 ll.293–300.

Note: Numbers in bold refer to members of the obkom buro other than the first secretary who attracted protest votes of 12 percent or more of all delegates.

were viewed in Moscow as a sign of the "inability of the first secretary to win over the aktiv."

A second subgroup from the list of 46 regions (of 107) earmarked for supplementary investigation consisted of regions where the votes were directed not against the first secretary at all but at other members of the regional leadership (see table 2.2).

Such a state of affairs may have arisen for various reasons. In some instances a buro member may have had an especially abrasive personality, one which antagonized the aktiv. It is also possible that such protest votes were orchestrated by the first secretary and his inner circle, who were either intent on deflecting criticism from their own poor showing or wanted to use the vote to intimidate a member of the leadership. It may be that something along these lines happened in Penza, where the heavy protest vote against the first secretary, Morschinin, was overshadowed by the much larger vote against the chair of the executive committee, who was, in light of the vote, sacked.[58]

Yet it would be unwise to overstate the role of the first secretary and his group in manipulating the proceedings. The various micro-institutional

Table 2.2. Obkom party conferences from October 1947 to May
1948 at which protest votes were directed at buro members other
than the first secretary (percent and, in parentheses, absolute number)

Region	First secretary	Second secretary	Chair of regional executive committee	Cadres secretary	Propaganda secretary
Talas (Kirgizia)	1.7 (3)	**27.1 (47)**	N/A	0.5 (1)	1.0 (2)
Chernovits (Ukraine)	1.5 (4)	**25.0 (66)**	**47.7 (126)**	8.9 (24)	6.6 (18)
Tambov	5.4 (24)	**18.0 (84)**	1.0 (5)	0.8 (4)	0.8 (4)
Cheliabinsk	4.2 (24)	**15.1 (85)**	**23.4 (131)**	10.1 (57)	**16.5 (93)**
Tula	7.0 (31)	2.5 (11)	**21.0 (92)**	**51.0 (223)**	5.0 (21)
Iuzhno-Kazakhstan (Kazakhstan)	0.7 (2)	2.5 (7)	1.0 (3)	**15.1 (41)**	0.3 (1)
Zakarpatia (Ukraine)	0.0 (0)	1.9 (5)	5.7 (15)	**15.6 (41)**	0.0 (0)

Source: RGASPI f.17 op.88 d.901 (see esp. 84, 158, 155).

Note: Votes over 15 percent are in bold.

procedures that were built into the electoral process were designed precisely to prevent such manipulation and to raise, where possible, the uncertainty of outcome. This uncertainty could find expression in a number of ways. In Tambov, in addition to the 84 delegates voting against the second secretary, Maiorov, 158 (33 percent) voted against the head of the agriculture department at the obkom and 155 (32 percent) against the head of the agriculture department at the regional executive committee, while a number of senior officials, including the deputy chair of the regional executive committee and the plenipotentiary of the ministry of state procurements, failed even to make it past the discussion stage.[59] These votes certainly counted for something. Shortly afterward, Maiorov was sacked. A note from the cadres department in Moscow made it clear that both the vote and what had been said by conference delegates had played a decisive role in the decision to get rid of him.[60]

The conference in Chernovits in 1948 saw a more serious rebellion. The event started well for the regional leadership, as a report from the department for checking party organs of the Central Committee noted of the first day that "criticism was weak." However, the delegates were put off by a statement from the incoming first secretary, D.G. Gapii, who in a blistering attack on the raikom secretaries threatened that "we will not stop at kicking them out of the party but will readily send them to the courts." In the words of the Central Committee's representative, Gapii's outburst "gave rise to rightful consternation on the part of delegates at the conference."[61] Although the delegates did not go so far as to vote against the new first secretary (who had yet to take up his post), they did aim their fire at other members of the leadership. At the discussion stage to approve the list of candidates, some delegates spoke out against including the obkom second and third secretaries, Ivanov and Maliarov. An angry debate ensued with no obvious sign of a resolution. In an unusual move the obkom leadership decided to interrupt the debate and reconvene the conference the next morning. In the meantime it sought instructions from the Ukrainian central committee, which, in turn, conferred with Moscow. In the end it was decided to give in to the mutinying aktiv and to block Ivanov's and Maliarov's candidacies. But the difficulties for the obkom leadership did not end there, for in the closed balloting other leaders were punished, with the cadres secretary, Riabik, having 66 votes against (25 percent) and the chair of the regional executive committee, Kolikov, 126 (48 percent).[62]

In addition to the forty-six regions which experienced electoral revolts there was a larger group of sixty-one regions whose elections were relatively devoid of drama. This can be explained by a number of factors. In some regions, the provisions for a closed ballot notwithstanding, the ubiquity of police spies and the prevalence of heavy-handed repression may have intimidated voters. On this question the evidence we have is too slender to warrant broader inferences. From our findings we can point, however, to another factor that appears to have played a role. In many of these regions we see signs of a new breed of leader who, while possessing some of the surface attributes of the hardened substate dictator, was also able to learn on the job and to respond to the institutional incentives presented by the elections by curbing his behavior and negotiating a new set of understandings with the aktiv, understandings that would allow him to get through the conference season without resorting to repression or fraud.

M.M. Stakhurskii, the first secretary of Vinnitsa in West Ukraine, serves as a good example. Having a strong propensity for one-person rule, for cultivating and overpromoting clients, and for effecting high rates of cadre turnover, Stakhurskii was, in many respects, a textbook substate dictator (see chapter 1). Stakhurskii's dictatorial tendencies were reflected in his dealings with both the rank and file and his inner circle. A Central Committee report of spring 1948 noted that Stakhurskii had little taste for consultative bodies or genuine debate: "The obkom buro is suppressed [by him], and collegiality is violated," while "criticism and self-criticism are viewed with suspicion by Stakhurskii, and he does not allow any room for them in the regional party organization. . . . [He] supplants the soviets and the economic organizations and runs things by means of orders and decrees."[63] But whereas in other regions similar charges against substate dictators were associated with conference revolts, in Vinnitsa they were not. In the elections Stakhurskii received only eighteen votes against (4.8 percent of all the delegates); other members of the buro had protest votes of roughly the same order.[64] These were decent results, so decent that the Central Committee decided to leave Stakhurskii alone.

Stakhurskii's strategy can be discerned from his carefully constructed opening speech. Whereas some substate dictators devoted most of their plenary reports to vituperative attacks on subordinates, Stakhurskii held his fire. It would not have been possible for him to avoid making critical remarks altogether—to have done so would have roused the suspicions of the Central Committee—but he was selective in his choice of targets. "In his plenary report," noted the Central Committee emissary, "Stakhurskii had very little to say about serious shortcomings in the work of the [current] obkom . . . and instead engaged in retrospective criticism, getting at raikom secretaries and heads of regional organizations who had long since departed the region." Stakhurskii's speech set the tone of the debate, which was largely "reduced to bland self-assessments by raikom secretaries and honorable mentions of the obkom." Only at the end of the debate did the criticism pick up, but even then it was very general in character.[65] Although the atmosphere at the start of the conference had been fraught, Stakhurskii went out of his way to defuse the tension and to avoid antagonizing the potentially most explosive element on the obkom, the raikom secretaries, by signaling that their positions were secure and that they would be treated with dignity.

Unable to overtly manipulate the election process, Stakhurskii responded by tempering his behavior. An electoral mechanism designed to funnel up local knowledge on regional conflicts and cover-ups had given him a strong incentive to reach an accommodation with the aktiv. This incentive took a very clear form: for a regional leader an electoral revolt was a perceptible blow to his local prestige, to say nothing of the possible effects it might have on how he was viewed in Moscow. Although a large protest vote did not necessarily end a career, it could have unpleasant consequences. While Vinnitsa under Stakhurskii is one example of such adaptive behavior, there were numerous others. Like Stakhurskii, substate dictators like Boitsov in Stavropol' and Churaev in Kharkov found that they were able to negotiate the 1948 electoral campaign without undue drama by sending out clear signals to their aktiv that they would be listened to and treated with respect.

The conferences of 1948 represented the high-water mark of the revolts against regional bosses, but the protest votes did not end there. At the next round of elections in 1951 there were, again, a number of electoral standoffs. In Iaroslavl' in February 1951 many of the delegates, especially secretaries of the raikoms and gorkoms, began to attack the obkom first secretary G.S. Sitnikov for his use of "threats and intimidation" and his "faulty mode of leadership, running things by means of orders and commands, for being rude, and for generally treating people badly." In the closed ballot seventy-seven delegates (18 percent) voted against him, a tally that outstripped the no votes of any other member of the buro.[66] The events in Iaroslavl' were taken seriously in Moscow. The Central Committee secretary, Malenkov, requested that the result be circulated to the other secretaries.[67] In part perhaps because such a result was now more unusual, the results did real damage to Sitnikov's credibility in Moscow and to his subsequent career. Eighteen months later he was removed from his post and put on a retraining course in Moscow; he would never be used in a leading party position again, instead being reassigned to midlevel managerial posts in the economy.

Although regional electoral revolts would continue into the mid-1950s, the elections of 1948 marked a peak, after which the number of revolts began to fall. One reason was that the elections had taught many regional leaders a lesson. In most cases the main driver behind the revolts had been the raikom secretaries. Not only had they been at the sharp end of the most vicious attacks by the obkom leaders but, as the party's line managers in the districts, they were also best able to coordinate other members of the aktiv against the obkom leadership. The conferences of 1948 taught substate dictators the benefits of mollifying the raikom secretaries if they wanted to forestall similar revolts in the future.

In their original design regional party elections addressed the dictator's agency problem by opening up the black box of regional politics to central scrutiny and doing so in a way that was consistent with the prevailing ideological principle of "Bolshevik democracy." Running regional conferences was a major administrative exercise. Central Committee representatives had to be sent in, auditing commissions convened, delegates transported, closed ballots organized and, where necessary, follow-up investigations set up. The center was willing to carry these costs because elections provided valuable information on the effectiveness of regional leaders in an ideologically palatable form. Yet while this may have been their original intention, their effect was often quite different, for they gave regional leaders an incentive to curb their behavior and find common cause with the aktiv. Elections thus helped turn regional leaders away from the model of the substate dictator and toward a new form of leadership that would come into its own in later years.

ASSAULTS FROM ABOVE

One consequence of the center's more lax regional policy from 1945 (covered in chapter 1) was the growing autonomy of local party leaders. Far from being terrorized and downtrodden, many became quite brazen. One measure of this attitude was their occasional abuse of the monetary reform of December 1947 (see chapter 3) and their involvement in a series of regional theft scandals, the most spectacular of which, the Ul'ianovsk Affair of 1949, led to the expulsion of the obkom first and third secretaries and the eventual dismissal of over a thousand leading functionaries in the region.[68] From the middle of 1948 Moscow's regional policy grew harsher. While the reasons for this new approach remain unclear, it had two immediate effects. The first was a seemingly mundane reorganization of the Central Committee apparatus which saw the replacement of Andrei Zhdanov by Georgii Malenkov as the man in charge of the Central Committee bureaucracy.[69] The second was the Leningrad Affair.

The opening shot of the Leningrad Affair was a resolution on 15 February 1949 by which the Politburo dismissed the Central Committee

secretary, Aleksei Kuznetsov, the chair of the RSFSR council of ministers, Mikhail Rodionov, and the first secretary of the Leningrad obkom,
Petr Popkov, from their posts. Later that year all three, along with the
head of Gosplan and Politburo member Nikolai Voznesenskii were arrested, and in October 1950 they were executed. As was true of so
many purges of the Stalin era (such as the "Ezhovshchina" and the
"Zhdanovshchina," in both of which the key mover was neither Ezhov
nor Zhdanov but Stalin) the Leningrad Affair was a misnomer. It was
aimed not at a particular territory but at a phenomenon: the violation
of a key postulate of Stalinist decision making. While Stalin tolerated
and tacitly encouraged the cultivation of networks by his provincial
leaders he had less patience for the consolidation of strong patronage ties between regional leaders and members of the supreme leadership in Moscow. We get a glimpse of this from the Politburo resolution
of 15 February, which noted that the first secretary of the Leningrad
obkom, Popkov, had

> started to bypass the Central Committee and to engage in various du-
> bious, underhanded, and self-serving schemes, which were channeled
> through the self-styled "patrons" [shefy] of Leningrad such as com-
> rades Kuznetsov, Rodionov and others. . . . The Politburo believes that
> such nonparty methods must be nipped in the bud for they are an
> expression of antiparty cliquishness [grupovschina], they sow distrust
> between the Leningrad obkom and the Central Committee, and they
> may well lead to the detachment [otryv] of the Leningrad organization
> from the party, from the Central Committee.

The most senior victims of the purge were associated with the recently
deceased member of the Politburo Andrei Zhdanov. To the extent that
Zhdanov had served as first secretary in Leningrad from 1934 to 1944
his ties were naturally concentrated in Leningrad and it was here that
the purge began.[70] Not all of the high-profile casualties of the purge,
however, came from Leningrad. Rodionov, for example, had never
worked in Leningrad. His association with Zhdanov appears to have
come from Gor'kii, where Zhdanov had served as first secretary before coming to Leningrad and where Rodionov had served as obkom
secretary from 1938 to 1946. As an Orgburo resolution of 23 March
1949, "On the work of the Gor'kii obkom," put it: "The RSFSR council of ministers and its former chair, Rodionov, have followed a per-
nicious path of tutelage over Gor'kii and in their wrongful behavior

have inculcated the attitudes and practices of clientelism among local leaders."[71] In fact, the Leningrad Affair soon widened into a broader purge of the regional apparatus. Leaders in other regions who had at various points either worked in Leningrad or had ties to the so-called Leningrad group, were arrested. These included the first secretary of the Crimean obkom, N.V. Solov'ev, the first secretary of the Iaroslavl' obkom, I.M. Turko, the first secretary of the Novgorod obkom, G.Kh. Bumagin, the first secretary of the Karelian–Finnish central committee, G.N. Kupriianov, the second secretary of the Riazan' obkom, P.V. Kuz'menko, the second secretary of the Murmansk obkom, A.D. Verbitskii, and the second secretary of the Penza gorkom, N.K. Smirnov.[72]

In principle, the chain of blame and culpability could have been never-ending. Anyone involved in appointing former Leningraders in another province or who had themselves been appointed by them was suspect. This, after all, was what had happened during the Great Purges. At the end of 1949 the head of the industrial department at the Velikolukskii obkom, who had earlier worked in Leningrad, was relieved of his post. The dismissal triggered an inquiry into the circumstances under which a former Leningrader had been appointed. The former secretary of the Velikolukskii obkom, Boikachev, who was at the time attending a course in Moscow, was reprimanded not only for having sanctioned the appointment but for having brought into the region a group of functionaries from Leningrad.[73] At the beginning of 1951 the second secretary of the Riazan city party committee, Borisov, who had also previously worked in Leningrad, was sacked and expelled from the party. The first secretary of the Riazan obkom at the time, Aleksei Larionov, was accused of extending protection to Borisov and escaped punishment only with some difficulty.[74]

Unlike the Great Purges a decade earlier, however, these trails of guilt by association tended to peter out. Consider the following case. In September 1949 in the city of Vladimir the chair of the Vladimir city executive committee, a former official from one of the Leningrad district executive committees, I.M. Bogard, was sacked. Shortly afterward the first secretary of the Vladimir obkom, P.N. Alferov, was reprimanded on account of his involvement in Bogard's appointment.[75] Alferov was naturally unnerved. At the beginning of 1950, when forced to act on an allegation that one of his obkom secretaries, Morozov, was a protégé of the Leningrad leaders, the cowed Alferov, rather than taking the trouble of looking into the matter and establishing whether there was any truth to the allegation, instantly requested that Morozov be fired. However, Morozov was saved by the Central Committee, whose investigators, on finding that the allegations were not substantiated, dismissed the case. Notwithstanding Alferov's knee-jerk response, all charges against Morozov were dropped.[76]

Why weren't the Central Committee investigators frightened in the way Alferov was? There were a number of targeted network purges in this period, not only in Leningrad but also in Georgia, Estonia, Perm, and Cheliabinsk. Why did these purges not spread as those preceding them had in the late 1930s? There appear to be two reasons. First, senior officials in the Central Committee who were responsible for making appointments had a vested interest in protecting their appointees and, by implication, themselves. Whether or not they were actually patrons of these appointees, they were always vulnerable to such a charge. They thus had a strong incentive not to rock the boat, to play safe. On this issue A.N. Larionov, then deputy head of the cadres administration, was quite candid in January 1947: "Sometimes we won't propose a candidate for months, and when we do, we will do it very cautiously, with hesitation, and doubts. The whole process is riddled with uncertainty, a lack of decisiveness, for when we eventually put a person forward there will always be a fear, a fear that he will fail [*boiazn', chto on provalitsia*]."[77] Even after the appointment any official from the Central Committee had an interest in giving cover to their appointee, lest they themselves be held accountable for the latter's mistakes or misdemeanors.[78]

The late 1940s also saw the emergence of another institution that could short-circuit a potential purge. As with the consolidation of new rules on elections this new institution was anchored in the regime's ideology. Obkom first secretaries appointed in the wake of the Great Purges had been overwhelmingly young, and a clear majority of them (71.4 percent) lacked a higher education. In addition, over the course of the war millions of young soldier-recruits had been admitted into the party with little political vetting or training. Some of these new recruits had worked their way into relatively senior administrative positions in the party. To kill two birds with one stone, after the war the party launched a campaign to raise the educational and ideological profile of its regional cadres. Specialized top-up courses on ideology were set up for regional party leaders with an incomplete higher education who, on graduation, were to be awarded a higher degree. The curricula of these courses had a strong ideological content, with core courses on dialectical and historical materialism, political economy, and the history of the Bolshevik party.

An event of signal significance was a decision of the Politburo on 25 October 1948 to set up courses, under the auspices of the Central Committee, for the retraining of territorial first secretaries and their equivalents in the governmental apparatus.[79] From November 1948 to the first half of February 1949 (that is, before the Leningrad Affair) no fewer than twenty-one first secretaries from the RSFSR and Ukraine were released from their duties in order to attend these courses and by the beginning of 1950 over a quarter of territorial first secretaries from the Russian Federation and the Ukraine were doing the same. Assignment on these courses started the ball rolling on a large-scale rotation of first secretaries.

One important effect of the accelerated rotation of first secretaries was the creation of a safety zone for cadres who had fallen out of favor. Those who had committed blunders in post could now be moved on, ostensibly for retraining, without the need for a wider purge. Once they had weathered the storm they could be released from the Central Committee courses to lower-profile and less demanding positions elsewhere in the nomenklatura.

The effect on regional leadership of the change in central policy in mid-1948 and the sudden upsurge in repression at the time of the Leningrad Affair can be indicated graphically. The relationship between Moscow and the regions after the war can be divided into two phases, the dividing line for which was 1948 (see table 2.3).[80] Two contributory factors for the surge in turnover around 1948 were the obkom elections that year and the introduction of "soft rotation" through temporary assignments at the Higher Party School. Under cover of the new policy, errant first secretaries were reassigned to Moscow, before being allowed to vanish into the lower ranks of the nomenklatura. As with regional party elections, a new institution ostensibly designed for one purpose, the creation of a politically conscious elite, was redeployed for another, namely, protecting senior regional cadres from repression.

From table 2.3 we can also observe another tendency, namely, that 1949 saw a peak, associated with the Leningrad Affair, in the number of

Table 2.3. Turnover of territorial first secretaries, 1944–1951

	Number of territorial first secretaries	Turnover	Turnover as percent of total	Reasons secretaries were removed			
				Incom-petence	Compro-mised themselves	Total	Percent of turnover
1944	169	34	20.1	13	1	14	41.2
1945	171	39	22.8	10	—	10	25.6
1946	173	39	22.5	10	—	10	25.6
1947	171	32	18.7	4	1	5	15.6
1948	167	58	34.7	12[a]	3	15	25.9
1949	167	46	27.5	8	6	14	30.4
1950	175	50	28.6	15	2	17	34.0
1951	175	52	29.7	15	1	16	30.8

Source: RGANI f.5 op.29 d.15 ll.62-63.

[a] The figure for 1948 includes one secretary replaced for "violating directives of higher agencies."

secretaries removed for having "compromised themselves." After 1949 the volume of explicitly political charges associated with this label declined and was overshadowed by another category, that of "incompetence." This formulation enabled the Central Committee to get rid of cadres who were clearly not up to the job—the contested autocrats of chapter 1—without invoking political charges. As with the policy of soft rotation this enabled the center to remove regional leaders without inadvertently triggering a destructive purge.

After the war the majority of substate leaders addressed the problems of authoritarian control and authoritarian power sharing by becoming, in effect, substate dictators. This meant an overwhelmingly coercive approach to the aktiv and the use of a range of techniques, from formal and informal exclusion to overpromotion and kompromat, in order to establish pliable ruling groups. In this chapter we have observed the limits of the substate dictator. In extremis they were balanced by powerful factory directors like Zal'tsman, MGB heads like Goglidze and, especially in the national territories, by heads of the state apparatus. These constraints were as much about institutions as they were about individuals. Powerful regional actors could devise new rules, for example, by forming shadow nomenklaturas or by drawing on the policy of indigenization, in order to stand up to their obkom first secretary.

For its part, the center developed new institutions for managing regional cadres. One of these was the regional party election which supplied the center with information on the effectiveness of the obkom secretaries in "leading the aktiv." The other was the party courses at the Higher Party School, ostensibly intended to raise the political consciousness of regional leaders. Both institutions were firmly rooted in the regime's ideology, according with long-standing tenets on Bolshevik democracy and on the need to inculcate leading cadres with Marxist-Leninist dogma. In both cases the delegation of power to regional leaders would also have another effect, for it enabled these leaders to redeploy the institutions for new ends which were quite different from those for which they had originally been intended.[81]

3   Inside the Nomenklatura

ON 29 AUGUST 1951 the Central Committee secretary, Georgii Malenkov, received an appeal from a party official in Kherson, Ukraine, N.D. Glushkov, for a radical overhaul of pension provisions for party employees.[1] Gushkov's proposals did not get far, but they do give us an insight into the identity and self-image of officials in the party apparatus. Citing the privileges enjoyed by employees of the industrial ministries, Glushkov asked, "How can the work of any of these agencies compare in scale, in seriousness, and, indeed, in overall significance with our party work? We all know that the very best people go into the party apparatus. Once in post there is a further winnowing, so that only those who are truly valued are kept on. . . . Party work, no less leading party work, is simply on a different plane from that of any other body."[2]

Like any successful revolutionary movement, the early Bolshevik regime had its share of "true believers," people who were willing to subordinate their material self-interest for the cause of the Revolution.[3] As the Soviet state evolved, the number of true believers probably fell.[4] By the late Stalin era true believers were supplemented by a second and probably larger group of loyalists, those who joined the party and entered the ranks of the party bureaucracy because they thought it was in their material or career interest to do so. Judging by Glushkov's comments, we cannot be sure which category he belonged to. Perhaps he genuinely saw himself as a political shock-worker, a cadre in a party movement with a uniquely political vocation, or he may have been saying these things because other powerful people were saying them, and he was canny enough to realize this was the language he needed to use in order to get what he wanted. It may well have been that in Glushkov's case both rationales were at play. Yet whether Glushkov believed or not in what he was saying is of secondary importance to our purpose here. The more crucial point is that in order to achieve his goals Glushkov appealed to the conventions of the ruling ideology, of which the leading role of the party was the first and the most important.[5] The ideology was a language spoken by political actors that knitted the ruling elite together.[6]

The terms of this language were not fixed. With Stalin's declaration in the mid-1930s that class exploitation had ceased and that the population now consisted of "nonantagonistic classes," the Bolsheviks' fixation on the class struggle had subsided, and former practices of class discrimination were progressively dismantled.[7] Despite this fluidity, Soviet regional party cadres in the late 1940s still inhabited what we can think of as a resolutely ideological world. This state of affairs was reflected in an increasingly bitter ideological conflict with the West and in the unfurling of policies, such as a massive campaign against "theft of socialist property" as well as campaigns against "speculation" and against the enlargement of private plots on collective farms, which were anchored in the second principle of the ideology, the supremacy of socialist over private ownership of the means of production.

After the war it was not uncommon for officials from a variety of state organizations to lobby for improved salaries and working conditions.[8] But the tone of Glushkov's request and the grounds on which it was registered were quite specific. For a functionary like Glushkov, the idea, recently expounded in relation to Soviet youth after the war, that "consumption, not ideology" was the main marker of their identity would have represented a false dichotomy.[9] While many party officials certainly took a great interest in matters of consumption, they often presented their privileges as just reward for their superior status as carriers of the party's revolutionary ideology.

So far in this book we have considered the strategies of regional leaders and showed how they tended to produce narrow, asymmetric ruling networks. We also examined the constraints under which they operated, in the form of other regional actors who commanded significant resources, and demands from below, expressed at regional elections. We move on here to examine the social and ideological environment in which regional party leaders operated. By the late Stalin era most regional party organizations had become socially stratified. Some authors distinguish seniority of office, that is, one's formal position in a hierarchy, from seniority of person, that is, one's age, length of service, and level of education.[10] What we see in the postwar period is an alignment of the two forms of seniority. In other words, those higher up in the party organization now tended to be older, to have served longer in the apparat, and to be better educated.

One reason low-ranking figures in the party apparatus such as Glushkov lodged complaints was that the schedule of salaries in the party bureaucracy, as well as the allocation of more hidden benefits and privileges, had become noticeably unequal, more so than in the 1930s. Comparative studies of one-party systems suggest that one reason for their relative resilience and durability is the institutionalization of a stable system of salary and income differentials within party organizations, which provides party officials at the lower rungs with a long-term incentive to stay on and build their careers around the party organization.[11] However, the Soviet Union in the late 1940s did not offer a fully stable or predictable environment for party functionaries. Many party officials understood that the elaborate edifice of co-optation would count for nothing if one was expelled from the party and thrown out of the nomenklatura. Moreover, for most of these officials in the early postwar years exclusion remained a very real possibility. One reason was that although explicitly political charges, which questioned one's loyalty to the regime, were now less widely used than in 1930s, Soviet functionaries still had to contend with extremely repressive, top-down campaigns which caught hundreds of thousands of party members in their net. It was in this regard that regional party principals could come to their rescue by making use of powers of protection granted to them in the wake of the Great Purges. To the extent that these powers were skewed toward protecting members of the regional elite rather than ordinary rank-and-file members of the party, they contributed to a second form of stratification which meshed with the social and economic to produce increasingly consolidated elites at the regional level.

SENIORITY

By July 1952 the corpus of regional first secretaries across the Soviet Union was older than the cohort Stalin had wiped out in 1937.[12] Nearly all of the incumbents in 1952 were people whom, then as relative youngsters, Stalin had placed in senior regional posts on the eve of the war. The vast majority had not only been appointed to these posts under Stalin but also had joined the party and received their education under him.[13] In what was still a deeply traditional society these leaders were on any plausible measure junior to the statewide dictator. It may have been partly for this reason that Stalin does not appear to have felt politically challenged by these leaders or by the regional party organizations they headed and that he was content, for the most part, to let them age in peace.

By the early 1950s most regional party leaders sat at the top of party bureaucracies marked by two forms of seniority. The first, seniority of office, concerned their formal titles, designations, and ranks. Most regional party apparats had approximately ten distinct job designations among career officials and eight among clerical staff. As in other political bureaucracies, the simplest way of interpreting the rank order of positions was by looking at their basic salaries (*oklady*), which in the case of full-time officials were normally layered into seven or eight grades and among clerical staff five or six. In 1946 instructors at rural and urban raikoms earned 650 to 850 rubles a month, not much more than the average salary across the population as a whole that year, 475 rubles, an average that was in any case depressed by the monthly money income of collective farmers of around 100 rubles.[14] From this base, salaries for regional party functionaries rose in steady increments of around 100 to 200 rubles, eventually reaching that of the obkom first secretary who, depending on which of the four categories of obkom he led, earned from 1,400 to 2,000 rubles a month.[15] This schedule of salaries, which coincided with the official designations and job specifications for party functionaries, marked out the official hierarchy of regional party positions.

The second form of seniority was seniority of person, which took three forms. First, if one consequence of the lack of major, statewide purges after 1938 was that regional leaders had grown older, so too did those functionaries working under them. The share of territorial first

Table 3.1. Age of territorial[a] party officials in USSR, 1941, 1945, 1952 (percent)

	Age on 1 January 1941		Age on 1 January 1945		Age on 1 July 1952	
	36–45	46 and over	36–45	46 and over	36–45	46 and over
First secretaries of territorial party organizations	—	—	76.8	8.3	46.8	51.6
All secretaries of territorial party organizations	42.4	0.7	—	—	57.1	36.9
Heads of department of territorial party organizations	—	—	59.7	3.8	59.6	26.5
First secretaries of local party organizations[b]	50.0	2.1	—	—	59.7	25.8

[a] Obkom, kraikom, and republican party organizations.
[b] Okruzhkoms, gorkoms, and raikoms.

secretaries over the age of forty-six had risen from under 10 percent in January 1945 to over 50 percent in 1952 (see table 3.1). Although not as marked, the increase among other categories of officials, such as ordinary obkom secretaries and heads of obkom departments, was sizeable too. Of particular note, however, is the alignment of seniority of office and age. More or less in rank order, the share of officials over the age of forty-five in 1952 descended in accordance with their position in the regional party hierarchy.

A second form of seniority of person concerned individuals' party tenure, or *stazh*. Data on length of service suggest that a growing proportion of regional party leaders had apparat tenures of at least ten years, that is, from the eve or during the very first stages of the war (see table 3.2). Again, this seems to have occurred at all levels. Yet, once again, if we consider the right-hand column, we see a general alignment of length of service with seniority of office. Unlike the situation on the eve of war, when a cohort of young and inexperienced cadres were propelled to the top posts at the obkom, by the end of Stalin's life occupancy of the most powerful positions tended to vary with length of service in the party apparat.

Table 3.2. Tenure in apparat of territorial[a] party officials in USSR, 1945–1952 (percent)

	On 1 January 1945, length of service in years		On 1 July 1952, length of service in years	
	5–10	Over 10	5–10	Over 10
First secretaries of territorial party organizations	48.8	29.2	39.5	49.5
All secretaries of territorial party organizations	50.2	19.2	44.9	38.8
Heads of department of territorial party organizations	30.7	8.5	46.0	20.5
First secretaries of local party organizations[b]	44.3	14.2	42.3	33.7

[a] Obkom, kraikom, and republican party organizations.
[b] Okruzhkoms, gorkoms, and raikoms.

There was, in addition, a third type of seniority of person. Many years ago Sheila Fitzpatrick noted the large share of leading cadres on the eve of the war who had earned a higher education, especially in engineering.[16] Among obkom first secretaries, however, despite the import of their role, the proportion with a higher education had been relatively low, at roughly a quarter.[17] During the war there was little improvement. After it, the regime seemed intent on making a difference and achieved considerable success, raising the proportion of first secretaries with a higher education from 29.8 percent on 1 January 1945 to 56.3 percent on 1 July 1952. Unlike other forms of seniority of person, in this case there was little alignment with seniority of office, in that more ordinary obkom secretaries and department heads had a higher education than first secretaries.[18]

Instead, the seniority of obkom first secretaries operated on another educational plane. In summer 1946 the Central Committee launched a concerted campaign to raise the ideological qualifications of its party members. One reason was that an estimated two-thirds of the party's membership had joined during the war, at a time when their exposure to Marxist-Leninist propaganda was limited.[19] This meant that local party machines experienced major difficulties in assimilating, training, and deploying new party members. The Central Committee passed two resolutions, one on 26 July 1946 on ideological work among the mass membership and the other on 2 August among leading cadres.[20] The second of these ordered the formation of a Higher Party School in Moscow, set up under the auspices of the cadres administration. It was to run three-year courses for senior territorial officials under the age of forty, and nine-month "top-up" courses (*perepodgotovki*) for those in posts at lower levels.[21] As we saw in chapter 2, this was supplemented by a Politburo resolution of 25 October 1948 which set up a specialist ten-month, top-up course for obkom first secretaries at the Higher Party School.[22] From September 1948 until the beginning of 1950 more than a quarter of territorial first secretaries in the Russian Federation and Ukraine left their posts to attend these classes in Moscow. One consequence was that the proportion of first secretaries whose higher education was gained at party schools shot up from 4.0 percent on 1 January 1945 to 48.6 percent on 1 July 1952, while those with an education in engineering almost halved, from 50 percent to 29 percent. And here there is a correlation between the proportion of higher education awarded at a party school and one's rank order in the regional party hierarchy (see table 3.3, right-hand column).

Closer examination of the Higher Party School top-up courses reveals certain peculiarities. Of the 750 hours on the curriculum well over half were devoted to short courses on dialectical and historical materialism as well as to highly politicized histories of the Bolshevik party and of the USSR. From what we know of these courses the quality of the education was not high and the pedagogic requirements were low. Other than general admonishments on avoiding nepotism and

Table 3.3. Proportion of territorial[a] party officials whose higher education was gained through a party school (percent)

	1 January 1945	1 July 1952
First secretaries of territorial party organizations	4.0	48.6
All secretaries of territorial party organizations	13.1	37.4
Heads of department of territorial party organizations	6.4	25.1
First secretaries of local party organizations[b]	10.4	20.9

[a] Obkom, kraikom, and republican party organizations.
[b] Okruzhkoms, gorkoms, and raikoms.

komchanstvo (communist arrogance or haughtiness) the Soviet regime had provided party bosses with relatively little positive guidance on how they should conduct themselves.[23] What these courses now gave students was a proficiency in the preferred language, idioms, and manners of the political elite. In addition, as in any educational system, the courses gave those enrolled an excellent opportunity to mingle and to network. Living together for nine months in the same buildings and receiving training from leading lights on the Central Committee, the students were given a considerable amount of free time, which they were encouraged to spend engaged in reading and "comradely discussions."[24] This situation provided both a setting for the forging of lasting relationships and a propitious environment for group cohesion and social integration into the wider nomenklatura.

The most basic form of hierarchy at the regional level was seniority of office, the formal ranks of officeholders as expressed in their titles and salary scales. In the early postwar period seniority of office became more closely aligned with seniority of person in the form of a person's age, length of service, and party education. As we shall see later in the book, the more established and long-lasting these forms of seniority became, the more likely were they to generate the norms of deference and respect that could help turn bureaucratic into status hierarchies.

CO-OPTATION

The Soviet economy has been characterized as an economy of shortage. Shortages were not only ubiquitous but also strategically manipulated by the state in order to placate and reward certain social groups. Its control over resources allowed the state to manage and to selectively ease shortages for specified groups of officials, thereby confirming their sense of privilege and status superiority. On the basis of this system, each stratum of the population received a package of goods and services, including salaries, top-ups, accommodation, medical treatment, and access to education, that was set according to that stratum's perceived usefulness to the state.[25]

The origins of this system went back to the early 1930s, when, beginning with the introduction of bread rationing, the Soviet state adopted more far-reaching forms of redistribution designed to reward those groups deemed essential to the industrialization effort. In this system regional leaders were placed on the lists of the most deserving.[26] Although centrally regulated rationing was formally ended in 1935, the various dislocations and shortages in the Soviet economy gave rise to forms of spontaneous rationing at the local level. On some occasions this form of localized rationing was used to avert social unrest and thereby attend to the problem of authoritarian control, while in others it was used to reward and cohere local elites, thus addressing the problem of authoritarian power sharing.[27]

After the war a similar process was at work. Despite efforts in Moscow to regulate rationing and make it more uniform, systems of redistribution at the regional level were often quite opaque. In addition to the formal schedule of allocations which was set by the center, there was a patchwork of informal in-kind benefits which varied from region to region. What resulted was a constant tug of war between the central state and the regional state as to who controlled the key levers in the machinery of redistribution. The more open and transparent the rules regulating elite assignments, the easier it was for the central state to steer the distribution of goods to meet its preferred ends. By contrast, the more opaque the system of privileges and the more complex the patchwork of benefits, the easier it was for local elites to establish diverse redistribution schemes that addressed their needs.

In the early postwar period regional party elites enjoyed what we might think of as three forms of remuneration. The first, noted earlier, consisted of base salaries (*oklady*) along with a financial top-up (*dotatsiia*) of 105 rubles a month for food, which was paid out of the party budget.[28] This schedule of salaries, which coincided with the official designations and job specifications of party functionaries, corresponded with the formal hierarchy of regional party posts.

A second layer of benefits, also approved by Moscow, consisted of in-kind assignments of foods and goods. Formalized in a Central Committee resolution of July 1943, such allocations were part of the broader system of official rationing introduced at the beginning of the war.[29] The major principle behind it was that skilled and other highly valued workers and officials were given ration cards which allowed them to purchase, with money, restricted amounts of basic necessities at low, state-subsidized prices through worker supply departments and other parts of the closed distribution network.[30] Rations corresponded with ranks and in the provinces the top category was strictly reserved for the very highest echelon of the regional elite.[31] Normally these took the form of food and manufactured goods assignments (*limity*), which, while they were distributed at no cost to recipients (and hence were known as *besplatnye limity*, or free assignments) and were in effect in-kind benefits, took the form of books of coupons (*limitnye knizhki*) that were calculated on the basis of their monetary value.[32]

As much as the center sought to regulate these in-kind payments, there was considerable variation from region to region, often depending on the economic profile of the area. So, for example, in 1946 the second secretary in Krasnodar, a predominantly agricultural region, received, apart from a base salary of 1,600 rubles and a top-up of 105 rubles, an in-kind food assignment worth 1,400 rubles and a manufactured goods assignment worth 500 rubles a quarter. In Molotov, an industrial center, the obkom propaganda secretary had, in addition to the base salary of 1,800 rubles a month and the party top-up, the equivalent of 1,000 rubles of food plus manufactured goods to the tune of 2,000 rubles a quarter, that is, four times as much as the secretary in Krasnodar.[33] "Despite the fact that the basic principles for allocating assignments have been in place for over ten years," noted a Central Committee report of May 1946, "the circle of functionaries to whom assignments are extended, the monetary value of these assignments, along with the norms for calculating these assignments, appear to be arrived at in a different way in each region."[34]

The third layer of benefits was the most murky and impenetrable, in part because it operated either on the margins of or outside the law altogether. In some regions there was a system of illegal subscriptions (*abonementy*) for hard-to-get goods, especially consumer goods, which were distributed through special stores, while in others such goods could be made available to members of the nomenklatura without quotas or indeed without any formal documentation at all.[35] There were, in addition, direct appropriations by regional elites of floating assets, which were off Moscow's radar altogether. Sometimes regional party organizations simply requisitioned assets, only to engage then in various forms of illegal exchange.[36] Among the most common examples was the transfer of war booty and "trophy property," secured as part of the war reparations from Germany.

In the context of the postwar devastation, the most common examples of obkom officials requisitioning resources revolved around the construction of homes and personal residences for members of the regional elite. Often this involved mobilizing the workforce and using the building materials and transport services of state enterprises, sometimes to build quite extravagant homes.[37] One of the most notable features of these illicit appropriations was that even when the center became aware of them, it was usually powerless to stop them. A central report in 1947 noted a major program under way in Armenia for the construction of villas for members of the republican elite. "In the construction of their personal homes," the report noted, "[republican leaders] use building materials, workers, and transportation facilities that belong to collective farms, to state institutions, and to cooperatives." When the Armenian leaders were instructed to put a stop to these activities they ignored the order and went on to rescind further directives from Moscow on the formal return of these villas to the institutions which had financed them.[38]

An examination of the terms of this exchange suggests that regional elites had little compunction in behaving as they did, in part because they viewed these benefits as "rights of office," rights which, in the case of obkom heads, accrued to them as a result of their role as political and ideological leaders. In fact, after the war many party cadres were quite unabashed about making their nomenklatura prerogatives known. Rather than concealing them, they were often quite demonstrative both in acquiring and in showing off these benefits, which signaled their status superiority over other groups. This attitude helps explain a pattern of behavior among local elites that in other respects might be regarded as an affront to norms of decency and fairness.

Sometimes local elites sanctioned building programs or the transfer to their possession of intact villas and mansions in city centers in full view of ordinary citizens. One such example is the Pukhovichskii district in Minsk, which, having been destroyed during the war, saw three hundred of the seven hundred buildings that went up in 1947 earmarked for regional bosses, and this at a time when 216 families of war invalids in the district were still living in dugouts.[39] In another case, in August 1945 three secretaries from the Vladimir obkom and the chair of the Vladimir regional executive committee took possession of three prize cars, a Packard, a Khorkh, and a Mercedes, which they had lifted from a special echelon of trophy cars that had passed through the region. They proceeded to drive these in full view of the general public.[40]

Toward the end of 1947 the central leadership sought to wrest back control over these perks and privileges with a coordinated array of economic reforms. In tandem with the end of rationing, these reforms were to replace the complex system of in-kind benefits by means of a unitary monetarized system and to turn over "closed" distribution points for open trade. The key starting point was the abolition of rationing on 14 December 1947. In order to eliminate the gap between commercial and ration prices and to establish a "full-value ruble," an accompanying money reform, as we saw in chapter 1, aimed to confiscate surplus cash from citizens, on the pretext that much of it had been gained through illegal speculation during the war. The ostensible goal of these reforms was that any good could be purchased in any quantity so long as the buyer had sufficient money.[41]

These two reforms were accompanied by a third one, a radical change to the system of supplementary benefits for party officials. A directive from the Council of Ministers and the Central Committee of 23 December 1947 noted as follows: "In connection with the abolition of rationing the current system of the free issuing of food and industrial goods to leading soviet and party functionaries will also be abolished."[42] Payments in kind, which had taken the form of the assignments of food and manufactured goods, were to be replaced with direct monetary payments that could be used by the recipients to purchase goods of their choice in state stores and markets.

As it related to regional party elites, the reform was intended to have three short-term effects. First, it replaced all in-kind benefits with a temporary money allowance (*vremennoe denezhnoe dovolstvie*), which normally amounted to two or three times the base salary.[43] Second, the reforms were intended to shut down the network of differential-access stores. The directive of 23 December 1947, signed by Stalin, prescribed that "all closed specialized food and industrial goods stores and depots serving leading soviet and party cadres, should henceforth be opened for general trade."[44] Third, the reforms were to encompass officials at lower levels of the party apparatus who had not previously benefited from assignments by giving raikom and gorkom secretaries a major hike in their basic salaries.[45] In replacing in-kind benefits with money benefits, creating a unified money system denominated in the same units of account as the rest of the economy, and formally raising the payments to lower-ranking party cadres, the central leadership aimed to make the system of payments more transparent, to align it with the formal hierarchy of party ranks, and thereby make it more amenable to central control.

But this is not what happened. As in the late 1930s, forms of spontaneous rationing soon emerged. In some cases, such as the selling of bread, some stores, especially in the provinces, reached their purchasing limits within hours of opening, so that lists of entitled recipients were quickly resurrected. As they compiled these lists, local party and state notables were allowed to exceed purchasing norms while ordinary workers suffered.[46] In addition, with the abolition of rationing regional elites began to reproduce the priority system that had existed before by recreating new closed channels of trade.

The easiest way of doing this was to persevere with the differential forms of distribution that had originally sprouted up in the wake of the earlier abolition of rationing in 1935, as food and goods were delivered through one's place of work, usually through in-house buffets, snack bars, canteens, and specialist shops.[47] But local authorities also made do with more improvised forms of limited-access distribution. In February 1948 in Ulan-Ude in the Buriat ASSR a special ad hoc distribution point for the provision of food was set up for fourteen republican functionaries, including five obkom secretaries, the chair of the council of ministers and his four deputies, the chair and deputy chair of the presidium of the supreme soviet, the second secretary of the Ulan-Ude gorkom (the obkom first secretary doubled as the gorkom first secretary), and the minister of state security.[48] Another investigation by the ministry of state security into trade in Poltava in 1949 found that in the courtyards of head offices of four regional organizations, including the obkom, "closed shops" had sprung up and were selling white bread, a prestige commodity that tended to be unavailable to the rest of the population. From 1 August to 24 November 1949, 82 tons of white bread had been sold on these premises, while only 34.6 tons of white bread had been distributed from the seventy-two other stores in Poltava that sold bread. Meanwhile, another of the closed shops in the city distributed other high-demand foods, such as flour, sugar, fish, meat, and fruit to members of the regional elite, who included officials from the obkom and Komsomol and from the regional and city executive committees, editors from the regional newspaper, and functionaries from the regional administration of the MVD (Ministry of Internal Affairs).[49]

The key factors determining the levels of transparency of elite benefits were whether they took the form of money or in-kind payments, whether they were conducted through free trade or closed stores, and the overall assortment of benefits, in other words, whether they took one, a small number, or many forms. The efforts by the center in December 1947 to claw back control over the system of redistribution were of little avail, as the underlying realities of the shortage economy and of regional elites' efforts to take control of forms of redistribution and side payments reasserted themselves.

Regional party cadres like Glushkov cloaked their various perquisites as a system of rights conferred on them by their special ideological role as members of the party's vanguard. To the extent that it underscored their status superiority over other groups, some regional cadres went further by going out of their way to show off their consumption of prestige goods. But this also presented the central leadership in Moscow with a conundrum. After all, another core ideological tenet of the regime was its egalitarianism. In the 1930s the central leadership had trod a very careful line on this question, trying to reconcile the need to reward effort and to accommodate its elites without appearing to betray the ideals of the Revolution.[50] In the late 1940s the problem would reemerge in a slightly different form. A series of scandals—some reported by KPK inspectors, some by Central Committee functionaries, and some by the regional press—illustrated the affront to communist norms, in the context of widespread material hardship, of ostentatious consumption.[51] Just as regional leaders responded to the electoral revolts of 1947–48 by adapting their behavior, so too did some see the benefits of behaving more discreetly by resurrecting closed distribution networks and by building residential ghettos and remote country dachas that were well out of the public's gaze.

THE POLITICS OF EXCLUSION

According to the "promotion contract" model of the communist party, the matching of rewards to nomenklatura rank created a long-term incentive for low-level officials to seek promotion and to build a career in the party bureaucracy. Rather than through one-off cash transfers, the party was a "promotion machine" that "created a nexus between economic incentives and the political stability of the regime."[52] Some have argued that this feature of one-party regimes helps explain their relative stability and longevity as compared to other forms of dictatorship.[53] As we have seen, most regional party organizations had relatively clear-cut hierarchies and an elaborate system of rewards to woo new recruits and to retain their loyalty. These rewards included monetary remuneration, payments in kind, including cars, apartments, country houses, and the use of special shops, and various forms of privilege, such as access to information and ease of travel. To make budgetary allocations more transparent and the party less dependent on state subsidies, the December 1947 money reforms envisioned transferring the party to a system of self-accounting in which regional party organizations were to be made liable for their end-of-year balance sheets and were allowed to dispose of any surplus they accumulated. To boost their revenue, the regional party organizations took over lucrative publishing businesses and raised their income from membership dues. Indeed, according to some scholars it is this new fixation on generating profits that helps account for the surge in party membership in 1950s.[54]

The difficulty with this account is that it does not explain why a young cadre would have pursued a career in the party in the first place. After all, the system of supplements for party officials was introduced only to make up for the shortfall in their base salaries relative to their counterparts in the ministries. In the early postwar period obkom first secretaries earned roughly half what directors of large enterprises and heads of regional ministerial administrations did.[55] Industrial ministries and enterprises had direct control of economic resources, which they could trade in unplanned exchanges. Why join the party bureaucracy if you could earn so much more as the director of an enterprise or the head of a factory shop?

Two factors may help explain the party bureaucrat's choice. The first has to do with ideology. As we saw in the case of Glushkov, the ruling ideology stipulated that the party was to exercise a leading role in society. Undoubtedly some people believed this claim and may have had a near-religious faith in the party and its ideals. For them, that faith may well have been cause enough to serve the party. Others may have had a more skeptical or pragmatic bent. Irrespective of their beliefs, the party's leading role in society was an ideological convention that could be used to achieve various goals. If you believed in it, working for the party was a reward in itself. If not, the leading role of the party was a source of power in dealing with other actors and organizations.

But there was also a second source of power. Party officials had at their disposal a specific resource that was denied to other actors. From 1946 to 1951 approximately three-quarters of a million individuals, roughly one in eight members, were expelled from the communist party for various forms of misconduct.[56] Expulsion from the party affected people in different ways. Some who had devoted their lives to the Bolshevik cause were so devastated that they fell ill, dropped into severe depression, became socially isolated, and even, in some cases, committed suicide.[57] To many, rejoining the party would turn into a lifelong quest in pursuit of what they viewed as a moral and existential rebirth.[58] For others, especially those in senior managerial positions, expulsion from the party could mean a drop in status but also, more tangibly, being cut off from the steady flow of nomenklatura privileges to which they and their families had grown accustomed. Expulsion was not the only sanction available to the party. There was also a wide array of warnings (*preduprezheniia*), instructions (*ukazaniia*), putting on notice (*postanovka na vid*), and reprimands (*vygovory*).[59] Like expulsions, reprimands could elicit various reactions. For some supply officials (*tolkachi*) a reprimand may have been just an ordinary job hazard, one that with the right connections they could quickly expunge from their party record.[60] For most officials, however, such punishments were to be avoided. Having a party reprimand could represent a serious obstacle to future promotion, and getting it removed required, in most cases, considerable bureaucratic effort.

In chapter 1 we saw that regional party leaders could use the threat of exclusion from the party as a powerful tool against other officials. Yet expelling a rival also carried certain dangers. If the victim was on the nomenklatura of a higher-level committee, the sacking would need to be cleared with it. In addition, there was always the chance that the expulsion might be appealed and that the appeal would reach the collegium of the Commission of Party Control in Moscow. Even if it were unsuccessful the inquiry could drag up all manner of embarrassing information that the regional party leader would much prefer be kept under wraps.[61]

In the late 1940s control over exclusion would emerge, in a rather circuitous way, in another guise, not as a threat but as a source of protection. In this form it would prove to be particularly valuable, not least because, even after the worst of the Great Terror of 1930s had passed, the regime remained extremely repressive. This meant that protection was not a theoretical or abstract resource but a very real one that might palpably affect your life in crucial ways.

The years 1946–47 witnessed a series of draconian campaigns against theft, against the expansion of private plots on collective farms, and against speculation.[62] The most virulent was the theft campaign, which, along with the related category of abuse of office, claimed 181,316 party members, or roughly a quarter of all those expelled, in 1946–51.[63] The theft campaign was one of the most profoundly ideological of all Stalin's campaigns. One of its chief aims was to defend socialist property, a term the dictator had coined in the early 1930s. Stalin reasoned that just as capitalism was underpinned by private property, so socialism required its own form of property. In the 1930s the dictator had been willing to throw the full repressive weight of the state behind socialist property, even if that meant death by shooting.[64] In June 1947 Stalin could not go that far because the death penalty had just been revoked, but the new decree still raised the minimum term for theft of state property from six months to seven years. It could be applied for appropriation of the most meagre amounts of food, cloth, industrial materials, or assets of any kind that could be loosely designated as belonging to the state. Convictions at the height of the campaign, from 1947 to 1949—1,408,879—were roughly on the order of convictions for counterrevolutionary crimes—1,344,923—at the peak of the Great Purges of 1937–38. By the time of Stalin's death half of the inmates in all the labor camps were serving terms on charges stemming from the June 1947 theft decrees.[65]

It was against the ferocity of these decrees that regional party bosses could act as a vital line of defense. The origins of their power went back to provisions agreed on in the immediate aftermath of the Great

Purges. On 1 December 1938 the Politburo decreed that the arrest of party members could henceforth take place only with the consent (*soglasie* or *soglasovanie*) of the first secretary of the corresponding territorial party committee.[66] Given that arrests could now take place only on the say-so of the party secretary, for the duration of Stalin's reign these rules could be used as a means of blocking the prosecution of party members.[67]

Many local party organizations were too disorganized to coordinate with the local justice agencies as they were supposed to.[68] Ordinary party members were sent to the camps in large numbers without having the issue of their party status resolved. Although we have no statewide data, surveys in the Velikolukskii, Murmansk, and Voronezh regions showed that up to two-thirds of ordinary communists in these regions were being prosecuted in court without the knowledge of the local party agencies, who were not even subsequently informed.[69] Yet first secretaries were much more likely to step in when members of the nomenklatura were charged. In fact, the best predictor of an intervention by a party secretary appears to have been the seniority of the accused and their rank in the regional party hierarchy.

Some of the best examples of this dual-track system concerned cases in which rank-and-file communists were convicted of a crime whereas members of the nomenklatura escaped punishment even though they had committed the same crime. In 1946 a large-scale theft at the Krasnorechenskii distillery in Ul'ianovsk was uncovered. While the rank-and-file members of the party received harsh sentences, ranging from long custodial terms to the death penalty, the director of the plant, after pressure was exerted by the obkom, was given a sentence of three years, and even that was suspended in view of the amnesty then in force. When the director's sentence was overturned by the RSFSR supreme court, the presiding judge, along with the chair of the regional court, were summoned by the obkom cadres secretary and warned that the new punishment would need to remain noncustodial. When the trial judge objected, he was curtly warned by the obkom secretary that this was the position of the obkom buro and that should the judge defy the obkom he would be expelled from the party.[70]

In another case, also from Ul'ianovsk, the obkom first secretary, Terent'ev, expressly forbade that criminal proceedings be started against the head of a district executive committee who was accused of misappropriating goods and siphoning them off to the district elite. Despite protests from the regional procurator, Terent'ev stood firm, and the prosecution was stopped.[71]Another example of the lengths to which party leaders would go to defend their own people comes from a theft case in Krasnoiarsk. In 1947 the director of a gold-mining firm, Sergeev, was charged with the theft and possession of prized consumer goods. Despite the efforts of the regional party committee to secure his immediate release, the charge came at a bad time, just after the June decree. In the event, Sergeev came out of it as well as he could have, getting seven years, the lowest mandatory sentence under the new law.[72] The kraikom then decided to sustain the battle by other means. On the insistence of the kraikom second secretary, Butuzov, Sergeev was freed from custody and placed under surety of three party members. He then went into hiding. Despite a complaint by Procurator-General Safonov to one of the Central Committee secretaries in May 1948, Sergeev was never found.[73] Moreover, Butuzov came out of the affair unscathed and was promoted two years later to first secretary of the kraikom.

A second campaign in which the dual-track system of justice was used to protect regional cadres was the money reform of 14 December 1947. The reform, which involved the withdrawal of old denominations and their replacement with new ones, was confiscatory, hitting in particular those with cash holdings. Funds held on the day of the reform in the state savings bank were to be exchanged at more favorable rates. Many Soviet citizens, especially peasants, who rarely made use of the savings bank, found that their cash savings were wiped out. Given the direct threat to their personal holdings, many officials with good connections found ways around the reform. The most common ruse was to deposit the cash with the savings bank and have the transaction backdated, so that it appeared as if the funds had been held by the bank before the new policy was announced. As we saw in chapter 1, some officials managed to have larger sums broken up into smaller parcels of under three thousand rubles which, under the provisions of the reform, were to retain their full value. The full extent of these operations is unknown, but they appear to have been widespread. According to statistics assembled at the Central Committee, by the end of March 1948 criminal proceedings had been instituted against more than two thousand people in twenty-six regions.[74] In view of the strong incentive of regional leaders to hush up such embarrassments, the actual level of such violations was likely higher.

Outsmarting the currency reforms normally required the complicity of a wide circle of financial, banking, and law enforcement officials as well as the cover and patronage of more senior leaders. In the crackdown on the currency violations of early 1948, some powerful individuals were caught in the net.[75] In general, however, only a small fraction of those prosecuted by law enforcement agencies were prominent regional leaders. This does not mean that regional leaders were not involved in the abuses, only that they tended, on the whole, not to be prosecuted. The point was noted in the following report of the Central Committee's administration for checking party agencies early in 1948: "For some reason, certain party agencies in the regions appear to be dragging their heels in cases involving violation of the currency reforms, and in particular they have taken under their wings certain 'bigwig' [bol'shie] party and soviet functionaries, while apportioning all the blame on hapless second-order officials."[76] Another report read: "Many obkoms are treating in a totally liberal way party and soviet leaders who have deceived the state and compromised themselves in the currency reforms. Thus, while many financial officials are being prosecuted, a large share of leading party and state officials are left unpunished."[77]

The theft campaign and the money reforms are two examples of a more general phenomenon. In many regions two spheres of justice had been created. As Procurator-General Grigorii Safonov would later assert, the resolution of December 1938 had originally been intended to thwart illegal arrests of the kind that had spread during the Great Purges. It was not meant to throw a blanket of protection over party members, but this, it was now clear, had been its main long-term effect.[78] This led to a number of technical and procedural difficulties for justice officials.[79] Yet the biggest problem, as a senior official from the all-union Procuracy noted, was that the ultimate decision on whether to institute criminal proceedings against party members had, in effect, been "removed from the competence of the justice agencies" and placed in the hands of party officials.[80]

Throughout 1948 and 1949 local procurators complained about the interference of party officials in specific cases.[81] Generalizing from them, the chief procurator for rail transport observed in February 1949 to

Safonov, "There are cases where party functionaries leap to the defense of those who have committed crimes, they object to us passing their files to the court, and they simply insist that the cases be taken out of the hands of the justice agencies or that they be just stopped."[82] From the point of view of the justice agencies, the dual-track system of justice undermined the legitimacy of the law and made it hard for justice officials to do their job. The overall effect of the December 1938 rule had been to create two legal jurisdictions, one for members of the nomenklatura and the other for everyone else. According to the procurator-general in a report to the Central Committee, the cumulative effects of "local influence" had been to create a situation in which "there are, in essence, two criminal codes [in Russia], one for communists and another for everyone else. There have been a number of instances where, for one and the same crime, the party member remains free while the non-Communist languishes in prison."[83]

Ranged against each other were two distinct institutional logics.[84] Justice officials pointed to provisions in the Soviet Constitution on the independence of the courts, they grumbled about the existence of two separate spheres of justice, and complained that judgments were being made by party officials with scant knowledge or understanding of the law. Against them was the institutional logic of the party, whose main advocate at the center was the Commission of Party Control. Underlying its position was a view that, given the party's "leading role in society," it was the party that should ultimately determine whether a member should be expelled and, by implication, prosecuted. As Belova and Lazarev put it, "The unique and in many respects superior position of the Soviet Communist Party dictated that its members could be disciplined only by the party itself."[85] It was on these grounds that on a number of occasions in the late Stalin era the KPK and its de facto head, Matvei Shkiriatov, made it known that communists should be prosecuted only on condition that their case had first been resolved by their party organization. In the most high-profile case, in April 1950 Shkiriatov, alarmed by the large number of party members who were being automatically expelled following criminal convictions over which the party had no control, insisted in a letter to 103 obkom secretaries that trials against communists could not go ahead unless the case had already been considered by their party organization.[86] In some provinces the instruction was then replicated in regional-level directives ordering procurators to refrain from prosecuting party members until the suspect had been expelled from the party.[87] Two months later Shkiriatov announced to a meeting of obkom party collegiums, "We must consider the case of communists independently of the trial. In my view we should not be bound or constrained in this matter. . . . [A]fter all, the courts do not always get these things right."[88]

In the contest between the two logics it was the KPK's that usually prevailed. To an extent this was unsurprising given that the KPK was lodged in the Central Committee, and its staff were part of the Central Committee bureaucracy.[89] Unlike the heads of the justice agencies Shkiriatov had been a full member of the Central Committee since 1939.[90] In fact, from the time of the Leningrad Affair in 1949 Shkiriatov had begun to appear on platforms with other members of the Politburo "as if he ranked with Central Committee secretaries."[91] Given the higher standing of their organization, officials from the KPK had no problem admonishing or rebuking their counterparts in the justice agencies.[92] In the run-up to the XIX Party Congress in October 1952 Shkiriatov's fortunes rose still further. Admitted to the new Central Committee Presidium, he presided over a change in the party's statutes which permitted local party committees to be even more brazen in interfering in court cases.[93]

Some scholars have argued that the emergence of a two-tiered system of justice is evidence of corruption and of a "darker 'Big Deal'" between the regime and its regional party organizations.[94] There is certainly plenty of evidence to suggest that some of the most flagrant cases of intervention involved scandals, such as the enormous theft case in Ul'ianovsk in 1949, in which senior party officials, including in this case the obkom first secretary, Terent'ev, stood to benefit from the scam.[95] But often there was another, deeper rationale, one which stemmed from the regional party's role in the wider institutional architecture of the Soviet political system. In many cases Stalin had delegated power to his regional principals with a mandate that, within certain limits, they could exercise discretion in forming regional networks. In the late Stalin era these leaders appropriated these powers and used them to protect members of their own networks from some of Stalin's flagship policies. "Protecting cadres represented an unarticulated, local response to anti-criminal repression in the late 1940s," writes Juliette Cadiot.[96] Party interventions were a means by which "members of the party and of the nomenklatura sought to circumvent the ferocious repression of the state . . . and to preserve a semblance of stability and tranquility for party cadres in a highly repressive context."[97] Most often, when it came to a contest between the implementation of statewide policies by the justice agencies and the prerogative of regional leaders to use whatever means to cohere their regional elites, the central apparatus sided with the latter.

In chapter 2 we saw how institutions introduced by the central state for one end were hijacked by regional leaders for another. In this chapter we have encountered two more processes of this kind. A transparent system of remuneration drawn up in Moscow was subverted by opaque forms of regional redistribution. Further, the right of party secretaries to grant sanctions for arrest, originally intended as a safeguard against arbitrary repression, turned over time into a source of local patronage and protection. Each of these cases belongs to a particular form of institutional change known as conversion, the redeployment by agents of existing rules for new goals, functions, and purposes.[98]

While co-optation was important, in a country as steeped in repression as the Soviet Union was under Stalin, protection and the power of exclusion were more so. In fact, Moscow was surprisingly relaxed in letting regional leaders wield their powers of exclusion as they saw fit. Despite repeated attacks on "nepotism" and on "family circles," the central leadership was loath to take concerted action against regional leaders. Save for the Leningrad and the Mingrelian Affairs there were few attacks on local networks, and those that did take place rarely led to expulsions from the party. Rather than undercutting them, the statewide dictator recognized how much he needed these regional networks if the system was to operate effectively.

The years after the Great Patriotic War were a period of social as well as institutional change. There was stratification at the regional level and a growing alignment of formal rank in the party with the age, length of service, and levels of political education of officeholders. This system of seniority was reinforced by various prerogatives such as privileged access, which varied with one's rank, to a package of nomenklatura benefits. Given the leading role of the party, party officials could present these privileges as a "right" grounded in their leadership role. At the same time, in view of the regime's egalitarian ideology, obkom first secretaries learned that it was best to conceal ostentatious displays of wealth from public view, just as they had understood from the regional party elections that it was wise to temper their treatment of the raikom secretaries. By early 1953 these processes of social and institutional change had become sufficiently engrained that they would prove to be surprisingly untouched by one otherwise momentous event that was about to happen in Moscow.

II
INTERREGNUM

4 Moscow, Center

ON 7 OCTOBER 1953 I.K. Efendiev, a veteran security agent from Azerbaijan, addressed a thirteen-page letter to the newly appointed first secretary of the Central Committee, Nikita Khrushchev. The purge of the all-union Ministry of State Security in July 1951 had yielded a stream of arrests and interrogations of former secret police officials such as Efendiev, who himself had been in prison since 1952. Many had triggered denunciations of former bosses, so why Khrushchev seized on this particular letter remains unclear. In this case, however, he acted quickly, circulating it to all the members of his cabinet and ordering a full-scale inquiry.[1] The Central Committee report of 12 December 1953 confirmed the substance of the letter, concluding that in Azerbaijan Bagirov had turned the manufacture of kompromat into a system of rule through which he tended to promote those on whom he had the goods. The consequence was that the upper reaches of the Azerbaijan elite was littered with individuals with "black spots" in their past. The ostensible purpose of the party-based system of cadre selection had been turned on its head. Rather than recruiting cadres for their competence or loyalty to the party, Bagirov had sought out those who had "failed in their previous work . . . so that, in relying on them, he was always sure to have his way."[2]

The Transcaucasus, of which Azerbaijan was a part, was not a typical Soviet region. Sharing external borders with Turkey and Iran and being within reach of the vast oil fields of the Caspian, it had been even before the Revolution a favored haunt of infiltrators, double agents, and externally sponsored insurgency groups. It was also the only Soviet region in which the upper reaches of the territorial party leadership were dominated by former secret police officers, many of whom had served an extended apprenticeship in the Cheka, the state security police, in the 1920s.[3] From Khrushchev's perspective, however, sitting in the Kremlin in the autumn of 1953, the goings-on in Azerbaijan had special significance. The elevation of the Ministry of Internal Affairs (MVD) into a superagency that could dig up, store, and make use of kompromat represented a form of governance that the recently deposed head of the secret police, Lavrentii Beria, had tried to implant across the country in the months after Stalin's death. With a broad network of clients lodged in regional offices of the MVD, Beria was the one statewide leader besides Khrushchev whose support had a truly all-union reach.[4] With Beria's arrest at the end of June, this all-union network, led, no less, by a member of the country's ruling cabinet, had been closed down, and the events in Azerbaijan represented one of the final chapters of this story.

We have focused thus far on events at the regional level. We have looked at how regional leaders responded to pressures from above by establishing networks, in most cases ones which enabled them to negotiate their own challenges of authoritarian power sharing and control by deploying resources provided by regional party organizations. We now turn our attention to a major change at the center. The death of Stalin in March 1953 unleashed a succession struggle that would have sweeping effects on the dynamics of regional rule. One effect was the appearance of a new model of governance associated with Beria. Another was the adoption of a string of reformist policies at the center. According to some historians, Khrushchev's assumption of power inaugurated a "decade long triumph of Soviet reformism" along a number of policy dimensions.[5] Other scholars have gone further and, on the assumption that these reformist policies had earlier been blocked by Stalin, have grouped them under the umbrella term "de-Stalinization."[6]

There are, in our view, two problems with this approach. First, as important as Stalin's influence was, the lack of reliable information on high-level decision making may have led some scholars to exaggerate what one individual was capable of.[7] As we have suggested in earlier chapters this overestimation of Stalin's powers may have combined with an underestimation of levels of institutional innovation and of the delegation of power under Stalin. One consequence of this has been an inclination to overlook important continuities between the late Stalin and Khrushchev eras. Second, while some authorities have tended to observe signs of de-Stalinization across a broad spectrum of policy areas, including agriculture, the Gulag, nationalities policy, criminal justice, welfare policy, industrial relations, literature, and the arts, we suggest that the rationales and motivations at play in each of these fields were too diverse and heterogeneous to warrant compression into a single concept.

Recent scholars have rightly observed that the term "de-Stalinization" was never used by officials or public figures in the Soviet Union. In the political sphere attacks on Stalin were framed in terms of another concept, that of the "cult of personality."[8] Critiques of the cult of personality tended to converge on two axes: attacks on "one-person rule" as opposed to "collective leadership" and criticism of abuse of power, especially in the form of excessive use of coercion or repression.[9] In the immediate aftermath of Stalin's death, many of the attacks on the cult of personality in the regions were directed not at Stalin but at substate dictators, broadly along the lines of criticisms that had been leveled against them in the late 1940s. After Khrushchev's Secret Speech of 1956, in which for the first time he publicly denounced Stalin's abuse of power, it was more likely that activists and officials at regional party meetings would attack Stalin himself as well as the repression that had been perpetrated under him.[10] Yet these attacks would generally have little effect on the dynamics of regional governance, on the selection of regional leaders, or on the composition of local elites.[11]

Far more significant for modes of governance in the regions were two other factors. First was a campaign waged by Khrushchev to bring about a radical increase in agricultural production. This would have an immediate, palpable effect on the incentives facing many regional leaders, including those in largely urban areas. Second was a subtle redefinition by Khrushchev of the terms of political exclusion. Under Khrushchev the number of expulsions from the party fell dramatically, so that by the end of the decade they were at roughly a quarter of levels in the late Stalin era.[12] But the decline in expulsions did not mean an end to the politics of exclusion, only that the mechanisms had been recalibrated. Capitalizing on innovations in the Stalin era, Khrushchev refined a technique for politically excluding politicians without having to expel them from the party. This tactic would be especially apparent in 1953–54, when he embarked on a major cull of regional party secretaries, in what would become the largest purge since the Great Terror of 1937–38.[13]

TWO MODELS CLASH

In dictatorship, repression can be used as an instrument of authoritarian control by crushing rebellions and compelling the population to submit to unpopular policies. But repression can also be used as a means of solving the dictator's power-sharing problem. Under Stalin, the threat of repression, realized from time to time, served as a useful means of disciplining and controlling those around him.[14] Repression could also be applied against regional leaders. With the exception of two specific cases—the Leningrad and Mingrelian Affairs—toward the end of his life Stalin does not seem to have perceived a threat from this group. Moreover, as we noted earlier, in his declining years the nomenklatura appeared to have come up with various institutional devices to protect themselves from the dictator's capricious and unpredictable behavior and mood swings.

Following Stalin's death this uneasy institutional truce was broken and the specter of a sudden breakout of violence reemerged. Although the dictator was gone, the resource of violence in the form of a poorly monitored security police was now up for grabs. Concerns on this score were heightened by the uncertainties of the succession, which put relations among the country's leaders under strain. Fears that violence would be used to resolve leadership differences reached a climax in June 1953. At this point, a majority of the statewide leadership, worried that Beria was pitching newly invigorated regional branches of the MVD against their party counterparts, carried out a preemptive coup.

From the very beginning Beria was at a disadvantage. His background in the Cheka in the 1920s, his leadership of the commissariat of internal affairs in 1938–45, and his continuing patronage of senior officers from the secret police meant that he was the Presidium member most closely identified with the agencies of repression. Beria tried to allay the concerns of other leaders by presenting himself as a liberal statesman who was intent on reining in the secret police.[15] However, Beria had two difficulties. First, one of his major adversaries was the former minister of state security Sem'en Ignat'ev, whom Stalin had tasked with picking off Beria's clients in the MGB leadership. After Stalin's death, Beria-led investigations into recent abuses pointed the finger at Ignat'ev.[16] However, in mid-March Ignat'ev returned to the Central Committee apparatus as secretary.[17] Beria's continued persecution of Ignat'ev, which saw Ignat'ev stripped of his secretaryship on 5 April and expelled from the Central Committee on 28 April crossed an important threshold and was presented by some members of the leadership, not least by Khrushchev himself, as a violation of party norms.[18]

In addition to portraying himself as an advocate of order, socialist legality, and human rights, Beria had another card up his sleeve. Aware that regional offices of the ministry of internal affairs were unable to compete with regional branches of the party as agencies of mobilization and propaganda, Beria represented himself as a champion of the rights of the national minorities, especially those on the country's western peripheries. Building on speeches he had made in the late Stalin era, Beria began to push for a new, more full-blooded form of indigenization, one which would privilege titular national languages as the language of official republican-level communication and assertively promote national cadres to nomenklatura positions. In doing so, Beria sought a constituency of support among midlevel officials, including ones from local party organizations and, as Fairbanks put it, to "recruit within the [regional] party elite without controlling the [Central Committee's] party organs department—of cracking open the nomenklatura of that department from the outside."[19]

Yet Beria also had a second difficulty, one which had a more clearly expressed regional dimension. As much as he tried to pass off his reforms as an effort to restore socialist legality, he could not avoid the fact that his patronage network was almost entirely confined to the Ministry of Internal Affairs.[20] On becoming USSR commissar of internal affairs in 1938 Beria had positioned his clients as heads of regional and republican branches of the commissariat, a tactic Stalin would check in later years.[21] On Stalin's death, Beria had little option but to do the same thing. One reason was that he and his network had failed to penetrate the civilian party hierarchy: of the 120 voting members of the Central Committee elected in mid-March 1953 only five were unmistakably Beria's clients.[22] Beria required an alternative patronage network in an institution that he knew well and where he already had some expertise and contacts. On 19 March he approached the Central Committee Secretariat with proposals for the wholesale replacement of MVD chiefs in all fifteen republics, twelve ASSRS, six krais, and forty-nine Russian regions, and shortly afterward he came up with names for new MVD heads across Belorussia and Ukraine.[23]

One of the best-known examples of the difficulties he faced comes from L'vov, which, being located on the western fringes of the Ukraine, was one of the prime targets of Beria's policy of accelerated indigenization. Among Beria's first acts in Ukraine was to replace the minister of internal affairs there, T.A. Strokach, with his acolyte P. Ia. Meshik and to appoint as the new deputy minister S. Mil'shtein, one of Beria's oldest associates from the Caucasus. The deposed minister, Strokach, was transferred to head the regional branch of the MVD in L'vov in western Ukraine. In April Strokach was asked by his successor as minister and Beria's client Meshik to pass along data on the national composition of the party organizations in L'vov. Given that the party in L'vov had been shored up by communists from outside the province and some even from outside the Ukraine, this information was highly sensitive and could be used to discredit the party as an organization of nonindigenous outsiders.[24] Strokach's concerns grew when Meshik put in an additional request for information on the shortcomings and deficiencies in party work in the region. Strokach took the matter to the obkom first secretary, Z.T. Serdiuk. It so happened that Serdiuk was one of Khrushchev's oldest associates, having worked with Khrushchev from his earliest days in Ukraine. Serdiuk also had the distinction of being the only regional leader outsider the Russian Federation who was also a member of the all-union Central Committee, in his case as a candidate member.[25] The information Meshik required was lodged in the special sector at the obkom, but Serdiuk steadfastly refused to release it. Instead, he approached the first secretary of the Ukraine, L.G. Mel'nikov, for guidance. In what would prove a fateful decision, Mel'nikov sided with Beria and ordered that Serdiuk pass on the data. Still, however, Serdiuk refused. "The Central Committee—that is the law for a Bolshevik, not some order from Beria," he would later recall. In what was a clear sign of his own limited authority, Meshik was forced to take the matter to Beria, who threatened Strokach, the regional MVD head, over the phone for not doing more to retrieve the information from the obkom. Strokach was sacked by Beria on 12 June and recalled to Moscow. In a manner that uncannily resembled Beria's attack on Ignat'ev at the Central Committee, Meshik, the republican minister of internal affairs, began to hound Serdiuk, the obkom leader. At a meeting of the Ukrainian central committee he threatened him with arrest, finally reducing Serdiuk to tears and inducing him to beg the Ukrainian second secretary, Kirichenko, to intercede on his behalf.[26]

Serdiuk and Strokach were both saved by Beria's arrest and rewarded for their resolve.[27] The events in L'vov underscored the wider significance of the Beria affair. From Serdiuk's point of view the request from Meshik was illegitimate for, as he reportedly put it to Mel'nikov "since when has the obkom had to report to the MGB?"[28] Serdiuk appears to have been under great duress, but his adherence to the party chain of command and, in particular, to the "priority of the Central Committee" made it hard for Beria's MVD to make inroads in the province.[29] In the end, in what must have been a major blow to his authority, Beria was himself sucked into the conflict and reduced to shouting threats over the telephone.

The events in L'vov reveal something more general about the nature of Beria's MVD-based strategy. After all, the MVD had an agent network and possessed kompromat of its own. But this was not the kind of information Beria needed here. What Beria required were general statistics on party cadres, including on the national composition of cadres, and these data were jealously guarded by the special sector at the obkom. The struggle in L'vov was to a large extent about control of information, one of the key sources of the party's power. Direct evidence of this is limited, but we do have an allusion from a speech given by Lazar Kaganovich at the July 1953 meeting of the Central Committee plenum: "Why was it that Beria was always . . . protesting? It was because he didn't want the Central Committee to know *his people* and, thereby, for the Central Committee to control *him*. He himself wanted to control the party. Let's look at what has been said about L'vov, *where they have materials on obkom secretaries [kogda imeiut materialy na sekretarei obkomov]*. What does this mean? It means placing the party under the control of the MVD, it means that the MVD has a hold on communists, raikom secretaries, obkom secretaries."[30]

It is doubtful Beria contemplated the application of mass repression against party officials across the country in a repeat of what had happened in the Great Terror. He must have understood that this would have unleashed a maelstrom that, lacking Stalin's authority, he was unlikely to be able to control. Much more useful as a means of governance was the threat of repression against individuals, supported by the use of kompromat. This, in effect, had been the system that had endured in Azerbaijan and very possibly in other regions of the Caucasus. After Stalin's death, Beria judged that he might be able to extend this mode of governance-through-kompromat to other parts of the country. Ranged against each other were two models of rule, each with its own type of information and its own type of sanction, the threat of repression in the case of the MVD, and the threat of political exclusion in the case of the party. The nullification of this alternative model of MVD rule was one of the most important consequences of the Beria affair.

After Stalin's death and Beria's removal, the institutional arrangements for kompromat began to change. Carrying on a trend that had begun after the Great Purges, expulsions on explicitly political grounds, such as anti-Soviet agitation, ties with alien elements, and hidden social origins continued to dwindle, falling to a few hundred a year by the mid-1950s.[31] Moreover, there were now changes to the way in which personal information was collated. One Central Committee report of 15 June 1955 noted that the party's cadre forms inherited from the Stalin era had "replaced proper political vigilance with harmful suspiciousness and cultivated the condemned practice of a biological approach to cadres." The report observed that the country was now dominated by a generation of people who had been politically socialized after the consolidation of Soviet power, and it asked why cadre forms continued to have questions about service in the imperial army or in the tsarist police, on support for the White Army, participation in the 1920s opposition, and so forth. Similarly, the report noted that the question of whether a respondent or their relatives had ever been convicted of a crime was, in view of the flagrant abuses of the justice system under Stalin, only compounding an earlier injustice. As the report stated, "In their time very many Soviet people, and among them tens of thousands of communists and members of the Komsomol, faced criminal prosecution for quite the wrong reasons."[32]

Yet the fact that information that had once been used for Stalin-era kompromat was being downgraded did not mean that blackmail was no longer used. Once de-Stalinization proper got under way, it was now, conversely, the fact that a leader had been a perpetrator of Stalin-era repressions that became the main source of kompromat. Nearly all senior politicians from the late Stalin era were in one way or another complicit or actively involved in the use of repression. The key thing was to gain control of information on their abuses. For much of the 1950s the main repository of information on "unlawful prosecutions" was the high-level rehabilitation commissions, which were controlled by an institutional alliance of the party and the Procuracy. Through the Procuracy and, in particular, through its head, Procurator-General Roman Rudenko, an old client, Khrushchev would show himself to be an adept at this game.

To highlight the role of the new, post-Stalin kompromat the case of Frol Kozlov is instructive. At the beginning of 1949, as the Leningrad Affair took off, Kozlov was transferred from Kuybishev, where he had served as obkom second secretary, to head the party organization at the huge Kirov plant in Leningrad. Later that year he was appointed second secretary of the Leningrad gorkom, where he served directly under Vasilii Andrianov and where he was credited by some, along with Andrianov, with seeing through the Leningrad purge. It was a measure of Kozlov's success in this role that he was promoted to first secretary of the Leningrad gorkom in 1950.[33] Yet this close association with the Leningrad Affair would soon turn into a problem. One of the first repercussions of Beria's arrest and of the Central Committee plenum in July 1953 was the reopening of the files connected with the Leningrad case.

At the beginning of 1954 Kozlov's position was precarious. A sizeable portion of the regional party organization had turned against him for his role in the Leningrad repressions, where many had lost friends and relatives only years earlier. This much was reflected at the February 1954 obkom conference, where 125 delegates (19 percent of the total) voted against Kozlov in the obkom election.[34] On 25 April *Pravda* published an attack on Kozlov for his insufficient self-criticism and for failing to address shortcomings in the regional party organization.[35] All along, Kozlov was aware that submission of the report of the Central Committee commission into the Leningrad Affair was imminent. Khrushchev had earlier shown confidence in Kozlov by endorsing his promotion as first secretary of the obkom during a visit to Leningrad in December 1953, but now Kozlov needed Khrushchev's support even more. On 3 May the Procuracy's report on the Leningrad Affair, written by Rudenko, was presented to the Presidium of the Central Committee, where Kozlov was to all intents and purposes exonerated. Four days later Khrushchev addressed the Leningrad party aktiv, making it quite clear that Kozlov should not be held at fault for what had happened in the city.[36]

The nature of Kozlov's dependence on Khrushchev was widely understood by those around Khrushchev and became a structural feature of Kozlov's position that limited his room to maneuver. One of the most acute observers of this structural dependence was another of Khrushchev's acolytes, Dmitrii Shepilov, who accompanied Khrushchev on the earlier visit to Leningrad, in December 1953. In his book *The Kremlin's Scholar* he wrote,

> After Stalin's death, I, as editor in chief of *Pravda,* accompanied Khrushchev to a meeting of party activists in Leningrad. . . . [T]he meeting's presidium, of which I was a member, received many notes demanding that Andrianov and Kozlov be brought to justice for violating socialist legality, smashing the Leningrad organization, and deliberately defaming its members. During the breaks, many party activists asked me, "Why is Frol Kozlov still secretary? Why aren't Kozlov and Andrianov made to answer for what they did?" . . . I told Khrushchev about the notes and what had been said to me at the meeting. "It's my impression," I said, "that the communists here are unanimous about the need to dismiss Kozlov immediately as Leningrad secretary. I think Kozlov himself recognizes that he has no respect or support among the *aktiv.*" Khrushchev was silent. I continued along the same lines, citing more facts and arguments. "All right, all right," Khrushchev said, "we'll see." . . . Speaking at the meeting the next day, Khrushchev made an astounding statement: "As for Comrade Kozlov, if you support him, the Central Committee will too." I soon realized that Khrushchev made frequent use of such tactics. He chose some failed and discredited official, appointed him to a high post, rewarded him with various titles, and made him into his most loyal and obedient servant. This protégé

understood that his welfare, titles, posts, and entire comfortable life depended totally on his benefactor. One word from the latter, and all was lost.[37]

The main feature of Kozlov's dependence on Khrushchev was that it was based on a new structural device that had appeared since Stalin's death, the strategic assignment of blame for Stalin-era repressions. Other politicians, such as Malenkov, were later implicated in the Leningrad Affair on Khrushchev's instigation, and Khrushchev could have, at any stage, decided to turn up the heat on Kozlov.

In fact, Khrushchev's attack on Malenkov at the January 1955 Central Committee plenum and the hints he dropped about Malenkov's role in the Leningrad Affair spawned a new wave of attacks on Kozlov.[38] According to the Central Committee official Storozhev, "After the January plenum, it has been hard for comrade Kozlov to work as a secretary of the Leningrad obkom. In the organization they remember what role he played in the destruction of the [Leningrad] 'anti-party group' and in getting rid of cadres."[39]

Such a state of affairs was ideally suited to Khrushchev. Knowing that he had strong leverage over Kozlov, he continued to promote him, first bringing him into the new Russian buro of the Central Committee in March 1956 and then making him a candidate member of the Central Committee Presidium in February 1957. Shortly afterward, during the "Anti-Party crisis" in June, Kozlov would repay Khrushchev's faith in him by playing the key role in enlisting support for his patron.

The defeat of the Anti-Party group, as Khrushchev, the victor, would come to label them, was a decisive moment in the battle for power after Stalin. Although Khrushchev had emerged as the first among equals shortly after Stalin's death, he was for a number of years hemmed in by a number of institutional constraints. Of these the most important was the need to win a majority on the Presidium, the country's cabinet. Confronted with majority opposition to his leadership on this body, Khrushchev appealed to the party's "parliament," the Central Committee. A key constituency on the Central Committee was the RSFSR obkom secretaries, especially those with voting rights. As it turned out, at the time the Presidium was meeting in Moscow most of these obkom secretaries were gathered in Leningrad to celebrate the city's 250th anniversary. The key role in rallying them to Khrushchev's cause and in

First Secretary of the Central Committee and master of ceremonies Nikita
Khrushchev (*left*) aboard a steamship on the Volga in 1957. The first secretary of
the Leningrad obkom, Frol Kozlov (*standing at center*), looks on as Khrushchev
speaks. One of Khrushchev's most loyal lieutenants, Central Committee Secretary
Averkii Aristov (*far right*) appears to be smiling at Khrushchev. Seated beside
Khrushchev is the Central Committee secretary and Presidium member Mikhail
Suslov. *Source:* RGASPI.

making arrangements for them to go to Moscow was performed by
their host in the city, the first secretary of the Leningrad obkom, Frol
Kozlov.[40]

Save for a small number of Stalin-initiated purges, the use of political
charges against senior party officials was no longer commonplace in
the late Stalin era. And yet Stalin's death had thrown up a mass of new
opportunities for kompromat. Frol Kozlov's case is just one example
of how Khrushchev used the rehabilitation process to generate a qualitatively new form of kompromat which could assure him the loyalty
of a key regional leader.[41] As head of the Central Committee apparatus

and champion of the Central Committee's right to resolve policy issues as well as of its prerogative to decide the moral culpability of those who had committed violations and crimes under Stalin, Khrushchev was well placed to take advantage of this resource. The Soviet political system, even after Stalin's death, was a sufficiently low-trust environment that simple acts of appointment or promotion were inadequate to secure loyalty, especially when the stakes were high. Khrushchev used the same structural device that Efendiev had complained about in Azerbaijan, except that now he turned it on its head, using a different type of information and threatening a different kind of punishment.

PRESSURE FROM ABOVE

The selective release of compromising information on Khrushchev's opponents, such as Malenkov as well as Molotov and Kaganovich, has been widely documented.[42] However, planting unpopular first secretaries like Frol Kozlov, whose complicity in Stalin-era repressions was well known throughout the country, would have sullied Khrushchev's reputation as a de-Stalinizer and undercut the authority of regional party organizations. Khrushchev needed to gain leverage over his regional party bosses, but he also recognized that, once in post, these leaders would have to command respect and authority in order to govern properly.

Earlier scholars saw Khrushchev's victory over the majority opposition on the Presidium in June 1957 as a result of two factors. First, there was the widening of the selectorate, the group to which policy makers were held to account. Much as Stalin had done in 1920s, Khrushchev, when faced with opposition on the Presidium, referred the conflict to the party's quasi-parliamentary body, the Central Committee.[43] The second factor was that Khrushchev had used his preeminence on the Central Committee apparatus to appoint clients to posts—especially as obkom first secretary—whose job entitled them to a seat on the Central Committee. This way Khrushchev was able to gain a majority on that body.[44] Evidence to support this thesis included the very high rates of turnover among obkom officials after Stalin's death and a meticulous reconstruction of Khrushchev's followers which suggested that they figured prominently among the new appointees.[45]

There are two problems with this approach. First, Khrushchev did not, as some contemporaries supposed, have a free hand in making these appointments.[46] The posts of all regional party leaders, and particularly those with voting rights on the Central Committee, were on the nomenklatura of the Presidium, where Khrushchev was heavily outflanked. This cast of seasoned, wily politicians would have scanned the lists of nominations with a keen eye for Khrushchev's associates. Khrushchev's cause would also not have been helped by the fact that until March 1955 the head of the Central Committee's party organs department, which supervised the nomination and appointments process, was the Central Committee secretary Nikolai Shatalin, an old ally of Malenkov's. Figures on high turnover also sometimes confuse positions that were subject to approval by the Central Committee with positions with voting rights on the Central Committee.[47] But even if we confine ourselves to the former, an examination of new first secretaries in the Russian Federation from 1953 to 1956 (the only republic in which obkom leaders held membership on the Central Committee) shows that in the sixty-six obkoms Khrushchev appointed clients to only seven first secretaryships.[48]

But there is a deeper, more critical problem with this approach. Khrushchev had himself served as territorial leader in Moscow and Ukraine, and in that capacity he would have understood how important it was for regional leaders to put down social roots, to win over the aktiv, and to build viable local networks. Parachuting in an ultraloyal client who had trouble establishing himself with the local party organization, in mobilizing the workforce, and in meeting economic targets would have done his reputation little good. Like Stalin, Khrushchev realized that regional leaders would have to be afforded a certain amount of leeway in order to win over local elites and mobilize the local workforce. This often meant agreeing to leaders who were not necessarily known to him but who had demonstrable qualities that might enable them to govern their regions effectively.

Like Stalin, Khrushchev had an agency problem, but the solutions that the two leaders came up with were quite different. As we have seen, Stalin's strategy had been to delegate but to temper acts of delegation with institutional controls such as elections, rotations, control agencies, and carefully targeted purges. Khrushchev's approach was altogether different. Khrushchev began by "territorializing" administration and ensuring that authority over appointments, budgets, and much else besides was transferred to the regions. Far from decentralizing, however, power was to be vested in the dictator's regional principals, the ob-kom secretaries.[49] Unlike Stalin, Khrushchev had an ingrained belief not only that these party leaders would remain loyal to the center and responsive to Moscow's commands but also, crucially, that they could be relied on to supply honest and uncontaminated information to the center about what was going on in their regions. To this end, in a move that would have fateful consequences, he relaxed many of Stalin's institutional controls.

To the extent that Khrushchev recognized that there was a problem, it was to him one of bureaucracy, of excess paperwork, and of overconcentration of decision making in Moscow. In these areas Khrushchev proved himself to be especially active. First, in July 1953 he slashed the Central Committee's nomenklatura from 45,000 to 25,300 posts, and three years later, on 1 June 1956, he halved it again to 12,600 posts.[50] Second, under Khrushchev the center's share of the overall budget expenditure fell from 77 percent in 1950 to 40 percent in 1960.[51] Third, in order to further reduce the information overload at the center, the organizational structure of the ministries was reformed. By the XX Congress in 1956 the prime minister, Bulganin, could report that coal, timber, iron, steel, food, textiles, transport, and construction, along with various other ministries, had been transferred from all-union to union-republic (that is, with joint all-union and republican ministries) or republican administrations.[52]

While the underlying theme of all these policies was to bring decision making and political leadership "closer to production," they were never envisaged as a loss of central control. Instead, political leadership was to be concentrated in local party agencies that were to remain under Moscow's tutelage. In one of the first reforms, district agencies of the ministry of agriculture were closed down, and the political directors of the machine-tractor stations (MTS) were replaced with party raikom-based "secretaries for the MTS zone."[53] The importance of stationing party officials at the MTSs was supposed "to enhance the importance of party lines of control and communication" and to "concentrate communication within party channels."[54]

In industry the importance of the party as a conduit of central control would become apparent somewhat later. As we saw in chapters 1 and 2, in most regions under Stalin local party officials had pivoted toward the agricultural sector, leaving industrial coordination to the central ministries. Khrushchev's desire to gain for the party as effective a role in running industry as it had in agriculture was one of the reasons for dismantling the industrial ministries and for the establishment of 105 regional economic councils (*sovnarkhozy*) in the summer of 1957. With a full remit for industry and construction, the sovnarkhozy had limited jurisdiction over agriculture, transportation, and retail trade. Unlike the remote ministries that "do not know what is going on in their own factories," the obkoms and the local party agencies were, in his view, perfectly placed to synchronize activities and to see projects through to completion.[55] Local party organizations would indeed play a leading role in staffing the sovnarkhozy and in liaising between them and local enterprises.[56] In dismantling the central industrial ministries, Khrushchev had in mind not decentralization per se but an arrangement whereby the ministries were replaced by the regional party apparatus as the main channel of central control.[57]

The one part of the dictator's agency problem that Khrushchev fully understood was that he needed agents, that is, regional party secretaries, who were subject to central control. He also had an intuitive, populist feel for the problems of overcentralization. He recognized that the center was overwhelmed with information it was unable to process, and to solve that problem he launched a vigorous campaign against paperwork and bureaucracy.[58] He also understood that parachuting in individuals from Moscow whose only criterion for leadership was their association with him was hardly sufficient to enable them to run their regions properly.

Yet Khrushchev had a naïve, almost childlike understanding of how organizations work. In the Russian Federation all the sovnarkhozy bar three were matched to the size of the regions.[59] This created a form of "yardstick competition" whereby obkom secretaries were to be assessed on the basis of the results of their sovnarkhoz.[60] Agency theory suggests that if an agent is held responsible for results he or she will have an incentive to distort the upward flow of information on activities in their domain.[61] Stalin seems to have understood this problem, which is why he tried to set up independent, honest-broker agencies to supply reliable information to the center.[62] By contrast, Khrushchev seemed to believe he could both increase the pressure on regional principals to achieve results and expect them to act as truth-tellers. Any hope Khrushchev entertained that regional party secretaries would stand up for the wider interests of the state were quickly dashed. To most, the need to fulfill the regional plan trumped all other considerations. Asked to reveal hidden production capacity obkom leaders, together with sovnarkhoz chairs, submitted heightened, unrealistic investment plans and lower production targets.[63] From the middle of 1958 the trend toward the deconcentration of industrial administration was reversed as, in a long and tortuous process, the sovnarkhoz scheme was gradually dismantled.

However, it would be in agriculture that Khrushchev's complete misunderstanding of the agency problem would truly come back to bite him. An epidemic of falsification of statistics and distortion of data, which came to light after the Riazan scandal, would lead to a major crisis in Khrushchev's leadership, one that would bring about a complete reconfiguration of his relationship with regional leaders.

The vesting of ever more decision-making powers in the hands of regional party leaders was accompanied by a redefinition of the terms of political exclusion. Consolidating a trend that had begun in the late Stalin era, Khrushchev introduced a new language to detoxify the labels used against dismissed party leaders. In the late Stalinist era the most neutral pretext for firing a leader was "incompetence," but this was now superseded by a new, more anodyne formulation, "failure of leadership."[64] Stripping away all political insinuations from the charges and quashing any doubts about political loyalty enabled the Central Committee to remove not only individual leaders, as in the late Stalin era, but also whole batches of them, in centrally coordinated sweeps. There was a sharp rise in replacements of territorial first secretaries in 1954 and 1955, much of the increase accounted for by the growth in the number of party leaders who were dismissed (fig. 4.2). A large proportion of those dismissed were removed under the new rubric of "failures of leadership" (fig. 4.3). This rather bold move allowed for the dismissal of groups of regional leaders who were regarded to have failed in their job but who, having been fired, could now be moved on to low-pressure sinecures within the nomenklatura without any danger.

The deployment of a less ideologically charged nomenclature was closely coupled to a second move. Khrushchev ruled that, where possible, regional bosses should not be replaced individually, on an ad hoc basis through occasional Central Committee resolutions, but that their

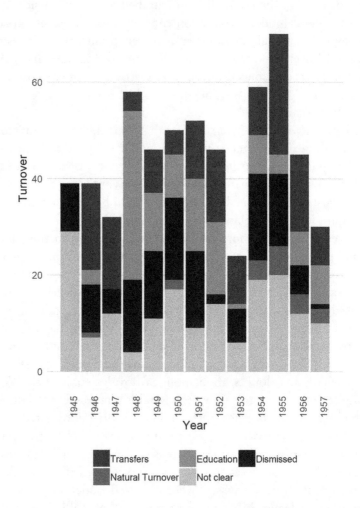

Figure 4.2. Departures of territorial first secretaries in the USSR, 1945–57. The term "territorial first secretaries" refers to first secretaries of obkoms, kraikoms, and union and autonomous republics. All totals and subtotals for 1953–57 are based on complete data, as are all totals and the subtotal for "Dismissed" for 1945–51. Since other subtotals for the USSR as a whole are not available for 1945–51, we have extrapolated these from complete data on 91 territories (i.e., out of 165 to 171, depending on the year) from the RSFSR and Ukraine that are available. Totals and subtotals for 1952 are based on data from RSFSR, Ukraine, Georgia, and Moldovia. For coding rules, see appendix H. *Sources:* Resolutions of the Politburo, Presidium, and Secretariat of the Central Committee, RGANI and RGASPI; RGANI f.5 op.29 d.15 ll.62–63.

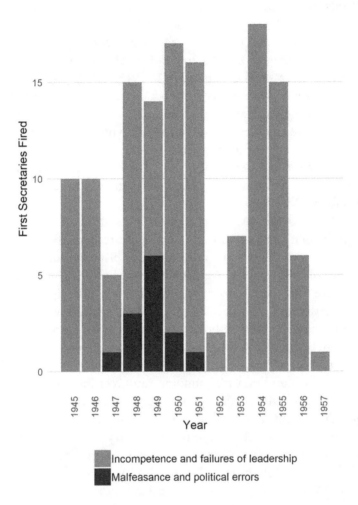

Figure 4.3. Dismissals of territorial first secretaries in the USSR, 1945–57. The term "territorial first secretaries" refers to first secretaries of obkoms, kraikoms, and union and autonomous republics. The graph is compiled on the basis of complete data with the exception of the total for 1952, which is based on data from the RSFSR, Ukraine, Georgia, and Moldavia. "Failures of leadership," an adaptation by Khrushchev of the category of "Incompetence," became the default category from December 1953. "Malfeasance and political errors" includes abuse of office, scandals, and political errors. For coding rules, see appendix H. *Sources:* Resolutions of the Politburo, Presidium and Secretariat of the Central Committee, RGANI and RGASPI; RGANI f.5 op.29 d.15 ll.62–63.

removal should be timed to coincide with regular obkom plenums and, where possible, with the biannual party conferences at which party elections were held. Ideologically, the synchronization of removals and appointments with the party's internal, democratic processes underscored the advantages of the party model of "democracy" and "accountability" over Beria's "repressive" MVD model.[65] In some cases, Khrushchev could use the party's democratic conventions to tighten the screws on a particular dependent, as he did in the case of Kozlov, whose candidacy, as we have seen, triggered protest votes in Leningrad. More important, for the purpose of properly installing a new leader, carefully coordinated elections were a more amenable way of introducing and familiarizing a new candidate with the aktiv than through a naked instruction from Moscow.

There was a third strand to Khrushchev's strategy. In September 1953, in the first frank assessment of agriculture since collectivization, Khrushchev announced that some of the key principles of Stalinist agricultural policy would be overturned: these included lowering taxes on collective farms, lowering procurement plans, and wiping out farm debts owed the state. But Khrushchev argued that this investment came with strings attached. First, there would have to be a rapid increase in production, to which Khrushchev promised to put things right "within the next 2–3 years."[66] Second, there would need to be a new model of leadership. The condition for pumping resources into agriculture was that appropriate party leadership was required. In those areas racked by debt, that meant replacing the regional first secretaries.

Khrushchev was quick to take regional party bosses to task. In December 1953 two first secretaries of predominantly agricultural districts, V.I. Nedosekin from Tula and S.A. Vagapov from Bashkiria, were sacked for incompetence. By mid-January the entire obkom buros from Iaroslavl', Astrakhan, Briansk, the Crimea, Kalinin, Molotov, Voronezh, Kostroma, Novgorod, and several other regions were ordered to Moscow and hauled over the coals at the Secretariat.[67] By the end of January their leaders had been removed, most of them on the grounds that they had "failed to provide leadership."[68] Within the space of a few weeks ten Russian regional party committees had lost their first secretaries, largely on the grounds that they had accumulated major debts to the state.[69]

Under the neutral rubric that they had failed to exercise leadership Khrushchev was able to effect a major cull of regional party leaders without invoking political charges or questioning their loyalty to the regime. There was no hint of sabotage or wrecking or of deliberately undermining the state. Instead, regional party bosses were rebuked for their "low expectations," for "not creating tension in their work," and for their "inattentive approach" to subordinates.[70] The consequences of failure were relatively innocuous. Most departed first secretaries were moved on to unglamorous, low-key positions in the nomenklatura. In terms of both signaling and substance this was a step change from the ad hoc rotations of the late 1940s because it amounted to what was, in effect, a new form of exclusion, a bloodless collective purge of senior party functionaries.

Although there was no outright repression, Khrushchev ensured that regional leaders operated in a high-pressure environment. Sackings and new appointments were confirmed at regional party conferences and overseen by senior Central Committee officials.[71] The conferences revolved around the failures of the regions to secure the goals laid out at the September 1953 plenum, and speakers, led by the Central

Viktor Churaev had a key role in Khrushchev's purge of the regional party organizations in 1953–54 and would go on to head various cadres departments at the Central Committee until 1961. This photograph is from 1962. Courtesy of Russian State Archive of Photographic and Cinematic Documents in Krasnogorsk.

Committee representatives, were scathing in their criticisms of poor spring sowings, delayed harvests, and the failure to bring new lands into cultivation. In light of the recent purge of obkom leaders, new first secretaries were put on notice that their tenures hinged on turning around agricultural production.[72]

Khrushchev's agricultural reforms, initiated at the September 1953 Central Committee plenum, supplied a pretext for the mini-purge that took place at the beginning of 1954. Amidst continued criticisms of regional secretaries for their agricultural failings, Khrushchev, in order to increase the pressure on the first secretaries, oversaw the appointment of second secretaries in some of the country's most important regions.[73]

Khrushchev set out some clear production targets to warrant the major investments in agriculture. By the XX Party Congress, scheduled for early 1956, wheat and dairy yields were to double. This created a metric against which regional leaders were to be judged. Themselves operating under immense pressure, they would resort to tried and tested party mobilization techniques and to a degree imitate Khrushchev himself in turning up the heat on those beneath them. Khrushchev created conditions which were conducive, especially in the agricultural regions, to a new breed of substate dictators. One of the paradoxes of the early phase of Khrushchev's rule was that the end of the personal dictatorship at the center was accompanied by a major boost to substate dictators in the regions.

The post-Stalin transition at the center involved conflict, including over the most fundamental resources of the state. Traditional approaches to the relationship between the center and the regions have tended to focus on the "cadres weapon" and the power of appointment, but this may have been less important than deeper struggles over the power of exclusion, control of information, and ideology. The institutions Khrushchev and Beria headed, the party apparatus and the Ministry of Internal Affairs, represented different models of governance. His association with de-Stalinization notwithstanding, one of the reasons Khrushchev triumphed over his adversaries was that he was able to negotiate the early post-Stalin transition with the greatest degree of ideological continuity, especially in regard to the leading role of the party and the need to maintain the party's perceived democratic practices.[74]

There were other underlying continuities. As we saw earlier, one of the main innovations of the late Stalin era had been the insertion of various protections for members of the nomenklatura. Khrushchev went a step further by altering the mechanics and revising the lexicon of political exclusion. As a measure of the unity of the party's ranks and of the greater emphasis on persuasion and education, there was a sharp contraction in the volume of expulsions from the party. When he wanted to get rid of adversaries or poorly performing regional leaders he tended to sack them. But altering the terms in which he did this and deploying milder, less toxic formulations enabled him to carry out sweeping bloodless purges, an option that would have been fraught with risk under Stalin.

Previous studies of Khrushchev's policy toward regional leaders have tended to focus on how he used appointments to bolster his power position in Moscow. But this fixation on Kremlin politics obscures a deeper truth. Even leaders who enjoyed special ties in Moscow had a day job to get on with. For most of these people the key issue was not whether they were Khrushchev's clients but how they could secure the loyalty of subordinates and forge workable networks in their new province so that they could make their region a success. Regions were complex political ecosystems. Senior party leaders, not least Khrushchev, understood that they could not simply plant party leaders in a region without taking some account of how they would get on there. In order to govern, a new provincial first secretary had to learn how to work with local leaders, build up coalitions, and do his best to win over the rank and file.

III
KHRUSHCHEV

5   The New Art of Survival

THE STRATEGIES PURSUED by substate dictators in the late Stalin era had relied on certain resources, but these were now dwindling. First, the new leadership began to deemphasize a primary form of political exclusion, expulsions from the party. From 1953 expulsions began a steady decline, and by the early 1960s they had fallen to a quarter of the levels in the late Stalin era. Soviet leaders hailed this as testimony to the party's newfound adherence to the principles of persuasion and education over exclusion and coercion.[1] Second, the traditional stock of political charges like concealment of social origin, which had been previously used for kompromat, also narrowed. Although, as we saw in chapter 4, there was a new source of blackmail, now tied to control of information on complicity in Stalin-era abuses, control over these processes was closely managed by the center.[2] Third, the steady consolidation of office and personal seniority, supported by norms of deference and respect, made it harder to engage in the Stalin-era tactic of overpromotion.

In chapter 4 we considered the dictator's agency problem from the center's perspective. We now return to how it was dealt with in the regions. One of the most notable features of regional politics in the mid-1950s was that forms of governance and the composition of elites were largely unaffected by the dramas of de-Stalinization. By contrast, Khrushchev's demand that regional leaders, even in industrial areas, achieve a sharp increase in agricultural yields and do so quickly would have a more tangible impact. At the end of 1953 Khrushchev carried out a purge of regional leaders, making it clear that the tenure of those who remained was dependent on a step change in agricultural production. In turn, most obkom leaders understood that the attainment of hyperambitious targets required cutting corners and breaking rules. One option pursued by some leaders was to take a gamble and "go for gold." This involved applying maximum pressure on one's inner circle and on the aktiv in the expectation that the inevitable leaks and defections would be disregarded by Moscow.

Not everyone could be a national champion. Given that fulfilling the new quotas normally involved breaking rules, those leaders who were not able to rise to the very top were best advised to keep members of the ruling coalition and of the party aktiv on side. They knew that alienating members of the regional elite was especially dangerous, as the latter were privy to high-grade insider information that could be used against them. Many regional leaders began to change their strategy. Although the consolidation of hierarchies at the regional level had stifled the use of overpromotion, it brought some benefits. In particular, substate leaders could draw on the emerging norms of seniority at the regional level as a source of loyalty. Moreover, they could use information gleaned from regional elections and other institutions originally established to control *them* to judge the mood of the aktiv and to work out how they might adjust their own behavior. Instead of all-out conflict, this second group of leaders began to settle on a path of accommodation and tactical flexibility.

SUBSTATE DICTATORS

In January 1956, on the eve of the XX Party Congress, the majority of obkom leaders were individuals who had earned their spurs in the war and early postwar years. Among them was a class of veteran first secretaries who, as a result of the policy of rotation, had served stints as obkom leaders in several regions. Most of these leaders had been trained to implement the will of the center, as measured in their ability to maintain order and fulfill the agricultural plan. The fact that in January 1956 they were still in post, having survived Khrushchev's mini-purge of 1953–54, suggests that fulfilling plans was on the whole one thing they could do well.

An examination of obkom meetings on the eve of the XX Congress suggests that while there were discussions of the cult of personality these largely tended to target, as they had in the late 1940s, dictators at the regional level. Among the most frequent targets of such criticism were the veteran substate dictators. Criticisms of their leadership had much in common with the criticisms of Stalin at the forthcoming congress, in that they focused on the twin evils of replacing collective with one-man decision making and the predisposition to crudeness and coercion, albeit in this case interpreted metaphorically. In a career stretching back to 1938, M.Ia. Kannunikov had served as first secretary in three regions (Kirov, Kuybishev, and Iaroslavl') before taking over in Pskov in 1951. "One can think of numerous cases where, in order to have the smallest of matters decided, we have to go to the obkom secretary," noted a member of the Pskov obkom in January 1956. "Everything goes to comrade Kannunikov in the knowledge that the man has only to open his mouth for a decision to come into effect."[3] "No issue, not even the most trivial, can be decided in our kraikom other than by one person," lamented the head of the sovkhoz administration in Krasnoiarsk in January 1956 of the kraikom first secretary, N.N. Organov, who, prior to taking over in Krasnoiarsk in 1952, had been first secretary of the far eastern Primorskii krai from 1947 to 1952. "We begin, of course, with consultation . . . but in the end we always have to go to the first secretary."[4] Before becoming first secretary of the Stalingrad obkom in 1955, I.K. Zhegalin had served as first secretary of the Krasnovodskii obkom in Turkmenistan from 1943 to 1945 and as first secretary of the Groznii obkom from 1949 to 1955. One raikom secretary depicted Zhegalin's leadership as follows: "When comrade Zhegalin convenes a conference he will resort to phrases such as: 'We will be shot of you,' 'you are past your sell-by date,' and 'you're of no use to us.' . . . In June this year we convened a local conference. Zhegalin turned up and began to mouth off at everyone. After a couple of hours of this ordeal he finally left us in peace."[5]

These veterans had been in the obkom business for years and understood they would ultimately be assessed on their record in plan fulfillment. In alienating the aktiv they always ran the risk that information about rule violations might be leaked to the center. Perhaps boosted by Khrushchev's recent intervention, they appeared to calculate that so long as they achieved their plan the center would disregard complaints about their leadership style and crude, aggressive behavior and let them stay in office. In most cases they were proved right.[6] For veteran sub-state dictators the default position was to go on the attack and to risk defections in the hope that overfulfilling the plan would trump all other considerations. Yet this rationale and way of thinking were not just the preserve of the Stalinist old guard. The early Khrushchev era saw the arrival of a new generation who, no doubt inspired by Khrushchev's calls, opted for a similar path.

One of the best examples of this kind of behavior was the forty-four-year-old A.P. Pcheliakov, who, in February 1952, took up his first post as obkom first secretary of the medium-size, largely agricultural region of Kirov in the Volgo-Viatka economic zone five hundred miles east of Moscow. Pcheliakov exhibited a heightened responsiveness to Khrushchev's calls to party leaders to demonstrate leadership, to take initiative, and to do what was required at all costs in order to attain a steep rise in production.

Born in 1908 in the small village of Krasnaia Sloboda in the Tatar Republic, Pcheliakov removed to Moscow by the mid-1920s, and there he took up a number of menial jobs before enrolling as a student at the engineering and economics institute in 1930. In nomenklatura terms his breakthrough came when he was appointed head of the department of ferrous metallurgy at the Sverdlovsk obkom in 1941.[7] After that he quickly progressed to first secretary of the Nizhny Tagil city party committee in 1946, to second secretary of the Stalingrad obkom in 1949, and to Central Committee inspector in 1951. In Nizhny Tagil Pcheliakov enrolled in a correspondence course at the Higher Party School in Moscow, by means of which he earned his higher education. As events would show, there is little evidence that his education did much to widen his horizons or moderate his outlook.

The mood in Kirov on Pcheliakov's arrival was one of apprehension. His predecessor, I.T. Bykov, had been dismissed for shortcomings in his leadership, and the standing and reputation of a number of local functionaries had been hurt in the process. His new colleagues greeted Pcheliakov nervously and, despite Pcheliakov's declarations to the contrary, they were right to be worried.[8] Pcheliakov's tenure coincided with the appointment of another regional leader, the new head of the regional ispolkom, A.M. Bueverov. This was a bad omen, as double appointments tended to presage considerable cadre turnover. Before long, Pcheliakov had plunged into conflict with Buevorov. Their relationship was complicated by the fact that Pcheliakov had not been consulted on Buevorov's appointment and that, before assuming his new post, Bueverov had held the same post at the Central Committee—inspector—as Pcheliakov, which led to status friction between them. The Central Committee's intention may well have been to place Bueverov as a high-status counterweight to Pcheliakov, but this arrangement was clearly not to Pcheliakov's liking. Within a few weeks the two were at loggerheads. The scope of the conflict soon widened, spreading to Bueverov's regional executive committee. Pcheliakov may have envisioned such an outcome, for in September 1952, a bare six months after his appointment, Bueverov beat a hasty retreat to Moscow. At this point, Pcheliakov began to round on Bueverov's associates in the oblispolkom. One of the targets of this offensive, A. Khodyrev, wrote a letter to Stalin on 17 September 1952 complaining that, in the wake of Bueverov's departure, Pcheliakov had demanded a purge of the regional Komsomol leadership and the dismissal of a number of district-level functionaries.[9] According to Khodyrev, these moves had begun to grate on the aktiv. Khodyrev reported that "among the aktiv there is talk of a 'slaughter of cadres.'"[10]

Pcheliakov's approach to his rank and file is exemplified by his treatment of the first secretary of the Murashinskii district, A.S. Reshetnikov. Appointed in July 1952, Reshetnikov had an unblemished party record, with no reprimands and two awards.[11] Yet conditions in the district, which was located at the northern tip of the oblast, were tough, and, from a very low starting point, Reshetnikov found it hard to turn things round. According to Reshetnikov, "Rather than discussing things, Pcheliakov has opted for a path of rudeness, threats, punishments, and sackings." In one instance, on 11 May 1953 Pcheliakov had said to him curtly, "You are handling the sowing badly. We'll give you five days—if you don't turn things round we'll send you packing."[12] Reshetnikov survived this encounter, but a year later, at a meeting of the obkom buro on 7 July 1954, he approached Pcheliakov for advice on how to get into the regional party school. "In the presence of two MTS directors from our district and other comrades, Reshetnikov

First Secretary Aleksandr Pcheliakov of the Kirov obkom in 1954. Courtesy of Russian State Archive of Photographic and Cinematic Documents in Krasnogorsk.

reported, "Pcheliakov began to berate me so sharply that I was quite taken aback." "Let us not talk of teaching you," Pcheliakov continued, "but of kicking you out."[13] After being "dragged through the mud" and "called all manner of things," the following month Reshetnikov was fired and handed a strict party reprimand. The pressure took its toll on Reshetnikov. Shortly afterward he collapsed from nervous exhaustion and was hospitalized. But Pcheliakov was still not sated. He ordered a department head from the obkom to go to the hospital to verify Reshetnikov's state of health. Ill and out of work for three months, Reshetnikov, against the advice of his doctors, began to look for new employment and commenced the long, slow process of a party appeal.[14] Even now, however, his path was blocked by Pcheliakov, who overrode a decision to admit him to the regional party school.[15] "When all the annoying and hurtful things against me had been exhausted," Reshetnikov recalled, "comrade Pcheliakov called me a double-dealer, he said that my true nature had been revealed and that not only should I be sacked but also expelled from the party."[16]

The Reshetnikov case was not an isolated incident. As the Central Committee official Tischchenko, who attended a party conference in the Soviet district in Kirov, commented, Pcheliakov was "outrageously rude," insulting kolkhoz heads, treating the raikom secretaries "like dirt," and in general resorting to the methods of the fictional prerevolutionary landowner depicted by the nineteenth-century Russian poet Nikolai Nekrasov, who wielded blows to "smash the teeth, twist the jaw, and draw glints of fear from one's eyes." Pcheliakov reportedly went around saying, "You are a provocateur, you are a waster" and threatening officials with expulsion from the party.[17] At the party conference of February 1954 some rank-and-file functionaries accused Pcheliakov, in the words of a Central Committee official, of "bellowing at people, being rude, . . . behaving in a haughty and arrogant manner, not hearing people out or taking the opinions of others into account." His low standing with the aktiv was reflected at the obkom election, where he received seventy-six votes against (16 percent of the ballots cast).[18]

Nevertheless, Pcheliakov persisted with his policy of mass sackings. In 1954–55, in a region with 42 districts, 40 raikom first secretaries were replaced, 40 heads of ispolkoms, 51 second secretaries, 103 party secretaries for MTSs, and 83 MTS directors. A fair number were removed for relatively trivial reasons, including poor short-term results and being out of the office when Pcheliakov came to visit unannounced.[19]

Pcheliakov was not especially interested in winning over the popularity of the aktiv, but like any dictator he required a small clique of loyal, dependable cadres in order to push through his policies. One strategy for gaining loyalty that, as we saw earlier, had been widely used in the late Stalin era, was overpromotion. One example of the tactic was the election of the obkom secretary for ideology in January 1956. Pcheliakov nominated Letiagin, the first secretary of the Kotelnicheskii raikom, for the position:

> COMRADE LETIAGIN: Comrades, members of the obkom, I request that my candidacy be withdrawn. This really is too much for me, and I just don't think I am up to it.
> COMRADE PCHELIAKOV: I think that the comrades will take note of this. Let us vote. Who is in favor of electing Letiagin obkom secretary, put up your hands? Who is against? Any abstentions? None. [Letiagin] has been unanimously elected.[20]

Pcheliakov also persisted with officials who were unpopular with their aktivs. One example was the first secretary of the Bogorodskii raikom, Volkov, whose candidacy was rejected by a third of the delegates at the

district party conference in 1956. At the party conference the following year the head of sector at the RSFSR buro, Verushkin, concluded
that Volkov "does not have any authority in his district" and yet for
some reason Pcheliakov "persists with him."[21] In addition, Pcheliakov,
defying the head of the regional executive committee, appointed one
of his own clients, Trapeznikov, as deputy head of the committee and
even made him a member of the obkom buro.[22] A grateful Trapeznikov
trumpeted his allegiance to Pcheliakov, eliciting the following charac-
terization at the obkom plenum: "[Trapeznikov] tries to show, comrade
Pcheliakov, that no one is closer to you, and that no one can ever be as
close to you as he is."[23]

Pcheliakov was aggressive with members of his inner circle too. In
place of Buevorov, I.P. Safronov was appointed as the new chair of
the regional executive committee, and shortly afterward he was joined
by a new obkom second secretary, S.E. Sanin.[24] Possibly building on
discontent among the aktiv, first Sanin, at the party conference in February 1954, and then Safronov, at the obkom plenum in March 1954,
ventured to criticize Pcheliakov. Pcheliakov responded with force, accusing the two of "insincerity" and "time-serving."[25] With Moscow's
support, Pcheliakov effected Sanin's demotion. However, Sanin, now
the head of the regional trade union, spoke up against Pcheliakov at
the January 1956 party conference, accusing him of suppressing criticism.[26] He was joined by another high-level opponent of Pcheliakov,
V.A. Moshchakov, the obkom secretary for industry. Moshchakov accused Pcheliakov of pursuing an incorrect cadre policy and of devot-
ing insufficient attention to industry. Pcheliakov was prone, claimed
Moshchakov, to get even with any raikom official who showed signs
of initiative or who dared to question him, leading to unacceptably
high levels of turnover.[27] Pcheliakov labeled Sanin's and Moshchakov's
speeches demagogic and blocked their publication in the main Kirov
newspaper.[28] As in 1954, the aktiv were given a chance to vent their
disapproval at the obkom election, where 67 of the 514 delegates voted
against Pcheliakov. For the second time running he garnered the highest proportion of no votes at an obkom election.[29]

Pcheliakov seems to have been unruffled by the opposition. The
main reason appears to be that, at a time when Khrushchev staked his
prestige and political reputation on agricultural growth, Kirov had fast
become one of the Russian Federation's leaders in agricultural pro-

duction. Over the next two years Khrushchev himself would point to Kirov's successes, observing that it was one of the five most improved regions in the Federation for milk yields and the most improved for meat.[30] Against this, the various cavils and complaints flowing in from the region could be cast aside. As a matter of party etiquette the Central Committee used the occasion of the XX Party Congress in February 1956 to invite Pcheliakov in for a word but confined itself to the following gentle message from the Central Committee secretary, Dmitrii Shepilov, to Churaev, head of the party organs department: "Churaev: please avail yourself of Pcheliakov's presence at the [XX] Party Congress to tactfully and in a comradely way talk to him at the department about the shortcomings in his methods of leadership and give him some sensible [tolkovyi] advice. D. Shepilov."[31] Pcheliakov epitomized a new brand of substate dictator who merged the aggressive, quasi-military culture of the war and postwar years with Khrushchev's high-stakes strategy of meeting the plan at all costs. After Stalin, the hectoring, intimidating leadership culture of his era was carried over, a continuity often reinforced by the precedent Khrushchev himself set. At the same time, substate dictators under Stalin had to secure the loyalty of, at the very least, a small clique of regional power holders in order to implement their policies. What appears striking about Pcheliakov is that he whittled down this clique to a bare minimum. Lacking some of the network-creating resources available to his predecessors in the late Stalin era, he set off on a course that approximated what we might think of as a permanent purge.

CONTESTED AUTOCRATS

Not all individuals were cut out for life as regional first secretaries. We have seen how in the late Stalin years some obkom leaders were branded by those around them as overeducated, cosmopolitan, and liberal and denigrated as being weak, indecisive, and out of touch. After Stalin, fewer of the "overeducated" candidates made it as obkom secretaries, but there was now a supply of contested autocrats from another source. Under Khrushchev, many contested autocrats were, in effect, the illegitimate offspring of substate dictators. Most were clients of former provincial dictators who had now departed from the region, leaving one of their dependents in charge. As we saw earlier, many of these dependents had been picked out precisely because some kind of weakness—a blemish in the past—had made them vulnerable. With their protector gone, the new incumbent was exposed to attacks from disconcerted members of the regional elite, some of whom were resentful that a former client of the first secretary who may have been their underling not so long ago had now risen above them.

A good example comes from Krasnodar krai, where V.M. Suslov was appointed first secretary in 1952. Born in 1910, Suslov had joined the party in 1939 and, by the end of the 1940s, had risen to the midlevel position of head of the agricultural department at the Krasnodar kraikom. In 1951 N.G. Ignatov, the first secretary of Krasnodar and a substate dictator par excellence, decided to elevate the forty-one-year-old Suslov over the heads of the other secretaries and install him as his right-hand man and second secretary.[32] Working so closely with the fiercely demanding Ignatov appears to have done little to instill in Suslov the initiative or decisiveness that might have turned him into a strong leader in his own right. In October 1952 Ignatov was promoted to Moscow as secretary of the all-union Central Committee and seems to have had a hand in Suslov's appointment as his successor. While his elevation may have suited Ignatov, for it allowed him to retain a foothold in Krasnodar, it put Suslov in a predicament. Years later Suslov recalled this early phase of his leadership: "In that first period I comported myself perhaps not exactly as a first secretary should have. This was due not just to my inexperience but also to the fact that, as I took over the reins, I found I had under me people who earlier had been my bosses."[33]

Certain guarded statements by Suslov at the kraikom plenum which confirmed his departure as regional first secretary in February 1957 hint at his relationship with his inner circle. Suslov acknowledged, for example, that he had been forced to leave in post officials whom he knew to be poor workers merely because they enjoyed the support of other powerful members of the buro. Suslov recalled how, following Krasnodar's formal adoption of a "socialist obligation," a centrally imposed target for a one-year plan, district heads had successfully rallied together and exerted pressure on members of the kraikom buro to have their targets lowered. "Buro members then put pressure on us to back down, and I relented," Suslov confessed.[34] From Suslov's testimony we can surmise that buro members had client networks in the districts, networks which allowed raikom secretaries to lobby effectively for the over-the-plan targets to be scrapped. In general, while raikom secretaries had an interest in lower targets and the obkom first secretary, whose success was measured by overall levels of growth, had a clear interest in higher targets, members of the buro tended to be caught in the middle, as their wish to do well by their region vied with the need to protect their clients in the districts from being saddled with unrealistic goals. In Krasnodar the balance had shifted to the raikom secretaries. This fact was clearly not to the liking of the Central Committee and appears to have convinced Moscow that Suslov was not made of leadership material. In 1957 he was demoted to the relatively obscure position of institute director at the academy of agricultural sciences, where he remained until his death in 1969.

One of the hallmarks of contested autocrats was that they were unable to exercise their right to appoint whomever they wanted. Far from overpromoting junior officials, as was the wont of substate dictators, they were unable even to get rid of poor ones or to appoint their own favored candidates. A second indicator was that rather than persevering with high growth targets set by the center, which was invariably in their career interest, they succumbed to pressure from local officials who lobbied for lower, more realistic plans. Broadly speaking, contested autocrats failed in the art of survival under Khrushchev. For their part, oligarchical networks enjoyed great autonomy from their leader, but they sometimes resented the breakdown in discipline and a decline in the region's influence in Moscow and were willing to trade in their autonomy for a more powerful leader who might also have more clout in the capital.

All things being equal, oligarchical networks were more likely to exist in larger regions with powerful subregional centers, like Krasnodar, or where there were large all-union enterprises. Soviet administrative structure was supposed to have anticipated this problem by ensuring that all major players in a region sat on the obkom buro, where the first secretary could keep an eye on them. Yet even the best designed of administrative structures could do little good when the authority of the first secretary was somehow diminished.

Krasnodar was a large, agrarian region. An example of a contested autocrat in a major industrial region is Sverdlovsk, one of the most prominent industrial centers in the country, and its first secretary, A.M.

Kutyrev.[35] Kutyrev had a different background from Suslov in that he had served as first secretary in Murmansk from 1945 to 1950 before arriving as second secretary in Sverdlovsk in 1950. In June 1951 he had taken over as acting first secretary from the incumbent, V.I. Nedosekin, while the latter started a retraining course. Kutyrev then replaced Nedosekin full time in 1952.[36] Kutyrev's leadership style should be framed against that of his predecessors. His former boss, Nedosekin, had learned his trade, first as a second secretary and then as chair of the regional executive committee, from a classic substate dictator, V.M. Andrianov, who had led the region from 1938 until 1946.[37] This succession created a problem for Kutyrev. Although substate dictators were berated for grabbing power and for their crude, coercive approach to subordinates, they had the benefit of being decisive and providing a framework of authority in a region. But Kutyrev did not fit into this mold. Some years later Kutyrev, who found his first phase as leader of the region especially unpleasant, reflected on this point: "I don't much care for the style [of leadership] of Nedosekin and Andrianov, I like to give my functionaries more initiative."[38]

In April 1955 a Central Committee delegation led by the deputy head of the department of party organs for the RSFSR, M.M. Sevast'ianov, identified a number of shortcomings in the work of the obkom. Sevast'ianov called two meetings of the obkom buro.[39] These meetings paint a picture of a liberal, benign Kutyrev exercising little control over his colleagues. Buro members had two concerns. The first was the lack of discipline. "The buro is disorganized, and people do not fall into line, they just come and go as they please," complained the head of the regional MVD. "Discipline is weak and people just do as they wish," said the first secretary of the Sverdlovsk gorkom, agreeing with his colleague. Kutyrev was depicted as a man who was "not strict with his subordinates, is soft, and gets easily distracted." A second concern was the shallowness of Kutyrev's network in Moscow and his inability to battle in the region's interests: "He is not persistent with the ministries," noted one member; another commented that, whether owing to wariness or timidity, "he refuses to sign off on documents to the Central Committee."[40]

There were other signs of Kutyrev's failing authority. On 26 October 1955 a rather unusual conflict flared up between the party and Komsomol hierarchies in Sverdlovsk. In an unprecedented move the

Komsomol plenum rejected the obkom nomination of a new Komsomol first secretary in the region even though it had been cleared with Moscow. A large contingent at the Komsomol plenum opposed the obkom's candidate on the grounds that he was an outsider and argued that the position be given to the current second secretary, who was from Sverdlovsk. Kutyrev, who attended the meeting, admonished the opposition group, reminding them that they were expected to follow the lead of the party. On Kutyrev's insistence the matter was put to a vote. In a show of hands sixteen of the forty-five members of the regional Komsomol committee voted against Kutyrev's candidate, while two abstained, inflicting a major blow to Kutyrev's authority.[41]

On 15 November 1955 Sevast'ianov submitted a detailed report calling for Kutyrev's dismissal. Six weeks later, on 31 December, he was sacked, albeit under the mild heading of "on health grounds."[42] Kutyrev was never appointed to lead another region again. However, unlike Suslov, he retained a relatively high status in the nomenklatura system, eventually being awarded his pension in 1960, at the age of fifty-eight.[43] Kutyrev's problem was not his origin as an overpromoted client but the fact that he ran a large region with major subcenters and significant enterprises, conditions which facilitated the formation of a formidable oligarchical countergroup. Either because the traditional methods of overpromotion, kompromat, and political exclusion were not as easily available or, as he put it, "unlike Nedosekin and Andrianov, I like to give my functionaries more initiative," he was unable to forge a compact ruling group. In Sverdlovsk regional oligarchs flaunted their disapproval of their leader in the open. As would be true of any contested autocrat, he was unable to prevent an allied rebellion, one which, in this case, began to openly petition Moscow for his removal.

Sometimes a first secretary brought in from the outside had to work alongside a group of leaders who had been together for a number of years. The chances of regional oligarchs joining forces against an outside appointee were heightened if, for a variety of reasons, it was felt that the outsider did not fit in. That was the case in Kemerovo in the second half of the 1950s. In December 1955 the first secretary of the obkom, M.I. Gusev, left his post "on grounds of illness." In his place Moscow appointed the deputy head of the department of party organs of the RSFSR, S.M. Pilipets. From early on local officials indicated that they were not overjoyed with this move. Years later, E.Z. Razumov, who served as second secretary under both Gusev and Pilipets recalled that "sometimes the Central Committee liked to send out its own people to the regions. . . . [T]hat was their prerogative. In their view the locals were inbred and sometimes formed attachments that were not becoming of a first secretary. . . . Still, the Central Committee did send out functionaries who were weaker than they needed to be. They sent out Pilipets, for God's sake. In the Kuzbas we have a Pilipets round every corner."[44]

Pilipets's background and experience did not help. At forty-three, he was relatively young and, having spent most of his career in Moscow, was felt to lack the experience needed to manage a region of this size. Moreover, by contrast with his predecessor, who had been a full member of the Central Committee, Pilipets was only a candidate. This status put him, somewhat embarrassingly, a rung below a member of his own obkom buro, the chair of the Kemerovo sovnarkhoz, the forty-seven-year-old A.N. Zademidko. Indeed, further undercutting Pilipets's authority, Zademidko made a point of stressing that he was in charge of the regional economy and that he would not waste time bowing and scraping to the party authorities.[45] Aside from Zademidko, Pilipets had to deal with a group on the buro who formed a tight unit, having worked in the region for a number of years. It was not long before Pilipets's relations with two members of this group, the chair of the executive committee, V.S. Shapovalov, and the obkom second secretary, E.Z. Razumov, became so strained that the Central Committee was obliged to send out an inspector. At a closed meeting of the buro presided over by the inspector, Shapovalov and Razumov launched into a tirade against Pilipets, picking apart virtually every aspect of his leadership. Among other things he was accused of being weak, of making ill-judged appointments, and of an inability to implement his own decisions.[46] This meeting dealt a fatal blow to Pilipets's standing. Not long after he was dismissed for his "failure to provide leadership." The experience brought his political ambitions to a sudden end; although he was only forty-nine, he would never hold a nomenklatura post again.

Contested autocrats became exposed to leadership rebellions for several reasons. In some cases being resisted may have had to do with the circumstances in which a leader came to power. An overpromoted client was likely to lack credibility with the ruling group, many of whose members may once have known him as their subordinate. An outsider brought in from Moscow may have had to face a coterie of leaders who had worked together over a long time and cohered into a tight network. In other cases the presence of formidable counterelites may have stemmed from the size and economic structure of a region. A province with sizeable subregional centers and large all-union enterprises headed by powerful individuals could make a competent but unglamorous leader look weak.

Constrained by a powerful ruling coalition, the contested autocrat was often unable to manipulate cadre appointments and thus create a powerful network of his own. Alternatively the first secretary could be hemmed in by other powerful officials in the region, and in important policy areas such as the determination of the plan, he would find that they were able to lobby on behalf of client networks. The position of the first secretary may have been further undercut by an oligarchical group that had tired of indiscipline and a breakdown of order and by the first secretary's lack of contacts in Moscow.

ROUTES TO COMPROMISE

In the spring of 1957, a couple of months before the so-called Anti-Party Affair that would see Khrushchev consolidate his hold on power, the attention of the Central Committee was drawn to signs of disorder in the small Volga region of Ul'ianovsk, famous as the birthplace of Lenin, five hundred miles east of Moscow. The obkom first secretary at the time was I.P. Skulkov, who had been appointed in 1952 in the wake of a huge regional scandal.[47] In the interim Skulkov had ruled the region with an iron fist and ignored the obkom buro, tendencies that occasioned numerous warnings from the department of party agencies at the Central Committee.[48] In April 1957 Moscow's attention was drawn to the fact that Skulkov had issued party punishments to twenty-eight district leaders. The Central Committee demanded the minutes of the obkom buro meeting that had sanctioned the punishments. A follow-up review by the department of party organs showed that the minutes had been falsified and that none of the buro members listed as present had in fact attended. A Central Committee inspector was sent out. Other members of the buro seized on the visit to speak up against Skulkov. His actions were then condemned in public, opening the path for his removal in January 1958.[49]

The first secretary in Tomsk for most of the 1950s, V.A. Moskvin, was another textbook substate dictator. Before arriving in Tomsk Moskvin had served, from 1941 to 1946, as first secretary of the city party committee in Stalino, a large Siberian industrial center, where he seems to have acquired, under the sway of the obkom leader M.V. Kulagin, the toughness and inner resolve required to get his enterprises through the quarterly cycles of high-pressure "storming," the frenetic, last-minute attempts to meet plan targets.[50] In November 1951 Moskvin had replaced A.V. Semin, who had been removed for incompetence, as first secretary in Tomsk. For his part, Moskvin took this as the go-ahead to bring order to the region and, to this end, pursued a path of confrontation with raikom secretaries. His targets included the leaders of the city of Tomsk's Kozhevnikovskii district, whose raikom first secretary, F.T. Golovenko, and chair of the district executive committee, F.M. Plotko, lodged an appeal with Khrushchev. In a statement dated 24 November 1958 they referred to Moskvin's "rudeness and swearing, and the insults and humiliation he constantly heaps on us communists."[51] What particularly alarmed the center was a reference to Moskvin's data rigging of the agricultural procurement plan. A brigade sent to Tomsk found that on Moskvin's instructions district leaders had deliberately falsified the accounts by including estimated deliveries from future accounting periods.

Moskvin tried to fend off the criticism by pinning the blame on low-level officials, who received party punishments, but this backstabbing was of no avail. At the next obkom plenum he was brought to task by a group of indignant raikom leaders, one of whom proposed that Moskvin's party status be discussed.[52] The original defection by raikom leaders, which had alerted Moscow to the data rigging in Tomsk, followed by this sustained criticism made Moskvin's position untenable. In June 1959 the Central Committee removed him on the grounds that he was "unable to fulfill leadership," a clear sign that a leader had failed to carry the aktiv with him. The long-term effect of this episode on Moskvin's career was disastrous. Not long after, at the relatively young age of fifty-one, Moskvin was forced out of active service and given a pension, bringing his career in the nomenklatura to an end.

The Ul'ianovsk and Tomsk cases illustrate the intricate balance that substate dictators had to strike. They could follow the lead of Pcheliakov in the expectation they would become national champions in agriculture, which would protect them from revolts by the local aktiv and from leaks to the center by the local elite. But such a course was fraught with danger. In those regions that did not make it to the top, leaders were vulnerable to defections, as the Ul'ianovsk and Tomsk cases showed. Such defections were all the more likely now, in the mid-1950s, as substate leaders recognized that they would have to cut corners in order to meet the center's increasingly ambitious demands. To Moscow, the classic telltale signs that all was not well were large protest votes and unusually high levels of turnover. Alienating raikom secretaries and especially members of the obkom buro always carried the risk that they would tattle to the center and provide insider information on the goings-on in the region, information that was not otherwise obtainable in Moscow. The threat of insider betrayal was a particular problem now, for the more Khrushchev increased the pressure on obkom leaders to raise production, the more they needed the cooperation—and in many cases the collusion—of raikom secretaries in order to meet their targets.

Even the most hardened substate dictators now realized they would have to adapt if they were to survive. With regard to the process of adaptation, two cases are instructive. The first, Vinnitsa, we encountered earlier, under Stakhurskii (see chapter 2). From August 1955, the obkom came under the leadership of a new first secretary, P.P. Kozyr.[53] Born in Dnepropetrovsk in 1913, Kozyr had forged his early career in Turkmenistan, first fighting the Basmachi in the NKVD cavalry and then editing a newspaper there. After the war, in 1946, he moved to Vinnitsa, where he was appointed raikom first secretary. In Vinnitsa Kozyr quickly gained a reputation as an able leader, one who was especially effective in meeting his district procurement plans. Stakhurskii soon took him under his wing and, with the latter's backing, he was promoted to first secretary of one of Vinnitsa's two city party committees, thereby gaining admission to the oblast elite. Earmarked as leadership material, he was then sent off to Moscow on a two-year course at the Higher Party School from 1950 to 1952, after which he returned to Vinnitsa, eventually becoming obkom secretary.

As part of Khrushchev's agricultural strategy, Vinnitsa, from the beginning of 1954, was placed under heavy pressure to raise grain deliveries, the target for which was raised by 62,300 tons in 1955. When two obkom first secretaries, N. Bubnovskii and P. Doroshenko, were fired in quick succession, in August 1955 Kozyr, with his strong credentials for plan fulfillment, was put in charge. He quickly got to work, extending the brief of the obkom buro to technical agricultural matters (previously it had confined itself to personnel issues), purging local officials, and making free use of party reprimands. From the start Kozyr's leadership was marked by two traits. First, he retained his laser-like focus on fulfilling the plan and refused to tolerate efforts by raikom secretaries to moderate their quotas. Second, he quickly established a stranglehold on the obkom nomenklatura. Those raikom secretaries who made informal appointments without consulting the obkom were reprimanded, while those who lacked "party sharpness and persistence" and who were found to be frightened of "spoiling relations" with raikom buro colleagues were harshly berated. By 1959 Kozyr had effectively overhauled the region's complement of raikom first and second secretaries.[54]

Yet Kozyr showed he was willing to learn on the job. While he kept appointments on a tight leash, he was aware of the limits of the cadres weapon and of the dangers of overusing it. He soon began to observe some self-imposed constraints. He refused to engage in the classic sub-state dictatorial tactic of overpromotion, preferring instead to promote colleagues on a gradual, incremental basis, giving weight to the formal hierarchy that had emerged in the region. Although information on his use of kompromat is necessarily more sketchy, it appears Kozyr did not make use of it to any great degree. So long as his colleagues were effective and hardworking, he made it clear that he himself was quite relaxed about those who had committed transgressions.[55]

Kozyr also began to comport himself differently. Far from being abusive of the aktiv or treating it with contempt, he was careful to show respect. Raikom leaders began to draw a contrast between Kozyr's behavior and that of the head of the regional executive committee, Dement'ev. One district head remarked, "When the others come to our district they tend to say 'hello' and 'good luck' but not Dement'ev. From the beginning he will begin to curse and swear. He slights the heads of our district and humiliates them, as if he were dealing not with human beings but with inanimate objects or things." By contrast, notes Podkur, "alongside all the harshness and the high demands, Kozyr made a point of showing his officials respect. This quality was commented on by a number of district leaders."[56]

First Secretary Pavel Kozyr of the Vinnitsa obkom in 1962. Courtesy of Russian State Archive of Photographic and Cinematic Documents in Krasnogorsk.

A second example of a substate dictator adjusting his behavior to changing circumstances is that of A.I. Struev, who became first secretary in Perm in January 1954.[57] In certain respects Struev fits the bill as a classic Khrushchevian substate dictator. Unlike most of the other first secretaries discussed in the book, Struev was an unequivocal client of Khrushchev's and seems to have made great play of the fact.[58] Moreover, although Perm was a predominantly industrial region, with large defense, machine-building, and timber and paper industries, much to the consternation of obkom officials and in line with Khrushchev's directives, the overriding policy emphasis in the region was on agriculture.[59] At the regional party conference in January 1956 one gorkom first secretary complained, "Why is it that all manner of things are said here about the great achievements of our MTS directors, our heads of collective farms, and so forth, but nothing at all is said about our industrial managers?"[60] The following January Struev and all the members of the obkom buro were summoned to Moscow for an assessment of their performance. In spite of its being freely acknowledged that Perm was a major industrial region, the session at the RSFSR buro was devoted entirely to failures in agriculture. Struev's closeness to Khrushchev does not seem to have helped him much, as he was castigated for, among

First Secretary Aleksandr
Struev of the Perm obkom
shortly after his appoint-
ment in 1954. Courtesy of
Russian State Archive of
Photographic and Cinematic
Documents in Krasnogorsk.

other things, his inability to follow the lead of another industrial center, Cheliabinsk, which had become self-sufficient in grain and almost so in meat and milk.[61] Despite being a predominantly industrial region, the main axis of pressure was on the agricultural sphere.

In terms of his outward behavior Struev was no less brusque or intimidating than other substate dictators. His repeated threats to colleagues that whoever failed to achieve increases in agricultural production would lose their jobs or even be expelled from the party "only serve[d] to frighten people . . . and undermine their confidence," according to one raikom secretary in January 1956. Another commented that at an obkom buro meeting "so many nasty epithets were hurled at me that as I walked out I lost a sense of who I was."[62]

Like other substate dictators, Struev opted for a strategy that accentuated the dependence of a select group of officials on his leadership. Unarguably the best example of an overpromotion was that of Iu.D. Malkov, who, on Struev's instigation, climbed spectacularly from junior raikom first secretary to obkom agriculture secretary. This breach of an emerging nomenklatura ethic of waiting one's turn was clearly not to the liking of the party aktiv. At the oblast party conference in January 1956 Malkov was given a frosty reception. One of the raikom secretaries made his concerns quite plain: "Malkov is a junior official who has suddenly risen to the rank of obkom secretary. He needs to lead more effectively, to be less rude and to do less shouting. He is young and must bear that in mind. After all, it was not that long ago that he was one of us."[63] Perhaps Malkov's behavior did not help matters. "I know Malkov well from his earlier work, we worked together in the second Serginskii raikom for about four years and I can tell you straight away that I wouldn't recognize him now," recounted one of the raikom secretaries. "At the raikom he was one person but now he has become quite another. . . . [T]here he was a sociable party man, easy to get on with, while now he is dry, po-faced and inaccessible, even to us raikom first secretaries."[64] "Malkov has not been an obkom secretary long," noted another raikom secretary, "so it is remarkable how quickly he has acquired airs and graces, he will walk past you without so much as nodding, let alone shaking your hand."[65] His dependence on Struev only served to diminish Malkov in the eyes of the rest of the party organization, thereby sucking him into a vicious circle where he was compelled to draw on Struev's reputation in order to get things done. One raikom secretary recalled the following incident: "The phone rings. It's spring, and we're planting potatoes. It's Malkov on the line. 'Tell me, can you do the spring sowing this year?' What could I say? 'Perhaps you should tell me. You, after all, are our leader.' Malkov: 'We're disappointed in you. I'll to have to tell Struev. You will see, he will really let you have it [*on zadast pertsu*].'"[66] Malkov went on to secure the highest number of no votes at the regional party conference, 43 out of 724.[67] In the face of so much hostility he understood clearly that his only course of action was to stick as closely as possible to his patron.[68]

From 1956, however, two years into his tenure, various signs of tactical flexibility on Struev's part are detectable. In the first place, he came to recognize the limits of cadre replacement and the cost of high levels of turnover. In January 1957 Struev observed that turnover among the 1,197 collective farm chairs in the region had been steadily rising from 27 percent in 1953 to 35 percent in 1954 and 43 percent in 1955. Although by 1957 most (83 percent) were communists, they were woefully undereducated—two-thirds had only a primary or incomplete secondary education—and Struev observed that in most years 20–25 percent of the entire population of collective farm chairs were being removed for incompetence.[69]

Struev himself acknowledged the limited long-term benefits of large culls of raikom secretaries. "My preference is to punish one person to serve as a warning to others," he averred in January 1956.[70] "Does the mass replacement of raikom secretaries lead to good results?" he asked rhetorically in January 1958. "No, it doesn't, and we categorically condemn such practices. In the two-year period [since the last party conference] only three raikom secretaries have been removed."[71] In fact, notwithstanding the purge of obkom leaders that had accompanied the dismissal of F.M. Prass in 1954, the subsequent membership of the obkom experienced a surprising level of stability.[72] Indeed, certain members of the original elite condemned in 1954 were now recycled by Struev and restored to their former positions or to other high-level posts.[73] Moreover, having defended his client, Malkov, for over two years, in 1957 he sacrificed him, and in doing so pointedly stuck to the "order of precedence" by making the head of the department of agriculture, I.I. Petrov, the new agriculture secretary. In introducing him to the plenum, Struev placed great stress on the fact that Petrov, prior to his appointment at the obkom, had worked for four years as first secretary of one of the local raikoms.[74]

As in the case of Kozyr, Struev understood the benefits of moderating his behavior in order to win over the local aktiv. "I would like comrade Struev to take note that, in my view, there is on your part and in your statements and proclamations elements of rudeness, and we really need to reject this. We need to reject it and for you to be a more cultured obkom secretary," noted one raikom secretary in January 1956.[75] Struev seems to have taken such criticisms to heart. "I fully accept that there has been too much tension on our buro," he said. "We have too easily pinned labels on people. We shouldn't allow this any more. The buro will need to operate more calmly."[76] There was also a fall in the protest votes at the regional party conference in 1958: the number of votes against Struev fell from 26 (out of 724 delegates in 1956) to 17 (out of 761 in 1958), while the number of obkom candidates with 10 votes against or more fell from 6 in 1956 to 2 in 1958.[77]

First secretaries who were new to the job could sometimes make a relatively smooth transition to the new model of leadership. One can catch a glimpse of this in Kostroma, for example, over a two-year period from early 1954 to the beginning of 1956. One of the first provincial leaders to fall to Khrushchev's post-Stalin regional purge was the first secretary A.I. Marfin, who was axed in January 1954 for his "inability to show leadership." To take his place, Moscow sent a Central Committee functionary, the forty-six-year-old D.L. Sumtsov. Sumtsov was part of a new breed of leader who had made steady but unspectacular progress through the party ranks. His career had begun with a lengthy apprenticeship as raikom first secretary followed by a three-year stint as obkom secretary in his native province of Omsk. Before coming to Kostroma, Sumtsov had taken up a staging post as sector head at the department for party agencies of the Central Committee in Moscow. The career of the new second secretary in Kostroma, P.V. Il'in, appointed at the same time as Sumtsov, followed a similar arc. Indeed, before coming to Kostroma Il'in was transferred to Moscow, where he became a Central Committee instructor, a posting one rung below Sumtsov's. Their next appointments as first and second secretaries in Kostroma therefore accorded with the principle of seniority since Sumtsov, having held a higher post in Moscow, now assumed the higher office in Kostroma.

Sumstov arrived in Kostroma to discover a host of problems, especially in agriculture. Despite his mandate to turn things round he seems to have decided against a path of direct confrontation. One sign of his hands-off attitude was that the level of turnover in the region under his leadership was modest.[78] This conciliatory approach was also apparent in his dealings with obkom buro colleagues. Sumtsov came to Kostroma as part of a team of outsiders that, apart from himself and Il'in, included the new chair of the regional executive committee, M.M. Baranov, and a new agriculture secretary, I.G Leshchev. Displacing the former incumbents in a single coup had indicated Moscow's strong displeasure with their predecessors. However, rather than dispensing with their services, Sumtsov offered them a variety of symbolic and honorary positions as well as other compensations designed to maintain their place and status within the regional elite.[79] Moreover, Sumstov gained favor with the regional aktiv by giving phased, step-by-step promotions to positions that were fully under his control (that is, outside the Central Committee nomenklatura) and by finding sinecures for other, less prominent officials who were displaced.[80] In the end, those not grateful to him for promotion were thankful for having kept their place

Regular meetings of party secretaries were an important feature of party life,
socially as well as politically, in the mid-1950s. This photograph is of gorkom and
raikom secretaries attending a regional party conference in Murmansk in 1956.
Source: RGASPI.

within the regional nomenklatura. For the most part they were willing
to repay his generous treatment of them with their loyalty. In Kostroma
there was a different model of loyalty, one based not on overpromotion, kompromat, and exclusion but on care, respect, and gradual promotion for long-standing cadres.

Despite his efforts, Sumtsov was unable to turn the agricultural sector around, and the ever-impatient Central Committee soon set about
getting rid of him. It was at this point that the loyalty he had earned
in Kostroma came to the fore. In January 1956 the entire Kostroma
obkom buro was summoned to Moscow to appear before the Central
Committee Secretariat. To the evident irritation of the Central Committee secretaries, members of the Kostroma buro refused to play their
part in the centrally scripted charade to turn on Sumtsov. One member,
Il'in, the second secretary who had accompanied Sumtsov from Mos-

cow, even baldly declared that, in his view, Sumstov should be allowed to carry on as first secretary. This was not what the senior Central Committee officials had in mind. Given that Sumtsov's fate had already been decided, the obkom buro's overt defiance was quite futile but all the more remarkable for that. The action then moved on to the regional party conference, which was expected to rubber stamp the Secretariat's decision. Again, however, the Central Committee emissaries were in for a surprise. The mandatory criticism of Sumtsov, routine on such occasions, was unusually mild and guarded. Some participants even rose to his defense and rounded on Moscow for its lack of empathy and understanding.[81] One indication of the views of the aktiv was the obkom election of 22 January 1956. Somewhat unusually, although Sumtsov had already been dismissed as first secretary, he was reelected to the obkom. This was all the more odd in that, despite the Central Committee's coordinated assault on him, he received only 28 votes against out of 414 ballot papers. By contrast, his one main detractor in Moscow and at the regional party conference, Leschev, who was perceived to have violated local norms, emerged as the villain of the piece, receiving 50 votes against. Il'in, who had stood by Sumtsov all along, was supported by all 414 delegates.[82] Although both Sumtsov and Il'in were eventually transferred out of the region to middle-ranking positions in Omsk (where Sumtsov had started his career) and Moscow, respectively, the speeches at the oblast party conference and the results of the closed ballot suggested that, in a relatively short period of time, Sumtsov had managed to capture the support of members of the ruling network and of the aktiv and that they were willing to support him even in the face of Moscow's disapproval.

In the late Stalin era regional leaders had been drawn to governing through small, highly asymmetric networks and to thrive on norm violation and conflict. After Stalin, this system would be reinforced by various impulses, the most important of which was Khrushchev's insistence on sharply increased production targets, for which regional first secretaries were to be held responsible. The post-Stalin environment presented obkom leaders with a choice. One option was to follow the lead of Pcheliakov in Kirov. His strategy, however, was fraught with risk. High levels of cadre turnover and the overuse of party reprimands not only attracted Moscow's attention but also could lower morale.

More important, most regional leaders knew they required the cooperation and very often the collusion of raikom secretaries if they were to achieve their all-important targets. From the perspective of the rank and file, the aktiv, there were also advantages in avoiding conflict. After all, even victory over a substate dictator could be double-edged. As pleased as they might be to be rid of one leader, taking on a new first secretary sent in from the outside might mire the region in an endless cycle of conflict. These threats induced regional actors to meet each other halfway. For party leaders this meant adhering to conciliatory norms in their relations with the aktiv. Rather than needling and berating them, they began to show care and respect and to harness the stabilizing forces of office and personal seniority. Unlike the original substate dictators, who had induced loyalty through blackmail, deception, and the violation of social norms, a new type of leader, intent on finding paths to compromise, began to capitalize on the moderate power gradations of the local nomenklatura and on the attendant hierarchical ethics of deference and mutual respect.

6 Substate Nationalism

THE TERMS "ETHNIC," "national," and "nationalism" cover a wide variety of identities and forms of collective action whose boundaries are not always easy to discern.[1] Broadly speaking, ethnicity refers to a community which shares some combination of a common myth of descent, a language, a religion, and an association with a specific territory. Nationality, by contrast, is a modern, secular form of mass identity, normally fostered by intellectuals and politicians, that possesses a degree of coherence that enables its members to be mobilized for common political goals. The most important difference between an ethnicity and a nationality is that the latter operates within the modern discourse of nationalism, a doctrine which holds that humanity is divided into nations and that loyalty to one's nation supersedes all other loyalties. Theorists of nationalism are divided as to the point at which nation building or the pursuit of national policies becomes full-blown nationalism. Some argue that for a movement to qualify as nationalist it must articulate explicitly political demands and that sooner or later these are likely to converge on calls for an independent state.[2] Others see nationalism as a process. On this view, the formation of a national consciousness is no less a form of nationalism than are calls for a sovereign state, as the formation of an independent state is a national goal only to the extent to which it promotes a core nation. Yet the idea of the nation has itself to be continuously replenished and filled with ethnocultural content.[3]

The early post-Stalin era witnessed various campaigns to raise the political or cultural autonomy of national groups, campaigns that fell short of demands for a full-blown sovereign state.[4] At the beginning, immediately after 1953, these campaigns rode on the coattails of the center's policy of reinvigorated indigenization, designed to promote ethnoterritorial elites and cultures. By 1958, however, Moscow had decided that some of these activities had crossed an important threshold, leading to major republican purges. From the center's perspective, the litmus test of nationalism was when an ethnoterritorial elite presented its interests as being opposed not only to those of other ethnoterritorial groups but also to those of the Soviet Union as a whole.

One reason the regime became so alert to the dangers of ethnic mobilization was the potentially acute problem it presented to authoritarian control. Ethnic mobilization meant going over the heads of the party membership and appealing to the wider titular ethnic group. In some cases this meant that collective action based on national goals could spread very quickly. The most striking example of this was in Georgia in 1956, where mass demonstrations involving tens of thousands of protesters presented a major problem of social order, one which had to be put down through brute military force coordinated from the center.

The demonstrations in Georgia had neither clear leadership nor an articulated political program. By contrast, in the two most important examples of nationalism in the 1950s, in Latvia and Azerbaijan, the main driver for change came from within the republican party elite. In both cases republican leaders set out political goals which went quite clearly against the wishes of the center. This raises a question: Why were experienced republican party leaders willing to violate one of the cardinal rules of the Soviet system and defy Moscow? We suggest that their actions are best explained in terms of the concepts set out in this book. In one case, Azerbaijan, the republican leadership resorted to a nationalist discourse as a means of addressing the problem of authoritarian power sharing by rallying members of their ruling coalition around national principles. In the other case, Latvia, the republican leadership pursued a nationalist agenda in order to defuse the problem of authoritarian control by winning over the largely hostile and alienated titular ethnic community. In both cases what separated their solutions from those deployed in nonnational settings was that the leaderships resorted to specifically national tropes—around the issue of language—in order to establish a consensus at the upper levels and reach out beyond the ordinary party aktiv to the wider population.

NATIONALITIES POLICY AFTER STALIN

There was no new nationalities policy as such immediately after Stalin's death. In its place was a series of Central Committee Presidium resolutions on the western borderlands promulgated at the end of May and at the beginning of June 1953, accompanied by "notes" (*dokladnye zapiski*) from Lavrentii Beria that were to be debated at the relevant republican and regional party plenums. All four resolutions concerned areas acquired by the Soviet Union as a result of the Molotov-Ribbentrop pact and were drawn up in response to proposals from Beria that highlighted the failure of the security police, the MGB, to deal with the nationalist underground or to fully stabilize Soviet rule in these territories. Beria called for an alternative approach which lessened the emphasis on repression and involved more sustained efforts to engage the wider population.[5] After Beria's arrest in late June the Presidium resolutions were rescinded and copies of Beria's notes removed from the archives.[6] Although the new leadership formally distanced itself from the resolutions on account of their association with Beria, the main thrust of the new policies was maintained.

The Central Committee resolutions centered on two principles. First, as the resolution on western Ukraine put it, the party obkoms there had failed to recognize that the "fight with the nationalist underground cannot be carried out by mass repressions and Chekist military operations alone," for the "unthinking application of repression leads only to resentment." Despite brutal local conflicts with partisans and waves of forced collectivization and deportation that had seen over half a million people arrested, killed, or deported from West Ukraine and 270,000 from Lithuania, nationalist sentiment in both territories remained strong.[7] Instead of the gendarme methods of the late Stalin years the regime now leaned toward more constructive methods of engaging the local populations.

Second, under the guise of a return to Leninism the regime reactivated the policy of indigenization. Initially introduced in 1920s, indigenization had afforded national minorities the characteristic forms of statehood, such as their own territory, culture, language and ethnoterritorial elites. Throughout the Stalin era the regime had continued to cleave to these principles, but there had in recent years been a number of reverses. One was the creeping policy of Russification and the growing use of the ideologically charged language of "bourgeois nationalism" to hold back the activities of titular national intelligentsias.[8] Another was that in a number of republics, especially in the western borderlands, the regime had fallen short of its nationality quotas for the titular ethnic group, especially in the obkoms and republican governments.[9]

The Presidium resolutions of 1953 referred to the "distortions of Soviet nationalities policy" that had been committed in recent years. Their general theme was best exemplified by the resolution on Lithuania, which lambasted the practice of "giving over leading positions to those who are unable to speak the local language and who do not know the customs, culture, or way of life of the Lithuanian people." It called for a return to "one of the central goals of Soviet power in the national republics—the training and promotion of national cadres."[10]

One solution was to launch targeted affirmative action policies, a pillar of indigenization, or *korenizatsiia*. In Lithuania the Presidium overturned a preexisting policy that had reserved second secretaryships at district and city party committees for non-Lithuanians, presumably to keep an eye on the Lithuanian first secretaries.[11] Yet the new approach ran into a structural problem. In the Soviet system one could promote a representative of the local nationality to a senior position only if they were already a member of the party, but too few members of the titular national groups were joining the party.[12] The authorities were caught in a vicious circle: they could not raise the appeal of the communist regime among the local population by promoting native cadres, as locals were refusing to join the party. The only way to break the impasse was to find policies that might appeal to the titular ethnic group. To reach out to the wider indigenous population the administration would need to present these policies in an idiom that they might understand and identify with, and in general this was a national idiom.

The Central Committee resolution on western Ukraine drew attention to the near universal use of Russian as the language of instruction at higher educational institutions in that region and to how this not only alienated the local intelligentsia but also gave ground to charges of "political Russification," which feeds the "bourgeois-nationalist underground."[13] In line with the principle of indigenization, native languages continued to be used as languages of instruction (especially in primary schools), in the press, and in cultural production, but from the early 1930s Russian became the dominant language of government, the party, large industrial enterprises, and higher education everywhere except in Armenia and Georgia.[14] But the policy had clearly bred resentment, and now, with the various signs of relaxation after Stalin's death, this resentment was bubbling up to the surface. The Presidium resolution on Lithuania noted that the "absence of official correspondence in Lithuanian only creates further distance between the authorities [*vlast'*] and the people and encourages further alienation from the Lithuanian intelligentsia." The resolution called for the "banning of official correspondence and paperwork [*deloproizvodstvo*] . . . in non-Lithuanian languages" and stipulated that "meetings of party buros and plenums at all levels . . . be held in Lithuanian."[15]

Although Beria kick-started the initiatives, the commissions which formulated the resolutions were led by senior central and republican leaders whose positions were unaffected by Beria's departure.[16] Moreover, prior to Beria's removal the resolutions and Beria's notes were discussed at republican congresses and local party plenums, where they were opened to debate and where they found, as was most probably Beria's intention, considerable resonance. With some adroit maneuvering to decouple the policies from Beria, the regime pressed on with the main thrust of the new policy. As had been the case in 1920s, the new policy included a recognition that the different strands of nationalities policy—especially on appointments, education, and language policy—were intertwined. In some areas, especially in Central Asia, the main brake on indigenization was the generally low level of education, a factor that limited the supply of politically trained, literate cadres. In the newly occupied territories to the west the bigger problem was the lack of support for the new regime. To secure these new territories, Moscow, in accordance with the new policy, had to promote native cadres and make joining the party more attractive to them by offering major concessions in the fields of language and cultural policy.

To compensate for these concessions Moscow came up with an important institutional innovation: the Slavic second secretary. Rather than referring to an individual, the "second" was a complex ensemble of rules and practices that replaced the more primitive and direct forms of rule, such as plenipotentiaries and republican buros of the Central Committee, which had been prevalent in the late 1940s.[17] Although individual Slavic second secretaries had been placed in the Baltic republics in the postwar period, as an institution consisting of a variety of mutually reinforcing elements one can pinpoint its emergence quite precisely to December 1955 with the appointment of Dmitry Iakovlev as second secretary in Azerbaijan.[18] From then on it became the norm for second secretaries to be recruited from the Central Committee and, in particular, from the department of party organs, where, at any one time, up to eight or nine sector heads or inspectors were being prepared for future service as a second in one of the twelve non-Slavic republics.[19] On arrival in the republic they would be endowed with appropriate status rewards, such as an Order of Lenin and candidate membership of the Central Committee and a position on the USSR Supreme Soviet. The institution of the second was never explicitly articulated or codified in a policy statement or a resolution. Yet the appointments did follow a clear institutional logic: second secretaries were to serve as mediators who could help the local nomenklatura "correctly understand" what Moscow was demanding, and here the fact that they had served in the Central Committee apparatus and were close to the decision-making process in Moscow was supposed to help.[20]

The appointment of second secretaries also followed the institutional logic of the nomenklatura in another way. As discussed above, most territorial leaders in the late Stalin era consolidated networks through their strategies of overpromotion, political exclusion, and kompromat. Each of these strategies relied on the party leader's control of key departments, especially the party organs department, and his line of access to the security police. In this regard, the fact that in many of the national republics it was increasingly the Slavic second secretary, not the first, who was placed in charge of these departments, served to block the classic network strategies of the substate dictator. As we saw in chapters 4 and 5, in the mid-1950s, shortly after Stalin's death, some of the traditional routes of network formation in the nonnational territories were being closed off. In the national territories these resources were further put out of reach by the fact that it was not the first but the second secretary who was now given priority access to them. Thus thwarted, some republican leaders turned to other options. In this regard, ethnic mobilization provided what appeared to be an instant solution to their problems.

NATIONAL MOBILIZATION

At around 3:00 pm on 4 March 1956, the day before the third anniversary of Stalin's death, a small crowd began to gather at the Stalin monument in Tbilisi. By evening there were an estimated thousand people reciting poems, making toasts, singing songs, and forming honor guards to the deceased leader.[21] The next evening, the day of the anniversary, there were ten thousand mourners in Tbilisi as well as crowds of two thousand in Sukhumi, twenty-five hundred in Kutaisi, and one thousand in Batumi. Rather than lessening, in the days that followed the numbers swelled, rising to twenty-five to thirty thousand in Tbilisi on 7 March, thirty-five to forty thousand on 9 March, and, according to some reports, an estimated seventy thousand demonstrators in Gori on the same day. The crowds were largely peaceful, but they presented a growing problem for authoritarian control. On 8 March in Krtsanisi a crowd of five thousand descended on the residence of the Chinese general and commander in chief of the Chinese Liberation Army Zhu De, who was visiting Tbilisi at the time. Reports suggested that some elements of the crowd launched bottles, stones, boards, and other objects at the security forces, injuring soldiers and some officers. Elsewhere on that day there were reports of officers and soldiers being beaten and cars being commandeered. The following day, 9 March, a crowd of two thousand picketed the headquarters of the Transcaucasian Military District, and one of ten thousand surged toward the buildings of the central committee and the council of ministers. In some districts anarchy reigned. General Major Bannykh, the head of the Transcaucasian Military District border troops, reported that Tbilisi "was in chaos. There was no order. Complete anarchy. All transport—cars and trucks, taxis, buses, trolleys—are in the hands of the crowd." Although the organizers of the protest promised to disperse the crowd after a speech by the republican first secretary, Mzhavanadze, by lunchtime they were unable to prevent a nucleus of hardliners, several thousand strong, from heading to the communications ministry that night. After early skirmishes a military unit in the building opened fire, killing twenty-one people and wounding many more. At two o'clock on the morning of the tenth the crowds were finally dispersed and the demonstration was halted. The next day armed soldiers were posted along the main streets of central Tbilisi with instructions not to let civilians pass or congregate.[22]

Most of the problems of authoritarian control discussed in the book thus far have involved electoral mutinies of the party aktiv. The events in Georgia of March 1956 represented a different challenge altogether. Here, the threat came not from the party rank and file but from the broader mass of the population. In fact, from the perspective of the ruling coalition the demonstrations marked a complete failure of party rule. As the crisis worsened, whenever the party leadership pulled the traditional levers of the party machine to restore order, nothing happened. Instructions from the Georgian buro on 6 March to employees of the central committee "to explain the historic decisions of the XX Party Congress" had little impact and seemed if anything to further antagonize their audience. Special meetings of all party organizations in Tbilisi on 8 March and a radio broadcast to party and Komsomol members the following day were similarly fruitless.[23] In fact, some of the most fervent attendees at the meetings were themselves from the cream of the party elite, members of the republican higher party school.[24]

Why did these demonstrations spread so quickly? And why could the party leadership do so little to stop them? The main reason was that the traditional terrain of party mobilization operated on a different plane from the issues that were now animating the crowds. At stake were not the tasks of economic construction or the implementation of current government policy but events interpreted in national terms by a large ethnic group. Three demands fueled the March demonstrations, each of which had a strong national coloring. First, for over two decades the tiny republic of Georgia—whose industrial production in 1950 comprised a mere 0.9 percent of the all-union total—had prized its connection, through a line of Politburo leaders that included Ordzhonikidze, Enukidze, Beria, and Stalin himself, to the corridors of power in Moscow. In Stalin's and Beria's stead, Khrushchev had appointed Vasily Mzhavanadze, an ethnic Georgian with no known ties to Beria and no track record of having worked in the republic or of holding senior office. While marking a clean break, Mzhavanadze represented a major loss of authority and prestige for the republic.[25] With Stalin's death,

Beria's fall from grace, and the installation of a political nonentity, the connection to supreme power had suddenly disappeared.[26]

Second, the republic was afflicted by interethnic tensions. This problem was related in part to the treatment of the two Georgian autonomies of Abkhazia and South Ossetia, where Khrushchev reversed a number of pro-Georgian policies on orthography and on the language of instruction in schools from the late Stalin era. Moreover, he replaced the first secretaries of the Ossetian, Abkhaz, and Ajarian obkoms, along with other senior officials, with local nationals and, once they were in post, backed these officials in their conflicts with the Georgian nomenklatura. There were also, in addition, tensions between Georgians and Russians as the Central Committee in Moscow received reports of newly arrived ethnic Russian workers being beaten and threatened, of female employees being harassed or even raped, of shop employees ignoring non-Georgian customers, and of fistfights breaking out between Russian servicemen and locals.[27]

A third factor, however, was to play the biggest role in the demonstrations, and it explains their timing. Shortly after the XX Party Congress in February 1956 many Georgians felt slighted by the lack of reference to Stalin in congress communications and by the pointed attack on the deceased leader by an ethnic Armenian, Anastas Mikoian. To pour oil on the fire, rumors of the Secret Speech, in which Khrushchev denigrated virtually every aspect of Stalin's leadership and, in particular, downplayed his role in the Second World War, also began to circulate.[28]

There are three ways to view the demonstrations of 1956 as national events. First, they were expressed in a national idiom. The mourning on the first, second, and third anniversaries of Stalin's death was attended by traditional national songs as well as speeches, poetry, and verse commemorating historic Georgian kings.[29] Second, the demonstrations were not confined to Tbilisi but extended all across Georgia. Large-scale unrest quickly spread to Gori, Kutaisi, Sukhumi, and Batumi, crystallizing the sense of a supralocal mass identity.[30] Third, although all the initial demands had to do exclusively with the commemoration of the "holy name and memory" of Stalin—restoring his name to public institutions, including references to him in public pronouncements, and organizing cultural events such as films and plays in his honor—

these demands were viewed through a national lens.[31] For many of his countrymen Stalin was first and foremost a Georgian. Given his international prominence, Stalin's name, image, and historical role were, to many Georgians, an instantly recognizable symbol of the Georgian nation as a whole. Hence the attacks on Stalin were quickly interpreted as a national slur.[32] One curious reflection of this response is the evidence of Georgians who lost relatives to Stalin's purges still campaigning to defend his name. "What surprised me the most," reported one participant, "were the members of repressed families, sons and daughters of repressed parents who were defending the personality of Stalin. ... [T]his was a mass protest of the Georgians, and they were defending Stalin as a Georgian."[33]

Some scholars distinguish these national actions from politically nationalist ones. This has the merit of recognizing that the March events were neither anti-Soviet nor directed toward independence or secession from the Soviet Union.[34] Some of the most radical demands made of the regime by the demonstrators were surprisingly conservative in institutional terms and were intended to protest specific policies, not to undermine Soviet power.[35] At the same time, the demands did quickly escalate. What began over the period of 5–9 March with a defense of Stalin and his name on 9–10 March turned into attacks on the current leadership and calls for their replacement.[36] Indeed, although by common agreement Mzhavanadze had not handled the situation well, he was promoted the next year and brought on as a candidate member of the Presidium, thereby satisfying the demonstrators' demand of having a Georgian at the very highest levels of the Soviet political system.[37]

These disturbances, fed by ever more radical demands, led to a major problem of authoritarian control. From the point of view of the regime the only way to thwart this outbreak of disorder was through repression. Even before the attack on the communications ministry, the authorities had arranged for martial law to be imposed that night and for troops to be deployed in the city. On the morning of 10 March armed soldiers were stationed at junctions in the city center and barriers and checkpoints set up on the highways. In anticipation of further disorder elsewhere in Tbilisi, party and Komsomol patrols were formed, police ranks reinforced, and KGB operational staff deployed across the city. Even after the immediate threat began to subside, the authorities remained alert to any form of collective action and instituted a new rule, which lasted for over a decade, banning gatherings of more than two people in the central streets of the republican capital. To further strengthen their grip the KGB lobbied for new branches to be opened across the republic.[38]

In Georgia in 1956 the mobilization happened so rapidly that it could be met only by force. In this centralized system the decision to employ repression was taken in and coordinated from Moscow.[39] Yet the punishments for those arrested and for the republican party leadership were surprisingly mild.[40] One reason was that the demonstrations were unorganized and appear to have had no leadership as such.[41] Although some party members joined the demonstrations on an individual basis, the republican party leadership had no role in organizing the demonstrations and did what it could to contain them. More significantly, as Kemoklidze puts it, Khrushchev did not have any alternative to keeping the Communist nomenklatura in Tbilisi intact since at the time "the Moscow leadership did not have any alternative Georgian elites whom they could trust."[42] In stark form this observation underlines the fundamental agency problem Khrushchev and other leaders faced in Georgia, as they did in other republics.

AUTHORITARIAN CONTROL AND POWER SHARING

In the spring of 1959 the Central Committee dispatched two high-level commissions to Latvia and Azerbaijan. While the ostensible purpose of the visits—to check on violation of party norms in the selection of cadres—was framed in quite neutral terms, these were no ordinary delegations. For one thing they were unusually large, with memberships drawn from across the Central Committee apparatus and the Committee of Party Control. Their deliberations were also highly secretive. Despite being headquartered in the republican central committee buildings, the commissions were kept in quarantine, adhering to a rigid schedule of interviews with the authors of complaints picked up in Moscow. What contact they did have with local leaders took the form of terse, one-to-one interrogations. After two weeks, the commissions left without so much as debriefing the local party leadership. For the Azerbaijani and Latvian party leaderships, the omens were not good. Only three months earlier a similar commission to Uzbekistan had led to the downfall of the republican first secretary, Sabir Kamalov. In

Azerbaijan the leadership was sufficiently worried to hold a preemptive republican party plenum to anticipate any forthcoming criticisms and to offload the blame onto a convenient scapegoat. In Latvia members of the leadership strained every sinew to activate their informal contacts in Moscow, only to find all their channels blocked.[43]

The Azeri and Latvian leaderships were right to be worried. On 8 June the head of the department of party organs of the union republics, Vladimir Semichastny, filed a damning report to the all-union party leadership accusing the Latvian party organization of willfully "distorting Leninist nationality policy."[44] The report claimed that, in what amounted to a crude national purge, non-Latvians in key governmental posts were being systematically driven out in favor of Latvians. It also argued that some republican leaders had become so "fixated with the nationalities question, artificially whipping it up," that it had begun to spread into every area of public life.[45] To separate the host population from non-Latvians, an informal system of ethnic segregation had formed: Latvian-only parties were organized, non-Latvian artists were prevented from putting on exhibitions, Latvian schoolchildren were forced to follow separate historical and geographical curricula and, in one school, were asked to wear special ribbons so that, in the words of their school director, "we can differentiate you from the Russians."[46] The candidate member of the Presidium, Nuritdin Mukhitdinov, was sent out to Riga to brief a meeting of the republican party buro on the report's findings on 20–21 June.[47] In the case of Azerbaijan, Khrushchev chose the final day of the all-union Central Committee plenum of 24–29 June to launch an intemperate attack on Azerbaijan's nationalities policy. On 30 June the entire Azerbaijani buro were summoned to Moscow. To dramatize the impact of the gathering, all republican first and second secretaries were invited to witness the Azerbaijani first secretary Mustafaev being mauled, first by the Central Committee secretaries and then, in turn, by members of his own buro.[48]

The showdown took place the next day, on 1 July. This was the first time the concurrent investigations into Azerbaijan and Latvia, which until then had been treated separately, were brought together, thereby setting the scene for wider reflections on nationalities policy. With the leaders of both republics in attendance, the Presidium considered oral presentations by Mukhitdinov on Latvia and by the deputy head of the party organs department, Ivan Shikin, on Azerbaijan.[49] By this point the fate of the two republican first secretaries had already been settled, but the meeting went further, signaling a new direction in nationalities policy.[50] Khrushchev's own position, especially in light of his earlier prominority stance, was tinged with ambiguity. Having championed indigenization since 1953, he continued to talk up some aspects of the policy. He was wary of bringing the nationalities question out in the open, lest it be used to stir up ethnic tensions. Radical interventions from the center were only likely to backfire, he cautioned: "That would just be a gift to our enemies, which would allow them to talk of some sort of crisis in our nationalities policy. That would be quite wrong and would only end up creating an artificial crisis."[51] For this reason Khrushchev counseled against framing the forthcoming debates at the republican party plenums in national terms.[52]

Notwithstanding these caveats, the session of 1 July marked an important shift. Khrushchev now identified the crux of the problem. He cut short the Latvian Kārlis Ozoliņš's statement that "there is no nationalist question in Latvia" with a curt interruption: "You are quite wrong, yes, there is."[53] Having endorsed indigenization earlier, Khrushchev was now alive to its dangers. "The path of national isolation is not the communist way," he mused, "for it will destroy the union and lead to us all being walled off within the borders of our national republics."[54] The problem, moreover, was not confined to either Latvia or Azerbaijan: "These lessons will be useful for all—for the Ukrainians as well as for the Tajiks. . . . Every nation, every party organization will have to fight its own form of nationalism."[55]

The turn against Azerbaijan and Latvia in July 1959 was significant because it pointed not to a single cause but to an array of factors that were troubling the leadership. It is these, taken together, that help explain why activities that only a short while earlier had been lauded as forms of indigenization were now being branded as nationalist. Three factors were in play. The first was evidence of systematic discrimination in Latvia and Azerbaijan against ethnic Russians and other nontitular nationals. Letters containing stories of everyday humiliation of ethnic Russians as well as, to a lesser extent, Ukrainians, Belorussians, Armenians, and Georgians residing in the two republics had streamed into the Central Committee. These letters spoke of nontitular nationals being refused service in shops, told not to speak Russian in public, denied residence permits, and refused entry to republican institutions of higher learning. One usually unstated implication of the letters was that this was part of a concerted effort to drive minorities out of these republics.[56] Second, there was now solid evidence from Latvia and Azerbaijan that these republics were defining their economic interests against those of other republics. In Latvia, in a bid for economic autarky, the republic, under the influence of Pauls Dzerve, the director of the Latvian Academy of Sciences' Economics Institute, tried to steer investment and production plans away from heavy industry and toward consumer goods and light industry, thereby undermining the case for large-scale inward labor migration and for the import of raw materials from other parts of the union.[57] In Azerbaijan, the chair of the council of ministers, Sadykh Rahimov, had opposed construction of the Kara-Dag to Tbilisi gas pipeline on the grounds that "this gas is ours, Azerbaijan's, and we cannot give it to the Georgians." Under Rahimov the republic also followed an Azerbaijan-first policy in relation to the supply of fuel oil, iron ore, and electricity provided to neighboring republics.[58]

But what most clearly exemplified the conflict between Moscow and the two union republics was the latter's defiance of the center on language policy. The issue first arose in Azerbaijan. On 9 May 1955 the all-union Council of Ministers had issued a decree exempting schoolchildren in the union republics (with the exception of the Russian Federation) who were not members of the titular ethnic group and who attended nonnative language schools from compulsory study of the republic's national language. Knowing that fluency in Russian was a condition of admission to institutions of higher learning and a virtual prerequisite for serious career advancement, some Azeri parents had taken to sending their children to Russian-speaking schools. For these children, often a small minority, the teaching of Azeri was often done after hours, so they either turned up at half-empty classrooms tired or missed the classes altogether.[59] To address this issue the Azeri buro, on 14 August 1956, passed a decision making the teaching of Azeri compulsory for all children, including nontitular nationals attending Russian, Armenian, and Georgian schools. The significance of this decision was that it directly contradicted the all-union Council of Ministers' resolution of 9 May 1955.[60]

To provide an ideological foundation for the 14 August resolution, the following week, on 21 August, the Azeri supreme soviet changed the republican constitution, making Azeri the "state language" of the republic.[61] This was the springboard for a number of initiatives passed over the succeeding months stipulating the mandatory use of Azeri, along with Russian, in official documents and in party and ministerial correspondence.[62] These developments in Azerbaijan reportedly inspired similar moves in Latvia. The latter indeed went further by requiring, at the end of 1956, not only that all officials in public-facing roles acquire conversational command of Latvian within two years but also that this expectation be strictly enforced through tests and examinations, with those who failed facing dismissal.[63]

Two years later, in the next confrontation with Moscow, it was the Latvians who took the lead. On 14 November 1958 Khrushchev's "Theses on Education" was published. Khrushchev's educational reforms were wide-ranging and primarily designed to modernize the curriculum and to update teaching techniques, making them more relevant to the changing demands of the economy. They also involved standardizing practices across republics, and it was this that would turn into a major sticking point. Previously Russian schoolchildren in the Russian Federation had been required to study only one foreign language, while all other pupils, whether in the Russian Federation or in the other union republics, were required to learn two, placing a heavy burden on an already overstretched curriculum. One common practice, already in use in Latvia, was for pupils in national schools to stay on an extra year, giving them more time to learn a third language. Khrushchev, however, hit on a new idea: in the union republics the principal language of instruction should be made a matter of parental choice; beyond that, pupils would have to choose only one other language. This idea overturned the long-standing position dating from 1920s that all indigenous peoples attend native language schools. Moreover, it opened the possibility that nontitular nationals in republics like Latvia might choose not to learn the language of their republic. The proposal flew in the face of the Latvian and Azerbaijani reforms of the previous two years. When it came before the Latvian supreme soviet on 17 March 1959, Khrushchev's thesis was rejected; six days later, emboldened by the Latvian precedent, the Azerbaijanis followed suit.[64] Of all the republics, Latvia and Azerbaijan were alone in taking such a stand. This meant that on two separate occasions first Azerbaijan and then Latvia had openly defied Moscow, passing laws which directly contradicted the center. It was this defiance, alongside evidence of ethnic discrimination and economic localism, that alerted the Central Committee to the fact that local interests were being defined in opposition to all-union ones. At this point acceptable indigenization came to be viewed as nationalism.[65]

Why Moscow chose to rein in the Azeri and Latvian leaderships is relatively clear. But this raises a second and more intriguing question. Why did either leadership pursue policies that went so flatly against those of the center? Unlike the Georgian events of 1956, the national movements in Latvia and Azerbaijan were led not by students or intellectuals but by seasoned party leaders. Why were these leaders willing to break the cardinal rule of the Soviet system and follow a path of serial insubordination?

The reasons behind this seemingly perverse pattern of behavior varied in the two republics. Some reasons had deep historical roots. Prior to 1918 no specifically Azerbaijani state had ever existed. The population of what became the union republic of Azerbaijan was overwhelmingly peasant and was characterized by what we might think of as a low level of national consciousness.[66] Indeed, the people who inhabited the region were known as Tatars for much of the nineteenth century and as Turks for much of the 1920s and 1930s. "Azerbaijani," the ethnonym favored by national leaders, was not universally adopted until the late 1930s. Moreover, it was only in 1937 that the spoken Turkic vernacular of the east Caucasus, which earlier had been known variously as Tatar, Caucasian Turkic, or Azerbaijani Turkic, would, now fully cleansed of Persian and Arabic elements, come to be known as "Azerbaijani."[67] By contrast, at the time of the Revolution the Latvians spoke a distinct language with its own literary tradition, and the population was characterized by high levels of literacy and urbanization. Most important, they experienced state independence in the interwar period.[68] One could argue that in a certain sense Azerbaijan was a state formation in search of an *ethnie,* a community with a common culture and a belief in common ancestry, while Latvia was an ethnie in search of a state.[69] The key goal in Azerbaijan was to fill territorial nationhood with ethnocultural content; in Latvia the national consciousness was highly developed but a lack of territorial state control was reflected in the limited ability of republican state bodies to control migration flows or economic policy and to recruit into the elite members of the indigenous population.

Here, however, we want to emphasize a different contrast, one grounded in the contrasting structural relationships that existed between party leaderships, party organizations, and the wider societies they inhabited. To understand this structural contrast we need to begin with two underlying factors that the Azeri and Latvian national movements had in common. First, in both republics the leaderships played on fears of an existential threat to the host "nation." In Latvia the concern was that ethnic Latvians would be wiped out in successive waves of Slavic migration. After Latvia experienced a major demographic collapse during the war, the large-scale Slavic migration that followed reduced the Latvian share of the population from 83 percent in 1945 to 62 percent in 1953. The sense of a nation being demographically overrun was exemplified in Riga, the capital city, whose Latvian population fell from 63 percent in 1935 to 44.5 percent in 1959, at the same time as the share of Slavs rose from 8.6 percent to 45.4 percent.[70] Latvia's second largest city, Daugavpils, where Latvians comprised 13 percent of the population, represented, according to Prigge, the "nightmare scenario" of a "heavily industrialised city in which the population of ethnic Latvians declined to such a small minority that its language and culture virtually disappeared."[71]

In Azerbaijan the sense of national danger had different sources. The first was territorial. While the boundaries of most Soviet republics had been fully settled in the 1930s, in Azerbaijan there were two enclaves whose status remained hotly contested: the Armenian-majority autonomous oblast of Nagorno-Karabagh in the southwest of the republic and the historic Azeri autonomous republic of Nakhichevan at the southern tip of Armenia. In the 1950s the Azerbaijani leadership became embroiled in vigorous exchanges over these territories.[72] The second source of national danger concerned language. Unlike neighboring Georgia and Armenia, where official business was conducted in the native language, Azerbaijan conducted it in Russian. The language problem became particularly thorny after Stalin's death, when Khrushchev eased restrictions on peasant movement to the cities. As Azerbaijani peasants migrated to the large cities and in particular to the capital, Baku, they found that Russian was a prerequisite not only to achieve a higher education and professional advancement but also for everyday interaction. Their lack of Russian exposed them to everyday petty embarrassments and humiliations. The result was that a growing number of Azeris had begun to send their children to Russian-language schools.[73]

A second factor that spurred national movements in the two republics was that the explicitly political claims being advanced, for example, on language use, on the issuing of residency permits in Riga, or on the ethnic composition of the nomenklatura, were linked to wider debates about education, propaganda, and national identity. The liberalization brought about by Khrushchev's Thaw was a propitious time for experimenting with national styles and for assembling a cultural canon in poetry, drama, painting, music, and other arts that could draw on writers, composers, and painters who had earlier been repressed.[74] The sudden loosening of constraints on cultural production and a recognition by the authorities of the effects this might have on the state's ability to mold popular consciousness was one reason ideological conflicts over the direction of mass culture, especially in Latvia, became so fierce. As the Stalinist ideology secretary, Arvids Pelše, pronounced in October 1957, in the midst of a dispute with the culture minister, Voldemārs Kalpiņš, "Each year in our republic two million go to the theater, nearly three million go to see films, millions of people read Soviet literature. Where there are millions, there is politics. That is why the Party organisation cannot stand on the sideline of artistic politics."[75]

Debates over language policy, territorial boundaries, and immigration, along with the use of instantly recognizable images and symbols, gave politicians a direct route to the wider population that was unprecedented in the closed world of Soviet politics. As the Latvian culture minister Kalpiņš later recalled, the "Latvian nation's era of revival" in 1955–59 was a "time in which the active participation of popular forces was permissible."[76] From the perspective of nationalist leaders like Edvards Berklavs in Latvia, this liberalization opened up the possibility of unrivaled personal popularity, a platform for a party-based populism. "As [Berklavs] raised these questions at the party congress," noted Krūmiņš in July 1959, "he would get rapturous applause, and in the republic they began to say that he was the man. . . . [T]here were widespread rumors that this person Berklavs will soon become our [first] secretary."[77] In Azerbaijan overtly nationalist leaders like the chair of the presidium of the supreme soviet, Mirza Ibrahimov, were feted in similar terms. It soon became apparent, somewhat to the consternation of his colleagues, that at public meetings Ibrahimov's speeches were being greeted with particularly loud and prolonged applause.[78] Reflecting later on the impact of the language law of August 1956, the chair of the council of ministers (and later Mustafaev's successor as first secretary), Veli Akhundov, commented somewhat acidly, "Some people, especially the youth and students, yielded to this [nationalist] sentiment. This explains the long, uninterrupted applause, every time comrade Ibrahimov speaks."[79] What distinguished substate nationalists such as Berklavs and Ibrahimov was their ability to articulate demands in an instantly recognizable register that would resonate with the wider titular ethnic community.

The nationalist movements in Latvia and Azerbaijan had in common the perception of an existential threat to the nation and a program of nation building across a range of cultural, educational, and commemorative fronts. Leaders such as Berklavs and Ibrahimov took advantage of these policies to build a strong personal following that extended well beyond the party aktiv. But there was also something fundamentally different in the two republics, and it is this that best helps explain why, for two quite different sets of reasons, seasoned leaders were willing to flout the center's will and risk political ruin.

Latvia represented, in the terms used in this book, the problem of authoritarian control. The difficulty here was that levels of Latvian entry into the republican party organization were minute. Without first being in the party, Latvians could not be promoted to senior positions in the administration. But, lacking the demonstration effect of Latvians successfully rising through the ranks, the reputation of the regime suffered, preventing Latvians from joining the party. Equally, it made little sense to have party documents in Latvian if the majority of party members could not read them; this too eroded the credibility of the regime. On 1 January 1953 the Latvian party comprised only 29.2 percent ethnic Latvians. Given that this figure included the so-called *Latovichi*, ethnic Latvians who had been born or raised in Russia and who had moved to Latvia at the end of the war (some of whom were not even fluent in Latvian), the number of homegrown Latvians in the party was even smaller.[80] This made it very hard for the party to reach out to the local Latvian population. As Berklavs, then first secretary of the Riga gorkom, commented at the June 1953 plenum, only eight hundred of the twenty thousand agitators in Riga worked in Latvian. This made it virtually impossible for the party's agitation and propaganda arm to make inroads into the wider Latvian community.[81]

The only way to break out of this impasse was to embark on policies that might hold genuine appeal for homegrown ethnic Latvians. Thus the national communists under Berklavs embarked on a set of policies on language and residency (both at the end of 1956) and on cadres (October 1958), moves that might help limit immigration and foster an environment in which native Latvians could prosper. The Latvian leadership could certainly point to some successes. There was a notable rise in the share of Latvians in the republican central committee, climbing from 42 percent in June 1953 to 69.5 percent in January 1956 and 75 percent in January 1958.[82] The national communists also point to their achievement in bringing down inward migration, which fell from 26,800 in 1956 to 7,400 in 1957 and 100 in 1958.[83] The underlying problem, however, remained unresolved. Latvians were willing to join the party only in very small numbers. From January 1957 to January 1959, at the height of the pro-Latvian policies, only 4,000 Latvians joined the party, marginally raising the Latvians' share of the party membership from 35.1 percent to 37.4 percent. In Lithuania and Estonia, by comparison, the native proportion of party members was 55.7 percent and 47.5 percent, respectively. The enterprise Avtoelektropribor was reportedly typical of the problem. Latvians failed to attend events and showed little interest in party matters. Party recruitment was reportedly in a dire state. For every 20 new admissions in 1959, only 1–2 were Latvians. According to the head of agitation and propaganda, Ivan Veselovs, such apathy prevailed because all events were held in Russian despite the fact that Latvians comprised the majority of workers at the enterprise.[84] The persistent underrepresentation of Latvians in the party was, according to the Latvian historian Daina Bleiere, the "Achilles Heel" of the national communists' program in Latvia.[85] Indeed, as he was later to reflect on it, it was this very concern that drove Berklavs's famous article "Conversations from the Heart," published in February 1959, which would cause such controversy in the republic.[86]

In Azerbaijan it was not the party's penetration of Azeri society that was the problem. After thirty years, the party was now well established. As its chair, Mirza Ibrahimov, told the presidium of the supreme soviet,

"This is no longer 1920. Today we have the numbers of [Azeri] cadres to fill all state positions."[87] Instead, the problem emanated from within the ruling coalition itself, and it took two forms. First, unlike Latvia, which had a number of well-known politicians from the 1940s, including Kalnbērizņš, Lācis, and Ozoliņš, on the republican party buro, the Azeri buro consisted of relative unknowns. The post-Stalin leadership in Moscow had dealt with the Bagirov problem by effecting a mass clearing out and filling the top leadership positions with obscure officials several steps removed from the previous administration.[88] The price of this maneuver, was that the new figures, such as Imam Mustafaev, the new first secretary from January 1954, and Sadykh Rahimov, the new chair of the council of ministers, had a low public profile and relatively little authority. To bolster their position they turned to figures from the Azeri intelligentsia, among them the national poet Samed Vurghun and the novelist Mirza Ibrahimov. As a member of the buro, Pasha Arushanov, noted in a discussion in January 1955, "No party worker . . . can be found who exceeds Samed Vurghun or Mirza Ibrahimov."[89] Although Vurghun's role was cut short by his death in 1956, Ibrahimov, who was appointed chair of the presidium of the supreme soviet, would play a crucial role in the national revival, driving the language law of August 1956, writing an inflammatory article in a Baku newspaper in October, and pushing through a resolution on the use of Azeri in state ministries in December.[90]

A second difficulty for the Azeri leadership stemmed from the exceedingly low levels of interpersonal trust on the buro, part of a long shadow cast by the previous administration under Bagirov. Under Bagirov it had been hard to advance even to midlevel positions without getting some black spots on your cv, and this was certainly true of Mustafaev and Rahimov, on both of whom there was kompromat going back to the 1930s.[91] From the late Stalin years Mustafaev and Rahimov had acquired an air of vulnerability which now colored relations with other members of the buro as well as with each other. Mustafaev himself had an almost pathological distrust of the KGB head, Anatoly Guskov, whom he suspected of building a dossier of slanderous materials against him. When early efforts to get Guskov removed failed, Mustafaev turned his ire on Guskov's deputy, Abdulkerim Alizadeh.[92] Mustafaev's suspiciousness was apparently pervasive. The party secretary, Mamed Iskenderov, related the following story: "We are afraid of visiting the CC CPSU apparatus. While Rahimov and I were in Moscow attending a meeting of industry workers, he suggested: 'Let's go to Shikin (the deputy head of the party organs department). If I go alone, Mustafayev might think that I'm going to complain about him.'"[93] Relations deteriorated to such an extent that in August 1955 Mustafaev was openly rebuked by the Azeri buro for "arbitrarily distrusting top officials," a criticism echoed by the all-union Secretariat in October.[94] Iakovlev, the second secretary, noted, "It appears that this suspicion and mistrust lead him away from the correct solution of the matter, from establishing proper business relations."[95]

Although they were selected precisely because of their remoteness from Bagirov, the buro of the Azerbaijani central committee was rendered dysfunctional by the pall of mistrust cast by the Bagirov years. Indeed, the Azeri buro was so riven by mistrust that only a special issue with a particular political charge could bring it unity: in the context of mid-1950s Azerbaijan that issue was language reform. As one correspondent, a researcher at the Institute of State and Language at the Academy of Sciences, Ramzi Yuzbashov, observed, "The question [of language] is a thousand times more important than the construction of the Mingechevir power station."[96] In Azerbaijan, unlike in Latvia, it was the problem of maintaining the ruling coalition—the problem of authoritarian power sharing—that drove the nationalist agenda and propelled the leadership to take such major risks in their policies vis-à-vis the center.

From the moment of Stalin's death Khrushchev championed a new, revived form of indigenization. That the policy was initially associated with Beria was unfortunate, but Khrushchev managed to distance himself from Beria by deemphasizing the anti-Russian tenor of Beria's rhetoric and by implementing indigenization not through the MVD, as had been Beria's wont, but through the party. Although Khrushchev rarely spoke on matters of nationalities, when he did, as at the XX Congress, his support for indigenization jibed with the wider policy of economic decentralization. Against this background, complaints from officials at the Central Committee that republican leaders were stirring up nationalist sentiments tended to be ignored by him.[97] It was only when evidence emerged that republican leaders were deliberately flouting central policies, in law as well as in practice, that Khrushchev changed tack.

The years 1958 and 1959 marked a change of course in the center's nationalities policy. In Lithuania and Azerbaijan the language laws were overturned and other key policies on residency and on the teaching of history were scrapped.[98] In addition to the earlier purges in Turkmenistan in December 1958 and Uzbekistan in March 1959, the next two years saw purges of titular party leaders in Kirgizia, Moldavia, and Tajikistan and the removal of two of the architects of the soft line on nationalities policy, Aleksei Kirichenko and Nuritdin Mukhitdinov.[99] The Party Program in October 1961 confirmed a new ideological orientation towards *sliianie*, the idea that "nations will draw still closer together, and their complete unity will be achieved," a move that understandably upset ethnic elites.[100] However, Khrushchev recognized the need to tread carefully. Republican party leaders were instructed not to bring up the subject of nationalism at republican gatherings, and, except in Latvia, the purges of ethnic elites were surprisingly restrained. Moreover, in most republics discrete pronational policies were allowed to resurface once the initial controversy had subsided.

From the perspective of republican leaders what nationalism offered was a register for popular mobilization. In the two republics where nationalism emerged as an explosive issue the reasons for doing so, however, were quite different. In Latvia the national communists recognized that the popular base for supporting the regime was exceptionally thin. If they could persuade the center of the need to broaden their appeal by focusing on issues such as language and culture they might lure more Latvians into the party and into the nomenklatura. In this they were primarily addressing a problem of authoritarian control, of how best to govern over a skeptical and unwilling population. In Azerbaijan the policies stemmed from a fundamental instability within the leadership—a legacy of the Bagirov era—which found that the only way to overcome enmity and mutual suspicion was through a policy that had true popular appeal. This was a solution to the problem of authoritarian power sharing.

7 Scandal in Riazan

OVER THE THIRTY years covered in this book the key turning point in relations between the authoritarian leadership in Moscow and their principals in the regions was not the death of Stalin in 1953 or the removal of Khrushchev in 1964 but a rupture that took place toward the end of 1960. The clearest outward sign of this rupture was the mass replacement and dismissal of provincial leaders (figs. 7.1, 7.2), which would turn out to be, in the words of one commentator, a "purge of regional leaders unprecedented in its proportions in the post-totalitarian era."[1]

Some have viewed this purge as a function of leadership competition in Moscow. In this view it was driven by the opportunities afforded Khrushchev by the upcoming XXII Party Congress in October 1961 to remove uncongenial regional leaders and replace them with those more amenable and loyal to him.[2] We suggest that the purge was the result of something deeper, a crisis in the agency problem faced by the dictator. The clearest manifestation of this was a pandemic of data falsification at the regional level that came to light at the end of 1960. Particularly troubling to the central leadership was that in most cases these distortions had been instigated by people who were ostensibly the dictator's most loyal agents, the regional party leaders.

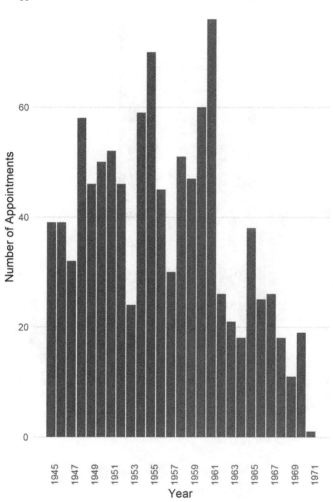

Figure 7.1. New appointments of territorial first secretaries in the USSR, 1945–71. The term "territorial first secretaries" refers to first secretaries of obkoms, kraikoms, and union and autonomous republics. The graph is based on complete data, with the exception of 1952, which is based on data from the RSFSR, Ukraine, Georgia, and Moldavia. Data for 1961 and 1963–64 exclude departures resulting from the bifurcation and reunification of regional party committees. *Sources:* Resolutions of the Politburo, Presidium, and Secretariat of the Central Committee, RGANI and RGASPI; RGANI f.5 op.29 d.15 ll.62–63

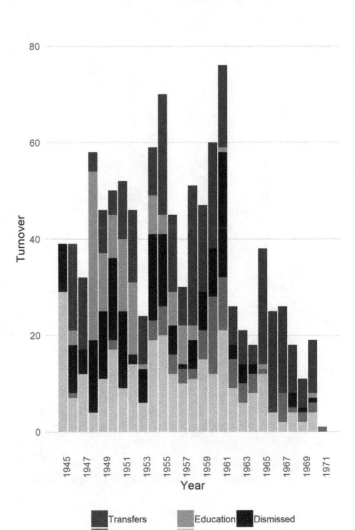

Figure 7.2. Reasons for the departure of territorial first secretaries in the USSR, 1945–71. "Territorial first secretaries" refers to first secretaries of obkoms, kraikoms, and union and autonomous republics. For the subtotals for 1945–51 and for 1952 see the figure 4.2 caption. Data for 1961 and 1963–64 exclude departures resulting from the bifurcation and reunification of regional party committees. For coding rules, see appendix H. *Sources:* Resolutions of the Politburo, Presidium and Secretariat of the Central Committee, RGANI and RGASPI; RGANI f.5 op.29 d.15 ll.62–63.

The moment of truth for Khrushchev was a scandal that blew up in Riazan, a medium-sized agricultural region two hundred kilometers southeast of the capital. Its proximity to Moscow had made it, in the words of its long-standing obkom leader, Aleksei Larionov, a "gold mine in the Moscow hinterland, a rich store of food for the workers of the industrial centers of the country."[3] Riazan had been held up by Khrushchev as a model region whose example could help propel the Soviet Union toward a great breakthrough in agriculture to rival the one Stalin had achieved with industrialization in early 1930s. In May 1957 Khrushchev promised that within a few years the USSR would match the USA in the production of milk, butter, and, especially, meat.[4] Impatient with the slow tempo of the sixth five-year plan (1959–60), Khrushchev opted for a new, hyper-optimistic seven-year plan, which was to commence in 1959 and run until 1965. He turned to Riazan as the standard-bearer for his new agricultural policies. Riazan was an

The awarding of Orders of Lenin at a session of the RSFSR supreme soviet on 28 December 1958. Here, Khrushchev's associate Central Committee Secretary Averkii Aristov pins an order to the banner of the Russian Republic. *Source:* RGASPI.

First Secretary Aleksei
Larionov of Riazan oblast
in 1958. Courtesy of
Russian State Archive of
Photographic and Cinematic
Documents in Krasnogorsk.

obvious choice, as Khrushchev had already collaborated with Larionov
and knew him well. More significant, if the Soviet Union was to catch
up with the United States in per capita consumption of meat, yields
would have to rise threefold. And in this respect Riazan had already
shown the way. From 1953 to 1958 productivity in milk in the region
had almost tripled. All that was needed was for Riazan to do the same
with meat.[5]

At the end of 1958 Khrushchev sent a special emissary to the region
to press for a "socialist obligation"—an ad hoc commitment by a local producer or party organization to a sudden over-the-plan increase
in production—of three plans, 150,000 tons, "a difficult but necessary
and honorable step" that would help enable the USSR to "catch up
with the USA." This was followed by a highly publicized visit Khrushchev made to Riazan in February 1959 and by a glitzy reception for
Riazan farmers later on that year.[6] The announcement on 16 December
1959 that Riazan had tripled its annual yield to a remarkable "three
annual plans" was greeted with a Soviet-style media frenzy, as national
newspapers led with front-page articles celebrating "Riazan's Victory"
and the "Achievement of the Third Plan." Brochures on the Riazan
story were printed in large runs and translated into the languages of

the USSR's fellow socialist states. Larionov's suicide in September 1960 and the spectacular, very public collapse of the campaign in Riazan was not merely an embarrassment for Khrushchev. The problem was that investigations revealed a massive fraud that centered on Larionov but was perpetrated by a wide regional network lodged in the regional party organization.

RIAZAN

Throughout 1959 and 1960 the Central Committee accumulated evidence that Khrushchev's agricultural campaign, in particular the campaign to increase the production of meat, was not going according to plan. There were two themes to these complaints. The first was that some regional party organizations appeared to have taken the campaign as a signal that they could revert to the strong-arm tactics and forceful requisitioning of the early 1930s. One directive of the RSFSR buro of the Central Committee showed how, in order to meet their quotas, collective farm chairmen and chairs of rural soviets were, with the help of local *militsiia* officials, often confiscating food stocks, carrying out illegal searches of people's homes, imposing unauthorized fines, beating collective farmers, arresting and falsely imprisoning peasants, and forcing farmers to sell cattle from their private plots. In some regions local authorities established norms for the forced sale of agricultural produce.[7] A second theme to the complaints, which normally emanated from functionaries of the state's various control bureaucracies, such as auditors, statisticians, and justice officials, was that local organizations were engaging in large-scale fraud. Although statistical distortion was a long-standing practice in the Soviet economy, the Central Committee's correspondents appeared to claim that it was now occurring on a greater scale than ever before.

Despite these complaints, for most of 1960 the Central Committee held firm in its position and enjoined local organizations to persist in efforts to meet the ambitious new targets. Where regional organizations ran into problems, they were for the most part assailed with slogans about the need to use more advanced agricultural techniques, from the sowing of spring wheat and the double harvest of maize to the more efficient use of weeding. One undercurrent of the Central Committee's directives was that, rather than going too far, some regional leaders were being too hesitant. This certainly was the stance behind the removal in June 1960 of the first secretary in Krasnodar, D.M. Matiushkin, who was castigated by Khrushchev's right-hand man, Averkii Aristov, for "always wanting to do good," for "showing kindness at the expense of party and state discipline," and for displaying undue "liberalism" in running the regional party organization.[8]

Following Larionov's suicide on 22 September 1960 it was no longer possible to hold this line. On 29 October Khrushchev sent out a set of notes, ostensibly to the Presidium but copied to all regional party organizations, which for the first time included an admission on the subject of cheating and falsification. For many regional party organizations these notes would mark a turning point. "Until we got that letter," wrote one anonymous correspondent from Zhitomir, "all the heads of the districts and of the collective farms simply assumed that the purchase of cattle by collective farms and its inclusion in our deliveries to the state were being done on the direct orders of the Central Committee."[9] Khrushchev warned that those found to be "bragging and even deceiving the state" would be punished. For the time being, however, subject to an ongoing inquiry, Khrushchev refused to criticize the Riazan party organization.[10]

The findings of the inquiry were eventually submitted to an extended meeting of the RSFSR buro on 2–3 December and then brought up for discussion at a specially convened plenum in Riazan on 3–4 January 1961.[11] The results of the inquiry and the high-level discussion that ensued would mark an important threshold for Khrushchev. Ahead of the forthcoming Central Committee plenum, convened for 10–18 January, Khrushchev released a set of so-called theses. For the first time, he conceded that the targets in Riazan had not been proposed, as had previously been claimed, from below by the region's state and collective farms but had been imposed from above by regional organizations, and that, in pursuing these targets, data in Riazan had been deliberately falsified. Moreover, he made it clear that the phenomenon of data inflation was not confined to Riazan but had also been found in a number of other regions. In calling for heads to roll, Khrushchev for the first time began to level charges of antistate behavior and antistate tendencies not only at state officials, as had been the case previously, but also at party officials.[12] This accusation laid the foundations for the forthcoming purge.

What explains Khrushchev's sudden change of tack? Why did he launch a purge of regional leaders, many of whom he had, until only recently, stoutly defended? What was it about the Riazan Affair that could have promoted such a radical turnaround? One factor may have been that Khrushchev was embarrassed. After all, he had repeatedly stood by and defended Larionov. "I know comrade Larionov to be serious and reliable," Khrushchev had proclaimed at the December 1959 Central Committee plenum. "He is not the kind of man ever to make an unrealistic commitment, to shine today only to come to grief tomorrow. He is just not that kind of man."[13] The scale of the deception may not have helped. An in-depth investigation showed that rather than the vaunted 150,000 tons of meat, Riazan had produced only 60,000 tons in 1959.[14]

Yet like many politicians Khrushchev was probably too thick-skinned to have pursued his new course of action out of mere embarrassment. Moreover, although the wide margin between the publicly proclaimed figure and the actual amount of meat was awkward, it was known only to a handful of people. Most members of the Presidium were fed the false assertion by Aristov, which was then repeated by Khrushchev, that Riazan had in fact achieved two plans, that is, 100,000 tons, and that the real blame for the whole fiasco lay with the meat commission headed by the agriculture secretary, V.P. Zenin, along with various officials from the sovnarkhoz and the regional executive committee.[15]

There are two distinct aspects of the Riazan Affair that are most likely to have prompted the center's new approach. The first was that the Riazan inquiry showed just how widespread the dissimulation was and how many organizations were involved in it. Officials from the region drew attention to the fact that fraud in Riazan had become a system, one that had fully enveloped the region's rank and file. "In every district there was falsification and deception, this was an entire system," asserted the obkom ideology secretary, S.G. Iakimov.[16] "At the obkom they gathered functionaries from the consumer cooperatives, the regional trade department, the agricultural administration, the state statistical agency, in a word *everyone*," reported the first secretary of the Shilovskii raikom, Tsyplakov, at the extraordinary convocation of the Riazan obkom on 6 January 1961. "The most terrible thing," concurred the head of the statistical administration, Ganiushkin, "was that drawn into the orbit of falsification was a wide circle of officials, starting with the kolkhozniks, but moving on to salespeople at the village general stores, kolkhoz accountants, and even newspaper reporters." Underlining this point, Aristov, who also attended the plenum, conceded that Moscow had received signals, including a very convincing one about suspicious goings-on in the Zapozhkovskii district: "Refuting it, however, was a letter signed by all the raikom secretaries, the raikom chair, the kolkhoz chairs, secretaries of party organizations, in a word about sixty people. . . . They signed, confirming that this was a slander, that it was all wrong. How could we not believe when so many comrades had signed?"[17]

Alongside the matter of rampant falsification was a second, connected but arguably more important factor. The Central Committee investigation appeared to imply that these large, disparate groups of individuals were being coordinated, protected, and inspired by the local party organizations, the raikoms. The raikoms were in turn integrated into a wider hierarchy of deception under the aegis of Larionov's obkom. In other words, the main agency that pulled the various threads of cheating and falsification together in Riazan was the regional party organization, with Larionov at its head.

In order to grasp this point we need to pause briefly to reflect on the three main forms of statistical deception that were uncovered in Riazan. The first involved buying up additional meat and cattle on secondary markets and submitting it as Riazan's own. Procurement agents roamed neighboring regions and even the markets and high street shops of Moscow in search of "meat for the plan." The RSFSR buro commission estimated that a total of 39,500 tons of meat were purchased in this way at a cost of 237 million rubles.[18] Although they ran against the spirit of the meat campaign, such purchases were, formally speaking, permissible under law. Reports of such activities had in fact been widely circulated throughout 1959.

The second main form of agricultural fraud involved cattle that had been placed for reassignment (*na perederzhku*).[19] This practice drew on an RSFSR council of ministers resolution of August 1959 which allowed for cattle that were scrawny or underfed at the time of formal submission to the state procurement agency to be weighed but then kept on at the farms and fattened up for delivery at a later date, when they would yield more meat. The weight of the cattle on the census date was to count toward the plan for that year, while the additional weight put on after that date would be included in the following year's plan. But the system was abused. The RSFSR buro investigation discovered numerous cases in which the weight of the cattle was fully double counted. Although not ideal, regional officials often cited the August 1959 resolution authorizing the reassignment and appeared to take some comfort from this that what they were doing was actually legal. Originally capped at 10,000 tons, the amount of cattle reassigned in Riazan rose in 1959 to 31,200 tons.[20]

The most dangerous form of deception and the one that involved the highest level of risk was the so-called nongoods transactions (*bestovarnye operatsii*).[21] Under existing rules, to spur production, regions were allowed to allocate half of their over-the-plan meat directly to the local population, normally through consumer cooperatives. In Riazan, however, most of this meat was not passed on to the population at all but resold by the cooperatives back to the kolkhozy and sovkhozy, who in turn resubmitted it to the procurement agencies as new meat, thus creating a potentially never-ending supply of recycled meat.[22] Nongoods transactions were especially worrying to the authorities because they entailed out-and-out fraud by a ring of officials within the state apparatus. To work effectively, the nongoods transactions required the active connivance of farms, procurement agencies, consumer cooperatives, trading organizations, retail outlets, and accounting offices, and they always involved the drawing up of fake receipts for nonexistent meat.[23] For these reasons, nongoods transactions were sometimes referred to as a type of "pure deception" (*priamoi obman*), and in official surveys of the various forms of cheating and statistical falsification they were invariably listed first.[24]

The RSFSR buro commission calculated that nongoods transactions in Riazan in 1959 accounted for 16,800 tons, but this figure is most likely an underestimate.[25] Bestovarnye operatsii were taken sufficiently seriously that an inquiry into their extent and distribution across the region was carried out. The districts with the highest levels are given in the accompanying table (see table 7.1).[26]

Closer examination reveals that these districts had one thing in common: their leaders constituted the spine of the regional political system. All were raikom first secretaries, had known Larionov for years, and had been cultivated and promoted by him, and all can be regarded as members of his ruling circle. Over the previous five years, Larionov had turned to N.N. Kabanov (Sasovo), P.A. Marfin (Spasskii), M.V. Tsyplakov (Shilovskii), V.N. Zigalenko (Riazan), and F.S. Ponomarev

Table 7.1. The five districts in Riazan province with the highest
volumes of nongoods transactions in 1959 (tons)

	Meat submitted toward the obligation for 1959	Part consisting of nongoods transactions
Sasovo District	10,090	2,129
Spasskii District	8,023	1,800
Shilovskii District	7,471	1,035
Riazan District	9,041	766
Skopinskii District	6,521	613

Source: RGANI f.13 op.1 d.793 l.14.

(Skopinskii) to win approval for new socialist obligations, to kick-start
agricultural campaigns, and to lead the drive for meat. All five occupied
the top seats, among district first secretaries, in the regional party hierarchy, and three, Kabanov, Zigalenko, and Ponomarev, were members
of the obkom buro.[27]

The structural importance of this group to Larionov and his agricultural campaigns was exemplified by the role of Kabanov. Before coming to Sasovo, he had been a longtime player in district-level politics,
having held prominent positions, first as head of the *raiispolkom* (the
executive committee of the local soviet) and then as first secretary in the
Zakharovskii district from 1943. With Larionov's approval, Kabanov
joined the obkom buro as a candidate member in 1952 and by the end
of the decade had become one of his most reliable allies. "Kabanov
was held up as a model raikom secretary," reflected the secretary of the
Riazan Knowledge Society, I.I. Aturin. "His method of work was widely
described in the press and presented as an example for others to follow."[28] Larionov also turned to Kabanov when he sought a local leader
who could reliably dissemble on behalf of the meat campaign. At an
obkom plenum in January 1960 Kabanov boasted that his Sasovo district had submitted 2,700 tons in 1958, had just totted up 10,293 tons
in 1959, and was now relishing the prospect of meeting its obligation
of "around 14,000 tons" in 1960. "No sooner has the tractor ploughed
a furrow," commented the head of the regional KGB, Oleinik, sarcasti-
cally, "than [Kabanov] claims he has finished the sowing."[29]

Larionov's relationships with the five raikom first secretaries varied, but all were characterized by high levels of mutual dependence.

In any district where nongoods transactions had become widespread, Larionov was reliant on the district first secretary to maintain each link in the long chain of district-level collusion together. The example of Ponomarev, who had been first secretary of the Skopinskii district since 1949, a year after Larionov's own appointment as obkom first secretary, is informative. On 8 April 1960 an instructor in the procurement office in the Skopinskii district, Aleksei Evtiukhin, wrote two letters, one to the Committee of Party Control and the other to Khrushchev himself, noting that at the beginning of the year he had observed a scenario relating to the meat campaign that was "directly out of Ostap Bender [the con man from Ilf's and Petrov's famous satirical novel *The Twelve Chairs*]." "Through the network of village general stores," Evtiukhin continued, "they have bought and sold [the meat], exchanged papers, given out assignments, the accountants have been off to the state bank and back, in short all is ready, the collective farms have fulfilled the plan, the village stores have registered a turnover of over a million rubles and profits of over 160,000, and all this has been done in a matter of three to four days. (All is fine apart from one small detail.) What about the meat? Where is the meat?"[30] Within five weeks Ponomarev had organized a crushing response to Evtiukhin. At a general meeting on 13 May at which he assembled forty-three participants, Ponomarev plied the thirteen speakers with confidential and disparaging information on Evtiukhin's past. One by one the speakers, including collective farm chairs and heads of local councils, proceeded to paint Evtiukhin as a drunkard and a moral degenerate. They all called for Evtiukhin's immediate expulsion from the party. Ponomarev also played a lead role in gathering over sixty signatures from local dignitaries denying Evtiukhin's claims and asserting that the man was a slanderer. In the face of all this pressure, Evtiukhin became frightened and backed down.[31]

In any district with a high volume of nongoods transactions there was a chance that the fraud might unravel given that the webs of deception were by their nature widely spread. In such districts Larionov depended on the first secretaries to hold the circles of collusion together. In the Skopinskii district Ponomarev was, in effect, the central coordination point of a Soviet-style *krugovaia poruka,* a circle of collective responsibility in which all members are held jointly accountable for the actions and obligations of the group. First, acting in his capacity as raikom first secretary, he provided the authority and cover to embolden the various actors in the bestovarnye operatsii. Then, when an insider defected, Ponomarev, as the district party leader with access to confidential information and to the party's organizational resources, marshaled the krugovaia poruka into a coordinated and effective character assassination.

Beyond this upper tier of five first secretaries there was a second layer of some dozen raikom secretaries whom Larionov sponsored and on whom he relied for his strategic objectives.[32] Between 1956 and 1960 there was a remarkably low level of turnover among the eighteen raikom secretaries who belonged to one or another of these two groups. Indeed, of the eighteen identified in 1956, fifteen were still in post in May 1960.[33] For all Larionov's bluster, he was surprisingly unwilling to get rid of this corpus of district first secretaries. Furthermore, despite the fear in which he was supposedly held by his subordinates, Larionov was reluctant to resort to applying the traditional weapons of party punishment—the reprimand or severe reprimand—against them. In January 1959 he proudly declared to Mylarschikov, the emissary sent by Khrushchev to elicit the original ill-fated socialist obligation, as well as to the whole obkom plenum, that in the previous five years not a single party functionary under him had been reprimanded.[34] Far from reprimanding or punishing them, Larionov rewarded a select group of district first secretaries by incorporating them into his obkom buro.[35] To the extent that he integrated these first secretaries into his power structures, regularly interacted with them, and was mutually dependent on them, we can regard them as members of his ruling coalition.

The relationships of lying, falsification, and deceit had formed over a number of years. "All this became possible," wrote the first secretary of the Riazan gorkom, N.M. Pakhomov, "due to the fact that over a long period, beginning in 1954, the regional party organization . . . has supported precisely those who have engaged in illegality and cheating."[36] The continuity of raikom first secretaries was significant because these officials were the chief conductors of the mobilization campaigns and those ultimately entrusted with holding the district networks of deception together. In this way, the involvement of so many people in the frauds and the key integrating role of the district committees were closely intertwined. From Moscow's perspective, however, the Riazan case represented a catastrophic failure of the agency relationship that the center had with one of its most trusted regional principals. It demonstrated how the whole party organization had, in effect, become a machine for the promulgation of falsification.

Larionov's public image was that of a classic substate dictator, one who made ample use of coercion in his bid to achieve procurement targets. When it came to the physical acquisition of meat, the overwhelming use of force—late night raids, house searches, the requisitioning of food stocks—just as in the 1930s, played a predominant role.[37] Statistical deception, however, tended to rest on other factors. While the threat of arrest or expulsion from the party may have played a role in getting a single individual to sign off on a false registration document, it was not enough to hold together the circle of officials needed for truly large-scale fraud. What oiled the gears of the fraud machine in Riazan was an extensive regional network consisting in the main of strong ties to raikom first secretaries. For all his threats and bluster, Larionov never sacked or punished a member of this circle; instead, he encouraged and promoted them, admitting them into his ruling coalition. In return, Larionov became increasingly dependent on members of this group to lie and fabricate on his behalf. The practices of mass deception observed in Riazan in 1959 hinged on relations of mutual dependence between Larionov and this subgroup of raikom secretaries. Their origins reaching back to the relatively innocent violations of the early milk campaigns, these relations deepened over time. Through incremental promotions, this group now constituted the main power artery of the regional political system, and it was through this artery that the most egregious forms of deception, the nongoods transactions, were pumped through to the localities. These ties were not only extensive but also strong, to the extent that they were built on mutual dependence and high levels of risk. This is not surprising: comparative work on fraud, embezzlement, and statistical deception shows that it tends to be most effective when carried out through teams based on tightly knit, trust-based relationships.[38]

OTHER SCANDALS

Even before Riazan, officials in Moscow had been well aware of irregularities in the regions, including double counting and the purchase of cattle and meat on secondary markets. Any substantive action to combat these activities, however, had been blocked by the first secretary. On 11 October, three weeks after Larionov's suicide, the Central Committee Presidium, at a session chaired by Frol Kozlov and held, notably, while Khrushchev was away, considered violations in the procurement of cattle in the RSFSR and Kazakhstan. On 1 November the RSFSR buro widened its remit with a resolution on data inflation in four Russian regions other than Riazan.[39] In subsequent months further inquiries revealed a picture of cheating and the manipulation of data in dozens of regions across the RSFSR and Ukraine as well as in Kazakhstan, Tajikistan, Uzbekistan, Azerbaijan, Armenia, Latvia, and Belorussia. Cases of fraud were uncovered in construction and in industry as well as across the agricultural spectrum with the massaging of figures on cotton, grain, maize, milk, poultry, and wool.[40]

When set against these other cases, Riazan was clearly unusual. Having been deployed by Khrushchev at plenums and congresses as a mouthpiece for his agricultural policies, Larionov had enjoyed a long, close, relationship with the Soviet leader.[41] In embarking on his most radical campaign Larionov had also benefited from assurances and special protection from Moscow. The slow gestation of widespread, systemic fraud in the region going back at least to the milk campaigns of the mid-1950s and possibly even to the late 1940s, may have all helped put Riazan in a category of its own.[42] In this regard Riazan does not fit easily into any of the regional categories used in this book.

However, a series of other investigations into regional abuses do help shine a light on the variety of network dynamics, and they do so in a way that is compatible with our broader regional typology. To the extent that these inquiries and the voluminous reports they yielded were necessarily focused on regions where scandals had occurred, they were self-selecting and cannot be held to reflect the development of networks across the whole range of Soviet regions. Yet picking up on two case studies discussed earlier in the book—one involving the archetypal sub-state dictator A.P. Pcheliakov and the other the transitional or adaptive leader Mikhail Stakhurskii—we get a glimpse of how these regional network-types fared in the face of acute pressure from above.

Pcheliakov, the first secretary in Kirov, was an unreconstructed sub-state dictator, one whose default position was to harass, intimidate, and sack subordinates (see chapter 5). In Kirov the pressures of the meat campaign were no less pronounced than those in Riazan, and Pcheliakov was, if anything, even more coercive than Larionov. In Kirov, however, the network surrounding Pcheliakov was narrower and more tentative than its counterpart in Riazan. Lacking such a network, officials in Kirov were far less inclined to engage in the high-risk types of fraud so prevalent in Riazan.

For much of 1959 Kirov was locked in a head-to-head battle with Riazan for the position of national meat-producing champion. Indeed, in the second quarter of 1959 Kirov, not Riazan, was awarded the prestigious Red Banner for agriculture by the RSFSR council of ministers. However, Kirov's declaration, on 20 October, that it had delivered 60 percent more meat than at the equivalent stage the previous year was no match for the dramatic news of the "second plan" from Riazan days earlier, and the Red Banner for the third quarter was duly presented to Riazan.[43] By the end of the year Kirov had notched 97,000 tons of meat, well below Riazan's vaunted 150,000 tons.[44]

Given the pressure put on by Pcheliakov and the apparent connivance of the center, many district leaders in Kirov undoubtedly massaged their production figures. An RSFSR buro resolution in early 1961 reported that no fewer than nineteen of the twenty-eight districts in Kirov had engaged in "padding, deception, and fraud" in 1960. Yet the spread of statistical falsification across Kirov would never rival the levels in Riazan. A Central Committee team concluded that thirty-one hundred tons of meat were submitted through reassignment at the end of 1959, ten times lower than the figure in Riazan. The statistic for *bestovarnye kvitantsii* (receipts for nongoods transactions), under one thousand tons, was even more modest and amounted to less than one-fifteenth the official estimate in Riazan.[45] Pcheliakov may deserve some sympathy for asserting, in the full glare of a hostile obkom audience in February 1961, that "with the exception of two to three cases of the issuing of nongoods receipts . . . there were no *pripiski* [instances of cheating], and there was no deception of the state in our region in 1959."[46]

There may be a number of explanations for the limited scope of fraud in Kirov, but perhaps the most cogent one is related to Pcheliakov's leadership style and to the narrow, asymmetric ruling network through which he governed the region. Unlike leaders such as Struev and Kozyr, Pcheliakov was a substate dictator in the old Stalinist mold. In the late 1950s this was reflected in three traits. First, Pcheliakov was inclined to dismiss officials, often en masse. As the first secretary of the Kirov gorkom, Moshchakov, put it to Pcheliakov: "Under your leadership five to seven members of the buro have been fired at any one time."[47] "Let's have a look at all the people who have tried to criticize Pcheliakov and see where they are now," suggested the head of the Red October collective farm Prozorov. "All gone! And among them, it must be owned, there were some pretty decent people."[48] But Pcheliakov took out his anger even more sharply on the raikom secretaries. In the late 1950s there was an especially high rate of turnover among district party leaders, and Pcheliakov made unstinting use of party punishments against them.[49]

Second, his working relationships with most officials was starkly confrontational. Among his obkom buro colleagues, Pcheliakov's bluntness was legendary. "You really know how to put a man down," the obkom secretary, Liamov, remarked.[50] Pcheliakov was known to interrupt raikom secretaries with dismissive, long-winded retorts, and those who chose to answer back were subjected to mini-inquisitions.[51] More generally, Pcheliakov's ties with those around him were imbued with suspicion and distrust. According to the second secretary, Shatalin, "Pcheliakov exudes distrust, he displays an excessive cautiousness and even suspiciousness toward certain members of the obkom buro, toward regional and district leaders."[52] A report from the Committee of Party Control to Khrushchev commented that "Pcheliakov sought to revive the illegal methods of 1937–1938" by ordering the head of the regional KGB to have "the phone conservations of an obkom secretary and of an executive official tapped and [that he] arrange that certain obkom officials be shadowed and secretly photographed."[53]

Third, Pcheliakov maintained an exceedingly narrow ruling network. At the obkom and in the raikoms he relied on a thin base of strategically located clients and agents to coordinate and supervise his military-style agricultural offensives. At the obkom the two key figures were the secretaries Zakhvataev and Bulatov, old-school Stalinist procurement agents who believed in achieving their goals through maximum pressure and force.[54] But it was at the raikom level that the contrast with Riazan was sharpest. Here, Pcheliakov's campaigns hinged on two secretaries, Brysov and Chemodanov. Yet, although both had been in the region for some years (Brysov had been raikom secretary since Pcheliakov's appointment in 1952), neither was promoted to the obkom buro or integrated into Pcheliakov's ruling network. In this respect, one of Pcheliakov's main lines of defense had, again, a ring of truth to it: "I had no 'sons' and 'stepsons.' The last nine years have shown that. I had no special ties with anyone, there were no family ties, really there was nothing of the sort [*net nikakoi semeistvennosti, nichego net*]."[55]

Despite the heavy pressure on officials at all levels in Kirov to meet extraordinary targets for meat production, they were less willing than their counterparts in Riazan to take the risk of resorting to statistical deception. For any act of statistical distortion to stand a serious chance of succeeding, it required the complicity of a large circle of people fulfilling complementary but interconnected functions. Fraud and deception on the scale witnessed in Riazan depended on a belief among its instigators that they could count on others in their circle to cover up for them. Such belief was unlikely to exist unless it rested on relationships built up over time that involved some level of trust. Yet through his actions, which included the bullying, sacking, and expulsion of officials, Pcheliakov in effect cut off such trust-based relationships at their root. While getting rid of opponents and expelling them from the region may have helped him maximize his short-term goals, they did little to broaden the network of officials who might take the risk of lying, fabricating, and distorting on behalf of the regional drive for meat.

Stakhurskii was quite a different kind of leader from Pcheliakov. Like any up-and-coming obkom secretary, Stakhurskii had adhered to the two principal tenets of success, first, meeting his plan targets and, second, fostering strong ties to his superiors—who in his case were in Kiev—during his first two major postings, in Vinnitsa and Poltava (see chapters 1 and 2). Yet unlike Pcheliakov he had taken great care to mollify his aktiv and to forge tactical alliances with members of the regional elite, thereby averting electoral rebellions and avoiding insider defections. This strategy had put Stakhurskii in good stead with the center. In 1955 Stakhurskii was transferred from Poltava to Khabarovsk, and two years later he was appointed first secretary in Zhitomir, in central-western Ukraine, between his former territory of Vinnitsa to the south and Belorussia to the north. It was as first secretary in Zhitomir that Stakhurskii was confronted with Khrushchev's latest campaign.

Toward the end of 1958 Zhitomir was singled out by Khrushchev as a laggard province, one that had fallen behind neighboring regions in the race with the USA in meat production. By comparison with

First Secretary Mikhail
Stakhurskii of the Zhitomir
obkom in 1958. Courtesy
of Russian State Archive of
Photographic and Cinematic
Documents in Krasnogorsk.

Vinnitsa, the Ukrainian front-runner whose meat yield from the public
sector had doubled from 1953 to 1957, Zhitomir's had grown by a
paltry 7 percent, making it the worst-performing region in the republic.[56] Notwithstanding Stakhurskii's earlier resolve to reach compromises with his aktiv, in response to such pressure he quickly fell in line.
At the beginning of 1959 and again in 1960 Stakhurskii signed up to
what were clearly unfeasible targets and began to apply pressure on his
subordinates. According to one insider, "Stakhurskii proceeded to give
strict instructions that in the bid for more meat only those who have
fulfilled their obligations be encouraged while those who have failed
should be branded (that's the word, branded [tak i skazano: kleimit']) a
disgrace." The gap between what Khrushchev demanded of the region
and what it could produce was so great that Stakhurskii began to look
for shortcuts. In a series of private communications he aligned himself
ever more closely with practices of tinkering, cheating, and statistical
distortion. Thus, for example, in response to a clearly unfeasible injunc-
tion to double the number of sows in the region in a year, he reportedly
insisted that "it's of no concern to me how you do it, just make sure

we get those sows." Under Stakhurskii, falsification was not restricted to data on meat. Even though later checks would reveal that the grain campaign for 1959 had fallen short, Stakhurskii announced that not only had they been met but also that the quotas in the region had been fulfilled ahead of time; and in November 1960 he heaped praise on the Emilchinskii district for its reportedly phenomenal maize harvest, whose results, it turned out, were also fabricated.[57]

To implement these frauds Stakhurskii relied on three individuals, the agriculture secretary, Shapran, the chair of the regional executive committee, Kremenitskii, and the deputy chair of the committee, Oberemko. At obkom seminars the three men reputedly guided functionaries on which bazaars to buy meat from and authorized buying trips to Moldavia and Belorussia. But they went further than this, involving themselves in nongoods transactions as well. On 29–30 December 1959 they ordered local functionaries to fulfill the plan "at any price." When told it was not clear where such cattle could be bought, their response was simple: "That's not our problem, get them wherever you can, you have your opportunities, it's just a matter of knowing how to use them." As the Central Committee's correspondent put it, this retort was a "direct cue to cheat."[58]

The methods used in 1959 drew on a repertoire from the Stalin era. Those who refused to buy up cattle for the plan were labeled criminals and disruptors of the state plan. When a local official balked at inputting unconfirmed data, Shapran reportedly shouted, "You are just hoarding the harvest in order to engage in swindling and theft—that is a kulak tendency." And when, in the last two months of 1959, local collective farm chairs agonized over whether they could fulfill the plan for meat, the demands became more shrill and were accompanied by threats from the obkom that, unless they complied, they would lose their jobs and be expelled from the party.[59]

Under acute pressure from above, Stakhurskii quickly reverted to subdictatorial type. The demands made by Khrushchev were so stark and unrelenting that worries about local rebellions or insider complaints quickly receded from view. Unlike Riazan or Kirov, Zhitomir was not competing for any prizes, so the targets were, in general, not quite as outlandish. Even here, however, relying on force was not enough. From the end of 1958, as the campaign got under way, Stakhurskii must have understood that the only way of reaching his improbable targets was through fraud.

The danger of applying extreme pressure, as Stakhurskii had first understood back in the late 1940s, was that it was likely to trigger defections. Albeit in different ways, this is exactly what happened to both Pcheliakov and Stakhurskii, and it was to prove their undoing. In 1960 the Central Committee received 5,281 complaints from Kirov, a large number of which concerned Pcheliakov's leadership. "Hundreds of letters on your unsuitable [*negodnyi*] style [of leadership] have come to the Central Committee," M.T. Efremov, the deputy head of the party organs department in Moscow, reported back to Pcheliakov. "Workers and communists are showing their distrust in you."[60] Pcheliakov's fate was sealed with a brief attack by Khrushchev at the January 1961 Central Committee plenum and by a *Pravda* editorial on 30 January. He was sacked two weeks later on 12 February. In Stakhurskii's case there does not seem to have been a similar torrent of complaints. Instead, a well-informed anonymous letter, almost certainly from a highly placed disaffected insider, triggered a formal Committee of Party Control investigation that confirmed most of the letter's claims.[61] One day after Pcheliakov's dismissal Stakhurskii was fired, ending his career as obkom leader, which had spanned fifteen years and four regions. The manner in which he was removed underlined the benefits of his original strategy in the late 1940s, which had hinged on finding ways of conciliating the aktiv and incorporating members of the region's ruling elite. The danger of the maximalist position to which he had now sunk was that, when the center changed course, as it did toward the end of 1960, he was left woefully exposed.

To the extent that we are reliant on detailed Central Committee investigations into these scandals, investigations that were by their nature selective, we are unable to say how typical the network dynamics they revealed were. We do know, however, that data falsification was a general feature of the Soviet economy and had been at least since the 1930s. To protect their enterprises and their collective farms, directors and their bookkeepers had long known the benefits of creative accounting to show that they had achieved their plan. With Khrushchev's madcap drive to push up production beyond ordinary limits, the incentives to massage these figures increased. Examination of one continuous run of data over a twenty-year period by Mark Harrison suggests that "in the second half of the 1950s the number, complexity, and value of frauds grew rapidly."[62]

Our case studies suggest an additional pattern. Where significant cheating occurred, the obkom first secretary was the prime mover. Normally he relied on an alliance that included an obkom secretary and a select group of raikom secretaries. Achieving targets involved the physical appropriation of goods on one plane and fraud on the other. While the former relied on force, the latter depended on other factors. The most radical forms of deception—the bestovarnye operatsii—tended to rely on the ability of the regional leadership to draw district leaders and other key figures, from auditors, bookkeepers, and state statisticians to journalists and procurators, into a wider trust network, one which, from the perspective of the center, was viewed as an insidious breakdown of central control.

KHRUSHCHEV'S PURGE

Ahead of the January 1961 Central Committee plenum on 5 January Khrushchev circulated his "theses" in which, on the basis of the now-completed Central Committee inquiry, he offered his analysis of the Riazan and other recent data-fixing scandals. Although Khrushchev followed two separate lines of attack, what they had in common was that in both the blame was now attached squarely to regional party officials. First, Khrushchev berated regional leaders for pushing unfeasible targets. In Tula only 49,000 tons, or 38 percent, of the socialist obligation for state and collective farms had been fulfilled; in Kirov the figure was not much higher, at 75,000 tons, or 65 percent. In an act of breathtaking duplicity Khrushchev proceeded to blame regional party officials in Riazan for "imposing" a target of 150,000 tons when local farmers had ostensibly pressed for a more reasonable and sustainable one of 75,000–80,000 tons. Khrushchev was aware of the damage these shortfalls had done to the reputation of the party. At the plenum itself, twelve days later, he warned: "If we take up obligations so easily but don't implement them, who will believe us? Are we a party of chatterboxes? Such a party will not be respected."[63]

In addition to dreaming up inflated and unfeasible targets Khrushchev now directly blamed regional party officials for coordinating the machinery of deception. Khrushchev offered the following examples.

In the Tian' Shan'skii obkom in Kyrgizia the central authorities had allocated ten tons of butter to support workers at the local coal mine. However, with the support of the obkom secretary, Isaev, this butter was recycled and submitted as part of the region's socialist obligation for milk. Although he was given a ticking off and a party reprimand in March, the incident did Isaev little harm and may even have improved his prospects, for, as Khrushchev noted sourly, the following September Isaev was promoted as the republican minister of internal affairs. In Poltava, with the connivance of the obkom secretary, the chair of the Lenin collective farm, S.K. Baiko, had used a state credit of 622,000 rubles and 376,000 rubles of the farm's own money to buy 622 head of cattle. Emissaries from the farm had roamed neighboring collective farms and the markets of Poltava handing over thick wads of cash in amounts varying from 10,000 to 30,000 rubles in exchange for cattle. The obkom not only colluded in these offenses but had nominated Baiko for the title of Hero of Socialist Labor and deputy of the Supreme Soviet. "How could the leadership of Poltava have presented this guy for an award?" Khrushchev asked. "These are not political organizers but cattle traders. We need to wage a decisive battle against such people who have a party card but who bring nothing but shame to our party." For his complicity in the affair, the obkom first secretary, Nikolai Rozhanchuk, was sacked at the beginning of February. The language used and punishments proposed by Khrushchev in his theses were almost Stalinist in tone: "What can we say about these leaders, many of whom call themselves communists? These people are enemies of the socialist state. . . . That is why we need to banish these people, to expel them from the party."[64]

The Central Committee investigations of the autumn of 1960 had laid bare three problems with the agricultural campaigns of the previous year. First, they had involved cases of coercion and serious physical abuse. In a throwback to the 1930s, food was being expropriated from farmers by violence and intimidation. Some Stalin-era first secretaries, many of whom had taken up senior positions in the party hierarchy during the war or in the late 1940s, probably had few compunctions about using violence or turning a blind eye to subordinates who used violence to fulfil the plan. In Tajikistan cattle and meat were simply taken by force. Brigades of collectors requisitioned chickens, eggs, wool, and meat without payment and often under extreme duress.[65] In the Pavlodar region in Kazakhstan a Central Committee report noted that "obkom functionaries . . . in pressing subordinates toward deception . . . dangle the threat of sackings and of expulsion from the party." In one case noted in the report, a raikom first secretary threatened a sovkhoz director with expulsion from the party if he did not sign off on a nongoods transaction of four thousand tons of grain. In another, a control official was hauled into the police station at three o'clock in the morning and ordered to authorize a fake receipt.[66] Some of the most startling incidents of the use of force for the physical acquisition of cattle meat took place in Riazan. "The districts were obliged to hand over [the cattle], everything was done by means of threats and fear," recalled the first secretary of the Skopinskii raikom, F.S. Ponomarev. "From 7 until 22 December [1959] we had one long St. Bartholomew's night [massacre], [Larionov's meat commission, headed by the obkom agriculture secretary, V.P. Zenin] would phone at four or six in the morning and tell us to give them more meat." "This band did everything to ensure the plan was fulfilled," recounted the obkom secretary, I.V. Gusev. "They would call the raikom secretaries at eleven o'clock at night and demand that they deliver six hundred tons of meat by nine the following morning." "The meat commission," confessed one of its members, Shval'b, "was really just a screen. We would arrive at seven in the morning and stay on until nightfall. If any of the raikom secretaries began to pose problems, there would be pressure."[67]

Second, the campaigns had scrambled incentives. The classic model for achieving an economic breakthrough consisted of three elements. The leader laid down a taut and hyper-ambitious target; a select group of shock workers demonstrated that this target could be met; and the party apparatus mobilized the rest of the workforce to "do as the shock workers do." However, because Khrushchev was pushing for targets that were clearly beyond reach, he merely rewarded those who lied best. By contrast, the impact on honest workers could be devastating. One example comes from Stakhurskii's region of Zhitomir, where, in 1959, the most productive milkmaids in the region had yields of eighteen hundred to two thousand liters per cow. For the following year a wildly unrealistic socialist obligation of four to five thousand liters was agreed to. But when the same milkmaids were able to produce only nineteen hundred to twenty-two hundred liters per cow they were branded as laggards and publicly humiliated. Some of the most valued members of the rural force lost their motivation, and many decided to abandon their vocation, depriving the regional dairy sector of some of its most skilled and highly rated workers. Stakhurskii's determination to meet his own plan targets came at the cost of deincentivizing his subordinates: "Any normal person will get satisfaction from his ability to achieve a target. But with us that feeling is reserved for the obkom secretary, Stakhurskii . . . while those on the front line, in the districts and collective farms, have only the bitter taste of failure in our mouths."[68]

The third and biggest problem, and the one Khrushchev dwelled on in his January theses and in his speech to the Central Committee, was that the frauds had been perpetrated by the political vanguard in every region. Only the obkoms and, in the districts, the raikoms had the breadth of contacts, the organizational resources, and, ironically, the political prestige to pull them off. It was this realization that triggered the sweeping purge of regional party leaders in 1961. Obkom first secretaries who "refused to break out of the vicious circle of their own ideas" were indeed the main target of Khrushchev's speech at the January 1961 Central Committee plenum. In addition to Riazan and Kirov, in the Russian Federation alone there followed a housecleaning of obkom leaders in Briansk, Tula, Tiumen', Smolensk, Astrakhan, Sakhalin, Tataria, Saratov, Kalinin, Kaliningrad, Omsk, Vologda, U'lianovsk, and Iaroslavl'.[69]

Not all of the charges against these leaders centered on data fixing. Most often there was a mix, albeit one in which data falsification played a prominent role. In Tiumen' the Committee of Party Control found that the first secretary, V.V. Kosov, had organized the arrest and imprisonment of an ordinary citizen over a traffic row and lavishly overspent on the refurbishment of a railway carriage. Nevertheless, the bulk of the charges against him related to data padding in industry, in cattle procurement, and in grain production. Tiumen' is a good example of how the obkom was used to provide cover for data fixing. When the regional procurator, Ponomarev, got wind of reassignments and the double counting of grain, he was scolded severely by Kosov and told that "he had violated the norms of party life." Similarly, when the head of the statistical administration protested over data irregularities he was informed by the obkom that "unless he retracts his letter, he would not only lose his job, but he won't be able to get work elsewhere in the region, as without the agreement of the obkom no employer would take him on." Kosov was removed on 23 May 1961.[70]

In other regions the obkom managed to pass the blame onto the raikoms. In Rostov the newly appointed first secretary, A.V. Baskov, pinned the blame for a nongoods transaction and fake receipts for ninety tons of meat on a local raikom leader who, along with the second secretary and the director of the state farm, had "created a krugovaia poruka." The three were sacked and expelled from the party, and "severe party punishments" were imposed on an unspecified number of other officials.[71]

In some cases the manipulation of statistics created room for outright theft and self-enrichment. One of the best examples comes from Tajikistan. Here, the role of the republican first secretary was to regulate the number of nongoods transactions and fake receipts by setting rates of statistical distortion that were high enough to allow for personal enrichment but low enough to deflect the attention of the center. To this end, according to one well-placed official, the first secretary, Ul'dzhabaev, had set out a tariff of optimal levels of data falsification for each district.[72] On 29 April Ul'dzhabaev was dismissed for "deceiving the party and the state, and for the organization of mass cheating in cotton procurements," for which he was also expelled from the party.[73]

The purge in the lead-up to the XXII Party Congress in October 1961 was the largest single clearing out of first secretaries since the Great Purges of 1937–38, and the manner in which it was achieved tells us much about how the purpose and meaning of the party purge had changed in the meantime. The purge of regional first secretaries in the late 1930s had been a *political* purge designed to root out powerful provincial leaders whose loyalty in the event of a crisis, especially one sparked by a war, Stalin was unsure of. The purge of 1960–61 was an *administrative* purge. In initiating it, Khrushchev was questioning not the loyalty of regional functionaries, either to him or to the Soviet system, but their capacity to achieve an economic breakthrough. He was alerted to this problem by the data-fixing scandals which highlighted what was, with respect to these leaders, a breakdown in the dictator's relationship with his principal agents in the provinces.

This difference was reflected in how the purge was carried out. The early signs of the purge looked ominous. To oversee it Khrushchev appointed G.I. Voronov, himself a former obkom first secretary from

The run-up to the XXII Party Congress in October 1961 was a time for study and propaganda as well as for purges. Here, an obkom secretary in Kemerovo oblast, Z.V. Kuz'mina, is leading a study group on the new Party Program with workers from the West Siberian Metallurgical Plant. *Source:* RGASPI.

Chita and Orenburg whom Tatu characterized as a "fanatical 'purger.'"[74] Shortly thereafter the journal *Kommunist* criticized in veiled form "the leaders of the Tula, Kirov and Riazan provinces. . . . These people are not political organizers but careerists, people who have wormed their way into the party; they bring shame to the party and must be expelled from the party and turned over to the law."[75]

First Secretary P.A. Leonov of the Sakhalin obkom discusses the new Party Program with fishermen from the *Ost* trawler in 1961. *Source:* RGASPI.

At a regional celebration on 6 July 1963 the first female cosmonaut and Hero of the Soviet Union, V.V. Tereshkova, is greeted by well-wishers at a parade in her home province of Iaroslavl'. To the left of Tereshkova is the first secretary of the obkom, F.I. Loshchenkov, and to the right, by her raised hand, the chair of the regional executive committee, V.F. Toropov. *Source:* RGASPI.

In practice, however, the purge was quite clearly circumscribed. One of its most striking features was that, despite all the talk of "antistate deception" and of the culprits having "followed a criminal path," the punishments were surprisingly mild. In Riazan although five leading officials were expelled from the party and a number received reprimands, none were prosecuted.[76] Elsewhere, expulsions from the party were few and far between, and prosecutions were even rarer.[77] In fact, despite a sweeping campaign against fraud, embezzlement, and statistical deception in the spring of 1961, which saw the criminalization of data fixing in May, the number of prosecutions was modest and left the prime movers behind the scandals of 1960, the party secretaries, almost completely unscathed.[78] The leniency of the punishments reflected the delicate balancing act that the center had to perform in limiting the fallout from the Riazan scandal. The culprits were usually so deeply embedded in their regional political networks that fully rooting them out would have required a mass purge, something the leadership was no longer willing to countenance. In any case, as the Riazan example made clear, regional leaders were only trying to achieve what they believed the center, and Khrushchev in particular, wanted them to do.

The Soviet system now had the institutional tools, developed since the war, to dispose of senior officials—even, as in this case, in a mass action—without invoking political charges or involving the agencies of repression. This aspect of the purge is reflected in figure 7.9, which shows the numbers of obkom first secretaries who were fired, according to the types of punishment they received. An overwhelming majority of those fired were removed under the neutral formulation of incompetence and failures of leadership, which, building on the precedent of the late Stalin era, Khrushchev had elaborated in 1954. Even more strikingly, a number of regional leaders such as Stakhurskii in Zhitomir and Khvorostukhin in Tula lost their positions under formulations that had no clear negative associations at all.[79]

At the XXII Congress in October 1961 Khrushchev, in a conciliatory gesture, remarked on the first secretaries who had lost their posts in the run-up to the congress:

> It is no secret that we have comrades who in their time were properly valued and were elected to leading positions which some of them have now filled for decades [*v techenie tselykh desiatiletii*]. In that time some of them have lost their creative edge, their ability to come up with new approaches, and have become a block to progress. . . . But the fact that these people have not been reelected does not give us grounds to turn against them. Where a communist has worked well for his allotted term—he must command our honor and respect [*chest' emu i slava*] [applause].[80]

Khrushchev's speech also highlighted one other aspect of the purge. One key difference from the turnover of cadres in 1953–54 was that this was not a rotation per se, as it had been for many first secretaries then. This time around it had a different flavor. As in 1954, many of those targeted hailed from the post-1938 generation of obkom secretaries. But for a number of leaders—including the outgoing first secretary

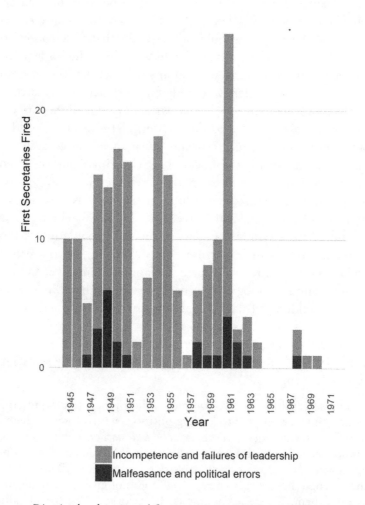

Figure 7.9. Dismissals of territorial first secretaries, USSR, 1945–71. The term "territorial first secretaries" refers to first secretaries of obkoms, kraikoms, and union and autonomous republics. The graph is based on complete data, with the exception of 1952, which is based on data from the RSFSR, Ukraine, Georgia, and Moldavia. For coding rules, see appendix H. *Sources:* Resolutions of the Politburo, Presidium, and Secretariat of the Central Committee, RGANI and RGASPI; RGANI f.5 op.29 d.15 ll.62–63

from Smolensk, P.I. Doronin, who had served as first secretary in Kursk from 1938 to 1948; the first secretary from Sakhalin, P.F. Chepliakov, who had served as second secretary in Azerbaijan from 1938 to 1944 and as first secretary in Groznii from 1944 to 1949; the obkom leader in Tula, A.I. Khvorostukhin, who had earlier been second and then first secretary in Irkutsk from 1944 to 1955; S.M. Butuzov from Penza, who had served as first and then second secretary in Krasnoiarsk from 1947 to 1952; and for Mikhail Stakhurskii, who had served with distinction as first secretary in no fewer than four regions—this was to be the end of the road.

The Riazan scandal and its aftereffects did enormous damage to Khrushchev's reputation. Earlier studies of this period have tended to view the U-2 Affair of May and June 1960 as a turning point in Khrushchev's administration, to the extent that it signaled the failure of Khrushchev's attempts to woo the West.[81] Nineteen sixty would prove problematic to Khrushchev in other respects. That year saw one of the worst harvests on record for Soviet agriculture.[82] It also saw, on 18 June, one of the most visible signs of the gradual collapse of the sovnarkhoz system: the establishment of republican-level sovnarkhozy in the RSFSR, Ukraine, and Kazakhstan replaced the regional level sovnarkhozy that had existed until then.[83] But more than these factors it was the Riazan Affair that would inflict lasting damage on Khrushchev's credentials. It delivered a death blow to the idea that a dictator in Moscow could bring about a great leap forward with the aid of substate dictators in the regions; yet, more than that, it showed that Khrushchev's most vaunted achievements were in fact based on a tissue of lies. The taint on Khrushchev's image would linger for years. When he was deposed in October 1964, one of the common refrains against him—one that figured far more prominently than the U-2 Affair or the failure of any particular harvest—was the Riazan scandal. It was mentioned several times at the plenum that sanctioned Khrushchev's departure and appeared at the very first Presidium meeting following his exit, in Brezhnev's notes.[84] As Brezhnev put it, rather pithily: "Riazan. Two–three plans. What a disgrace."[85]

8 Administrative Revolution

THE RIAZAN AFFAIR and the purge of regional leaders that followed may have signaled an end to the classic Stalinist model of great leaps forward, but it did not bring to a close Khrushchev's faith in organizational panaceas. In November 1962 Khrushchev launched his most radical but also most puzzling and least understood organizational reform. His proposal to cleave the regional party-state in two was far-reaching, for it entailed not only dividing the obkoms, the obkom buros, and the obkom bureaucracies but also having two obkom first secretaries in each region, one for agriculture and the other for industry. While this was by no means Khrushchev's first organizational experiment, each of his earlier administrative innovations had been predicated on the regional party organization as the main agent of change. What made this reform different was that it struck at the nerve center of the regional power network, the regional party apparatus. Even the purge of regional party leaders a year earlier, while it swept away regional potentates, often shaking up their clients and supporters in the process, did not, as this reform proposed to do, touch the institutional foundations of their power.

While those around him greeted Khrushchev's proposals with the customary enthusiasm and acclaim, within the bowels of the party-state bureaucracy there was considerable unease. Some traditional communists worried that by splitting the party into agricultural and industrial halves the party was surrendering its traditional role as a force for broader political and ideological leadership. Others were concerned that the division of the party might threaten the alliance of workers and peasants on which the Bolshevik state was founded or even herald the emergence of a two-party system.[1] Judging by Khrushchev's statements, however, including those he made in the relative seclusion of the Central Committee Presidium, nothing could have been further from the truth. Khrushchev remained a profoundly ideological leader, and in the realm of institutions this meant placing his faith in the party. As he would proclaim on the eve of the reform, "If the capitalists have the constant pursuit of profit followed by destruction and ruin, our bureaucrat need not worry about such things, because his position is secure. With us it is the party that [drives things forward]. . . . [H]ere we have administrative intervention, and who does the intervening? The party. It is not the [economic] apparatus but the party that needs to strengthen its control."[2] The division of the party apparatus did not mean that Khrushchev had lost his belief in the party. Instead, it was his final and in some ways most desperate response to the crisis in regional leadership that had been unleashed by the Riazan Affair and other scandals over the previous two years. Khrushchev was not interested in diminishing the role of the party, but he did want to find some way of containing his overly powerful regional leaders. A year earlier he had tried a purge, but all of the leadership, Khrushchev included, recognized that a "permanent purge" would only have lowered morale and depleted the stock of experienced cadres. The division of the party apparatus was his ham-fisted attempt to achieve the same goal through alternative institutional means, by using competing regional party organizations as a check on overly powerful regional leaders and their networks.[3]

As much as reining in his regional secretaries was an important goal for Khrushchev, it is unlikely it was the only goal of what turned out to be a many-sided reform.[4] Khrushchev's exact intentions, however, are secondary to our purpose here, which is to trace the effects of the reforms on regional leaders and their networks and to see what they can reveal about the nature of their power. On the ground the bifurcation of the party apparatus often had the effect of prizing open regional networks, as local politicians were forced to make choices about which alliances they should prioritize, which new regional bureaucracy they should join, and how they should best signal their continuing loyalty to powerful patrons in the context of mass organizational change. The institutional reforms of 1962 were to be a genuine test of the cohesiveness and resilience of the regional networks that had formed in the 1940s. What we find is that institutional changes ran up against and were often repelled by powerful informal status hierarchies that were able to quickly reconstitute themselves, even in a new organizational setting. Reforms that appear to have been about organization were in fact about society. At the same time, the rise of new centers of power at the regional level compelled regional leaders to further refine the skills of compromise, mutual accommodation, and negotiation they had acquired over the previous decade.

ORIGINS OF THE REFORM

The idea of dividing the entire party apparatus into agricultural and industrial branches seems to have formed in Khrushchev's mind while he was on holiday in Crimea in August 1962.[5] On his return to Moscow he tabled a motion to the Presidium on 20 August that "an expanded plenum of the Central Committee on industry be convened in November or early December."[6] On 10 September he elaborated his ideas in a paper which argued, with some logic, that a single party committee was often unable to run both agriculture and industry with equal interest and enthusiasm; and that the traditional tendency of party organizations to favor their agricultural duties had come at the expense of their management of industry.[7] With his typical impetuousness Khrushchev in effect decided the issue on 20 September, when, at a meeting of the Presidium and without waiting for the Central Committee plenum, he instructed regional leaders to discuss the division of the party apparatus and to present their thoughts on the matter to Moscow.[8] The reorganization was formally launched at the November plenum, with its final shape outlined in a Presidium resolution of 20 December.[9]

The overriding theme of Khrushchev's pronouncements in the lead-up to the reform was that the obkoms needed to rebalance their activities toward industry. The idea that in focusing its attention and resources on agriculture the party tended to lose sight of what was going on in industry was a concern that had plagued party leaders for over a generation. As Khrushchev would have been aware, it had assumed particular prominence on the eve of the war, in February 1941, at a time when the need to build up the USSR's military and industrial potential had been pressing. The answer then had been to set up specialized territorial branch secretaries to take responsibility for those fields of industry, transportation, and construction that were especially well represented in any given region.[10] Khrushchev now felt that he wanted not only to return to the spirit of that reform but also to take it to its logical conclusion by dividing the entire apparatus on the branch principle. To justify the move, Khrushchev pointed out that, although in terms of its output, value, and strategic importance industrial production now far outweighed the agricultural sector, the time and energy of most party organizations were still swallowed up by agriculture.[11] To underline this point, Khrushchev noted at the November plenum that only 14 of the 215 questions discussed in 1962 at obkom plenums in the 25 largest industrial regions in the RSFSR had dealt with industry.[12] In a faint allusion to the Riazan fiasco, Khrushchev also warned of the danger of "storming" and cautioned the party to "lead evenly, not in sudden bursts or jolts [rovno, ne ryvkami], without pouring all of our energies in a campaign, first throwing all of our efforts into one sphere, only then to quickly shift it to another."[13]

Industry dominated his speeches, but in the summer and autumn of 1962 the subject of agriculture and food supplies would not have been far from his mind. Despite a major surge in investment in the early 1950s, an already creaking, inefficient kolkhoz sector had been further undone by Khrushchev's ill-conceived experiments. By the early 1960s the effects of Khrushchev's liquidation of the machine-tractor stations and the transfer of equipment and technology to collective farms that were ill-suited to make proper use of them, his reckless striving for unfeasible records in livestock rearing and his assault on individual plots, which undercut one of the most valuable sources of agricultural produce, had begun to affect the country's food supplies. An exhaustive survey by the central statistical agency of the average food consumption of workers, engineers, and white-collar workers in some of the largest industrial regions across the USSR showed that the average diet of employees in 1961 consisted overwhelmingly of bread and potatoes.[14] Discontent flared into open protest in June 1962, when the government announced a hike of 30 percent in the retail price of meat and meat products and of 25 percent for butter.[15] In various parts of the country anti-Soviet leaflets and graffiti denouncing the government and calling for strike action began to appear.[16] The worst protests erupted in Novocherkassk, where, on 1–3 June, a wave of strikes and demonstrations spilled over into violence as workers stormed key administrative buildings. The government responded by sending in armed troops, who shot and killed twenty-three demonstrators, wounded dozens, and rounded up the ringleaders. On Khrushchev's orders two of his closest associates, A.I. Mikoian and F.R. Kozlov, were sent to the city to help quell the disturbances, and the matter was brought up for lengthy discussion at the Presidium.[17] Although the declared aim of the reform of the regional party apparatus in November 1962 was to accentuate the need to manage industry, the requirement to do something about agriculture was a close second.

Despite the intended goal of the reform—achieving greater parity and focus in the party's management of the economy—it had inescapable effects on the power of regional party leaders and their networks. Depending on the economic and demographic profile of the region, the obkom secretary might be deprived of up to half of the territory, population, and economic activity that had previously been under his authority. The reform cut off the source of his power in other respects as well. Given that with a few small exceptions the whole obkom apparatus—including the all-important department of party organs, which controlled the assignment of personnel—was now divided, the obkom secretary's powers of patronage were also seriously curtailed. And the erosion of the first secretary's source of power did not stop there. As grandiose as the division of the party apparatus was, it was not the only major administrative reform implemented in the autumn of 1962.[18] Closely tied in to the new reforms was a major overhaul of the system of party control, which was converted into a nationwide Commission of Party-State Control under Aleksandr Shelepin. The new commission replaced the old committees of party control that had overseen the disciplining and punishing of party officials. One feature of the new system was that each divided obkom would have, as one of four secretaries, a secretary who would double as chair of the regional commission of party-state control.[19] The overall effect of these reforms was to limit the incumbent obkom first secretary's control of two traditional sources of power, namely, exclusion and kompromat. The first secretary no longer had sole control over the bureaucracies that controlled patronage, the collection of information, and the application of party punishment, but, in addition, he could no longer resort to exclusion as easily as before, as now there was, in theory at least, another source of power in the region to whom an excluded official could turn.

Another institutional change blunted the power of the obkom first secretary. The Riazan scandal had sparked an interest in the issue of deception and fraud in the party and state apparatus, leading, as we saw in chapter 7, to a campaign in the spring of 1961. A string of major scams in 1961 in Kirgizia, Uzbekistan, Kursk, L'vov, and Orel embracing in each case up to fifty or sixty senior officials awakened the regime to the related but distinct problem of bribery and corruption in public administration. A closed letter from the Central Committee of 29 March 1962 reported that senior officials, many of whom were members of the party, had fallen in league with "large-scale plunderers, operators [temnye del'tsy], and swindlers." The culprits had used a range of methods, starting with presents and gifts, carousing, drinking bouts, and gambling, to "envelop and break down senior officials, turning them into coconspirators in their criminal actions."[20] Special attention was paid to the fact that some party committees had "failed to react to signals" and, even worse, had "actively shielded communists and taken them under their wing." The letter stated that active participation by communists or their collusion in acts of theft and plunder, along with "a liberal attitude toward such acts," would be viewed as a "serious crime against the party and the state" that was liable to "expulsion from the party and prosecution."[21] The eventual outcome of this campaign was a Presidium resolution, published on 20 December 1962, the same day the arrangements for the division of the party were finalized, that reversed the long-standing practice going back to 1938 whereby investigating agencies had to seek preliminary permission from the relevant party committee before arresting or starting a criminal case against a communist.[22] Originally introduced as a device to protect communists from "unfounded arrests and prosecutions" of the kind that had proliferated in the Great Terror, the practice had become, as we saw in chapter 3, a means by which senior party officials became, in effect, gatekeepers of the criminal justice system, the first line of defense who could shield powerful communists from prosecution. As well as signaling that Moscow had become impatient with the various

Table 8.1. Obkom and kraikom apparats divided as a result of the November 1962 party reforms

Union Republic	Total number of obkoms and kraikoms	Divided apparats	Unaffected apparats	Proportion of divided apparats (percent)
RSFSR	76[a]	42	34	55.3
Ukraine	25	19	6	76
Belorussia	6	6	—	100
Uzbekistan	8	4	4	50
Kazakhstan	18	14[3][b]	4	77.8
Kirgizia	1	1	—	100
Tajikistan	1[c]	—	1	—
Georgia	3[d]	—	3	—
Azerbaijan	2[e]	—	2	—
Total	140	86[75][b]	54	61.4

Source: Regional'naia (2009: 487–93).

[a] Includes five autonomous oblasts whose apparatus was not divided.
[b] In most territories where the apparat was divided there were two first secretaries. However, in eleven of the Kazakh oblasts—all under krai subordination—there was only one first secretary even though the apparat was technically divided. These oblasts formed agricultural obkoms; their industrial bureaucracies were placed under the authority of a specially created krai buro for industry and construction.
[c] Gorno-Bakhadshanskaia autonomous oblast.
[d] Abkhaz and Adzharskii autonomous republics and the South Ossetian autonomous oblast.
[e] Nakhichevan autonomous republic and the Nagorno-Karabakh autonomous oblast.

exemptions and status privileges that had been extended to powerful party functionaries, the new rule stripped back one more power of obkom leaders to exercise leverage over party members.

Khrushchev invested his full authority in the campaign, overriding resistance from powerful regional party organizations.[23] Despite this show of resolve, however, the final shape of the reform agreed to on 20 December departed quite significantly from Khrushchev's original plans (see table 8.1).

In light of Khrushchev's determination to press ahead with the reform and the strong personal interest of most regional leaders to resist it, the number of deviations discloses something about the distribution of power in the country. Three groups of regions and republics were able to resist the plans.[24] The largest, most important group was the national territories, including union republics, autonomous republics, and autonomous oblasts.[25] The reason for their success was due almost entirely to the nationalities policy that had formed under Khrushchev in the late 1950s (see chapter 6). "The Republic," as Khrushchev conceded at the Presidium session "is a different case altogether . . . because here we have unified republics, and naturally there has to be centralized leadership across all branches and across the whole life of the republic."[26] A second category consisted of strategically important oblasts along the borders of the Soviet Union. Thus, for example, the only exceptions in Ukraine were the six westernmost regions—Volynia, Transcarpathia, Roven, Ivano-Frankovsk, Ternopol'sk, and Chernovyts—where until very recently armed conflict had raged between the government and insurgents and the regime was reluctant to undermine its tentative hold on power.[27] A third category was made up of regions with no meaningful potential for industrial (or, more rarely, agricultural) development, such as the five almost exclusively agricultural regions in the Virgin Lands and, at the other end of the country, the cities of Moscow and Leningrad. In the end, the full division of the apparatus was carried out in just over half (75 out of the 140) of obkoms and kraikoms.[28]

SENIOR SECRETARIES, JUNIOR SECRETARIES, AND THEIR NETWORKS

Notwithstanding the intention to shake up the regional apparatus and to tamper with the institutional foundations of the first secretary's power, the reorganizations were thus frustrated at the very first stage: in all, barely over a half of the Soviet Union's regional leaders found that they had to share power with another first secretary. But there was also another, more serious issue. In the vast majority of regions which were divided, the reforms clashed with an entrenched status hierarchy that enabled first secretaries not only to control the reorganization but also, for the majority of local officials, to see who was still in charge and to act accordingly.

In order to demonstrate the underlying continuity of a status hierarchy, we deploy a typology of regional first secretaries that attempts to build in questions of status and elite networking. As we shall see, in the majority of divided regions the standard model was for the incumbent first secretary to stay on in the region and to take on the leadership of the more important obkom as dictated by the economic and demographic profile of the region: in predominantly agrarian provinces the former first secretary tended to move to the agricultural obkom and in urban regions to the industrial obkom. For the sake of brevity, where the former first secretary stayed on in the region and went on to head the larger obkom by population, we refer to him as the senior secretary and to the new head of the adjacent obkom as the junior secretary; in turn, the obkom headed by the senior secretary is referred to as a Category I obkom and the adjoining obkom as a Category II.[29] These categories are complicated by two difficulties. First, in sixteen of the seventy-five divided regions, the incumbent first secretary either died or was moved (usually promoted) in the interim, meaning that there was no incumbent first secretary to speak of.[30] Even in these cases, however, we will show that one of the two first secretaries was, in terms of his status and ranking, clearly the senior. The other difficulty is that in some regions the incumbent first secretary may have chosen, usually because of his expertise and background, to opt for the smaller region by population. However, even in these cases, as we shall see, there was in the vast majority of cases a very clear ranking of the two first secretaries.

We will show the ongoing persistence of status distinctions by looking in depth at the forty-two regions in the Russian Federation that were divided. In a majority of cases (twenty-seven out of forty-two) the senior secretaries were incumbents who ended up in the obkom that matched the economic and demographic profile of the region (see table 8.2).[31] There were two exceptions to this rule. A second group of incumbent first secretaries ended up in mixed regions whose populations were predominantly rural but whose party membership was urban. In each of these cases, however, the question of seniority was clarified by the fact that the incumbent first secretaries were also members of the Central Committee, a key position with a national profile and very high status.[32] The most troublesome area is Category D, where there was a disjuncture between the destination of the senior secretary and the population profile of the region. Despite the fact that most of the population lived in towns and cities, in most of these cases the incumbent was still posted to the agricultural obkom, probably because of his expertise and background in agriculture.[33] In most cases the disadvantage

Table 8.2. Senior secretaries in the Russian Federation, early 1963

Region[a]	Obkom category: agriculture/ industry[b]	Population: rural/urban (000s)	Party membership: rural/urban (000s)	Alignment between senior secretary and regional profile?
A. Predominantly rural populations				
Altai Krai	I/II	1,667/981	64/43	Yes
Belgorod	I/II	958/289	28/20	Yes
Kaluga	I/II	619/332	23/22	Yes
Kirov	I/II	1,339/496	38/33	Yes
Kostroma	I/II	633/394	32/17	Yes
Krasnodar Krai	I/II	2,185/1,343	72/68	Yes
Kurgan	I/II	830/217	38/14	Yes
Kursk	I/II	1,147/360	34/21	Yes
Lipetsk	I/II	847/326	29/23	Yes
Omsk	I/II	998/736	40/39	Yes
Orenburg	I/II	1,017/938	48/44	Yes
Orel	I/II	740/201	27/14	Yes
Penza	I/II	1,015/517	38/34	Yes
Riazan'	I/II	952/504	35/34	Yes
Smolensk	I/II	770/318	27/23	Yes
Tambov	I/II	1,082/463	38/34	Yes
Tiumen'	I/II	736/417	21/19	Yes
B. Predominantly urban populations				
Cheliabinsk	II/I	783/2,364	25/102	Yes
Gor'kii	II/I	1,626/2,045	44/127	Yes
Ivanovo	II/I	412/930	16/60	Yes
Kuibyshev	II/I	895/1,515	34/100	Yes
Leningrad[c]	II/I	583/4,211	17/342	Yes
Perm	II/I	1,154/1,915	21/78	Yes
Primor'e Krai	II/I	442/990	18/50	Yes
Sverdlovsk	II/I	902/2912	23/141	Yes
Iaroslavl'	II/I	553/780	21/42	Yes
C. Mixed populations[d]				
Briansk	I/II	958/606	24/32	Mixed
Kalinin	I/II	936/846	42/57	Mixed
Saratov	II/I	1,244/631	52/77	Mixed
Stavropol' Krai	I/II	1,122/575	33/42	Mixed
Volgograd	I/II	1,097/875	57/61	Mixed
Voronezh	I/II	1,553/878	54/68	Mixed

(continued)

Table 8.2. (*continued*)

Region[a]	Obkom category: agriculture/ industry[b]	Population: rural/urban (000s)	Party membership: rural/urban (000s)	Alignment between senior secretary and regional profile?
D. Nonaligned regions				
Chita	I/II	409/599	14/25	No
Irkutsk	I/II	727/1,374	20/60	No
Kemerovo	I/II	618/2,328	23/103	No
Krasnoiarsk Krai	I/II	1,078/1,242	28/60	No
Moscow[c]	I/II	1,559/3,085	50/225	No
Novosibirsk	I/II	1,011/1,411	39/64	No
Rostov	I/II	1,486/2,027	55/118	No
Tula	I/II	695/1,226	23/66	No
Ul'ianovsk	II/I	666/451	29/28	No (Industrial)
Vladimir	I/II	579/870	23/43	No

Sources: RGANI f.13 op.2 d.477 ll.37–40; *Regional'naia* (2009: 560–94).

[a] Unless otherwise stated, the regions referred to are oblasts.
[b] Category I refers to the obkom headed by the senior secretary and Category II to the second obkom; thus "I/II" means that the senior secretary took over as head of the agricultural obkom while the industrial obkom was taken over by the junior secretary.
[c] The Moscow and Leningrad obkoms, not the Moscow or Leningrad gorkoms, neither of which was divided.
[d] Regions where the majority population lived in the countryside but most party members were located in the towns and cities.

of leading the smaller obkom was compensated for by the fact that the officeholders were incumbent first secretaries and held higher nomenklatura positions as members of the Central Committee.[34]

The division of the obkoms in the Russian Federation was conducted along lines which privileged incumbent first secretaries. In a majority of cases they ended up heading the larger obkom by population and party membership; in a second, smaller group, the former incumbents, all of whom were also members of the Central Committee, took over the larger obkom by population. In these cases officials within the region would have been left in no doubt, after the reorganization, as to the identity of the most powerful person in the region. Where former first secretaries were put in charge of the smaller obkom, normally on grounds of their specialism or expertise, the resulting hierarchy may have been harder to read. Even here, however, former first secretaries were also members of the Central Committee. In all thirty-six cases in which the former incumbents stayed on, they recruited as junior secretaries officials from the region whose status and prestige were plainly lower than theirs.[35] Following the reorganization most regions settled into a clear hierarchy in which one of the first secretaries, invariably the incumbent, emerged as a senior secretary while the other took up the role of his junior. The former were accorded seniority by their previous position as first secretary; by their membership of the most vaunted and prestigious political body in the country, the Central Committee; or by the fact that they now led the largest of the two obkoms.[36] In general, at its highest reaches the preexisting hierarchy was thus left more or less intact.

The process by which junior secretaries were appointed offers valuable insights into the exercise of power in the regions. Usually senior secretaries appointed as junior secretaries long-standing subordinates from the region, for example, second secretaries or chairs of executive committees, who were a rung below the former first secretary in the nomenklatura hierarchy. Although subordinates, they held positions that were sufficiently powerful to command authority in their own right, which facilitated the smooth administration of the territory. In a number of cases, however, and in common with the traditional application of overpromotion, appointments were made in breach of the principle of nomenklatura seniority, as officials lower down in the pecking order were promoted over the heads of the former first secretary's immediate deputies.

The following examples are instructive. In Krasnodar the incumbent who took over the larger agricultural kraikom, G.I. Vorob'ev, was accused by officials from the Central Committee of appointing weak but dependent individuals to leading posts, including the secretaries of the agricultural kraikom, the chair of the agricultural executive committee, and the second secretary of the industrial kraikom. "He has surrounded himself with submissive and obsequious people," noted one Central Committee report, before adding that, despite formidable protests and objections from the party agencies department of the RSFSR buro, Vorob'ev had insisted on "dragging in" a patently flawed candidate as second secretary of the industrial obkom.[37]

Penza is a good example of what appeared to be the deliberate bypassing of nomenklatura seniority in appointments.[38] The incumbent at the time of the reorganization was L.B. Ermin. The circumstances of Ermin's arrival in the region in August 1961 were significant, for he had replaced a previous first secretary, S.M. Butuzov, who had been subjected to a fierce attack by Khrushchev for his failures in agriculture. These circumstances had afforded Ermin, who had previously worked as an instructor at the Central Committee, the right to bring in his own team, including the new second secretary, G.V. Miasnikov, and the chair of the regional executive committee, G.L. Smirnov, to clear up the situation.[39] However, with the division of the obkom in 1963 Ermin took these people with him to the larger agricultural obkom, while the former obkom secretary for industry, B.A. Matkin, took over the smaller industrial obkom. While Matkin had amassed twenty-two years' experience working in factories, his appointment was unusual as he had next to no experience of leading party work. It was only in the spring of 1961, eighteen months before the reorganization, that he acquired his first position in the party, making the transition from factory director to obkom secretary for industry. Matkin's limited party credentials suited Ermin well. Lacking major nomenklatura connections of his own, Matkin fell under the spell of Ermin, a candidate member of the Central Committee since 1961, and was quickly slotted in as his junior secretary.

A more blatant violation of the nomenklatura order occurred in Sverdlovsk. The incumbent at the time of the reorganization was K.K. Nikolaev, a veteran regional official who had served for fourteen years as chair of the Sverdlovsk regional executive committee before assuming the first secretaryship in May 1962. Nikolaev's position in Sverdlovsk had been cemented in 1961 by his election to the Central Committee, and he duly stepped in as first secretary of the larger industrial obkom. But a question mark with regard to the agricultural obkom remained. The theoretical front-runner to lead it was the second secretary, V.I. Dovgopol'.[40] Dovgopol', however, had a touchy relationship with Nikolaev. Nikolaev opted instead for his colleague and deputy over many years, A.V. Borisov, while Dovgopol' was made second secretary of the industrial obkom. Other factors may have endeared Borisov to Nikolaev. One was that in 1961 Borisov had received a formal party reprimand for "illicit exchange of flats." The significance of this episode was highlighted by the fact that the reprimand was lifted only on the eve of Borisov's appointment as first secretary, in December 1962.[41] Disgraced or compromised officials often were useful to first secretaries, and in this case underlined Borisov's status as Nikolaev's dependent.

In general, senior secretaries had considerable leeway in placing dependents as junior secretaries and also in other leading positions. But filling the upper tier of posts was only part of the story. In popular parlance the obkom was the regional party machine or bureaucracy that was led by senior politicians and staffed by administrators. Khrushchev's off-the-cuff proposals on splitting the obkoms involved a number of unforeseen consequences to which the leader himself had probably given little thought. One of these was that for every region not only would the senior leaders need to be divided but so too would their permanent staffs and the wider regional party committees. Detailed examination of six divided obkoms suggests that even though the apparat was supposed to be divided equally, larger numbers followed the senior secretary, irrespective of whether he headed the industrial or agricultural obkom or even whether he headed an obkom that was smaller by population size or party membership.[42] Analysis of individual cases suggests that this state of affairs was the result of the skill and ingenuity of the senior secretary in working the appointments system as well as of the preferences of the cadres themselves. Given a choice, senior officials tended to attach themselves to the more powerful man. A case in point is that of A.I. Alekseev from Penza. On the eve of the bifurcation Alekseev was the head of the department of propaganda and agitation at the Penza obkom. Alekseev had two offers. The first was from the junior secretary at the industrial obkom, B.A. Matkin, to head his obkom department of propaganda and agitation. The second, from the senior secretary, L.B. Ermin, was to work as head of the rural council of trade unions. The formal prestige of the Matkin position was greater, as the post boasted superior working conditions, and it was a more natural avenue to later high-level promotions. Alekseev, however, decided to stick with the Ermin offer. Ermin, as Alekseev would later admit, was the main player in regional affairs, and, for him, this fact outweighed all other considerations. As things turned out, Alekseev was proved right, for Ermin stayed on in the region and was to act as his patron late into the Brezhnev era.[43]

STATUS ON DISPLAY

The most obvious test of whether the senior secretary could master the regional network was his relationship with the junior secretary. Where the junior secretary slotted into the regional hierarchy as, in effect, the second in command, and where members of the regional elite could observe him complying with informal norms of deference and subordination to the senior secretary, they usually recognized that it was in their interest to do so too. Broadly speaking, junior secretaries tried to conform to the emerging norms of the nomenklatura hierarchy relating to their senior secretaries. In turn, senior secretaries tried to steer clear of conflict and to demonstrate respect for and tolerance of their junior secretaries and the second-category obkoms they headed.

The most common settings for putting these norms on display were the obkom plenums. After the bifurcation, branch obkom plenums were held separately, but one factor which helped enhance the visibility of the new norms was the practice of obkom delegations, usually led by the first secretary, visiting each other's plenums. During these visits the guest first secretary was often asked to say a word, while the report of the host was addressed, in part, to the visiting delegation. Such home and away speeches often imparted a spirit of compromise and set a tone of mutual accommodation which was regarded as central to assuring cooperation, especially now, in the context of divided government. At the same time, to minimize friction and uncertainty such speeches could also be used to underline, in the most public of fashions, exactly who was in charge in the region. For example, in Tula, the regional first secretaries, I.Kh. Iunak (agricultural obkom) and O.A. Chukanov (industrial obkom), had something of a history. In October 1960 Chukanov, as second secretary, had been appointed first secretary in the region. However, he had been knocked off his perch by a chance occurrence. In July 1961, while en route to his summer vacation in Gagry, Khrushchev decided to make an impromptu stopover in Tula. The visit went badly for Chukanov. "Comrade Chukanov, it seems to me, just does not get agriculture," lamented Khrushchev in a note to the Presidium on 20 July. "Actually, I can hardly carry on a conversation with him."[44] Within a few weeks he was fired. His place was taken by an outsider, the former chair of the Dnepropetrovsk regional executive committee, I.Kh. Iunak, who had a strong track record in agriculture. Chukanov, in the meantime, had landed the second-tier position of head of administration at the Tula sovnarkhoz. When it came time to appoint a junior secretary Iunak went over the head of the most eligible candidate, the second secretary G.I. Kamaev, who had spent three years working at the Central Committee and was in many ways his own man, in favor of Chukanov, who had recently been sneered at and ignominiously demoted by Khrushchev. In April 1963 the plenum of the agricultural obkom, headed by Iunak, was attended by a large delegation from the industrial obkom. In his speech the host first secretary, Iunak, went out of his way to emphasize the relationship of cordiality and mutual assistance that persisted between the two obkoms: "Our meeting here today, attended by up to 35 members from the industrial obkom, is, in effect, a joint plenum of our two obkoms. . . . I can tell you quite plainly that the buro of the industrial obkom and comrade Chukanov personally are doing everything in their power to resolve as quickly as they can any problems or difficulties connected to the fulfillment of the state plan and to ensuring that all of industry's obligations to support agriculture [*v poriadke shefskoi pomoshchi*] are fully met." What slightly complicated matters in Tula, however, was that although Iunak was the senior secretary (as the incumbent and a member of the Central Committee), the rural population of the region was only half that of the towns and cities. Iunak also used his speech to banish any doubts about who was boss in the region. Having shown respect and reverence toward the industrial obkom, he spoke of "a certain rupture" between the noble intentions of the industrial obkom and the actual behavior of industrial and construction organizations in the region. He then underlined his primacy in the region by, in effect, issuing an order to heads of department at the industrial obkom and to first secretaries of the industrial district committees, who were technically in Chukanov's jurisdiction, to lean more heavily on heads of enterprises who were not doing enough for the agricultural organizations. "This is not bowing respectfully, it is not a request," he stressed. "It is an order [*zakonnoe trebovanie*], and you must treat it as your obligation."[45]

In Sverdlovsk the issue of who was in charge was even more clearcut. Having been appointed first secretary of the united obkom in May 1962, K.K. Nikolaev was not only the incumbent but also the head of the powerful industrial obkom of one of the most important industrial centers in the country. As guest speaker at the agricultural obkom plenum on 13 August 1963 he ranged freely over matters which technically lay outside his brief, matters such as the shortage and procurement of fodder, the slaughter of cattle, and the assignment of labor by agencies under the command of the agricultural obkom.[46] At the agricultural obkom plenum on 5–6 March 1964 Nikolaev criticized the rural agencies for their incorrect use of automobile tarpaulins (*avtomobil'nye pokrishki*), and he spoke in favor of greater specialization of agricultural production on farms near urban centers.[47] Justifying his interference in the affairs of the agricultural obkom, Nikolaev said, "We have common goals, it is not as if the interests of agriculture are somehow divided from those of industry."[48] Nikolaev was no doubt motivated by the goal of ensuring there was an adequate food supply for a major urban center, but his involvement in agricultural matters also had other roots. Prior to becoming obkom first secretary he had served for fourteen years as head of the Sverdlovsk regional executive committee, in which capacity his work had centered on agriculture. Moreover, the current first secretary of the agricultural obkom, A.V. Borisov, had earlier worked under Nikolaev as his deputy at the regional executive committee. Borisov could not deny his former—and, for all intents and purposes, his current—boss his desire to speak on whatever matter he chose.

Despite the mutual interest of senior and junior secretaries in reaching compromise and maintaining harmony, sooner or later small-scale tensions and misunderstandings were likely to emerge. A good case in point was Kursk, an overwhelmingly agricultural region where the dominant figure was the former first secretary since 1958 and now head of the agricultural obkom and member of the Central Committee, L.G. Monashev. From the very beginning Monashev overshadowed his counterpart at the industrial obkom, the former head of the Kursk sovnarkhoz, S.I. Shapurov. At the very first regional industrial party conference on 8 January 1963, ostensibly presided over by Shapurov, it was Monashev, the agricultural first secretary, who took the stage and began to issue directives on the development of industry.[49] Later on that year, at the plenum of the industrial obkom of 13 November 1963, Monashev admonished the region's industrial party organizations for failing in their obligations to agriculture.[50] As the regional second-in-command, Shapurov took these criticisms in his stride: "Comrade Monashev has rightly spoken of the unsatisfactory pace of building on rural construction sites and of the inadequate help given by our enterprises to the countryside. We . . . shall take all necessary measures to ensure that our socialist obligations in these areas in 1963 are . . . fulfilled."[51] The Kursk agricultural obkom plenum of 28 December 1963 went by in a show of mutual respect. All the same, various turns of speech and linguistic nuances laid bare the underlying power relationship between

Monashev and Shapurov. The junior secretary referred reverentially to the senior by his first name and patronymic, Leonid Gavrilovich [Monashev], as would befit any social superior, but Monashev made do with the formal plain mode of address, "comrade Shapurov," in referring to his neighbor, thereby highlighting the latter's lower status.[52]

The growing evidence of disruption in food supplies in Kursk led to a souring of relations between Monashev and Shapurov. At the industrial obkom plenum of 4 March 1964 Monashev took the industrial trade agencies to task for the "slander against the party" brought about by the limited availability of food in the regional capital.[53] Monashev's speech was in fact quite tactless. As the person in charge of agriculture, it was he who was ultimately responsible for food supplies. His response, however, had been to pin the blame on the urban trade distribution network, whose activities fell within Shapurov's jurisdiction. On this occasion Shapurov was not ready to take the slur lying down. "The fault for all these difficulties which the people of Kursk are facing with food supplies," he reportedly grumbled, "lies squarely with the agricultural obkom."[54] Monashev was not deterred from hounding Shapurov in other areas. At the same plenum, on 4 March, he reproached the city council in Kursk, also subordinate to the industrial obkom, for not granting requests by agricultural obkom personnel for city-center accommodations.[55] At the next meeting of the agricultural obkom, on 12 June, the industrial obkom was criticized for its poor work in organizing construction on agricultural projects.[56] In the early Brezhnev period these simmering tensions would boil over into outright conflict.

Both at the point at which the reforms were announced and in the course of their implementation it was, in the vast majority of cases, a relatively easy task for officials in the regional bureaucracy and for ordinary rank-and-file communists to work out who was the junior and who the senior secretary, even in those cases where the senior secretary ended up in the smaller obkom.[57] Whatever Khrushchev's intentions in launching the reforms, the solidity of the local status hierarchies at the higher reaches lent an important element of stability to a process that could otherwise have easily been fraught with uncertainty. Yet as much as senior secretaries were able to introduce an element of order to this process there were also dysfunctional aspects to the reforms which required the senior secretaries to hone their skills in compromise, negotiation, and coordination.

COORDINATION

Conflicts of the kind observed in Kursk were a not unexpected consequence of Khrushchev's reforms. Maximum specialization of the party apparatus had come at a cost, for it had ignored not only the close formal linkages among different sectors of the economy but also the informal ties and connections that had helped suture its various segments together. Traditionally the role of the regional party committees and their secretaries had been to cut through bureaucratic blockages and to ensure coordination of diverse sectors of the economy through informal means. The subdivision of the party bureaucracy made it far harder to achieve this kind of coordination and instead gave rise to conflicts and opposition among the newly divided structures and the interests that began to form around them.

One of the primary examples of distinct sectors of the economy being coordinated through informal means was *sheftstvo,* the "tutelage" or "patronage" extended to a farm by an enterprise. Typically an enterprise might provide an adopted farm with a variety of benefits, such as assigning its own workers for seasonal labor, sponsoring and organizing over-the-plan building projects, or lending technical machinery or cars. Tutelage could entail certain benefits for the enterprise (above all, food direct from the farm), but it nearly always required administrative pressure from party agencies for it to be put into effect. A united obkom answerable not only for industrial production but also for the fulfillment of agricultural procurement plans and the supplying of food to the towns normally had a strong interest in fostering tutelary relationships. But divided obkoms, each of which represented one side in the relationship, had to expend additional time and effort bargaining over the terms and conditions of tutelary aid. Thus a new barrier to the successful integration of the industrial and agricultural sectors was created.

Worries over the fate of tutelage were among the most commonly voiced concerns at regional party conferences from 1962 to 1964. Party secretaries responded by assuring audiences that tutelage would be maintained and even extended. But the complaints persisted. Delegates worried that in the absence of party-induced compulsion enterprises had few incentives to carry on with tutelage. "When the obkom was divided, I genuinely thought that things might get easier," lamented one delegate in Kirov in 1964, "but now I see that that's not the case. All tutelage by industrial enterprises has basically stopped."[58] Difficulties in the practice of *sheftstvo* were one of the main reasons for growing tensions between divided obkoms in the wake of bifurcation.

Administrative pressure exerted by party agencies was also an important means of mobilizing specialists to work in rural areas. After decades of underinvestment, the countryside was rarely a destination of choice for teachers, doctors, or even graduates with an agricultural diploma. Generally speaking, such people went to the countryside only when ordered to by the party. With the splitting of the party apparatus, mobilization of this kind was harder to achieve. Industrial obkoms were often unwilling to sanction the transfer of what they regarded as their own people to the villages, while the agricultural obkoms lacked the authority or clout to pull leading cadres out of the towns. In these circumstances, according to the secretary of the Irkutsk agricultural obkom, Schetinin, attracting qualified personnel to the countryside often "required long, drawn-out negotiations."[59] The first secretary of the Tiumen' gorkom similarly spoke of the "diplomatic negotiations" involved in luring specialists out into the countryside.[60]

A major source of friction was the initial parceling out of industry among the obkoms. While in theory most industries were supposed to come under the control of the industrial obkom, some industrial enterprises, such as those charged with food processing, were usually placed in the hands of the agricultural obkom. Even here, however, much could depend on the location of the enterprise. Whereas food-processing enterprises in the countryside tended to be administered by the agricultural obkom, those in the towns were often claimed by the industrial obkom. A particularly bitter conflict over industrial jurisdictions sprang up in Stavropol', where the undisputed senior secretary, F.D. Kulakov, the first secretary of the agricultural obkom, had used his influence to seize control of all enterprises in the meat and milk, tinned goods, and wine industries, as well as all mining, chemical, and machine-building industries located in the autonomous oblast of Karachevo-Cherkessia, which was also administered by Stavropol' krai. The upshot was that the overall proportion of industry managed by the agricultural obkom exceeded that handled by the nominal "industrial" obkom: in all, the former administered 236 industrial enterprises with a gross output plan of 456 million rubles, while the industrial kraikom had authority over 158 enterprises with a gross output plan of 359 million rubles.

Kulakov's ambitions were such that he even had eyes on other krai structures which, in the initial allocation of functions, had been vested with the industrial kraikom.[61] Clearly unhappy with this state of affairs, the leaders of the industrial obkom decided to take a stand. On 23 November 1963 their first secretary, N.V. Bosenko, proposed, in a letter to the Central Committee, that all industrial enterprises in the territory of Stavropol' be returned to the industrial kraikom. Bosenko justified his proposal by referring to the various difficulties faced by the industrial kraikom in coordinating food supplies, and in particular the supply of meat and milk products to the krai's towns and, most embarrassingly, to its resort towns, such as Sochi, where many members of the Soviet elite holidayed. Bosenko also broached other issues which touched on the core interests of the agricultural kraikom, for example, suggesting that those staff working for the kraikom collective and state farm administrations be redeployed from the towns and "brought nearer" to the rural localities, a move that would have certainly gone down very badly with Kulakov's officials.[62] As Mikhail Gorbachev, who worked in Stavropol' at the time, observed, what ensued was an almost constant struggle between the two, "almost a daily 'tug of war' in which they were forever shadowing and trying to outfox each other."[63] Yet following the upheaval of the original bifurcation the Central Committee was loath to countenance yet more changes, even ones packaged as correctives. At a meeting at the Central Committee apparatus in Moscow, to which both Bosenko and Kulakov were invited, it was agreed that in exchange for a promise by Kulakov to sort out the supply of milk and meat to the resort towns, Bosenko would withdraw his proposals.[64] Notwithstanding the original goal of dividing the economic spoils in each region according to function, in Stavropol' it was the more powerful agricultural first secretary, Kulakov, who managed to wield his influence and connections in order to take over the lion's share of the economy.

A common point of controversy was the use of motor vehicles. An undersupply of cars, lorries, trucks, vans, and buses was a perpetual feature of the Soviet economy. A large portion of the relatively small number of automobiles in circulation lay idle, often because of their low quality or the lack of tires or other spare parts. As a result, there was often intense competition between rival agencies over their use and appropriation, especially during campaigns, for example, during the harvest. But the uncertainties surrounding the division of the party apparatus would open up new possibilities for conflict. Usually the bulk of motor vehicles was under the control of the obkom led by the senior secretary; in many cases, however, senior secretaries were also known to make incursions into the car pool of the second-category obkoms, leading to additional friction. A conflict of this kind in Penza reveals emerging mechanisms of compromise and mutual accommodation in the region.

In the aftermath of the reorganization of the apparat, party leaders in Penza were well aware that competition over motor vehicles might lead to conflict. In order to avoid such face-offs the buros of the two branch obkoms reached a locked-in agreement on 10 May 1963 whereby the distribution of any new cars in the region as well as the redeployment of existing cars could take place only with the express permission of both obkoms. This agreement was telling, for it reflected a general tendency in Penza for regional leaders to head off conflicts where they could through compromise. However, as events were to show, this was a decision that was easier made than implemented. On the first occasion in which the agreement was tested, during the autumn harvest of 1963, it fell apart. On 2 August 1963 the Penza branch obkoms petitioned the RSFSR buro of the Central Committee for permission to commandeer four hundred to five hundred additional vehicles from other Russian regions to help with the harvest in Penza. The request was justified with reference to the recent shortfall in the planned assignment of cars to the region. The shortage of cars, however, was a universal problem which afflicted all Russian regions, and the request was declined.[65] The first secretary of the more powerful agricultural obkom, L.B. Ermin, reacted by flouting the agreement of 10 May and instructing his subordinates to operate a "special regime" which gave them license to expropriate cars from the industrial obkom. Inevitably, the head of the industrial obkom, Matkin, reacted sharply and complained in a letter of 4 December 1963 to Ermin that despite the agreement of 10 May 1963 "the agricultural obkom and oblispolkom are now in a routine and willful way taking cars from users under our jurisdiction." Matkin noted that in October and November almost half of all the vehicles operated by the region's industrial enterprises had been expropriated in this way, leading to serious congestion and transportation blockages. Matkin urged Ermin "to cancel the incorrect directives on this question and to strictly abide by the joint resolution [of 10 May] on the joint use of motor transport." Although Ermin was clearly the more senior and more powerful secretary he understood that for the region as a whole to prosper he would need to obtain the cooperation of the industrial obkom—this indeed was what had motivated the original agreement. Accordingly, in deference to Matkin's request he ordered that once the "delivery of all agricultural goods [in connection with the harvest] has been completed the vehicles must be returned to their former users."[66]

One reason senior secretaries sought out routes to compromise was that while their most senior subordinates were willing to slot into the status hierarchy, this was harder to achieve lower down in the system. If senior, junior, and other obkom secretaries tended to show a greater willingness to abide by the principles of the nomenklatura hierarchy, midlevel leaders sometimes had other priorities. As in any bureaucracy, officials who were several steps removed from the obkom leadership were often more focused on their immediate tasks, such as meeting their individual plan target, than concerning themselves with the demands, often stated in more general terms, of their regional leader. Replicating the agency problem at the statewide level, some midlevel officials, in order to achieve their immediate goals, were liable to act in ways that ran against the interests of their senior secretary. This was a particular problem for midlevel officials who worked for the rival obkom in the region, the one that was not formally subordinate to the senior secretary. Reaching out and winning over these officials required a capacity for mutual accommodation and, more often than not, the support of the junior secretary.

In Irkutsk the senior secretary, Shchetinin, headed the agricultural obkom. Nonetheless, and despite its regionwide remit, after the reorganization the department for the municipal economy at the industrial ispolkom began to systematically favor urban over rural interests. Thus, for example, in the first four months of 1963 the department fulfilled 39 percent of its annual construction quota in the towns and worker settlements but only 1.6 percent in rural districts. What is more, these figures signaled a collapse in the department's performance in the rural sector, where plan fulfillment prior to the reorganization, in the equivalent period in 1962, had stood at a healthy 56.3 percent.[67] In Cheliabinsk the powerful and prestigious industrial obkom, also headed by the senior secretary, had relatively little leverage over enterprises in the

rural sector. Even where their products were parts of a single production chain, enterprises in the agricultural obkom simply ignored the
needs of their counterparts in the industrial obkom. Some of the worst
hit were farms on the edge of towns which, owing to their location,
were administered by the industrial obkom. Thus, for example, the regional administration for agricultural technology, which was under the
auspices of the agricultural obkom, sidelined the requests of suburban
farms, under the jurisdiction of the industrial obkom, for spare parts
and new technology as well as for processing consignments of milk.[68]

In the Soviet economic system the distribution of any so-called non-
funded good in short supply, whether flats, spare parts, new technolo-
gies, or raw materials, were driven by the current institutional interests of the holders of these goods, and these institutional interests had
changed as a result of the November 1962 reform. Often junior secretaries recognized and accepted these institutional interests and did
their best to accommodate them. In these cases their desire to reach a
mutual understanding with a senior secretary on the rational allocation of resources across a region was often trumped by the short-term
incentives facing their subordinates. "Of course we had our fair share
of arguments and disagreements," recalled the former first secretary
of the Tiumen' agricultural obkom, B.E. Shcherbina. "But most often
these were not about personalities or about the peculiar qualities of an
individual but about the need to defend one's interests."[69]

Conflicts of this kind could gnaw away at the underlying norms of
the nomenklatura hierarchy and, in particular, at the principle of subordination of junior secretaries to senior ones. This was one reason senior
secretaries found they had to veer toward some form of accommodation and compromise. Another was that as a result of the bifurcation
the membership of the obkoms suddenly increased, leading to a flow
of new obkom members into the system. A detailed examination of six
regions which vary by size, economic profile, and alignment of category
I and category II obkoms shows that if one sets aside those who did not
hold positions in the state or party (that is, those whose membership
of the obkom served a primarily symbolic purpose such as rank-and-
file workers, collective farmers, and schoolteachers), between 30 and
45 percent of the regional party committees elected after the reforms of
November 1962 consisted of new members who were not drawn from
either the former obkoms or the auditing committees.[70] This was to be

expected, given that with the division of the obkoms their combined membership had swollen. This promotion of new officials to obkom membership was to change markedly the configuration of the regional network as a whole. Some of the new members were economic functionaries, such as factory directors and chairs of collective farms, but a number of lower-tier officials were now also thrown into the mix. This included functionaries whose earlier careers had taken a turn for the worse but who were now given a second chance. The division of the apparat had opened up a host of new party positions for individuals whose careers had taken a detour out of the party. The need to bring these people back into the fold created an additional incentive for regional leaders to adopt a more conciliatory and inclusive approach.

KHRUSHCHEV'S FALL

According to Wintrobe, the dictator's dilemma is that he can't trust those immediately below him to tell the truth.[71] Khrushchev's underlings were unlikely to get killed for disagreeing with him, but he was prone to taking great umbrage when they objected to his plans. When Khrushchev had first broached the idea of dividing the party apparatus to Brezhnev, Podgornyi, and Poliansky, "everyone," recalled his son, "supported [it] enthusiastically and with one voice." "What a wonderful idea, it must be done immediately," they are reported to have said.[72] It was perhaps his inner circle's unwillingness to pass on information about the major problems encountered by the reform and about rising opposition to it among regional party secretaries that fed into Khrushchev's misplaced self-confidence and intransigence on this issue.[73] In fact, Khrushchev "continued to believe in his idea, and he strove to develop it yet further, insisting that, as a means of structuring party organizations, the production principle should now be extended to all krais and oblasts."[74] Behind the scenes, however, those around him and in particular those who were charged with implementing it believed it was a very bad idea. "Prowling the corridors during the three days of the [November 1962] plenum, journalist Nikolai Barsukov heard 'not one good thing about the reorganization, only bewilderment and outright rejection.' Yet when the voting started, it was adopted 'unanimously' and with 'loud cheers.'"[75]

It has been widely observed that of all Khrushchev's reforms that were condemned at the October 1964 plenum and that confirmed his removal as Soviet leader it was the bifurcation of the party apparatus that grated most. One measure of this dissatisfaction was that it was the first reform to be reversed. What the reconstitution of the obkoms demonstrated was that the division of the apparat had injected tension into regional networks, but on the whole it was a tension they could withstand. Invariably, at the top of the new hierarchy was the senior secretary, who now resumed his old post as first secretary of the united obkom. In the RSFSR, for example, this happened in thirty-seven of the forty-two divided obkoms.[76] The appointment of junior secretaries also followed a clear pattern: in general, those who had headed industrial obkoms went on to become second secretaries of the united obkom (twenty-seven cases), while those who had led the agricultural obkom became chairs of the newly united regional executive committees (eleven cases).[77] Similar tendencies were observed in the other republics with divided obkoms (Ukraine, Uzbekistan, and Kazakhstan), though here, on the whole, a larger share of senior secretaries were promoted or rotated out of their regions. The division of the apparatus and the reassignment of network positions was a process that was largely steered and controlled by the senior secretaries. Despite the formal division of the apparatus, senior secretaries were able to rely on a number of informal devices—for example, the subordination of the junior secretary to the senior secretary and the control of key network positions exerted by the senior secretary—to maintain unity within the regional network. At the same time, in order to maintain coordination and to mitigate the dysfunctional aspects of the reform most functionaries in the divided networks continued to adhere to an emergent nomenklatura ethic and to the idea that differences could be reconciled through compromise. Such continuity was an important precondition for the resurrection of networks in their former state after Khrushchev's removal.

IV
BREZHNEV

9 The New Course

NOT FOR THE first time in Russian history the specter of social and economic disorder forced a realignment of the country's political elite. The mayhem that followed the division of the obkoms did much to turn regional leaders against Khrushchev. The emergency import of grain from the West the year after was also a personal humiliation for the Soviet leader. More than anything, however, it was the wave of riots and strikes that began in 1960 and culminated in the Novocherkassk massacre of June 1962 which underlined the potentially hazardous problem of authoritarian control faced by the regime. It is not clear how far or how fast the Novocherkassk demonstrations would have spread had the administration not sent in troops to crush them. To forestall a recurrence, the security police was restored to a new, more prominent role. Its armory was bolstered in July 1962 via amendments to the law on crimes against the state, which contained stiffer provisions for acts deemed to constitute "anti-Soviet agitation and propaganda."[1] As would happen over thirty-five years later, at the time of the Russian economic crash of 1998, various segments of the power elite fell into line and agreed that the county needed to move in a new direction, which, in this case, involved helping to get rid of the leader.[2]

In quick succession Khrushchev's heirs reunified the regional party committees, dismantled the system of party-state control, dissolved the sovnarkhozy, and reinstated the central industrial ministries. The outcome was a classic party "vertical" connecting the Central Committee in Moscow to republican, oblast (regional), and raion (district) party committees in a clear and uninterrupted chain of command.[3] Yet despite the conservative aspect of these organizational reforms, the substance of many of Brezhnev's policies was quite novel and pushed the regime in a new, unexpected direction. First, in a departure not only from Stalin but also from Khrushchev, who had hoped to combat food shortages through a variety of low-cost, quick-fix solutions, Brezhnev oversaw a massive infusion of resources into the agricultural sector and adopted a more inclusive, conciliatory approach to the countryside.[4] Second, in a frank acknowledgment of the diminished motivational power of Marxism-Leninism, functionaries at the Central Committee apparatus turned to Russian nationalism as an agent of mobilization. Drawing on themes from the late Stalin era, Russian nationalist

The early Brezhnev era was a time of investment in infrastructure projects. Here, First Secretary A.G. Dankovtsev of Khakasskii obkom is opening the Abakan–Taishet railroad in 1965. *Source:* RGASPI.

The awarding of orders and prizes mushroomed under Brezhnev. On 8 January 1971 Secretary of the Central Committee F.D. Kulakov bestowed the Order of Lenin on the Volgograd region. The award was accepted by the obkom first secretary, L.S. Kulichenko (*center*), and by the chair of the regional executive committee, Iu.I. Lamakin (*to the right*). *Source:* RGASPI.

writers argued in stories and polemical tracts published in widely circulated books and journals that the core of Russian history was not class struggle at all but the unending conflict of the Russian people, its values and traditions, with those of the West.[5] Third, there was a new approach to repression. After a decade in the shadows, the security police (KGB) saw a reversal in its fortunes as a result of the events at Novocherkassk.[6] With the formation of a new fifth directorate and the appointment of Iuri Andropov as the KGB's head in 1967, the role of the security police was redefined, and the organization began to regain some of the credibility it had lost during the Khrushchev era. Its new role involved a shift from formal prosecutions toward prophylaxis (*profilaktika*), normally involving a "conversation" (*beseda*) and various forms of physical and psychological intimidation.[7]

One area in which Brezhnev exhibited his most radical side was in his treatment of regional leaders. In this area he came up with a new and quite novel solution to the dictator's agency problem. We have shown above how Brezhnev's predecessors dealt with this issue. As an established autocrat, Stalin had been a surprisingly disciplined delegator: he had handed power to regional leaders but also used a variety of institutional checks, including fixed terms, rotations, elections, a variety of control agencies, and the occasional targeted purge, in order to contain them. Khrushchev proceeded along a different tack. He dispensed with repression, reduced the administrative load on the center, and vested more power in his regional party principals. Like Stalin, however, he kept up the pressure on regional leaders by imposing high targets, conducting purges (albeit nonviolent ones), and retaining the system of cadre rotation. For all their differences, Stalin and Khrushchev had in common a proclivity to keep regional leaders under pressure through a combination of taut plans, cross-postings, and the occasional threat of a purge.

Brezhnev's approach would be quite different. In order to prevent regional leaders from coming under the control of local elites, the Bolshevik party from its early days had either sent out cadres from Moscow or rotated leaders from region to region.[8] In a striking departure the Brezhnev administration began to recruit regional leaders locally and keep them in post beyond what had become the standard term of office. To some extent this shift in policy was a function of the constraints now placed on Brezhnev by his fellow leaders. Concerned that he might abuse his powers of patronage, as Stalin and Khrushchev had, Brezhnev's fellow oligarchs placed strict limits on his powers of appointment at the regional level. For their part, regional leaders, who had played a major role in ousting Khrushchev, now also insisted on greater security of tenure. Their role in removing Khrushchev had shown they were a force to be reckoned with. When Brezhnev spoke enthusiastically about the "stability of cadres," he was, to a degree, making a virtue of necessity.

Yet closer examination of Brezhnev's cadre policies suggests that another factor was also at play. Running through Brezhnev's pronouncements was a concern with how obkom leaders should "exercise authority" and "command respect" in their region. Expanding on the policy of indigenization in the national republics, Brezhnev appeared to be arguing that only leaders familiar with the social and cultural traditions of their area would have the appropriate communicative skills and social ties necessary to run their regions effectively. In general, leaders who drew on local norms and customs were best placed to build the networks and to gain the authority they needed to govern their regions and, most often, these were leaders recruited from the regions themselves.

NETWORK RESTORATION AND
THE SETTLING OF SCORES

The division of the obkoms in November 1962 was one of the most radical administrative reforms of the whole Soviet era, as it cut to the marrow of the regional party as an organization. It was a measure of the strength of feeling over these reforms that the merging of the provincial obkoms was the very first organizational act agreed to by the new administration and that it was implemented almost immediately. Reuniting the obkoms was potentially a hazardous operation. After all, half of the first secretaries were to lose their posts, and a large number of positions in the regional party bureaucracy were to be axed. We have observed the consolidation of patterns of seniority of office and of person at the obkom (see chapter 3). It was a mark of the maturation of this system of seniority and of the norms of deference that flowed from it that the reunification of the obkoms was to prove surprisingly smooth and trouble-free.

The original aim of Khrushchev's reform had been to shake up routines and hierarchies, yet most regional leaderships had quickly settled into an informal rank order, as the rural and industrial first secretaries variously assumed their position as either senior or junior secretary. As was its prerogative, Moscow now took the lead in appointing the new first secretaries of the united obkoms. Although the category of senior secretary was never formally acknowledged, its reality is attested to by the fact that it was invariably this figure who was enthroned as the new head of the obkom.[9] The next step was to decide on the fate of the junior secretary. Here too Moscow's role is indicated by the fact that there was an unmistakable pattern to the appointments made across the country.[10]

Yet, beyond the top two positions, the Central Committee had neither the time nor the resources to draw up a precise appointments schedule for every region. Instead, they handed the more detailed and technical aspects of the reorganization to the senior secretaries. In making and then announcing major appointments, the latter were alert to the potential nuances and symbolism of their decisions. Merging the obkoms meant compressing two obkoms into one. Some full-time staff were destined to lose their jobs, while those members who failed to make it to the new obkom suffered a drop in status. It was at this point that the new first secretaries made gestures toward the coherence of the regional network and to the equity and fairness of the reassignment process. This theme was picked up by the former senior secretary and new first secretary of the Kursk obkom, L.G. Monashev, who justified the appointment to second secretary of the united obkom the former junior secretary Shapurov in the following terms: "We have to do this so that we are properly understood by the former industrial party organization [that is, Shapurov's obkom], so that its members can say to themselves: we have been merged, yes, but the posts have been equitably distributed. (Voices from the hall: That's right [*pravil'no*]!)."[11]

At the same time, there was always room for the new first secretary to seek retribution for perceived slights he had endured during the bifurcation. In fact, despite the praise he had heaped on Shapurov this is exactly what Monashev did in Kursk. Having publicly lauded Shapurov, Monashev soon had him in his sights. Rather than attack Shapurov directly he got the director of one of the leading regional factories to mount an attack at the first meeting of the united obkom on 25 November 1964.[12] At the next session of the regional party conference the front against Shapurov widened. Shapurov was forced to explain why he had two flats, one in Moscow (where he had come from in 1957) and the other in Kursk. The charge against Shapurov was an unwarranted slander, as he had in fact rented out his flat in Moscow, but it stuck all the same. There were also moves against Shapurov's onetime colleague the former chair of the industrial ispolkom. On the eve of the conference Monashev made it known that the colleague was descended from a "kulak family" (in fact, at the moment of his father's "dekulakization" the colleague was two years old). To avoid further complications the ispolkom chair ruled himself out of the running for a leading position on the obkom. The next wave of attacks came at the first organizational plenum after the conference, when a succession of speakers accused Shapurov of "setting our urban communists on a collision course with our rural party organization."[13] Shapurov readily acknowledged his purported mistakes and within a few months had beaten a hasty retreat out of the region.

Similar altercations between former junior and senior secretaries occurred in other regions.[14] In a majority of cases, however, the senior and junior secretaries not only stayed on in the region but were able to work together long after the reunification.[15] The reasons for this continuity varied. Most often relations were smoothed out when the secretaries reached common understandings over seniority: just as such agreements had enabled leading officials to slot into senior and junior positions after November 1962, so now they were able to take up positions in a clear rank order. New leaders were keen to signal to others working in the obkom that the general balance between the agricultural and industrial sectors would be preserved and that the circle of clients following the former senior and junior secretaries would be protected. Where possible, the sudden departure of senior figures, with their disruption to routines and the inevitable churn of clients lower down the administrative ladder, was to be avoided.

The continuity was not confined to the upper reaches of the regional elite. From December 1961 to December 1964 there had been unprecedented organizational turmoil. In the lead-up to the XXII Party Congress in October 1961 Khrushchev had carried out the largest single purge of regional leaders in the post-Stalin era. The bifurcation of 1962 and the reunification two years later presented enormous scope for bureaucratic conflict, tit-for-tat reprisals, and even mini-purges at the regional level. Despite this atmosphere of uncertainty the composition of obkom elites over this period appears to have been remarkably stable. In-depth analysis of a sample of eleven (out of seventy) obkoms in the RSFSR from December 1961 to December 1964 shows that on average three-fifths of the core elites elected at the end of 1961 were still in place three years later.[16] Given that in any normal year in 1950s and 1960s the usual replacements from illnesses, retirements, deaths, out-of-region transfers and promotions, sackings, and demotions was roughly on the order of 10–15 percent, these figures were not out of keeping with the long-term baseline for turnover in the post-Stalin era.[17] In the face of the largest organizational upheaval in the party's history, the composition of the obkom in our sample of regions remained remarkably intact, suggesting a deeper underlying level of network continuity.

BREZHNEV'S NEW COURSE

On 30 January 1967 the Central Control passed a resolution "On work with leading cadres in the Estonian Central Committee." The resolution decried the fact that too few cadres with experience in "the localities" (*na mestakh*) were being pooled in cadre reserves from which future leaders might be drawn.[18]

On the surface, the decree on Estonia, which was itself a union republic, could be viewed as an affirmation, following the vacillations of the Khrushchev years, of Brezhnev's commitment to indigenization, the promotion of titular nationals to executive positions in the national territories. Along with the reunification of the obkoms, the resumption of indigenization had been one of Brezhnev's first steps on taking office. Two years earlier he had signaled a return to korenizatsiia in Kazakhstan, a republic in which he himself had served as first secretary and where he continued to have strong ties. Under Khrushchev Kazakhstan had seen a drop in the admission of ethnic Kazakhs to the party, a fall in the number of Kazakhs taking up senior positions in the party apparatus, and, most strikingly of all, the replacement of an ethnic Kazakh, Dinmukhamed Kunaev, by a Uighur outsider, Ismail Iusupov, as the republican first secretary. After reportedly informing Iusupov that the "first secretary of Kazakhstan has to be a candidate from the local population," Brezhnev replaced him with Kunaev in October 1964. Over the next two years, from 1964 to 1966, the number of Kazakhs joining the party doubled, and over the next seven years, from 1964 to 1971, there was a noticeable rise in the number of republican central committee secretaries who were not only Kazakhs but also Kazakhs who had been raised and educated in the republic.[19] The resolution on Estonia appeared to put an official stamp of approval on the new policy.

Yet the resolution on Estonia had a more general significance too. Its logic ran in parallel to that which had informed the "territorialization" of administration in the early Khrushchev era. By the mid-1960s the Soviet Union, in existence for almost half a century, had had time to raise, train, and educate its own local elites, not just in the non-Slavic union republics, but in Russia and Ukraine as well. Having cadres who were imbued with the correct values and who were responsive to the wishes of the center was certainly to be welcomed, but it addressed only part of the agency problem facing the leadership in Moscow. The center also required leaders who could exercise authority in their region. Those leaders who knew their region's history and customs, who had extended local client and friendship networks, and who spoke the local language were normally the ones best placed to translate central policies to local circumstances.

The same logic that had applied to korenizatsiia was now extended to the Russian Federation. This point was borne out by a resolution of May 1967, on the heels of the Estonian resolution, titled "On the Omsk obkom." It called for the creation of local cadre reserves and for the appointment of local cadres who could "exercise authority" (pol'zuiushchimisia avtoritetom) among the local population.[20] As the senior Central Committee official N.A. Voronovski made clear on a visit to Omsk the following month, "After the October [1964] plenum of the Central Committee and [the] XXIII Party Congress our approach to cadres has fundamentally changed. . . . [N]ow our high expectations of cadres have to be matched by [showing our] full trust and respect toward them."[21] In other words, if provincial cadres were to develop genuine authority among the local population and, as it were, to be trusted from below, the least Moscow could do was to trust them from above.

One way of boosting the authority of cadres was to honor continuity, to value experience, and to eschew the "unjustified turnover of cadres."[22] These themes were at the heart of the new policy of "stability of cadres." But the Brezhnev administration was now going further. The transfer of regional leaders from Moscow and their rotation from province to province had been a feature of the party's personnel policy from the early days of the Bolshevik regime. Jettisoning this policy, Brezhnev began to champion the promotion of local leaders from within their home region.[23] From October 1965 to March 1971 two-thirds of first secretaries in the Russian Federation were selected from their home region, and over the next five years the proportion rose to five-sixths.[24] A corollary of the new policy was a drop in interregional transfers. From 1965 to 1976 the proportion of incumbent first secretaries who, prior to their appointment, had been transferred from another region dropped from 39 percent to 23 percent, while the number of those drafted in from the Central Committee apparatus also fell.[25] In Siberia the appointment of a former Central Committee apparatchik, Egor Ligachev, as the new first secretary in Tomsk in 1965 was the last known case of a Central Committee official being sent out in this way.[26]

In promoting local people as obkom first secretaries, Brezhnev was in effect extending the principle of indigenization to the Russian provinces.[27] The logic of the two policies was roughly similar. Local leaders were in the best position to know the history and customs of their region, to earn the confidence of local elites, and to cultivate the networks that they needed to govern. In the Russian Federation this tapped into the new "operative ideology" of Russian nationalism, which, through an oblique strategy of "politics by culture," valorized Russian traditions by idealizing the Russian countryside, Russian architecture, and Russian history.[28] But there was also a specifically regional aspect to this development. The early to mid-1960s saw the revival of *kraevedenie,* a multidisciplinary form of local study that involved the opening of local museums, the teaching of regional history at schools, and the preservation of local architecture.[29] Drawing on the "small homeland" (*malaia rodina*) movement of a century earlier—which had argued that the geographical vastness and diversity of Russia had made it hard for ordinary people to comprehend, let alone identify with, the state as a whole—a new breed of homeland nationalism now emerged that sought to build a wider Russian national consciousness by celebrating local identities and reinforcing attachments to one's region.[30] The promotion of native-born officials to obkom first secretaries was a natural outgrowth of this policy.

The second strategy for enhancing the prestige of local leaders was to secure the hierarchies that supported them. Detailed analysis of patterns of promotion in the Russian regions show that not only were the majority of newly appointed first secretaries promoted from within the region but also most were increasingly likely to have been promoted from the next-ranking position in the region, that is, from one spot below in the regional pecking order.[31] Moreover, under Brezhnev there was a growing tendency for obkom first secretaries to be chosen from among officials who had slowly climbed up the party ladder from the lowest rungs. By the mid-1970s a majority of obkom first secretaries had assumed their first party appointment at the bottom step, as either secretary of the district party organization or secretary of a factory party cell.[32] Most had steadily progressed up the career path from there. This system of gradational, step-by-step promotions served to align seniority of office with seniority of person, as measured by party service. As T.H. Rigby put it at the time, by these means "the seniority principle has been emphasized."[33]

Brezhnev also set an example by his own behavior. After the boorish Khrushchev, Brezhnev was more respectful of those around him, even where they had erred. Some of his associates even coined a term—Brezhnevite criticism—to reflect his more temperate and evenhanded form of rebuke. "Leonid Il'ich just knew how to reprove people, how to take them to task, and to do it in such a way that no one ever felt offended," recounted his son-in-law.[34] After the ceaseless haranguing of the Khrushchev years, Brezhnev's more considered manner was widely appreciated. At the reunification plenums at the beginning of 1965, senior and junior secretaries, in their bid to avert tensions, were often impeccably courteous and mutually respectful.

Achieving complex, often contradictory objectives—for example, attaining central economic targets while retaining the support of the local population—required not only the adroit manipulation of individual appointments or the cultivation of an appropriate etiquette or leadership style but also the development of institutions. When it came to governing the non-Slavic union republics one such institution, as noted earlier, was that of the Slavic second secretary. Rather than referring to an individual, the "second" was a complex ensemble of practices that replaced direct forms of rule, such as plenipotentiaries and republican buros of the Central Committee, which had prevailed in the late 1940s.[35] The seconds had been refined as a device to solve the center's agency problem: without alienating the republic's titular nationality, who would still be led by one of their own, they could ease the flow of information to the center by taking charge of the strategically important fields of cadre selection and by liaising with the security service. But an additional problem remained. Who would be the first secretary? The practice in the union republics since the late 1940s had been to appoint as first secretary a member of the republic's titular ethnic group. Ideally, the center preferred a leader who, while being a member of the titular nationality, was also Russified. The question was, to what degree?[36] While it appealed to the center to have someone who was

Russified and who could perhaps better understand Moscow's requirements, it also needed someone who could command respect among the titular nomenklatura. But how could they know who that person was? It was here that the institution of the party election could help out.

A good example was the appointment of a new first secretary in Lithuania following the death of Antanas Sniečkus in January 1974. The second secretary at the time was Valerii Kharazov, a typical second who had served in the department of party organs at the Central Committee before his arrival in Lithuania in the spring of 1967.[37] Moscow's favorite contender to take over from Sniečkus was the then head of the council of ministers, Juozas Maniušis.[38] The difficulty was that Maniušis, although an ethnic Lithuanian, had been brought up and raised in Russia and spoke Lithuanian only with difficulty. There was hardly any point in Moscow appointing a candidate who commanded little respect or support from the local nomenklatura.

As it happened, a combination of Maniušis as first secretary and Kharazov as the second elicited a sharply negative reaction from the republic's ruling circles. Members of Sniečkus's coterie arranged, via a contact, for Vladimir Shcherbitskii, the first secretary in Ukraine, to make a call to Brezhnev to express their concern.[39] At this point Kharazov, as second secretary, was tasked with canvassing opinion among the upper reaches of the republican nomenklatura. It soon became apparent to Kharazov that, should it come to a formal vote, a number of senior figures, including the head of the republican KGB, Juouzas Petkevičius, and the former head of the KGB, Kazimieras Liaudis, would break ranks and vote against Maniušis's appointment.[40]

In forty-seven interviews with fifty-five members of the titular nomenklatura, all recorded in a notebook, Kharazov carried out what amounted to a proxy but very real "election" of a leader to succeed Sniečkus. In that election, Maniušis did not get a single vote as the first preference to fill the post. Instead, another candidate, Petras Griškevičius, the first secretary of the Vilnius city party committee, netted twelve first-preference votes and twenty-nine second-preference votes as a possible candidate. Formal party elections, as noted above, tended to have a number of functions, but electing a leader was rarely one of them. Instead, they had been used by the center to monitor regional party organizations, to contain overzealous party principals, and, from the perspective of these leaders themselves, to operate as a signaling system that could help them moderate their own behavior. But here the function of the proxy election, carried out by the second secretary, was to enable the titular nomenklatura to actually elect a leader and, what's more, to do so in the knowledge that the center was most likely to accept their choice. In fact, despite being reproached for various ideological failings and nationalist leanings, concerns that were put to him at meetings of the Secretariat and Politburo, Griškevičius's candidacy was approved. When presented to the next meeting of the Lithuanian republican plenum his candidacy was greeted with applause.[41] Griškevičius went on to serve as the republican first secretary for the next thirteen years, until his death in 1987.

The Lithuanian case illustrates the dangers of appointing puppets with little grounding or acceptance in the local community. In the national republics the center had long known it had to pay heed to local wishes and sensitivities before making appointments. In some republics there were adaptations to this basic format. In Lithuania, Moscow permitted what was in effect a competitive election to yield additional information on what kind of candidate—and in particular what level of Russification—would be palatable to the local ruling stratum. However, the need to find leaders who enjoyed the support of the local political community was a general one. One way of doing so was to encourage continuity of personnel and to talk up the virtues of experience and seniority. Another was to recruit as leaders individuals who knew the history, traditions, and ways of their region and who could use these qualities to build a successful ruling network.

BREZHNEV'S PURGE

In order to enroll more workers and collective farmers and to make the party more representative of the working class as a whole, Brezhnev's predecessor, Khrushchev, had presided over a surge in the party's membership. From just under seven million members in 1953 the party had grown to almost twelve million in 1965. Concerned that it had perhaps opened its doors too widely and inadvertently let in too many careerists and chance elements, in July 1965 the Central Committee passed a resolution titled "On serious shortcomings in the Kharkov party organization." On the surface it appeared to be little more than a run-of-the-mill directive aimed at firming up the party's admissions policies. Seizing on what it viewed as the lax procedures in Kharkov, the Central Committee enjoined regional party organizations to vet candidates more carefully and to pay greater attention to their track records before the point of admission. The new policy initiated by the Kharkov decree duly led, over the next few years, to a dip in party membership and to a small spike in expulsions.[42]

In the Aesopian world of Soviet high-level politics the resolution on Kharkov also served a second purpose. The first secretary in Kharkov in 1965 was G.I. Vashchenko. Vashchenko was connected in a patron–client chain to a line of earlier first secretaries in Kharkov, including N.A. Sobol' (1961–63), currently the second secretary in Ukraine, V.N. Titov (1953–61), currently the Central Committee secretary in charge of cadres, and Nikolai Podgorny (1950–53), who by 1965 had become the second most powerful man in the Central Committee apparatus. The fact that the errors in Kharkov had "gone back several years," as *Pravda* made clear in an article on 28 August 1965, cast a shadow on all three of Vashchenko's predecessors, who were, on this seemingly thin pretext, all relieved of their gatekeeping roles in the party machine.[43] The resolution on Kharkov was an arcane but unmistakable signal to lower-level party functionaries that Podgorny, Titov, and Sobol' had been expelled from the higher reaches of the party's system of patronage.

In the complex symbolic language of higher-level Soviet politics, this point was reinforced by another seemingly obscure event. Of all the changeovers of regional party leaders in the first years following Khrushchev's fall only one was attended by a member of the Central Committee Presidium. Echoing Khrushchev's famous visit to Leningrad in November 1953, at which he presided over the removal of Malenkov's protégé, Andrianov, as obkom first secretary and anointed Frol Kozlov in his place, Brezhnev now took his turn. In December 1965 he visited one of the largest regional party organizations in the country, in Gor'kii, to oversee the replacement of M.T. Efremov by a new first secretary, K.F. Katushev.[44] The appointment, loaded with symbolic meaning, presaged the new policy of promoting local cadres. Katushev was born in Gor'kii and moreover had spent his entire adult life there. But the appointment of Katushev was also significant in another respect. At the time, he was a thirty-eight-year-old construction engineer whose first party appointment had come only eight years earlier.[45] Notwithstanding the new emphasis on incremental promotions, this was a classic example of overpromotion, one which underlined Brezhnev's role as a patron and, given the significance of the post and the media attention the appointment received, marked his effective coronation as the party leader in charge of cadres.[46]

For the sake of regime stability the center had to make it clear that one person or grouping was in charge of cadres, and in taking this step it resolved that that person would be Brezhnev. Yet this decision should not obscure the fact that in his first years in office Brezhnev was still a contested autocrat, one who was vulnerable to a rebellion from his fellow oligarchs. To reinforce this point, the ruling collective hedged Brezhnev's powers with a number of controls. In relation to regional leaders, two stood out. First, in order to prevent Brezhnev from using appointments of regional leaders to create a power base for himself, as Stalin and Khrushchev had done, strict limits were placed on the assignment of new obkom first secretaries. From January to November 1965 no new first secretaries were appointed in the Russian Federation. This trend toward lower turnover would continue over the next decade. By comparison with the previous ten years, from November 1964 to 1978 the rate of replacement of obkom first secretaries in the union republics fell by half, and in the Russian Federation it dropped by three-fifths.[47] The policy of lowering turnover acted as a brake on Brezhnev's powers of patronage and on his ability to pack the leadership with his supporters.[48] A second constraint was that even when new first secretaries were appointed, Brezhnev was, in effect, prohibited from appointing former colleagues as obkom leaders. Although Brezhnev was given discretion to elevate former associates from territorial party organizations to leadership positions in Moscow (from, among other places, Dnepropetrovsk, Zaporozhe, and Moldavia), he was not allowed, as Khrushchev had been from 1953 to 1955, to appoint former clients to obkom leadership positions.[49]

The prohibition had one important side effect. Lacking any prior relationship with them, Brezhnev now went out of his way to nurture these obkom secretaries. Upon their appointment, he would invariably arrange special meetings with them, and he maintained an open-door policy whenever they gathered in Moscow on official business. Moreover, he organized routine long-distance telephone calls with the secretaries, and he showered them with awards and prizes, each of which betokened more opportunities for face-to-face meetings.[50] "Brezhnev's great strength," writes one of his biographers, "was his ability to devote attention to his obkom first secretaries. He never regretted time spent on telephone calls. . . . [E]ven while on holiday he would spend two to three hours a day on the Kremlin line, chatting with the obkom secretaries, asking them about their needs and problems."[51] "Brezhnev welcomed 'our people' [the obkom secretaries] willingly, often until late, until eleven or twelve at night," recalled Egor Ligachev, the first secretary in Tomsk for the duration of the Brezhnev era. "Sometimes he would receive us in such large groups that we would have to squeeze into his office and, if there wasn't quite enough room, some of us would have to make do and squat by the windowsill."[52]

The rules of the Soviet political game nonetheless dictated that an incoming leader would have to carry out a purge of some kind. This was not just to firm up alliances or dispose of foes. A purge sent out a strong signal across the party apparatus that it was now Brezhnev who was first among equals. The low general rate of turnover masked a small number of strategically important replacements. Refining a technique developed by Khrushchev, Brezhnev pushed through a discreet purge in four of the five largest provinces (by party membership) of the Russian Federation.[53] Yet a purge of regional secretaries could be carried out only within certain limits, as Brezhnev's fellow oligarchs were keen to prevent him from using the general secretary's control over patronage to build a power base among the regional leadership.

In light of these constraints, what kind of purge could Brezhnev carry out? Earlier we saw that in 1965 Brezhnev implemented what amounted to a mini-purge of the Kharkov group, led by Podgorny. In terms of age and seniority, Brezhnev, along with other leaders such as Suslov and Kirilenko, were on the other side of a generational divide from a new cohort of leaders who centered on the Central Committee secretary, Aleksandr Shelepin, and the head of the KGB, Vladimir Semichastny.[54] Having been born in the Soviet era (that is, after 1917), a good ten to fifteen years after Brezhnev, all of these figures were unsullied by the repression of the 1930s as well as too young to have attained high office under Stalin or to be implicated in some of the worst excesses of that period.[55] Some had served on the front as newly conscripted soldiers, a powerful formative experience which divided them from more senior party figures who had sat out the war in the rear. Sensing a threat from this younger cohort, Brezhnev set about getting rid of them. Semichastny was sacked as head of the KGB in May 1967, and Shelepin lost his position as Central Committee secretary in September that year. Most of the others were sent out on ambassadorial postings.[56]

One member of this younger group was the regional leader Nikolai Egorychev, the first secretary of the Moscow city committee. Ousting Egorychev was in some respects a more thorny proposition than getting rid of Brezhnev's other targets. One reason was that Egorychev had a tight personal network in the Moscow city organization which embraced a number of raikom secretaries who, like him, were *frontoviki* (veterans of the Great Patriotic War who had served on the frontline) and who, after the war, had gone on to serve as party secretaries in Moscow's higher educational institutions. Another was that, unlike Shelepin and Semichastny, Egorychev was the head of a party committee, and party organizations, as we have seen, had elaborate procedures for electing and removing leaders. In this regard it was a particular nuisance that the Moscow city organization had, only a year earlier at the March 1966 party conference, elected Egorychev in a unanimous vote.[57]

The pretext for Egorychev's removal was a speech he made on the first day of the June 1967 Central Committee plenum. Initially, assuming that Egorychev had made the speech with Brezhnev's blessing, members of the Central Committee, including those from Egorychev's own Moscow gorkom, rushed to congratulate him. Picking up on a quick exchange of glances and murmurs behind him, however, Egorychev began to sense that something was wrong. The following morning the first secretary of the Uzbek central committee, Sharaf Rashidov, reproached Egorychev for raising questions related to defense, which was the prerogative of the Politburo, in the more open and public forum of the Central Committee. The next day, in a tense encounter, Egorychev was sacked by Brezhnev. Egorychev was then handed a prepared text he was expected to read aloud at an emergency meeting of the Moscow city buro, scheduled for 24 June.[58]

The sacking proved to be the easy part. Getting a supportive city party committee to turn against Egorychev required careful planning and coordination. What followed was a textbook example of a new form of political exclusion whose effects, while not involving repression,

First Secretary of the Moscow City Committee Nikolai Egorychev speaking at the XXIII Party Congress on 30 March 1966, a year before his ill-fated speech at the Central Committee plenum. Courtesy of Russian State Archive of Photographic and Cinematic Documents in Krasnogorsk.

were crushing nonetheless. On the eve of the Moscow buro meeting, its members were individually summoned to the gorkom and instructed to give their vocal support to Egorychev's decision to step down as first secretary. Egorychev's retraction the next day was followed by carefully choreographed denunciations from the head of the executive committee, Vasilii Promyslov, with whom Egorychev had had various run-ins in the past, and from the raikom first secretary, Raisa Dement'eva. The unkindest cut, however, came in a speech by Praskov'ia Voronina, Egorychev's own client and protégé who, with his support, had taken over as first secretary of the Bauman district raikom when he had vacated that position to become head of the city party committee. Voronina's charges of "Bonapartism" and of an unwillingness to listen to other buro members rang especially hollow as, in the past, she had, according to one of Egorychev's aides, always worshiped Egorychev. But now, as Egorychev himself would later recall, "Praskov'ia Voronina went out of her way to show that I was just some kind of son of a bitch."[59]

One of the most striking features of these speeches was that they were all read aloud from prepared texts from the same blue notebooks. "They poured out boiling water as per the instructions in their manuals," recalled one participant. The other curious aspect was that, in violation of established conventions for supposed organizational meetings of this sort, there were no representatives of the Central Committee in attendance. The status and position of these speakers help account for the anomaly. All three, along with the second secretary, Pavlov, who chaired the meeting, were themselves members (Pavlov and Promyslov) or candidate members (Dement'eva and Voronina) of the Central Committee, and, indeed, other than Egorychev himself, they were the only members of the buro who were. It later turned out that immediately after Brezhnev's sacking of Egorychev, all four had been summoned to the Central Committee building on *staraia ploshchad'* (Old Square) near the Kremlin and briefed on what to say by two senior party figures, Nikolai Savinkin and Mikhail Suslov. There was thus no need for formal representation from the Central Committee, as these four members were, in effect, proxies speaking on its behalf. For any member of the buro or, later, of the full party committee to have argued or quarreled with this group would have been tantamount to questioning the authority of the Central Committee.[60]

The plenum of the Moscow city committee, which opened on 27 June, was a subdued affair with no debates, questions, or applause. The plenum was chaired by Pavlov, who also gave the opening speech, which included a suitably severe appraisal of Egorychev's "political mistakes" at the Central Committee plenum. "It felt, however," recalled an aide, Valentin Davydov, "[that] Pavlov was preoccupied and that he had been severely worked over." With little notable enthusiasm the plenum

Photographs of the Moscow city plenum that rubber-stamped Egorychev's sack-ing were not permitted, but the layout of city and regional party plenums tended to follow a set pattern. This photograph of the Altai kraikom plenum is from 1972. *Source:* RGASPI.

proceeded to go through the motions of stripping Egorychev of his posts and anointing a successor. As much as the whole episode was pre-sented as an initiative from below, all the participants understood that it had been carefully staged and that any dissent or resistance on their part would have been futile. Egorychev's political exclusion was then reinforced by a carefully coordinated act of informal exclusion. "We went into the lobby," noted Egorychev's senior assistant, Iurii Lipinskii, after the gorkom buro meeting, "and all the secretaries and members of the buro were there, but we felt suddenly as if some kind of invis-ible wall had formed around us and that we were walking through a social vacuum. Nikolai Grigoverich and I walked through this void and no one, absolutely no one, dared come up to us!" In the succeeding months, Egorychev found that at public events or in chance encounters on his way to work former friends and colleagues would turn their heads or cross the road.[61]

From one of the most powerful positions in the Soviet system Egorychev was demoted to deputy minister of agricultural and tractor machinery, and in 1970 he was packed off on an ambassadorial posting to Denmark, where he served until 1984. Politically speaking, Egorychev had been neutralized. Although he was a prominent political leader, the mechanics of the purge reflected two secular trends in the nature of political exclusion. First, the charges against Egorychev were devoid of political content. There was no questioning of his political loyalty or issues raised around his class or social origins.[62] Second, although Egorychev was politically neutralized, his party status was unaffected. In fact, after the dramatic fall in expulsions under Khrushchev, by 1967, the time of the Egorychev episode, expulsions had become something of a rarity.[63]

The drop in expulsions from the party did not mean that political exclusion was no longer practiced. To some extent the Egorychev case shows how Brezhnev had turned political exclusion into something of an art form. Three aspects of the revised process of political exclusion under Brezhnev warrant further scrutiny. First, any purge involved not only dislodging a political principal but also rooting out his network. It involved not just getting rid of a leader but also extricating his whole circle, which could be destabilizing for a regional party organization. This particular aspect of the purge explains why carrying it out in public was important. Carefully staged acts of ostracism dramatized the aura of social exclusion and political contamination that hung over a victim. For good measure, the head of the KGB, Iurii Andropov, reportedly circulated a rumor that Egorychev was part of a Komsomol plot involving Shelepin, Semichastny, and others, something Egorychev always denied.[64]

Second, while the absence of expressly political connotations surrounding Egorychev's loyalty to the regime or his class origins meant that it was possible to disable him without having him arrested or expelled from the party, it also created a difficulty. In the 1930s and 1940s acts of expulsion could be carried out with relative ease, almost as if the system were working on autopilot, as they could freely draw on deep-seated reserves of feeling and emotion concerning matters of political allegiance and class identity. Now that these issues were no longer at play, the regime had to organize expulsion manually. As is evident in Egorychev's case, such a process could be elaborate and time-consuming, one for which, in this particular case, few members of the Moscow city party committee appeared to have any enthusiasm.

Third, precisely because it was harder to draw on these deeper well-springs of support, it was now more important to combine political exclusion with co-optation. For this reason it was deemed important that, while cadres like Egorychev were to be politically excluded, they should be allowed to hold on to a tranche of nomenklatura benefits. From 1965 to 1976 sixty-two obkom first secretaries were replaced under Brezhnev, but only three were so reduced in status that they fully disappeared from public view. The majority received transfers to Moscow, which, even in cases where this move represented a loss of status, "were in themselves immensely desirable not only because [in Moscow] lies the fountainhead of power but also because of the vastly superior conditions of life [there]."[65] Those cut off from senior portfolios, often in quite brutal and public ways, were allowed to keep their party membership or their nomenklatura benefits and even, for a time, their seats on the party's top bodies.[66] As Brezhnev himself reportedly told Egorychev, "Look, Kolya, I'm not talking about having you kicked off the Central Committee."[67] The key thing was that the officials had been moved to portfolios that held little power.[68]

There was a coda to the Egorychev story. As his replacement, the Politburo decided to appoint the head of the Soviet trade union organization, Viktor Grishin. Upon getting elected, Grishin invited members of the Moscow city apparatus to a small room off the main hall, where he warmly thanked them for their support. "But we all knew," remembers a gorkom secretary, "that Grishin had been chosen precisely in order to get rid of us."[69] Grishin obliged by sacking anyone who had worked with or been appointed by Egorychev, including five of the main gorkom department heads.[70]

Grishin's appointment was significant for another reason as well. At the trades union organization, which he had headed for the previous eleven years, Grishin had earned a reputation as a taciturn, private man who was, in the parlance of the day, a poor communicator (*chelovek nekommunikabel'nyi*).[71] "Unlike a great number of his party and Soviet colleagues," writes the editor of his memoirs, "Grishin did not suffer from a provincial inferiority complex. Therefore he did not feel the need to create around him a clan of those from his region [*zemliaki*] or to insinuate his own loyal supporters into key positions."[72] Compared with the eminently sociable Egorychev, who would drink with his clique of frontovik raikom secretaries and invite gorkom buro colleagues to his dacha over the weekend to play volleyball, Grishin was a loner.

In most regions the Brezhnev leadership sought to solve their agency problem by appointing good networkers who could build the solid, widely extended networks they required in order to govern. Moscow, however, was a special case. It was not only symbolically significant as the country's capital but had a high concentration of educated, ambitious politicians. The Brezhnev leadership was well aware that the Moscow gorkom could provide a platform for some form of political opposition in the future. In Moscow, therefore, rather than opting for a network builder it went for a network breaker. In a tradition that went back to the Stalin era, Brezhnev opted for a truth teller who had little need to ingratiate himself with his peers and who could be relied on to act as an honest, reliable agent of the center.[73]

Brezhnev's many years as an obkom secretary may have made him especially aware of the challenges facing a typical obkom leader. As his son-in-law Iurii Churbanov recounted, "On one occasion we chanced to have a conversation about the obkom first secretaries, and Leonid Il'ich put it as follows: 'Of course one can remove any secretary of a party committee at any time. Where there's a will you can always find a way. But before finding fault with our party secretaries, we must not forget the colossal responsibilities that rest on their shoulders.' And Leonid Il'ich went on to say that serving for over ten years as the head of an oblast party organization can only be done by those who have truly earned authority and respect among their colleagues and, most of all, with the population at large."[74]

Despite his reputation for control and micro-management and his speeches condemning family circles and nepotism, Stalin had always recognized the need for regional leaders to build viable networks if they were to govern properly. So long as they did not represent a political threat to him, he was generally content to let them do so. As a precaution he instituted a panoply of institutional checks involving control agencies, elections, rotations, and the occasional targeted purge. Although Khrushchev, unlike Stalin, was determined to relieve the administrative burden on the center and eager to delegate more power to his regional principals, he maintained the center's pressure on them, in the form of taut plans, fixed term limits for cadres, and major, nonviolent purges. Brezhnev's approach would be different. Instead of transfers and cross-postings he recruited obkom leaders from the regions. And once they were in post he let them stay there for longer, signaling that they could exercise greater discretion in running their own affairs. He did this because, as he put it to Churbanov in the quotation cited above, he recognized that being an obkom first secretary could "only be done by those who have truly earned authority and respect among their colleagues and, most of all, with the population at large." Moreover, unable to appoint his own clients, Brezhnev cultivated ongoing relationships with obkom secretaries based on meetings, telephone calls, and various rituals involving awards and prizes.

One of Brezhnev's main achievements was to reconfigure the practice of political exclusion. Although there were various constraints on the kinds of purge he could carry out, Brezhnev had no choice but to purge, so as to signal his position as "first among equals" in the Soviet political order. Ironically, purges of this kind served as a stabilizing force, for they made it clear to lower-level functionaries where the ultimate power resided in this system. Under Khrushchev, political exclusion had been decoupled from repression and, largely, from expulsions from the party. Yet in this regard too Brezhnev went further. The fact that exclusion and purges no longer carried deeper associations revolving around political loyalty and class identity had created a problem, as exclusion no longer carried the emotional force it had enjoyed in the 1930s and 1940s. Instead, it had to be applied manually, with considerable additional effort in the form of central management and coordination. Moreover, while the management of cadres still relied, as it had before, on a balance of exclusion and cooptation, the system had begun to lean more heavily on the latter.

10 Party Governors

IN PLACE OF any far-reaching organizational reforms, the Brezhnev regime made do with higher levels of economic and political freedom at the micro-level. On the economic plane this included the toleration of various forms of direct market exchange and the tacit acceptance of reciprocal exchange, that is, personal and often delayed exchanges enforced through custom or tradition. Although less commented on, there was also a parallel development in the state itself. Under cover of the new discourse of "noninterference" and "respect," regional leaders were granted greater levels of autonomy. Whereas in the economy this process unfolded behind the scenes, in the political sphere it was brought out into the open. Launched at the XXIII Party Congress in 1966, the campaign for "trust in cadres," which was the public face of the new approach, became one of the most enduring and recognizable refrains of the Brezhnev era.[1]

The fact that the new slogan turned on the idea of trust (*doverie*) was no accident. Ties of trust are ordinarily built on ongoing personal relationships.[2] By the Brezhnev era the Soviet economy had tacitly made use of such relations of trust—in particular through *blat*, the use of personal connections—for over a generation in order to make the bloated and overcentralized economic system work more effectively. Now it was the turn of the political system. The new emphasis on trust in cadres of the early Brezhnev period signaled a rolling back of the crude "administrative measures" of the Stalin and Khrushchev eras, which had relied on a blend of coercion and organizational pressure, in favor of a set of informal arrangements organized around personal relationships.

Trust in cadres marked the culmination of a transformation that had started in the late Stalin era. As in the late 1940s regional leaders still had to find solutions to the problems of authoritarian control and authoritarian power sharing. In both periods they did this by setting up some kind of protective network, usually courtesy of the resources afforded them by the Communist Party. But the institutional and social environment had now changed so that the standard strategies of the classic substate dictator were harder to activate. The result was that in many regions political regimes marked by asymmetric networks and heavy reliance on overpromotion, kompromat, and political exclusion ceded to a new form of rule.

All this mattered for the evolution of the Soviet system because by the mid-1970s the first secretaries of regional and republican party organizations had become the most important category of official in the USSR. They were the largest numerical group on the Central Committee, the party body of several hundred of the most powerful officeholders in the country. Regional and republican party secretaries also served as the single largest reserve from which members of the supreme leadership were chosen.[3] Before getting to the top, future statewide leaders such as Mikhail Gorbachev and Boris Yeltsin had served as heads of territorial party organizations under Brezhnev, with Gorbachev serving as first secretary in Stavropol' krai from 1970 to 1978 and Yeltsin as first secretary in Sverdlovsk from 1975 to 1985. Despite this we know relatively little about how regions were run under Brezhnev. The purpose of this chapter is to help fill this gap.

The chapter describes the model that most regions under Brezhnev were moving toward. While this transition was general, it did not unfold in an even or uniform way. Regional transitions followed varying timelines. Earlier in the book we saw that under Stalin there were signs of a shift from the two dominant regional models, those of the substate dictator and the contested autocrat, toward a new form of regional leadership. In many regions this new form of regional leadership was already in place at the beginning of the Brezhnev era. Before

Many obkom leaders under Brezhnev would later move on to top positions in the Soviet Union's supreme leadership. This meeting of construction workers on the Main Stavropol' Canal on 27 April 1972 is being addressed by the first secretary of the Stavropol' kraikom, Mikhail Gorbachev. *Source:* RGASPI.

assessing this model more fully, we begin the chapter by examining two late-starting regions, one led by a substate dictator and the other by a contested autocrat, and follow their truncated transitions, condensed into a brief period of conflict in the late 1960s, that would propel them toward the new model of regional rule.

SUBSTATE DICTATOR

In the mid-1960s Kabardino-Balkariia was one of sixteen autonomous republics (ASSRs)—regional-level national territories which accorded special rights to their titular minorities—in the Russian Federation, and one of only twenty in the USSR as a whole. With a population of 518,000, it had what was almost the smallest regional-level party organization in the RSFSR (sixty-sixth out of seventy). A decade earlier one of the two titular ethnic groups, the Balkars, who had been deported by Stalin during the war, had been allowed to return and, accordingly, the region reverted to its former title of Kabardino-Balkariia (having been called the Kabardinian ASSR from 1944 to 1957). Despite this development, some Balkars, who comprised 8 percent of the population, complained of continued ethnic discrimination against them by the Kabardin leadership. The first secretary of the autonomous republic in the mid-1960s was T.K. Mal'bakhov, a Kabardin and stalwart of the republican political establishment.[4] He had held that position since January 1956. As other regions in the late 1950s and early 1960s gravitated toward what we call party governor regimes, Kabardino-Balkariia clung doggedly to the classic model of the substate dictator. As was the case in other national republics, Moscow may have decided to give Mal'bakhov free rein to run the region as he wished. The case for doing so may have been strengthened by the delicate ethnic balance in the republic, one which involved reincorporating an ethnic group that until recently had been forced into exile.

Mal'bakhov's strategy, which cleaved closely to that of an earlier generation of substate dictators, rested on two pillars. First, he formed an inner network from a small ethnoterritorial group drawn from his home district of Tersk.[5] Among the members of the Tersk circle who were closest to Mal'bakhov were the obkom secretary, M.Kh. Shekikhachev; the head of the republican trade union organization, Rosa Sabanchieva; the secretary of the presidium of the republican supreme soviet, F.T. Arsaeva; and the head of the department of construction at the obkom, Pshikan Khapachaev. This Tersk group dominated some of the key strategic positions in the republic. Of the five Kabardins on the obkom buro, three (Mal'bakhov himself, Shekikhachev, and Sabanchieva) were from Tersk, and of the nineteen Kabardin deputies on the supreme soviet who held executive positions, twelve, or 63 percent, were also from Tersk.[6] While the obkom buro met relatively rarely and its cadre decisions were often ignored or rejected, Mal'bakhov regularly consulted an informally constituted grouping of his Tersk associates on appointments. "I assert," wrote one well-informed insider in a letter to the Central Committee, "that not a single cadre question is decided by comrade Mal'bakhov without the advice of comrades Sabanchieva, Arsaeva, and his other *zemliaki* [from Tersk]. This is well-known to all comrades in the republic."[7] Members of the Tersk group also acted as Mal'bakhov's most reliable agents. "They create a cult of Mal'bakhov," reported the same source, "they sow intrigues, organize anonymous letters, and try to frighten those who have the temerity to criticize Mal'bakhov."[8] The most assiduous in this regard was the ideology secretary, Shekikhachev, who appears to have been used by Mal'bakhov to hound a number of opponents, such as the former obkom secretaries I.L. Ul'bashev, Ch.B. Uianaev, and Kh.I. Khutuev as well as various raikom secretaries who had dared to stand up to Mal'bakhov. According to K.K. Uianaev, "Strictly speaking, comrade Shekikhachev is not a secretary of the obkom but a personal enforcer [*prokuror*], and he certainly does not seem to get up to work of an ideological kind."[9]

The second pillar of Mal'bakhov's power-building strategy rested on a mixture of overpromotion and kompromat. In order to accentuate their dependence on him, Mal'bakhov opted not only for individuals from Tersk but also for candidates with personal blemishes or a questionable past. One such was V.Z. Duduev, who, following an extramarital scandal while he was head of the republican Komsomol, was appointed, against the wish of the obkom buro, as second secretary of the Nal'chik (republican capital) gorkom and then as head of the capital's soviet executive committee. "At one of the plenums of the gorkom," recalled K.K. Uianaev, "[although] members of the gorkom knew that the obkom buro opposed the appointment of Duduev as gorkom secretary, [and] they were exasperated, they objected [*oni vozmuschalis, vozrazhali*], nevertheless, all the same, comrade Mal'bakhov insisted on dragging Duduev in as the new gorkom secretary."[10] To an outside observer it may have appeared that Duduev's main qualification was not his professional or work attributes but his personal connection to Mal'bakhov, a fact that made him highly vulnerable should Mal'bakhov have lost office. It was this extreme personal dependence on Mal'bakhov that turned Duduev from a run-of-the-mill colleague into a client. Willfully defying the wishes of the aktiv, Mal'bakhov demonstrated his power and brought Duduev into the inner sanctum of the republican political system. Other controversial figures from Tersk who received spectacular promotions in spite of opposition majorities on the obkom buro were Goriacheva (no initials provided), who became deputy minister of education, and M.M. Gukepshev, a relative of Rosa Sabanchieva, who was first installed as chair of the Nal'chik city executive committee before becoming head of the industrial-transportation department at the obkom.[11]

Much like other substate dictators, Mal'bakhov had an acerbic, confrontational manner. At public meetings he and his allies were unsparing in their attacks on those outside their network. When, at a meeting of the obkom plenum on 5 February 1968, the minister of agriculture, M.Kh. Khachetlov, and a candidate member of the obkom, N.F. Mishkov, tried to fend off criticisms from Mal'bakhov, they were sharply rebuffed. Mal'bakhov taunted the minister:

> MAL'BAKHOV: If I am not mistaken, I have understood comrade Khachetlov thus: we mustn't criticize [his] ministry or at the very least we should say that the ministry and the obkom are both at fault here. Is that right?
>
> KHACHETLOV: Yes
>
> MAL'BAKHOV: Well, tough (laughter in the hall). No, comrades, we shall all the same have to criticize the ministry of agriculture. . . . I take it that the members of the obkom have no problem with this?
>
> VOICES FROM HALL: No, no problem.[12]

As for Mishkov, the minister of health, V.Sh. Shogenova, one of Mal'bakhov's closest confidantes from Tersk, chided, "It has to be said that certain members of the party have committed *anti-party acts,* especially comrade Mishkov."[13] Mal'bakhov joined in: "I hadn't thought we needed to out comrade Mishkov. But if it comes to naming names then, of course, we have to start with his first of all."[14] "Mal'bakhov . . . starts shouting and is rude and persecutes those who criticize him," noted Uianaev. "That was the case with the former first secretary of the Zol'skii raikom, Anuar Keshtov [as well as with . . .] the first secretary of the Urvanskii raikom, Zh. Efendiev [both of whom were] dismissed for [their] troubles."[15]

In all these regards Mal'bakhov, in the mid-1960s, might be viewed as an archetypical substate dictator. From the late 1960s, however, there were three impulses to change, all of which emanated from the Central Committee in Moscow. Early in 1968 the Central Committee began to curb Mal'bakhov's hold on power in Kabardino-Balkariia. While falling short of a wholesale purge of Mal'bakhov and his Tersk network, the Central Committee began to strengthen its institutional checks on the republican leader. The strategically significant post of head of cadres at the obkom had been held by a Russian, Andrei Mel'nik, who had also been a member of the obkom buro.[16] Mel'nik had enjoyed a good relationship with the deputy head of the department of party organs at the Central Committee, V.I. Bessarabov, and had been used by the latter to keep an eye on appointments in the republic.[17] Until now, however, Mel'nik had been outflanked by Mal'bakhov and the Tersk group, who, in any case, usually bypassed the obkom buro when it came to cadres decisions. But in February 1968 this state of affairs changed. After twelve years as second secretary, the Tatar Gennady Khubaev, who had come to regard Kabardino-Balkariia as his "second homeland," was replaced by a fifty-year-old Russian, Nikolai Krupin, who had spent the previous ten years at the department of party organs at the Central Committee.[18] Although, as we have seen, the first traces of the new system of second secretaries in the national republics went back to the late Stalin era, as an ensemble of practices it took general hold in the middle of the Khrushchev era, around 1960–61.[19] Even then, however, it was not rolled out simultaneously across all national regions. In Kabardino-Balkariia it took until 1968 before the institution of a native first secretary and a Central Committee–trained Slavic second would be installed. Also that February a third Russian, the new local head of the KGB, Mikhail Timofeev, was voted onto the obkom buro.[20] With three Russians on the buro, all of whom occupied positions of power on republican administrative structures and all of whom demonstrably enjoyed the support of the Central Committee, the Tersk network was confronted with a powerful counterweight.

A second factor which altered the dynamics of elite politics in the republic was a demonstration-cum-riot at the central kolkhoz market in Nal'chik on 13 July 1968. The trouble started when a Russian policeman, V.I. Tokarev, apprehended a Kabardin, N.Kh. Maremukov, who, reportedly being in an inebriated state, smashed one of the windows in the militsiia office and shouted out that he was being severely beaten and that his life was in danger. At the same time, two other Kabardins, Tkhakakhov and Kunizhev, claimed, falsely as it turned out, that the Russian policeman, Tokarev, had also killed Tkhakakhov's brother, Alik. An angry crowd of two thousand to three thousand people quickly gathered outside the police station as a vanguard group of rioters caught up with Tokarev, who tried to flee by car, and killed him.[21] As the crowd began to give vent to anti-Russian feeling, Mal'bakhov, who had rushed to the scene, addressed the demonstrators in the local language, Kabardian, and eventually managed to calm them down. But Mal'bakhov's subsequent efforts to dismiss the disturbance as the work of hooligans, speculators, and criminals were in vain. An internal memorandum two days later acknowledged that the outbreak had been fueled by ethnic tensions, a view corroborated by a Central Committee report at the end of August.[22] The affair heightened Bessarabov's sensitivity not only to relations between Kabardins and Russians but also to the simmering tensions between the titular nationalities in the republic, the Kabardins and the Balkars. It also sharpened his department's attention to the quotas used by the state to regulate relations between the two ethnic groups. This limited Mal'bakhov's ability to remove certain Balkars, including Kh. I. Khutuev and Ch.B. Uianaev, from the republican elite, so that although they were sacked they retained their seats on the obkom.[23]

The appointment in 1968–69 of Slavic viceroys and the consolidation of nationalities quotas marked a refinement of long-standing techniques developed in the late Stalin era for managing national relations in the Soviet multiethnic state.[24] The third institutional check on Mal'bakhov would, however, prove to be the most significant. In the summer of 1969 the Central Committee took steps to clamp down on Mal'bakhov's Tersk network. It did so by, in effect, wresting the powers of social and political exclusion out of Mal'bakhov's hands. At a meeting of the obkom buro in August 1969 Mal'bakhov was forced to attack two of his dependents, the director of the "Skototkorm" trust, P.A. Shogenov, and the director of the Tersk cattle-fattening sovkhoz, Kh.Kh. Pshigoshev, both of whom he had earlier stoutly defended.[25] The two were dismissed, and criminal proceedings were initiated against the latter.[26] In a thinly disguised rebuke of Mal'bakhov a Central Committee report on Kabardino-Balkariia two months later lamented that "certain party committees have not always responded in a principled way to violations by leading cadres from the republic of party and state discipline."[27] The tables were now turned on the Tersk network. At the January 1971 obkom plenum Mal'bakhov noted that while the Tersk district had previously been "famous throughout the North Caucasus" for its agricultural successes, it had recently fallen on hard times.[28]

Mal'bakhov was not only structurally hemmed in by his centrally appointed overseers. He was also forced to step back from his earlier brusque, confrontational methods and to observe standards of

First Secretary Timbor Mal'bakhov of the Kabardino-Balkariia ob-kom in 1970. Courtesy of Russian State Archive of Photographic and Cinematic Documents in Krasnogorsk.

decorum that were becoming a feature of Soviet public life. Aping the new discursive norms set by Brezhnev and other leaders in Moscow, and in what could have been viewed as a rebuttal of his earlier style of leadership, in 1970 Mal'bakhov asserted, "We cannot entrust a leading position to a person if he cannot be sensitive and attentive to others, if he is not courteous and tactful. . . . Those positions which involve dealing with people are not suitable for the hard or callous individual."[29] The new emphasis on forms of tact and respect went hand in hand with an explicit appeal to the importance of seniority in public affairs. "It turns out," Mal'bakhov would tell the members of his obkom buro in 1972, "[that] I am more senior than you in terms of age and experience. But I am also more senior in terms of *my formal position* [*starshe i po dolzhnosti*]. Of course, this may not be to everyone's liking, but that is the way it is."[30]

Rather than unleashing a regional purge of the kind that Stalin or Khrushchev might have favored, Brezhnev's Central Committee drew on the existing repertoire of institutional controls on leaders in the national territories in order to muzzle Mal'bakhov. Yet it also went beyond these techniques by forcing him to act against his narrowly constituted territorial network and by getting him to temper his public persona so that it fitted in with the more restrained norms of the post-Khrushchev leadership. Forced to turn against his Tersk clients, Mal'bakhov was compelled to broaden the regional ruling elite to include ordinary colleagues whose ties to him were more conditional. As a result his leadership shed the attributes of the substate dictator and shifted toward the hierarchical ethics and wider, shallower network of the typical Brezhnev-era party governor. It was in this form that Mal'bakhov was allowed to stay on as the first secretary of Kabardino-Balkariia until 1985.

CONTESTED AUTOCRAT

Kirov province in the early Brezhnev period had the archetypal contested autocrat who presided over a divided elite that congealed around two rival networks. The obkom first secretary at the time was B.F. Petukhov, who had been parachuted in from the south in February 1961 following the dismissal of the first secretary A.P. Pcheliakov in one of the most celebrated data-fixing scandals of the era (see chapter 7).[31] As a southerner and an outsider, Petukhov irked some members of the local elite who felt he did not fully understand local conditions. After a series of fractious disputes, Petukhov found himself faced with a formidable opposition network, which had its base in the obkom bureaucracy. As we have seen, contested autocrats were often leaders who had been transplanted from the center or from another province and had little standing or support in the region. Accordingly, they quickly became the target of resentment and hostility. Measures of their weakness were that they were rarely in a position to elevate their own people to positions of influence, to implement ambitious plan targets, or to lobby effectively in Moscow.

The origins of Petukhov's Brezhnev-era disputes reached back to the division of the obkom apparatus in November 1962. As first secretary of the more powerful agricultural obkom—Kirov was a predominantly agricultural region—Petukhov embarked on a number of ill-advised policies on procurement and sowing practices that led to a fall in yields and productivity in 1963. His detractors were quick to blame the shortages on the fact that, as a southerner, Petukhov failed to grasp agricultural requirements in Kirov, a northern region.[32] On 28 February 1964 Khrushchev launched a broad attack on the Kirov leadership for its poor economic record, and on 12 March Petukhov himself was ordered to Moscow and reprimanded. A resolution of the RSFSR buro of the Central Committee of 13 March 1964 assailed Petukhov for the high turnover of cadres in his region and for a style of work that encouraged "cringing and servility [*podkhalimstvo i ugodnichestvo*]."[33] The resolution was publicized at the obkom plenum in April, and this paved the way for some sweeping attacks on Petukhov. Two of his sternest critics at the plenum were the raikom secretaries A.V. Podoplelov and N.P. Chemodanov, who, taking their cue from the Central Committee resolution, attacked Petukhov for fostering servility (*ugodnichestvo*) and nepotism (*semeistvennost'*).[34]

In November 1964 the Central Committee received a denunciation of Petukhov which prompted a second summons to Moscow and, in turn, a new round of hostile articles in the Kirov regional paper, *Kirovskaia Pravda*.[35] At the December 1964 plenum, which was charged with electing a reunited single obkom, one of Petukhov's critics from April, Podoplelov, embarked on an all-out attack on Petukhov for "not tolerating objections, overestimating his own abilities," and surrounding himself with "people who flatter and cringe"; others, meanwhile, attacked Petukhov for fostering toadies, cultivating cringing and servility, and being no less to blame for the woeful state of agriculture in the region than the recently departed and now widely vilified first secretary of the Central Committee, Nikita Khrushchev.[36] At the closed obkom ballot, 53 of the 491 delegates voted against Petukhov, while his closest supporters also attracted large protest votes.[37] Although Petukhov was eventually elected as first secretary of the united obkom, his authority had been dented.

Shortly after the reunification of the obkom a new opposition to Petukhov formed within the obkom buro. Podoplelov, now an obkom secretary, and Chemodanov, now head of the cadres department, were joined by two other disgruntled figures, the new second secretary of the obkom, P.G. Dobroradnykh (formerly the first secretary of the industrial obkom), and the new agricultural secretary, I.M. Kolupaev (the former second secretary of the agricultural obkom). While other members of the buro rallied around Petukhov, this group remained steadfast in its opposition. As a candidate member of the buro, Karecharov,

First Secretary Boris
Petukhov of the Kirov
obkom in 1966. Courtesy
of Russian State Archive of
Photographic and Cinematic
Documents in Krasnogorsk.

later recalled: "If the first secretary says 'yes,' this group always says 'no.'"[38] Petukhov would himself concede afterward that "within the buro there practically existed two buros . . . with the second consisting of comrades Dobroradnykh, Podoplelov, Kolupaev, and Chemodanov. . . . [Prior to meetings of the buro the four would gather at] comrade Dobroradnykh's house to debate the points and would then turn up at the buro to declare: 'We are against.'"[39] On one occasion Petukhov, in the presence of an instructor from the Central Committee, warned Dobroradnykh to "stop organizing a second buro."[40]

Eventually Petukhov did manage to have Dobroradnykh, his main opponent, dismissed. There ensued, however, a bitter standoff between Petukhov and the head of cadres at the obkom, Chemodanov. As in any obkom, the cadres department was the most important instrument of network building in the region, and Petukhov regarded control of it as a priority. For their part, his detractors, including Dobroradnykh, who remained a member of the obkom, charged Petukhov with treating "the department of party agencies [that is, the cadres department] as . . . his own fief."[41] Petukhov countered by accusing Chemodanov of being insubordinate and of having "false ideas of his own impor-tance."[42] I.P. Bespalov, who had replaced Dobroradnykh as second sec-retary in 1968, shortly after remarked, "Although the [head of the] *orgotdel* [the cadres department] is subordinate to the first secretary, Chemodanov has always seen himself as the first secretary's equal."[43] For a long time, Bespalov noted, Chemodanov "has neglected to go and see the first secretary to decide important questions. He seemed to reckon that people had to go cap in hand to see *him*." "That over the course of two whole years [Chemodanov] could not spare five minutes to go and see the first secretary to sort out various questions, what sort of behavior is this?" asked another member of the buro, Vorob'ev.[44] Al-though Petukhov did manage to have Chemodanov removed from the obkom buro in mid-1967, an attempt in early 1968 to have him fired as head of the cadres department was aborted.[45]

Petukhov's two remaining adversaries on the buro, Podoplelov and Kolupaev, continued to defy him. One buro member, Grachev, stated that "comrades Podoplelov and Kolupaev can't stomach the first sec-retary. They simply can't stand him. They use every opportunity to dis-credit him and have him removed. . . . Over a number of years now they have followed a separate line from the buro on a variety of key cadre questions."[46] In the meantime, two local scandals further polarized the regional elite as a number of disaffected officials gravitated toward the Chemodanov–Podoplelov–Kolupaev camp.[47]

Matters came to a head in the summer of 1969. In April Petukhov appeared to have finally secured the transfer of Chemodanov from the obkom cadres department to a secondary post at the ispolkom. When, however, Petukhov asked for the decision to be ratified at the meet-ing of the full obkom on 24 June he came in for a surprise. Before an enlarged audience which included Komsomol members and pensioners who were not members of the obkom, the decision was openly chal-lenged by Podoplelov, who proceeded to launch a personal, quite bitter tirade against the first secretary for his handling of the Chemodanov case.[48] In view of the sensitive subject matter Petukhov requested that it be discussed in closed session. Members of the audience who were not on the obkom were asked to leave the hall. Once the session re-sumed, in a series of pointed attacks first Chemodanov, then Kolupaev, along with a number of disenchanted officials such as Liamov and the former obkom secretary, Dobroradnykh, reprised a host of grievances against Petukhov, accusing him of engaging in political intrigue, stifling criticism, and trampling local democracy.[49] In what appeared to be a coordinated assault that picked up various strands of criticism from the late Khrushchev period, Chemodanov accused Petukhov of "surrounding himself with cringers and servile individuals [*podkhalimami i ugodnikami*] who constantly praise and admire him."[50]

These attacks initially caught the first secretary and his followers unawares. As the meeting progressed, however, a number of Petukhov's followers on the buro as well as members of the aktiv rallied to his defense. The retaliation was more clearly formulated at a meeting of the obkom buro the following week, on 30 June, where there was a groundswell of support for Petukhov and his office. Unlike the situation in Kabardino-Balkariia, where the impulse for change had come from above, in the form of a pincer movement against Mal'bakhov by the Central Committee, in Kirov the main force for change came from below, from Petukhov's peers and from members of the regional aktiv. The dissidents had, according to the buro member Derevskoi, "undermined the authority [*avtoritet*] of the first secretary and of the buro as a whole."[51] Another buro member, Karacharov, invited the others to imagine the following scenario: "Let's say that you, as the first secretary say one thing, while your head of department says something else, then, without doubt, you, as the first secretary, would immediately get rid of him. No first secretary can tolerate a person on the obkom apparatus who does not fall in line and fulfill his duties."[52] This clamor for restoring the authority of the buro sounded as strongly from the raikom officials as it did from other members of the buro. After the turmoil of the Khrushchev years rank-and-file officials began to speak up in favor of what one might think of as order-supporting norms in regional affairs. "Many of the [district] secretaries are telling me," admitted Grachev, "what's up with you [in the obkom buro], you really should be setting an example, why can't you bring the buro to order?"[53] "After our conversations," Petukhov himself recounted, "raikom secretaries often come up and tell me that comrade Kolupaev is pestering them: 'What shall we do about comrade Petukhov, look at what he is up to.' I'm simply embarrassed for you [Kolupaev] and embarrassed for them too."[54]

One of the specific accusations leveled at Petukhov had been that in wanting to unseat the first deputy chair of the soviet executive committee, Smirnov, he had resorted to "provocational tricks" by planting a complaint, ostensibly by a district secretary Kazakovtsev but in fact composed by him, that was designed to compromise Smirnov. When Chemodanov was asked, as head of the cadres department, to look into it, his review established beyond doubt that the "complaint was organized on the insistence of the first secretary, Petukhov" for which Petukhov was forced to recant at the obkom buro and Kazakovtsev was fired.[55]

In the eyes of the rank and file, however, the restrained use of kompromat, exclusion, and provocational tricks was the legitimate prerogative of the first secretary. These actions were not to be sneered at but were, in the appropriate circumstances, part of the rightful tool kit that the first secretary needed to bring order to the region. Rather than condemning Petukhov's underhanded actions in the Smirnov affair, members of the aktiv, such as the first secretary of the Verkhnekamskii raikom, Bryzgalov, sprang to Petukhov's defense: "[Smirnov was fired] and not a moment too soon. . . . It's another matter on whose initiative. It may have been Boris Fedorovich [Petukhov] or someone else who came up with the proposal, but in all honesty it *should have* been his call. What kind of obkom secretary is it who does not show initiative? You [that is, the dissidents] want to put the first secretary in an impossible position. If you had things your way, we raikom first secretaries would also have to cope with this kind of situation. The first secretary has always been and always will be the first secretary."[56]

In Kabardino-Balkariia the substate dictator Mal'bakhov was reined in from above through a series of directed actions by the Central Committee. In Kirov a divided ruling network had to contend, by contrast, with a craving for order, stability, and leadership from below. "Did you see how many members of the Komsomol were present, how many young people there were, who view the buro as a model? Pensioners were invited, but you still could not find it in yourself to announce that you had something to say, but that you would leave it to the closed plenum," remarked the buro member Sharov to Podoplelov at the meeting of 30 June.[57] "It is simply painful to hear how obkom secretaries [that is, Podoplelov and Kolupaev] could behave like this," declared the buro member Grachev. "The party has a number of pragmatic principles for assigning cadres. No one holds on to a post forever; if an issue is settled collectively, then for the disciplined party member that really should be it."[58] In reaction to the public hectoring of the Khrushchev years, there were now new strictures on keeping up appearances and on pressing disagreements behind closed doors. Podoplelov, Chemodanov, Kolupaev, and the others had breached the order-enhancing norms of the post-Khrushchev era and, in the words of Sharov, had "violated party ethics."[59] There was also a rejection of the linguistic tropes of the late Khrushchev era. "The word 'toady' has an absolutely clear meaning," noted the buro member Vorob'ev.[60] "We can't go around pinning the label on all and sundry," Petukhov pitched in. "This is an old, dirty weapon [*eto staroe, griaznoe oruzhie*]."[61]

Following the obkom buro meeting of 30 June the dismissal of Chemodanov was confirmed and both Podoplelov and Kolupaev were sacked as obkom secretaries. With this, the faction that had stuck like a thorn in Petukhov's side since 1962 was at last removed. When Petukhov eventually stepped down in 1971, his replacement was a local cadre, the second secretary I.V. Bespalov, whose appointment accorded with the regime's new policy of promoting local officials and adhering to the unwritten norms on seniority (see chapter 9). Bespalov had risen progressively up the hierarchy and was at the time of his appointment one step below Petukhov on the regional nomenklatura ladder.[62] Like so many RSFSR obkom secretaries of his generation, Bespalov enjoyed a long tenure, stepping down at the age of seventy upon Gorbachev's ascent to the leadership in 1985.

Accused of being excessively soft and liberal, Petukhov was unable to exercise his prerogatives and effect key cadre changes, including those which by rights lay within his jurisdiction.[63] While the center clearly wanted a strong leader in Kirov, so too did members of his obkom, who urged Petukhov to be more forthright and to make full use of the powers of his office. "The obkom buro spent a whole week chewing over that Nolinskii affair [of 1967]," observed Sharov, "but the whole thing should really have been settled in five minutes . . . and then look what happened. . . . Smirnov left the region only eventually to come back and then, after a week of wandering the streets in a drunken stupor, he has now been expelled from the party . . . whereas he really should have been kicked out from the very beginning."[64]

In the mid-1960s Kabardino-Balkariia and Kirov both appear to have been outliers. In Kabardino-Balkariia it may have been because of the sensitivities surrounding the return of an exile nation, the Balkars, in 1956 that the first secretary, Mal'bakhov, had been given unusually broad discretion in running his province. In Kirov the schism within the obkom went back to the disastrous legacy of the Pcheliakov years and the appointment of an outsider from the south with little experience in running a northern territory. Kirov was indeed the only region in the country where the reunification of obkoms at the end of 1964 led to such ructions that it featured in the national press.[65] In Kirov what eventually turned the dissident faction out was not so much Petukhov's own actions but the upsurge of support for stability and order from below. After the turmoil of the Khrushchev years, many regional aktivs threw their weight behind a package of authority-enhancing norms that included public shows of deference, the hiding of policy differences, and a carefully calibrated system of seniority based on stepped promotions.

PARTY GOVERNORS

Political networks in regions led by party governors were neither narrow nor highly asymmetric, as those of the substate dictators had been, but wider and more evenly graded, broadly following the contours of the formal party hierarchy. Party governors were more likely to use the ordinary instruments of party rule, such as marginal reallocations of personnel and conventional meetings of the obkom buro, to firm up their ruling coalition. Both the first secretary and his network adhered to the unwritten code, or "hierarchical ethics," of the regional elite. Unwritten norms in these regions might include promotion by seniority, the elevation of local officials rather than outsiders, and the maintenance of standards of politeness and decorum in everyday intercourse. Although the first secretary was not a dictator, he was normally regarded as a strong leader who could impose his will on local affairs. The leadership strategies and network dynamics of party governor regions can be fleshed out by considering two quite different examples, one from Krasnodar, a large agricultural krai in southern Russia, and the other from the Baltic union republic of Lithuania (see chapter 9).

In Krasnodar a powerful first secretary, Grigory Zolotukhin, was a textbook example of a party governor. From the moment he was appointed, Zolotukhin put his stamp on the region and was able to effect cadre changes at the lower levels with a minimum of fuss. But he was never allowed to become a substate dictator. In a mirror image of what happened to Brezhnev in Moscow, Zolotukhin was hedged in by a number of informal institutional controls. At the regional level these included restrictions on his powers of patronage over senior and midlevel officials. There were limits on how many people he could fire without attracting the unwonted attentions of the center; moreover, cadre movements were broadly expected to mesh with the system of seniority, limiting his capacity to promote and overpromote young cadres. In accordance with the new tone of the post-Khrushchev leadership, Zolotukhin also observed rules of propriety and decorum in his dealings with subordinates.

In addition to being the fourth largest region in the Russian Republic, Krasnodar was a major producer of grain, supplying one-thirteenth of all grain in the RSFSR in 1966.[66] One way in which Zolotukhin's appointment did differ from most others in the early post-Khrushchev period was that his was part of a small but strategically important tranche of replacements of four of the five largest party organizations in the Russian Federation in the year after Brezhnev came to power.[67] Unlike later, predominantly in-house appointments, Zolotukhin, who became first secretary in January 1966, was brought in from another province. Having served for eleven years as first secretary in Tambov, also a predominantly agricultural region, he was regarded as a heavyweight, one with excellent contacts in Moscow.[68] It was around this time that Zolotukhin joined Brezhnev's "rapid reaction force" of regional leaders who were regularly given the floor at party plenums and congresses.[69] At the XXIII Party Congress in March 1966 Zolotukhin was duly elected to full membership on the Central Committee. In the coming years it was taken as a reflection of Zolotukhin's considerable clout in the capital that he could boast of major over-the-plan increases in central investments in the region.[70]

Zolotukhin's appointment in Krasnodar was typical of the light Brezhnevite purge of regional officials that took place soon after Khrushchev fell. Zolotukhin replaced G.I. Vorob'ev, whose authority had earlier been eroded by a series of scandals.[71] Diminutive and having a slightly twisted face, Zolotukhin, nicknamed the Tambov wolf, was quick to make his mark and, in the words of one commentator, "did not leave any member of his circle in any doubt as to who was in charge of the Kuban [region]."[72] In January 1967 Zolotukhin effected a complete clearout of eight raikoms, removing not

First Secretary Grigory Zolotukhin of the Krasnodar kraikom addressing the XXIV Congress of the CPSU on 31 March 1971. Courtesy of Russian State Archive of Photographic and Cinematic Documents in Krasnogorsk.

only the first secretaries but also the second secretaries as well as the ordinary-rank secretaries in each case.[73] During 1967 Zolotukhin also ordered investigations and plenum debates on two of the most substantial party organizations in the region, the Krasnodar gorkom and the Adygei obkom.[74] The most incisive criticisms were of the gorkom of the third city in the krai, Novorossiisk, which eventually led to the sacking of its first secretary, N.E. Tupitsyn, on 13 May 1967.[75] Zolotukhin efficiently transmitted the economic demands placed on him by Moscow to his subordinates, singling out and publicly upbraiding plant managers and kolkhoz chairs who failed to meet their plan targets.[76] As Zolotukhin was wont to remind officials, he was not afraid to take "organizational measures" (*orgvyvody*) where need be, as he did in 1966 when he fired the director of the Krasnodar house construction industrial complex, V.D. Kiriakin, for "having made and then broken numerous promises on construction targets."[77] To observers in neighboring regions, such as the young Mikhail Gorbachev in

Stavropol', news soon filtered out that Zolotukhin was "on the case" in Krasnodar.[78]

Zolotukhin's show of strength was nonetheless carried out within clearly prescribed limits. Although he could readily dismiss raikom secretaries, there were constraints on his powers of patronage. With regard to midlevel and senior appointments Zolotukhin was forced to observe the established ladders of promotion. In contrast to the Stalin and Khrushchev era practice of overpromotion, which had seen the elevation of junior cadres over the heads of their immediate superiors as well as the regular appointment of outsiders, Zolotukhin complied with the seniority principle, whereby upward mobility was incremental and made from within the province. All of his appointments to the kraikom buro were of long-standing, senior regional officials whose previous post had been one step below on the regional nomenklatura.[79] In a manner that paralleled the institutional limits on Brezhnev's control of high-level cadres in Moscow, Zolotukhin was quite conservative in his leadership appointments.[80] Further, he insisted on behavioral self-restraint. Distancing his approach from the boorishness and petty tyranny of the Khrushchev era, he urged cadres to refrain from unnecessary shouting, swearing, or bullying. Six months after Brezhnev's speech at the XXIII Party Congress, Zolotukhin declared, "High expectations have nothing in common with bellowing, ordering people about and running things in an administrative way. Holding functionaries to account should not mean yelling, firing off punishments, or blowing up at people. . . . High expectations need to be matched by trust and respect—this is one of the most important principles of the cadre policies of our party, and this needs to be strictly enforced in our everyday life."[81]

Zolotukhin's feelings on this subject and on how the Soviet Union had entered a new stage of political development after the upheavals of the Stalin and Khrushchev eras was most clearly expressed in a speech he made in December 1969 in which he said,

> Certain comrades recall the times when there used to be what they refer to as "order" and, in essence, they suggest that we return to the tough administrative methods of the past. But such solutions are no longer feasible. The discipline that rests only on fear is not the sort of discipline we need. And this is not only because it would run against Leninist principles of socialist democracy or because it might undermine legality. We must look at the past in a sober light, and not lay it on thick, not idealize what happened. We well remember what the fear

instilled by administrative methods led to. It led to dishonesty, to suppressing the real state of affairs, to attempts to bury problems rather than to properly grasp and solve them, it led to deception and falsification. It also led to cadres playing safe and to the loss of initiative. Today our party is building its approach to cadres on the basis of trust . . . for our party and economic cadres have shown that they have the ability to solve complex problems for themselves.[82]

This was a restatement of Brezhnev's solution to the dictator's agency problem, only from a regional perspective. The experience of the Stalin and, even more so, of the Khrushchev eras had underlined the limits of what the center could control. One reason was that the most valuable information on the capacities and attainments of frontline officials was stored at the local level. Among the keenest lessons from Khrushchev's experiments was that any attempt to force the hand of local party officials through "administrative methods" was liable to yield an orgy of dishonesty, deception, and falsification of the kind that had reared its head in Riazan. "An atmosphere of trust," Zolotukhin reported, "has been established in the party. Nothing now prevents leaders at all levels from working creatively and from demonstrating their independence and initiative."[83]

By the Brezhnev era most of the Stalin-era techniques of network formation which had served an earlier generation of substate dictators were no longer available. Overpromotion ran against the stabilization of hierarchy which had begun in the 1930s and became entrenched after the war. Kompromat could no longer rely either on loosely formulated political charges, as in the late Stalin era, or on accusations of complicity in Stalin-era abuses, as under Khrushchev. In its most extreme version—expulsions from the party—political exclusion was also in decline. In general, network formation in party governor-led regions was more likely to follow the contours of the formal hierarchy of the party and to rely more heavily on co-optation. From region to region there were variations in how this transformation was achieved, often depending on such factors as the size of the territory, the structure of the economy, the social and ethnic profile of the population, and the ethnoterritorial status of the province.

For a different take on the party governor model, we turn to a very different example from one of the Soviet Union's smaller union republics, Lithuania, which we came across in the previous chapter. From 1974 the new first secretary in Lithuania was Petras Griškevičius. From the perspective of Moscow one of the most important functions of the titular nomenklatura, headed by Griškevičius, was to quell the emerging ethnopolitical movement in the republic. The action had come to a head in 1972 with an organized demonstration of five thousand people, the circulation of anti-Soviet leaflets in stairwells and mailboxes, and several reported self-immolations. With its penetration of Lithuanian cultural institutions and its command of the Lithuanian language, the titular nomenklatura was the most viable bulwark against this movement. Griškevičius and other members of the Lithuanian political elite may have even played up the challenge to authoritarian control in order to increase elite cohesion and to underline their indispensability to the center.[84]

As in other non-Slavic republics, control of cadres and of the secret police in Lithuania was placed in the hands of a Slavic second, who, in the case of Lithuania, was the Russian Valerii Kharazov (see chapter 9).[85] The presence of a centrally appointed figure with primary authority over personnel assignments and over the gathering of information meant that, as in other union republics, Griškevičius had to adjust his network-building strategy. He did so by resorting to a variety of informal practices, the most popular of which, following a precedent set by Brezhnev himself, was the organization of a hunting club. Griškevičius's hunting group displayed all the characteristics of an informal network. The first secretary selected the composition of the group and could decide on whom to evict and on what grounds, for example, if they turned up to the hunt drunk. Members of the upper elite were not allowed to hunt alone, only as part of the group. Their leadership of the hunt was ceremonially enforced by ritualized practices such as the awarding of a rifle or the right to take the lead in shooting. Via the hunt Griškevičius, following the pattern set by his predecessor Sniečkus, made sure that the informal life of the nomenklatura hinged on him. "Everyone who wanted a career had to hunt," recalled one participant; the "invitation to hunt was an offer to become an insider," remembered another. "Its main value," observes Grybkauskas, "was not the catch, but the capital accumulated in social networks."[86]

In its form of organization, which involved two separate hunting groups, the hunting club had a strong national inflection. The membership of the first group included figures such as M. Šumauskas, the chair of the presidium of the supreme soviet, and Kazimieras Liaudis, the former chair of the KGB, who were lower down in the formal pecking order than the ethnic Russian and second secretary, Valerii Kharazov, and the Russian-educated chair of the council of ministers, Juozas Maniušis, who were relegated to the second group.[87] The language of communication in the first club was Lithuanian and in the second Russian. This arrangement enabled members of the first group to agree certain matters beforehand. The group also included individuals outside the nomenklatura, such as Griškevičius's son and other family members.[88]

The networks of party governors tended to be broader and their power inequalities less steep than those of the substate dictator. Despite the cleavage between the two hunting groups, their mode of organization was relatively transparent. Unlike the secretive, small, and highly asymmetric networks of the substate dictator, the composition of the hunting groups broadly overlapped with the upper echelons of the Moscow-approved republican nomenklatura. Although Griškevičius was a strong leader who was able to fight for taut plan targets and to demonstrate his power by removing individuals, he practiced restraint. In general, he fitted in with Brezhnev's solution to the agency problem, based on a major delegation of power and a web of light-touch, informal controls. At the same time, the network he headed was more integrated than the divided networks of the contested autocrat: although they belonged to different groups, all the hunters were, after all, members of the same club.

There were a number of reasons for the eventual collapse of the Soviet system, among them economic decline, institutional failure, and the problems presented by geopolitical competition with the West.[89] Two of the most crucial factors had a strong regional or territorial dimension. First, the consolidation of party governor regions and the expansion of local horizontal networks meant that vertical channels of control began to silt up. The more local leaders invested in horizontal networks and the more these horizontal network links solidified, the more closed and impervious to vertical controls the local nomenklatura elites became.[90] Second, the spread—and demonstration effect—of nationalist rebellions in the second half of the 1980s quickly turned into an insuperable problem of authoritarian control.[91]

Although these were general trends reflected in the increasingly long tenures of obkom first secretaries, many of which were broadly coterminous with Brezhnev's own, one can pick up more nuanced signs of them in the two party governor regions of Krasnodar and Lithuania. After Zolotukhin left Krasnodar in 1973 he was replaced by Sergei Medunov, the former first secretary of the Sochi gorkom, whom Zolo-tukhin himself had promoted to head of the krai executive committee in March 1969. Along with Albert Churkin, Zolotukhin's second sec-retary, Medunov formed a clan that would in later years become a by-word for party-led corruption. Key linchpins in the Krasnodar corrup-tion network—who reputedly accepted hundreds of bribes—included the kraikom party secretary, Anatoly Tarada, the secretary of the Sochi gorkom, Aleksandr Merzlyi, and the first secretary of the Gelenzhik gorkom, Nikolai Pogodin. According to the lawyer Arkadii Vaksberg, "Thousands of letters were sent to the Kremlin . . . [and] each spoke of lawbreaking, extortion, misappropriation of state property, summary justice to anyone that crossed the authorities, and in every letter the fin-ger of guilt pointed at Medunov."[92] For his part, Griškevičius's policies helped foment relatively high levels of national consciousness in Lithu-ania, which, after his death in 1987, would see the Lithuanian commu-nist party secede from the all-union Communist Party in 1989 and go on to become the front-runner in the Baltic independence movement.

Conclusion

WE BEGAN THIS book by suggesting that an examination of substate leaders and their strategies can shed light on dictatorship and on how it changes over time. What we have learned from the Soviet case falls into two broad categories, one empirical and historical, the other comparative and theoretical. On the first plane, scholars have long viewed the death of the statewide tyrant Joseph Stalin as marking a decisive break in the trajectory of the Soviet state. Recent work has come to question this chronology. Some have pointed to the relaunching of the Soviet project initiated by the Great Patriotic War as an equally important divide.[1] Others have shown how Stalin, well before he died, systematically vested decision-making authority in committees on which he played no role, thereby easing the way for his succession.[2] In this book we point to a parallel act of delegation at the regional level. Unable to penetrate the inner recesses of local administration, Stalin handed over power on a provisional basis to regional leaders. Like any ruler in a dictatorship, substate leaders then had to address the dual problems of authoritarian power sharing—how to accommodate other members of the regional oligarchy—and authoritarian control—how to prevent rebellions from below.

Stalin's acts of delegation stemmed from an incentive problem.[3] The dictator needed trustworthy delegates whom he could control, but often these people lacked the authority or local ties to implement the center's decisions. Given that the qualities of submitting to the center and getting things done on the ground were not always compatible, the center looked for a balance. While this balance normally began with delegation, it went on to include a variety of trade-offs and institutional innovations. This central dilemma helps explain a number of persistent features of the Soviet state. One of these is indigenization—the policy of promoting national languages, cultures, and cadres—which enabled delegates of the center to gain authority over local populations. Another was the surprising willingness of the center, after the cataclysm of 1937–38, to let local leaders establish their own ruling networks, networks that, it understood, were intended to help them govern more effectively.

The bulk of the book looks at these questions not from the perspective of the center but from that of the regional leaders themselves. In addition to the problems of authoritarian control and power sharing, substate leaders faced two other challenges. First, they needed to fend off pressure from above and to ensure that local leaders and local party activists did not betray them to the center. Second, there was one important respect in which their hands were tied: against members of their regional elite, at least, they were not allowed to use repression. The book begins by showing how, under Stalin, most regional leaders addressed these problems by establishing particular types of networks: small, asymmetric groupings which tended to operate through four mechanisms: overpromotion, kompromat, and informal and political exclusion.

In order to make the structural dynamics of substate rule more comprehensible we began with a pared-down account of the strategic logic of the substate leader. To grasp change under dictatorship, we then added two layers of complexity. The first relates to institutional change. Whereas most scholars have focused on the surface and statewide forms of institutional change triggered by the death of the dictator—for example, the widening of the selectorate, the group whose support the dictator requires in order to retain office—we have highlighted deeper forms of institutional change that began while Stalin was still alive.[4] Although the Stalinist system was in many respects extremely centralized, a number of institutions originally designed in Moscow were systematically redeployed by regional leaders.[5] The second layer of complexity concerns wider processes of social change. From the 1940s the composition of regional party and state administrations became more stratified, more status conscious, and more socially conservative.

This social and institutional transformation meant that the Stalin-era system of substate dictators began to change. One reason was that some earlier sources of network formation began to dry up. The stabilization of regional hierarchies and of patterns of service and age seniority made it harder for regional leaders to resort to the classic Stalin-era tactic of overpromotion. Although the tactics of kompromat and exclusion remained open to substate leaders well into the post-Stalin era, they were now more circumscribed. Moreover, regional principals skillfully used information from institutions originally designed to control them to their own advantage by assessing levels of discontent, adjusting their own behavior, and averting damaging conflicts. The result was wider, shallower networks that were more closely aligned to the formal rank orders of the regional hierarchy. This laid the social and institutional foundations for a shift from the substate dictators of the Stalin era to the party governors of the Brezhnev administration.

While the main focus of the book is on the regional level, in some places (see chapters 4, 7, and 9) we shift our view to the center. We contend that Stalin, Khrushchev, and Brezhnev had quite distinct solutions to the dictator's agency problem, that is, to the fact that the most valuable information about tasks on the ground as well as about the actions, abilities, and preferences of those charged with carrying them out was locked up at the local level. Stalin dealt with this problem by delegating power to regional actors but hedging this act of delegation with institutional controls. Khrushchev's approach was altogether different. Although he had an intuitive, populist feel for the problems of overcentralization and to that end launched a vigorous campaign against paperwork and bureaucracy, he seems, unlike Stalin, to have had a naïve, almost childlike understanding of how organizations work. Khrushchev seemed to believe it was possible to load ever-greater responsibility for results on his regional party leaders while at the same time expecting them to provide honest, uncontaminated information about activities in their domain. As the epidemic of data falsification in 1960–61 would show, in this he would prove to be sadly mistaken. The book suggests that the massive purge of regional leaders which followed would mark a far more significant rupture in the regional system than anything that happened at the time of Stalin's death or, indeed, at any stage in the thirty-year period covered here. Unlike Khrushchev, Brezhnev recognized that there was an agency problem, one that he could not simply wish away, but unlike Stalin he was willing to cede far more ground to his regional agents. The result was a policy of trust in cadres and a proclivity, both in national and nonnational territories, to recruit cadres from their home regions, usually in accordance with an established order of precedence.

We have also sought to make a contribution to the comparative and theoretical literature on dictatorship. Recent work on comparative dictatorship has shown how Leninist one-party states like the Soviet Union shared, along with an institutionally related category of dictatorship, that of hegemonic or dominant party regimes, a propensity for longevity and regime resilience not present in other forms of nondemocratic rule.[6] This comparative scholarship has raised the question of why and in what ways the institution of the party facilitates the survival of dictatorship. Some scholars have pointed to the ability of the party as an institution to provide a relatively stable framework for distributing rents and negotiating policy concessions, thereby co-opting and defusing any potential opposition.[7] Other institutional scholars point to common organizational features of regime-sanctioned parties in promoting co-optation not through one-off cash or policy transfers but by making redistributions time-dependent and organizationally contingent on party service and seniority, thereby creating an enduring stake in the regime's survival.[8]

A second strand of scholarship stresses the historical origins of revolutionary regimes.[9] The most durable one-party regimes are those rooted in a period of sustained, violent struggle such as a civil war or a war of liberation. It is the identities, norms, and organizational structures forged during a prolonged period of ideologically driven conflict that consolidates partisan boundaries, mobilizes popular support, and ensures elite cohesion. The deeper forms of allegiance that result are better able to sustain a regime through subsequent moments of crisis than support earned through mere co-optation.[10]

By contrast, we argue that as the party matured the distinctive source of its power was neither repression nor co-optation but exclusion. The Soviet Communist Party was the first statewide organization to regularize this process of exclusion by making party membership an exclusive privilege, thereby turning expulsion, and the credible threat of it, into a powerful means of control.[11] While repression and co-optation did play a central role throughout the Soviet era, exclusion was a vital tool wedged in, as it were, between them.

The system of party-based exclusion had three characteristics. First, as in the case of the use of coercion by the state, it was often not exclusion itself but the credible threat of it that had the more pervasive impact. Expulsions from the party were linked to an array of punishments which fell short of expulsion but served to remind communists that their membership might be in jeopardy. Second, expulsion from the party meant ejection from the nomenklatura and all the associated perks, privileges, and preferential access it granted. But exclusion was not reducible to co-optation. For those who had devoted their lives to the party, exclusion could amount to far more than a loss in earnings or benefits: it could be a life-shattering blow leading to a drop in status, social isolation, depression, and, on occasion, suicide. Third, party-based exclusion could assume a number of forms. Formal expulsion from the party was the most visible and the most damaging. But there were other forms too. There were bouts of collective, informal exclusion—invariably staged at party meetings and orchestrated by party principals—which involved shunning, social ostracism, and aggressive verbal abuse. In addition, one of Khrushchev's most notable innovations was the introduction of a qualitatively new type of party purge. While they entailed the collective removal from their party posts of groups of leaders, these purges skirted the issue of political loyalty to the regime, allowing their targets to escape repression and retain their place in the nomenklatura. Such purges, later practiced by Brezhnev and Gorbachev, had a perversely stabilizing effect in that they signaled to lower-level functionaries across a vast, sprawling, party-state bureaucracy that it did, after all, have a center and that there were, after all, people in charge. In these ways party-based exclusion was a form of discipline that differed from repression and co-optation and served both to prolong and stabilize the life of this dictatorship.

A second feature of Leninist one-party states is that they were profoundly ideological. Most dictatorships, especially ones with ruling parties, have ideologies in one form or another. In the Soviet case, however, the ideology was unusually coherent and rigidly enforced. What we mean by ideology is that the elite shared a political discourse or language, one consisting of evaluative terms, such as working class, bourgeoisie, the party, and propositions or conventions, such as the leading role of the party, democratic centralism, and the superiority of public ownership of the means of production.[12] The internal coherence of Soviet ideology did not mean that members of the elite believed in it, although they may have, or that it was immune to change. Ideology was simply the language used by the elite as a medium of public debate and as a means of legitimizing their actions to each other. In any ideological system a key skill is to make innovations acceptable by rendering them compatible with the ideology's central conventions.[13] This was one of Khrushchev's greatest strengths. Because he was able to negotiate the post-Stalin transition with the highest degree of ideological continuity, especially as regards the leading role of the party, he triumphed over his rivals.[14] Similarly, in one of his most radical steps, the Secret Speech, he would go out of his way to frame Stalin's cult of personality as a violation of the teachings of Marx and Lenin.[15] Rather than drawing a boundary with Stalin's death, we point to a strong ideological continuity from Stalin to Khrushchev.

To some observers the cynicism that crept into communist elites after Khrushchev's Secret Speech and the defeat of the Hungarian uprising implies a fading of the ideology. Yet the emergence of varied beliefs and even the loss of faith need not signify ideological erosion. "The contrary," suggests Schull, "might be closer to the truth: the survival and indeed surprising stability of communist regimes for several decades depended to a large degree on a public discursive framework that assured predictability and overt consensus among its elites long after the faith had died."[16] These broad comparative and theoretical points pertaining to the Soviet Union will, we hope, serve as a benchmark against which scholars can compare other regimes.

With the disintegration of the Soviet system in 1988–91 the most far-reaching changes to the political organization of the post-Soviet space were the formation of fifteen successor states to the USSR and the dissolution of the Soviet Communist Party as the key point of integration at the substate level. Over the next decade Russia and the other large successor states with major regional subdivisions, especially in Central Asia, began to move in different directions. While the large Central Asian states such as Kazakhstan and Uzbekistan moved toward a form of centralized, bureaucratic authoritarian rule, in Russia the 1990s were a period of marked decentralization as regional elites seized economic assets and Moscow's efforts to impose administrative control over regional affairs were repeatedly frustrated.[17]

Growing concerns among the Russian political elite over the institutional and territorial integrity of the Russian state came to a head with the humiliating economic crash of 1998, which forced the Russian government to default on its debts and, in effect, declare bankruptcy. The response was a concerted drive for fiscal and administrative recentralization, of which the election of Vladimir Putin as president was the most visible expression. Although early efforts to bring regional governors to heel met with some resistance, this wilted in the face of the abolition of gubernatorial elections in 2004 and their replacement with a de facto system of central appointments controlled by the Kremlin. This arrangement was supplemented by the removal of barriers preventing the dominant statewide party, United Russia, which all regional governors, now appointed, were expected to join, from sweeping into most regions. There followed a shift from the decentralized substate authoritarianism of the 1990s to a centralized, party-based form of authoritarianism in the 2000s.[18]

Two contrasts can help tease out the comparative features of this new system. The first is between substate authoritarianism in democracies and in dictatorships. The problem for an authoritarian regional leader in a democratizing regime is how to hold on to power in the wake of competitive elections.[19] In a democratizing regime substate authoritarianism may be eclipsed by the spread of party competition from the statewide to the substate level.[20] But rather than dismantling substate authoritarian regimes, a statewide authoritarian leader like Putin had much stronger incentives to co-opt them and, with the help of his dominant party, integrate them into his administration. Moreover, in terms consistent with the findings of our study, rather than getting rid of the most powerful regional leaders, Putin kept them on, intervening only against latter-day contested autocrats, those "weakest governors who could not maintain popular support."[21]

The other contrast is between substate dictatorship in Russia today and the forms it assumed in the Soviet Union. In our terms, contemporary Russia is not a democracy or even a hybrid regime but an authoritarian state or, to put it more starkly, a dictatorship. At the same time, it is unmistakably a new kind of dictatorship, one that we may not yet have the concepts or terminology to fully understand.

Some of the differences between substate authoritarianism in Russia today and regional politics and administration in the Soviet era are obvious, others less so. Whereas substate dictators in the Soviet era created asymmetric networks of personal dependence on the basis of a preexisting party apparatus, regional leaders in Russia in the 1990s built their own political machines, first taking control of privatization and then manipulating subsidies, contracts, tax breaks, permits, regulatory exemptions, and legal protections to build their own clientelistic followings.[22] In the Soviet era noncompetitive party elections yielded information that the center could use to assess the competence and effectiveness of its regional leaders. Open, semicompetitive elections today play a greater role, not only in signaling levels of support for the regime but also as an indicator of regional leaders' effectiveness in mobilizing the vote and managing regional elites. Indeed, regional-level performance in statewide parliamentary and presidential elections appears to be the best predictor—trumping even economic competence—of whether a governor will be reappointed by the Kremlin.[23] Whereas in the Soviet Union the Communist Party monopolized control of information over cadres, making it a primary weapon for exclusion and kompromat, in postcommunist Russia this information has been "unlocked" and made the plaything of a wide variety of organizations in the public domain.[24]

And yet the structural impediments noted by Stalin in his conversation with Patolichev in 1946 are still in place. The center requires the support of regional leaders to maintain order, to implement policy, and to provide information on political conditions in the provinces. To that end, then and now, it affords regional leaders considerable leverage to rule their own domains, a fact of political rule in Russia that is unlikely to go away.

Appendix A

A Note on Dictatorship

There are two traditions of writing on dictatorship. The first is as a concept in the history of ideas. In this sense it has oscillated between two contradictory meanings, both with origins in Republican Rome: one as a temporary institution with fixed powers to restore a preexisting order; and the other as the usurpation of power by an individual or a collective, unencumbered by constitutional constraints, in the pursuit of new goals.[1] It was the second of these interpretations, in the form of "dictatorship of the proletariat," that was taken up by Soviet ideologists.[2] Other than as a tool of Soviet propaganda, however, the term "dictatorship of the proletariat" tells us nothing about how the Soviet system worked.

Our primary concern is with the second tradition, that of dictatorship as a tool of social science. In recent years social scientists have come to use dictatorship as an umbrella term to designate any regime that is not a democracy.[3] As a residual concept, it spans a vast array of political systems that no one definition could ever capture.[4] Beyond that, approaches to dictatorship have branched off in two directions. The first, inductive approach involves working from the observed traits of existing nondemocratic states and, on the basis of what appear to be distinct family types, assembling categories or regimes of dictatorship. Examples include Friedrich and Brzezinski (1956), Linz (2000), Huntington (1993: chap 3), and, more recently, Geddes (1999; 2003) and Geddes et al. (2014).[5] The second approach is procedural and minimalist. It is procedural in that it focuses not on the substantive outcomes of a political system but on its operation; and it is minimalist in that it focuses on a single criterion—how leaders are removed from office—as its basis for classification.[6] Two advantages of the second approach, as claimed by its proponents, are that it is based exclusively on observables, thereby limiting the scope for subjective judgments, and that, because it excludes traits such as responsiveness, accountability, political freedom, and participation from its definition of a regime, it makes it easier to explore empirically which causal connections may exist between regime type and various outcomes of interest.[7] Whereas the first, inductive approach allows for hybrid categories of dictatorship, the coding used by the minimalist approach is "clear and stark" and the categories mutually exclusive.[8] Examples of the minimalist approach include Alvarez et al. (1996), Przeworski et al. (2000), Gandhi (2008), Cheibub et al. (2010), and Svolik (2012).[9]

The inductive and minimalist approaches to classifying dictatorship have generated large data sets, involving major sunk costs. As a result, there has been some reluctance on either side to give ground, though this has been partially outweighed by the desire to arrive at a shared set of terms which might facilitate comparison. Geddes, for example, has embraced the category of monarchies (absent from her earlier classification scheme), altered her category of one-party states to the more widely used dominant party regimes, and introduced coding rules which allow for her seven-fold classification, which includes hybrids, to be converted into a simpler four-fold system, making it broadly commensurate with the categories used by exponents of the minimalist approach (compare Geddes 1999 and 2003 with Geddes et al. 2014).[10] The one area where Geddes refuses to yield is over personalist regimes, a Weberian category.[11]

The Soviet case highlights some of the difficulties in employing the category of personalist regime. As Svolik (2012: 31) observes, many personalist leaders emerge out of dictatorships dominated either by a leading party or by the military or, sometimes, both, but given that they rarely banish these organizations altogether on coming to power, establishing the occurrence or timing of the transition from one to the other can be difficult.[12] Consider the Soviet Union under Stalin. On nine of Geddes's thirteen coding rules (2003: 227), the Soviet Union in this period was a personalist dictatorship. This includes some of the most important features of any political system: we know, for example, that Stalin chose all members of the Politburo; that the Politburo was a rubber stamp for his decisions; that access to very high office depended on his personal favor; and that he personally controlled the security apparatus.[13] And yet Geddes (2003: 231) categorizes the Soviet regime in this period as a single-party dictatorship. Although the Soviet Union qualifies under fourteen of the fifteen coding rules for a single-party regime and is therefore classified as such—see Geddes (2003: 225–26)—it is not clear on what grounds this trumps the criteria for a personalist dictatorship, especially as the latter include what are arguably the most important facets of any political system. The inconsistency is underlined by the following comparison. Geddes argues that "most observers" are agreed that Milton Obote's administration in Uganda was a military regime while that of his successor, Idi Amin, was a personal dictatorship, largely on the basis that, under Amin, there was an extraordinary "concentration of power in the hands of a single man."[14] But surely *on these grounds* Stalin's regime of the late 1940s was also personalist?

While we do not discount the possibility that the concept of personalist dictatorship may be applied to political systems with low degrees of institutionalization, the Soviet political system was highly institutionalized, and its use there, as a result, only confuses matters.[15] Far more useful is the distinction between autocracy and oligarchic rule or, to use Milan Svolik's theoretical conceptualization, between "established autocracy" and "contested autocracy."[16] For our purposes this typology has two important advantages. First, it allows us to trace important developments within a regime type, of the kind described in this book, between a form of one-person rule under Stalin and collective rule under his successors. Second, this typology can be usefully extended to the substate level, where, in the terms used in the book, it correlates closely with our categories of the substate dictator and the substate contested autocrat.

Of the two approaches to dictatorship—the inductive and the minimalist—we lean toward the latter for categorizing statewide regimes. However, we see three weaknesses in this approach. First, in focusing on a single theoretical dimension—how leaders are removed—Cheibub, Gandhi, and Vreeland (CGV) extend the same measure of regime they use for democracy (i.e., where leaders are removed through competitive elections) to two categories of dictatorship, monarchies and military regimes, but they are unable to do so for other forms of dictatorship. This leaves one-party states in a residual limbo of "civilian regimes."[17] Labeling the Soviet Union as a civilian regime is to miss what drove this system and what gave it its identity. More than the armed forces in a military regime or the ruling dynasty in a monarchy, it is the party in the one-party state which penetrates society, generates support for leaders, and organizes public life. To identify it as a civilian regime is to miscategorize it.

A second difficulty concerns the unit of analysis. Most recent work on dictatorship focuses on three units of analysis: country-level, leaders, and leadership spells.[18] In this book we add a fourth, the substate level. But to focus on how substate leaders under dictatorship are appointed or removed tells us little; after all, in dictatorship regional and republican leaders are, in general, appointed and removed from above.[19]

Third, the theoretical categories of established and contested autocracy, which hinge on whether a ruling coalition can dislodge a dictator, are hard to pin down empirically, especially as most of the processes we are interested in are not easily observed. Instead, our approach rests on starting with the political strategies of the regional leader and, on that basis, constructing ideal types based on composites of what can be observed. Thus although we broadly adhere to a minimalist position at the statewide level, at the substate level our approach is inductive. The criteria for distinguishing the categories of substate dictator and contested autocrat are set out in the introduction and more fully in appendix D.

Appendix B

Units of Analysis

The Soviet state was a federation consisting of fifteen union republics.[1] While each republic enjoyed nominally equal rights, the federation was highly asymmetric. To illustrate this, we focus on a single census date, 1 July 1947.[2] That year the Russian Federation had sixty-six regional units (forty-eight oblasts, twelve autonomous republics, and six krai), the Ukraine twenty-five, and Belorussia twelve. Each of the Central Asian union republics was divided into oblasts, Uzbekistan with sixteen, Kazakhstan with nine and one autonomous republic, and Kirgizia, Tajikistan, and Turkmenistan with six, five, and four, respectively. By contrast, none of the other seven union republics (Armenia, Azerbaijan, Georgia, Estonia, Latvia, Lithuania, and Moldavia) had typical oblasts, although the Caucasian republics had national autonomies. We found no single criterion for delineating uniform units of analysis. Instead, our approach was to address the issue republic by republic following two broad principles. First, we tried to equalize our units of analysis in terms of population and party membership. Second, we avoided any double counting, so that if, for example, we counted a union republic or a krai as a unit, we discounted administrative subdivisions within it.

We divided our substate units into three categories. The first consisted of the sixty-six oblasts, autonomous republics, and krai in the Russian Federation. Although these varied by size and ethnopolitical status, all were on the same tier of soviet and party administration and possessed broadly equal powers. Although the krai had their own internal subdivisions (most often autonomous districts), they were roughly of the same size and influence as the larger oblasts. Including all three as units of analysis was relatively straightforward. The second group was the oblasts in the largest non-Russian republics with regional subdivisions (Ukraine, Belorussia,

Kazakhstan, and Uzbekistan). The main difference between these regions and those in the Russian Federation was that whereas party organizations in the Russian Federation fell directly under the jurisdiction of the all-union Central Committee (with a ten-year hiatus from 1956 to 1966, when they were administered by the RSFSR buro of the Central Committee), these regional party organizations were under the authority of their respective republican central committees and had to operate through them when dealing with Moscow. Despite this discrepancy, these non-Russian regions were roughly the same size, by population and party membership, as the oblasts, krai, and autonomous republics in the Russian Federation and are also treated as units of analysis. The third and most problematic category consists of the ten other union republics. As important players in the Soviet system these republics needed to be included in our research domain. Hence, although they occupied what was formally a different tier of administration from the Russian or Ukrainian regions, they form part of our universe of cases. They are divided into three subgroups. First were those union republics which had no regional subdivisions at all (the Baltic republics and Moldavia). To the extent that these republics were of the same order of magnitude in terms of population and party membership as many of the Russian regions, they too are treated as units of analysis. A second subgroup is the three Caucasian republics, each of which had its own national autonomies. Although we could have included these autonomies as units of analysis, doing so would have violated our double-counting rule. Instead, to the extent that the republics themselves were commensurate with the larger territories of the RSFSR, they too are treated as units of analysis.[3] The last subgroup is the three smaller Central Asian republics, each of which had a handful of oblasts.[4] We could have treated these oblasts as our objects of study. However, to the extent that these oblasts were, by population and party membership, extremely small and that the republics were themselves directly comparable to medium-size oblasts in the Russian Federation, these republics too are treated as units of assessment. Therefore other than the larger union republics of the RSFSR, Ukraine, Belorussia, Kazakhstan, and Uzbekistan, each of the other ten republics is treated as a unit of analysis.

As of 1 July 1947 (this figure grew in subsequent years following administrative reorganizations, especially in 1952 and 1954) our universe of cases consists of 139 territorial units.[5] These consist of oblasts, krais, and ASSRs (but exclude autonomous *okrugs* and autonomous oblasts) which were immediately below the union republic tier in the largest republics of the RSFSR, Ukraine, Belorussia, Kazakhstan, and Uzbekistan, along with those ten republics which either did not have regional subdivisions or which, in terms of their population and territory, were on the same order of magnitude as the other regions we study here.

Appendix C

Sample

Given the resources at our disposal, studying all 139 units of analysis (and more in subsequent years) in depth was not feasible. Instead, we selected a sample of thirty regions to reflect as closely as possible those aspects of the wider universe of cases (such as location, size by territory and population, ethnic composition, and economic structure) that were of interest to us. Initially we maximized the variance on six dimensions: regional size (by population); geographical location and remoteness from the center (by republic and by the ten geographic-economic zones used by Soviet administrators); urban population (i.e., rural–urban split); national-administrative status (i.e., oblast or krai as opposed to autonomous republic or union republic); ethnic breakdown of population; and structure of the economy (relative proportions of agriculture, light industry, heavy industry, defense, and resource extraction and the existence of large, all-union plants). The purpose of these data was not to advance causal hypotheses but to identify a sample that might allow us to draw broader inferences about our ideal types. For this we did not need longitudinal data; instead, we fixed on a single date, 1961, which fell almost at the midpoint of our study.[1]

As the project progressed, the sample was tweaked in two ways. First, in order to allow for the possibility that patterns of association affected by ethnic factors in national territories might differ from those in nonnational territories, we included, in addition to five regions in the non-Russian union republics, two autonomous republics in the Russian Federation (Chuvashia and Kabardino-Balkaria) and three smaller union republics (Estonia, Tajikistan, and Azerbaijan). Second, in an initial pilot study in the first year of the project we amassed archival data on dismissals of regional first and second secretaries from 1945 to 1967, paying particular attention to the reasons for dismissals, including scandals and amoral behavior, incompetence, and natural turnover. This is reflected in the two accompanying tables in the column on the far right, which includes contextual information on the turnover of first secretaries. Given our interest in conflict and scandal as a point of entry into the workings of regional networks, we listed the reasons for turnover, fixing especially on contentious dismissals which we could then follow up on. To correct for potential bias, we also included six regions which were politically calm and relatively free of scandal.

Our thirty regions were divided into two groups. The first consisted of four pilot regions, Moscow, Vinnitsa, Penza, and Cheliabinsk (see table 11.1), where we employed full-time researchers to carry out on-site research: Oleg Khlevniuk in Moscow, Olga Nikonova in Cheliabinsk, Valerii Vasiliev and Roman Podkur in Vinnitsa, and Viktor Kondrashin in Penza. This research was then supplemented by a more wide-ranging examination of the other twenty-six regions based on materials from Moscow and the Urals (see table 11.2).

Table A.1. Four pilot regions

Region	Zone	Population	Urban/rural (percent)	Ethnicity[a] (percent)	Economy[b] (percent)	Administrative status	Turnover and reasons[c]
Cheliabinsk	Urals	3.09m	77/23	81R/6T	50mb/21fm	oblast	S (1950) I (1954/61)
Moscow	Central	4.94m	59/41	94R/3U	41mb/22li	oblast	S (1949)
Penza	Volga	1.53m	36/64	86R/6M	65mb	oblast	I (1961)
Vinnitsa	Southwest Ukraine	2.16m	18/82	89U/6R	45mb/14li	oblast	Q

Sources: FirstBook of Demographics; archives.

Note: The figures for columns three and four are from 1961, the midpoint of our study. The figures for columns five and six are from the 1980s.

[a] R = Russians, T = Tatars, U = Ukrainians, M = Mordovians, K = Kazakhs, B = Belorussians, A = Azeris, C = Chuvash, E = Estonians, Kb = Kabardins, G = Germans, Ar = Armenians, Ta = Tajiks, Uz = Uzbeks.

[b] mb = machine building; fm = ferrous metals; li = light industry; w = woodwork and paper; f = fuels; m = ferrous metals; fp = food processing; c = chemical and petrochemicals.

[c] S = scandals and immoral behavior; I = incompetence; Q = natural turnover (health and retirement).

Table A.2. Sample regions

Region	Zone	Population	Urban/rural	Ethnicity[a]	Economy[b]	Administrative status	Turnover and reasons[c]
Azerbaijan	Caucasus	3.97m	49/51	83A/6R	29mb/25li	U/R	n/a
Chuvashia	Volgo-Viatka	1.14m	26/74	68C/27R	53mb/18li	ASSR	Q
Dnepropetrovsk	Donets-Dneiper	2.85m	72/28	72U/24R	37mb/32m	oblast	n/a
Estonia	Baltics	1.22m	58/42	62E/30R	28mb/20li	U/R	n/a
Gomel'	Belorussia	1.39m	31/69	80B/12R	43mb/15li	oblast	n/a
Gor'kii	Volgo-Viatka	3.66m	55/45	95R/2T	61mb/8li	oblast	I (1950)
Irkutsk	East Siberia	2.09m	64/36	89R/3U	30w/2.5mb	oblast	Q
Kabardino-Balkariia	North Caucasus	0.46m	40/60	58Kb/32R	47mb/20li	ASSR	Q
Kemerovo	West Siberia	2.9m	78/22	91R/2U	34f/21mb	oblast	I (1960)
Khabarovsk	Far East	1.15m	76/24	86R/6U	45mb/17w	krai	Q
Kirov	Volga-Viatka	1.84m	41/59	90R/3T	42mb/24w	oblast	S (1961)
Kostroma	Central	0.92m	43/57	96R/1U	35mb/24w	oblast	I (1946/50 1954/56)
Krasnodar	North Caucasus	3.91m	40/60	85R/4U	35mb/15li	krai	I (1960)
Kursk	Central Chernozem (Black Earth)	1.51m	23/77	97R/2U	41mb/14li	oblast	Q

Novosibirsk	West Siberia	2.38m	58/42	92R/2G	61mb/11li	oblast	Q
Orel	Central	0.94m	27/73	97R/1U	61mb/9li	oblast	Q
Perm	Urals	3.04m	61/39	84R/5T	39mb/17w	oblast	I (1954)
Riazan'	Central	1.46m	33/67	96R/1U	59mb/13li	oblast	S (1949/60)
Rostov	North Caucasus	3.45m	59/41	90R/4U	48mb/13f	oblast	I (1952)
Samarkand	Uzbek	1.17m	29/71	n/a	31li/25mb	oblast	n/a
Semipalatinsk	Kazakh	0.61m	42/58	n/a	37li/20mb	oblast	n/a
Stavropol'	North Caucasus	1.97m	33/67	78R/3Ar	39mb/19li	krai	I (1946/60)
Sverdlovsk	Urals	4.15m	77/23	89R/4T	50mb/15f	oblast	Q
Tajikistan	Central Asia	2.12m	34/66	54Ta/23Uz	39li/mb20	U/R	n/a
Tiumen'	West Siberia	1.12m	35/65	73R/8U	29mb/17w/16f	oblast	S (1955/61)
Tula	Central	1.9m	63/37	95R/2U	48mb/12c	oblast	I (1953/55)

Sources: First Book of Demographics; archives.

Note: Figures for columns three and four are from 1961, the midpoint of our study. The figures for columns five and six are from the 1980s.

[a] R = Russians, T = Tatars, U = Ukrainians, M = Mordovians, K = Kazakhs, B = Belorussians, A = Azeris, C = Chuvash, E = Estonians, Kb = Kabardins, G = Germans, Ar = Armenians, Ta = Tajiks, Uz = Uzbeks.

[b] mb = machine building; fm = ferrous metals; li = light industry; w = woodwork and paper; f = fuels; m = ferrous metals; fp = food processing; c = chemical and petrochemicals.

[c] S = scandals and immoral behavior; I = incompetence; Q = natural turnover (health and retirement).

Appendix D

Political Networks

A social network is any collection of actors (nodes) and a set of relations (ties) between these actors; it may vary by size (i.e., by the number of nodes) and by the purpose and strength of the ties.[1] A political network is a particular type of social network involving the exercise of power, either through influence (when one actor transmits information to another that influences the latter's behavior) or domination (when one actor controls the behavior of another by offering or withdrawing some benefit or harm).[2] Most network analysis is quite technical, involving precise measurement of nodes and ties, often with a view to assessing causal theories.[3] By contrast, our understanding of networks is looser. For us, a political network is an asymmetric arrangement of actors bound together by ties of dependence and by its own norms.[4] One reason we have shied away from more precise configurations of networks is that the relations we are most interested in, such as those of loyalty and trust, are not easily observable.[5]

As a research tool, network analysis has two advantages. First, it is an umbrella concept which has superseded earlier approaches and linked them to wider developments in the social sciences. A case in point is the idea of clientelist or patron–client relations. These refer to asymmetric relations of social exchange in which patrons provide dependents with protection, material rewards, and the prospect of promotion. As dependents are not in a position to reciprocate with like-for-like exchanges, they offer instead deference and loyalty. "Given their unequal resource holdings," writes one scholar, "clients can almost never repay their debts. They remain forever entangled in the patron's web of paternalistic authority."[6] Although patron–client studies were common in the 1960s and 1970s they have since been folded into the broader study of networks.[7] Second, although informal networks will emerge in all political systems, comparative analysis suggests that they are likely to emerge with particularly strong ties—as in trust networks—where exchanges are marked by high levels of pressure and risk.[8] This finding suggests that they were particularly likely to emerge in an environment marked by high-level pressure from above, as in the late Stalin and Khrushchev eras.

This idea is reflected in our network ideal-types. Our benchmark network, that of the substate dictator, has two features. First, the ties connecting members of the inner circle tended to be strong. Overpromotion, exclusion, and blackmail had emerged as solutions to a particular problem: how were politicians to meet demands from above in an environment marked by low levels of trust? These unlikely origins were the bedrock for some of the most hardy and resilient long-term relationships. Second, the substate dictator's core network tended to be compact and tightly knit but of medium size. Networks that were too large contained weak links that could snap, but those that were too small allowed insufficient resources or scope for a substate dictator to govern an entire region. Networks needed to be sufficiently broad to help the substate dictator meet a key requirement of the Stalinist state: the mobilization of people and resources at short notice.

Our second network ideal-type was that which emerged around contested autocrats. Normally perceived as passive and weak-willed, contested autocrats often had to contend with powerful alternative networks that could gel around either charismatic individuals or alternative institutions such as all-union plants or the state apparatus. While these alternative networks could take a variety of forms, they tended to operate independently of the regional leader. Sensing his weakness, other key actors were reluctant to get drawn into ties of dependence on the regional leader or to become his clients: networks around the regional leader were small and loose and marked by weak ties.

Our third category revolves around party governors. Networks in these regions had two key features. First, as was not the case in substate dictator regions, there was a relatively close fit between the ruling network and the formal executive, the obkom buro. The first secretary might leaven his inner circle with one or two personal dependents, but the inner circle was largely composed of organizational leaders who were ex-officio members of the regional cabinet. Second, the ruler's network was held together by a system of norms which prioritized seniority and a relatively stable system of status differentiation. In tandem with a central leadership policy which encouraged informal arrangements and understandings, these practices were elevated under Brezhnev into the regime's ideology under the banner of "trust in cadres."

Appendix E

Archival Sources

We have relied overwhelmingly on archives for our data. Given that we are interested in networks built on informal ties, why did we rely for our evidence on written, predominantly formal sources? After all, the most successful efforts at tracing networks in the Soviet Union have been through interviews.[1] The main reason is that nearly all the political leaders of interest to us (either as patrons or as clients) who reached positions of sufficient power from the 1940s to the 1960s are now dead. Moreover, none of the classic interview projects on the Soviet system, such as the Harvard Project in the 1950s, the Soviet Interview Project in the 1970s, or the forty-three interviews by Ledeneva, included politicians of any seniority. Thus we have followed a multitrack archival approach designed to address our research questions from a variety of perspectives. We have supplemented this with memoirs, biographies, and other publications that have appeared since the fall of the Soviet system.

The starting point of our research was a full and reliable picture of all appointments to the regions and of Central Committee resolutions on the workings of the regional nomenklatura. To this end, we compiled a list of appointments in the regions (*Regional'naia Politika*, 2009, 560–639); we put together a list of Central Committee resolutions on the evolution of the nomenklatura (RGANI, f.5 op.15, 30, 31; RGASPI f.17 op.122; and *Regional'naia Politika*, 2009, 130–69); and we looked at the obkom buros to examine the appointment procedures at the regional level (e.g., RGASPI f.17 op.102). Second, we traced the evolution of networks in the regions. Given our focus on moments of crisis and scandal in order to illuminate the dynamics of the regional power system, we assessed not only the dismissals of regional first and second secretaries but also the reasons for these dismissals (scandals and amoral behavior, incompetence, and natural turnover). We then followed these scandals via three means. First, we explored the discussions at the obkom plenums by looking at the *sektor informatsii, otdel organizatsionno-partinnoi raboty* (RGASPI f.17 op.51–8, 89–93, 102–6, 145–57), a unique complex of protocols of regional buros and stenographs of regional plenums and conferences. Since the holdings run to about fifty thousand files for our period, and these have to be flown to Moscow from the Urals, this repository had been virtually unused. We used our sample to whittle this figure down to a more manageable three thousand files. Second, we carried out an analysis of Central Committee investigations of scandals (RGANI f.5 op.15–16, 25–26, 30–31, 60–62; f.13 op.1, 2). Finally, we made use of the growing number of memoirs, biographies, and encyclopedias as well as secondary literature published since the fall of the Soviet system.

Our main strategy was to reconstruct networks through conflict. Conflicts could take a variety of forms. At the very lowest level a disagreement between a first secretary and the district aktiv could spark a complaint to Moscow which, in turn, could trigger a polite request to the regional party organization or possibly even a minor inquiry, both of which would find their way into the archives. At the next level up, conflict could be generated from within the regional elite, especially if the first secretary upset local notables by violating social norms. But conflicts which reached the highest pitch of intensity and which could erupt into scandals tended to do so when a regional leader had violated the center's rules. Broadly speaking, conflicts were allowed to fully bubble up to the surface only on Moscow's say-so because it suited Moscow's interest.[2] Centrally authorized investigations usually involved a number of lines of attack, allowing for cross-corroboration. Thus, for example, Central Committee brigades were dispatched to the province to follow paper trails, interview participants, and file lengthy reports, and these could then feed into the interrogation of entire obkom buros at the Secretariat in Moscow. These materials could be matched against the personal revelations aired at a subsequent obkom plenum.

To guard against selection bias we also looked at a wide range of relatively conflict-free regions. Whatever leadership turnover occurred here was due either to retirements or ill health or to the orderly transfer of cadres up the nomenklatura hierarchy. The reconstruction of networks here required a more piecemeal approach. Often this was based on a patient reconstruction of patronage alliances alongside routine reports from Moscow and comparative assessments by the Central Committee of a region's performance against that of others. For these regions what were often especially valuable were the relatively candid memoirs of participants published after the breakup of the Soviet Union.

Appendix F

The Nomenklatura

In its literal meaning *nomenklatura* is a "list" or a "schedule." In the early Soviet era the word was often used in this way to describe the lists of positions filled by party committees. As the Soviet state evolved, the word acquired two more metaphorical meanings. The first was as a collective term for those appointed to positions on these lists. As these lists encompassed all the most powerful posts in the Soviet system, in this first metaphorical sense nomenklatura came to stand for the Soviet elite. This elite was stratified by the level of party committee that approved an appointment. At the very highest level were appointments vetted and approved by the Central Committee of the CPSU. Thus if you worked as a regional official but your position was confirmed by the Central Committee, this was a mark of status and conferred on you the prestige of being "on the Central Committee nomenklatura." You were placed in a specific category of privileges, one step removed from those granted to individuals on the next nomenklatura down, that of the republican central committee, and two steps removed from the nomenklatura below that, of the regional party committee.

In its second metaphorical sense the nomenklatura referred to the official Soviet system of patronage. Collectively this referred to the process of upward mobility by which cadres followed well-regulated career paths controlled by the center. While the original totalitarian model assumed that the nomenklatura, as a system of patronage, was micromanaged by the Central Committee in Moscow and that this was one of the most important manifestations of the power of the center in this system, an important body of research in the 1960s and 1970s suggested that there were regional pockets of personnel circulation that operated with little or no interference from Moscow.[1] Further research, in the 1980s, went a step further by suggesting not only that the selection process had its center of gravity in the provinces but also that it was skewed in favor of certain factions—local patronage groups governed by norms of reciprocity— within those regions.[2] A third line of research asked whether such regional networks, if they existed, undermined or consolidated central control and came to the view that, somewhat paradoxically, they performed a positive function for Moscow by allowing statewide politicians to build consensual alliances through which central policies could be better implemented.[3]

One advantage of the nomenklatura system is that these lists give a relatively precise measure of the Soviet elite. The records department of the Central Committee showed that, on 1 January 1952, there were 142,819 leading cadres (i.e., whose appointments were approved by party committees) in the republics and provinces. The most important subcategory was the 18,949 cadres on the Central Committee nomenklatura.[4] This included two important groups at opposite ends of the spectrum. At the very lowest level were the district party first secretaries, who, despite the localized nature of their work, gained tremendous prestige from the fact that their appointments were approved by the Central Committee. At the pinnacle of the pyramid were the 907 secretaries of the union republic central committees, the kraikoms and obkoms (of whom 190 were first secretaries), and their 188 state equivalents, the chairs of the republican councils of ministers and of the krai and oblast executive committees.[5] A number of other influential regional leaders were only marginally below this higher stratum. These were the members and candidate members of the buros headed by these first secretaries; given that these buros had, on average, ten members, we can say that in January 1952 this upper echelon of regional-level officials consisted of around two thousand people across the country as a whole.

Appendix G

Regional Party Elections

According to the party statutes of 1939 and 1952, the regional party conference—the highest organ of the regional party organization—was to convene once every one and a half years. One of the conference's main functions was to elect a smaller obkom (the regional party committee) that was to run the affairs of the regional party organization while the conference was out of session. The obkom in turn convened plenums once every two to three months.[1] The 1939 statutes had formally introduced a new element to these elections, namely, that they "be conducted by closed [secret] ballot" and that instead of voting lists the voting should "take place by separate candidate," with all members of the conference being given the right to challenge or criticize each candidate.[2] The statutes did not explain the precise mechanics of the elections, however, and on this subject earlier accounts by Western scholars remained quite hazy.[3] In fact, the elections were regulated by a secret Central Committee Instruction titled "On elections of Ruling Party Agencies." The Instruction was approved on 3 April 1941 and subsequently replaced by a slightly amended version on 29 March 1962. Although the 1941 version of the rules remains classified, the 1962 version, which appears to be an only slightly amended version, is now accessible.[4]

One of the main themes running through both the 1941 and 1962 Central Committee Instructions was the distinction between open and closed ballots or votes.[5] Certain stages in the election of the obkom were to be conducted through an open vote. The process began with the presentation of an alphabetical list of nominations, each nominee to be individually discussed before the entire conference, which occasionally, in the larger regions, would have upward of six hundred to seven hundred delegates.

These lists came from the primary party organizations but were invariably coordinated by the party organs department. At this stage the majority of candidates were waved through, but it was common for individual nominees to be questioned or challenged. The issue of whether a nominee should continue to be questioned and, after the questioning, whether she or he should be included on the voting list for the closed ballot was to be settled through an open vote. Normally this meant a show of hands or, more commonly (as recorded in the documents), individuals in the audience shouting their approval or disapproval.[6] Although it was quite common for nominees to be challenged or questioned, it was rare for them to be blocked at this stage.

The next stage was the compilation of all the successful nominees on a ballot and the process of voting on this ballot. The Instruction was quite specific that the vote be closed, or secret (zakrytoe [tainoe]).[7] What this meant in practice was that a counting commission compiled a ballot or list (biulleten' [spisok]) with all the names that had progressed through the discussion phase; it then sealed the electoral boxes and handed a ballot paper to each delegate.[8] Every delegate had the right to reject nominees by crossing out their names and to add names as they wished, but in order to do so they would have to demonstratively go to a booth or some other place where they could mark down their preference.[9] The question of whether this was a closed or open ballot depended on how many people chose to exercise this right, as the greater the number, the higher the degree of anonymity. In the elections of 1948, where it was common for upward of fifty to a hundred delegates to cross out names, the process more closely approximated a closed ballot.[10]

There was one further stage in the election process. Once the obkom had been elected, it would normally convene a first organizational session, supervised by an official from the Central Committee. At these sessions the obkom secretaries and other leading figures in the regional party organization, such as heads of department and the editor of the regional newspaper, would be elected. This too would be done through an open vote, which normally amounted to people shouting their assent from the hall.[11] Given that obkom secretaries and heads of department were on the Central Committee nomenklatura, it was, in principle, extremely rare for a secretary to be blocked by an obkom at this stage. At the same time, it was conceivable, especially if the original candidate had attracted a heavy protest vote, for their position to be weakened and for them to be withdrawn shortly afterward or even for an alternative candidate to be found. Second, the first organizational obkom would vote for the obkom buro, again through a show of hands or via voices from the audience. Unlike positions on the obkom apparatus, membership in the buro was not on the Central Committee nomenklatura, and here the first secretary did have some leeway in whom he proposed.[12]

It might be conjectured that these rules bore little resemblance to reality. But this was not our finding from a view of the archives (see chapter 2 for more evidence). For a relatively typical example of an obkom election—from Perm in January 1956 and January 1958—that followed the 1941 Instruction closely (i.e., the parts of it that were reproduced in the now-accessible 1962 Instruction), see RGASPI f.17 op.56 d.2040 ll.306–34; d.2041 ll.29–30, 34–39; op.58 d.2246 ll.270–74, 307–11; d.2247 ll.28–34.

Appendix H

Coding Rules

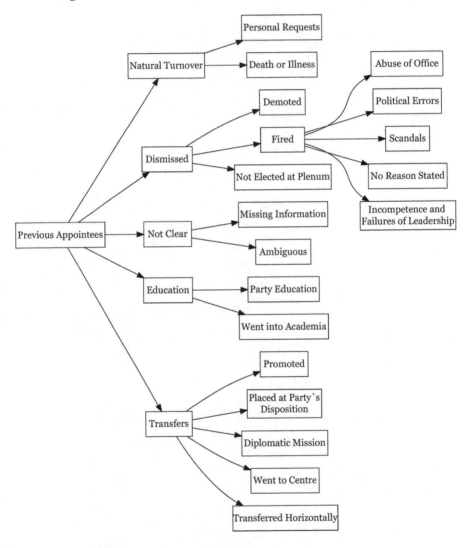

Diagram prepared by Darya Vanchugova.

Glossary

aktiv: Politically engaged rank-and-file members of the party.

apparat (apparatus): Party bureaucracy.

apparatchik: Official of the party bureaucracy.

ASSR: *See* autonomous republic.

autonomous republic (ASSR): One of sixteen (later twenty) smaller national formations (i.e., smaller than the union republics), most of which were in the Russian Federation, based on a titular ethnic group but often with a majority or near-majority ethnic Russian population.

bestovarnye operatsii; bestovarnye kvitantsii: Literally, "nongoods operations," that is, fake transfers between state agencies of nonexistent outputs which, while recorded on paper, did not occur in reality; *bestovarnye kvitantsii* refer to the fictional receipts used to cover up for such nongoods transactions.

Central Committee: Central Committee of the Communist Party of the Soviet Union. The term has two meanings. It refers, first, to the nominally elected body of from 236 (1952) to 426 (1976) (depending on the period) Central Committee members, who convened at regular meetings or plenums. Second, it applies to the bureaucracy of the Central Committee, which consisted of around 2,000 officials, or apparatchiks, most of whom were based at *staraia ploschad'* (Old Square) in Moscow. In lowercase, the term refers to the central committees of the union republican branches of the party.

Cheka: Acronym of the state security police (Vserossiiskaia Chrezvychainaia Komissia) from 1917 to 1922. Also used as shorthand for later incarnations of the security police, including the GPU, the NKVD, and, in the years covered by this book, the MGB and KGB.

Commission of Party Control (KPK): The party's internal control agency, charged with disciplining and expelling members and with overseeing the implementation of the Central Committee's decisions. Formed in 1934, it was renamed the Committee of Party Control (also KPK) in 1952.

Congress: Supreme decision-making body of the Soviet Communist Party, which met to approve the direction of party policy, to confirm the five-year plan, to amend the party rules, to pass new party programs, and to elect the Central Committee. In the period covered in this book there were six Party Congresses, the XIX (1952), XX (1956), XXI (1959), XXII (1961), XXIII (1966), and XXIV (1971).

CPSU: Communist Party of the Soviet Union, the country's single ruling party.

executive committee: Governing arm of the district or regional state apparatus (see *ispolkom*).

first secretary: Leading official on a party committee and, by implication, of the territory covered by that party committee, whether on the district, regional, republican, or all-union level.

frontovik: Veteran of the Great Patriotic War who served on the front. In the postwar years some *frontoviki* formed close bonds which could serve as a foundation for networking.

gorkom: City party committee of the Communist Party.

indigenization (*korenizatsiia*): The promotion in the union and autonomous republics of the language, culture, and elite of the titular ethnic group.

ispolkom: Executive committee of the state (soviet) apparatus, either at the district (*raion*) or regional (*oblast*) level.

junior secretary: The lower-ranking of the two first secretaries of the agricultural and industrial obkoms formed after the bifurcation of regional party organizations in November 1962.

KGB: Committee of State Security (Soviet secret police), formed in 1954, successor to the MGB.

kolkhoz: Collective farm.

kompromat: Kompromitiruiushchie materialy, or compromising materials.

Komsomol: Communist Youth League, the youth wing of the party.

korenizatsiia: See indigenization.

krai: Regional administrative unit, usually larger than the oblast and containing one or more ethnoterritorial subdivisions.

krugovaia poruka: A circle of collective responsibility in which all members are held jointly accountable for the actions and obligations of the group.

MGB: Ministry of State Security (Soviet secret police), formed in 1946 and dissolved in 1954; succeeded by the KGB. Also see Cheka and NKVD.

militsiia: Civil police force.

MTS: Machine-tractor station.

NKVD: People's Commissariat of Internal Affairs (1934–46); in the 1930s most often shorthand for the secret police.

nomenklatura: The term originally referred to the lists of key public positions and of those eligible to fill them that were controlled by party committees; in later years it broadened out to refer to the party-state elite, which enjoyed special access to a variety of goods and services. *See* appendix F.

oblast: Regional administrative unit, formed in 1929 as successor to the tsarist-era *gubernii.*

obkom: Regional committee of the Communist Party. The term could refer both to the elected members of the committee who convened at obkom plenums and to the full-time staff of the obkom, the regional party bureaucracy.

obkom buro: The supreme decision-making body of the regional party organization, normally consisting of nine, eleven, or thirteen members.

plenum: Meeting of a party committee (either the regional, republican, or all-union Central Committee) attended by all full-voting and candidate members.

Politburo: Supreme decision-making body within the Central Committee, in effect, the country's cabinet. Although the formal Politburo rarely met under Stalin, it convened regularly (as the Presidium) under Khrushchev.

Presidium (Central Committee Presidium): Supreme decision-making body in the Central Committee, which doubled as the cabinet from 1952 to 1966. Before and after it was known by its more familiar title, the Politburo. Not to be confused with the Presidium of the Council of Ministers or the Presidium of the Supreme Soviet, which were the top decision-making committees of the government and of the state structures.

pripiski: Cheating; the padding or inflation of data.

Procuracy: Soviet justice agency responsible for carrying out criminal prosecutions and for the supervision of legality.

raikom: District committee of the Communist Party.

raion: District-level administrative unit, one level below the oblast.

RSFSR: Russian Soviet Federal Socialist Republic, the Russian Republic, largest of the fifteen union republics (*see* Russian Federation).

RSFSR buro: RSFSR buro of the Central Committee of the Communist Party, established in 1956 and dissolved in 1966.

Russian Federation: The largest of the fifteen union republics that made up the Soviet Union, containing approximately half its population (*see* RSFSR).

second: Shorthand for the institution of the Slavic second secretary, which consisted of an ensemble of rules and practices and was used by the

Central Committee to supervise internal party affairs in the non-Slavic union republics.

Secretariat: Supreme administrative committee for managing the party's internal affairs, normally comprising the party committee's secretaries and heads of department. The most important secretariat in the country was the Secretariat of the Central Committee.

secretary: One of a number of senior party officials who sat on the Secretariat and ran the party's affairs.

senior secretary: The higher-ranking of the two first secretaries of the agricultural and industrial obkoms formed after the bifurcation of regional party organizations in November 1962.

sheftstvo: "Tutelage" extended to a farm by an enterprise, normally involving the assignment of workers for seasonal labor, the sponsoring of over-the-plan building projects, or the lending of technical machinery or automobiles.

sovkhoz: State farm.

sovnarkhoz: Regional economic council established by Khrushchev in 1957 to replace the central industrial ministries. Dissolved in 1965.

stazh: Seniority, i.e., number of years a cadre had been a member of the party or had held managerial posts in nomenklatura positions, either in the party, the state, or the economy.

titular nomenklatura: The ruling elite of a national republic (either a union republic or an ASSR), formed from within the titular ethnic group.

union republic: One of fifteen (sixteen until the dissolution of the Karelian Republic in 1956) national formations which together formed the Soviet Union. The largest was the Russian Federation (the RSFSR), but in addition there were two other Slavic republics (Ukraine and Belorussia) as well as three Baltic, three Caucasian, five central Asian republics, and the republic of Moldavia.

USSR: Union of Soviet Socialist Republics (the Soviet Union).

vydvezhenets: A person of low origin, normally a worker or a peasant, who was fast-tracked to a white-collar or senior executive position.

zemliaki: Persons originally from the same region or territory.

Notes

ABBREVIATIONS

d.	*delo* (file)
DAVO	State Archive of Vinnitsa Oblast
f.	*fond*
GAPO	State Archive of Penza Oblast
GARF	State Archive of the Russian Federation
KPSS v rez.	*Kommunisticheskaia partiia Sovetskogo Soiuza v rezoliutsiiakh i resheniiakh s"ezdov, konferentsii i plenumov TsK (1898–1986)*
l.	page number
OGAChO	State Archive of Cheliabinsk Oblast
op.	*opis'* (inventory)
RGANI	Russian State Archive of Contemporary History
RGASPI	Russian State Archive of Social and Political History
TsK VKP(b)	*TsK VKP(b) i regional'nye partiinye komitety 1945–1953*

INTRODUCTION

1. There are plenty examples of local authoritarian enclaves in multilevel (usually federal) democracies and democratizing regimes, e.g., Benton (2012), Gervasoni (2010), Gibson (2005, 2013), and Giraudy (2015). However, to the extent that they are ensconced in nondictatorial regimes we do not classify them as substate dictatorships. In line with current usage, we define statewide dictatorships in residual terms as "regimes in which rulers acquire power by means other than competitive elections," e.g., Gandhi (2008: 7). For a broader discussion of this theme, see appendix A.

2. We follow Rogers Brubaker (1996: 26–29) in preferring "substate" to the more common "subnational." Whatever else it was, the Soviet Union was never a nation. We agree with Brubaker that what was distinctive to the Soviet nationality

regime was precisely the degree to which nationhood and nationality were codified and institutionalized on the substate rather than the statewide level. Given that national units were at the substate level, to speak of subnational in this context would be doubly confusing. A fuller elaboration of how we define our substate units of assessment can be found in appendix B.

3. These terms were coined by Milan Svolik (2012). Phrased somewhat differently, the distinction also appears in Gandhi (2008: 164–65) and Geddes (2003: 50), among others.

4. Gregory and Harrison (2005: 723, 732–33). The term "revolution constraint" is from Acemoglu and Robinson (2006: 120–23).

5. We have in mind here nonviolent opposition in the form of speeches and protest votes at regional party elections. While violent opposition and social order problems in the form of insurgencies, uprisings, and urban riots did occur in our period, they tended to attract the attention of the center and were suppressed by army, NKVD, and MVD units under central command. On the latter, see, for example, Kozlov (2002: 58, 65, 108, 146, 149, 221), Baron (2001: 44, 46–48, 59–60), and Statiev (2010: chap. 9).

6. On the various meanings of the nomenklatura, see appendix F.

7. For a broader discussion of this theme, see Schelling (1960: 43) and Gambetta (2009: 37, 40–41, 59).

8. The male pronoun is used here advisedly. All substate leaders considered in this book, with the exception of Ekaterina Furtseva, the first secretary of the Moscow gorkom from 1954 to 1957, were men.

9. Lest we be accused of "actor-based functionalism," namely, the claim that institutions exist because they are expected to serve the aims of those who created them (e.g., Pierson 2004: 105–22 and Magaloni and Kricheli 2010: 130–31), we should stress that we are not saying anything here about why these patterns emerged, only that they were a widely observed empirical regularity.

10. These transitions fall into two categories: first, the transformation of one type of authoritarian regime into another (e.g., from a one-party regime to a military dictatorship); and, second, shifts within a regime. Our concern is with the latter. For more on transitions among authoritarian regimes, see Geddes et al. (2014) and Magaloni and Kricheli (2010: 125).

11. The terms "established" and "contested" autocracy, which are elaborated later on in this introduction, are from Svolik (2012: 54–70, 73–79, 96–99). Note that a specific version of this question was posed—but never properly answered—by the first generation of totalitarian theorists who wondered how a regime so dependent on rule by a single individual and on extremely high levels of repression might survive without either.

12. See Rigby (1959), Pethybridge (1962), and Roeder (1993: 24–27, 73–74).

13. Gorlizki (2002), Gorlizki and Khlevniuk (2004).

14. Terms of office were fixed not in a legal or constitutional sense but in the expectation that they would last for a set term of around five years.

15. Seminal early contributions include Ross (1973), Mirrlees (1976), and Jensen and Meckling (1976). For later summaries and extensions, see Moe (1984), Stiglitz (1989), Eggertson (1990: 40–45), and Laffont and Martimort (2002). For an application of agency theory to dictatorship, see Egorov and Sonin (2011: 904–9).

16. These information asymmetries are owing to the fact that agents will have better information than their hierarchic superior about the specific tasks assigned to them, as well as about their own actions, abilities, and preferences, which in most cases can be neither observed nor inferred from observable variables. On this, see Mirrlees (1976: 105–7), Stiglitz (1989: 241–42), and Eggertson (1990: 41). Asymmetric information is one part of the agency problem. The other is that agents may have different objectives from their principals. For more on this issue, see Laffont and Martimort (2002).

17. On the use of repression to prevent popular rebellion, see Wintrobe (1998: 33–37, 337), Acemoglu and Robinson (2006: 270–82), Davenport (2007), Svolik (2012: chap. 5), and Escribà-Folch (2013). On the use of repression to attain other economic or ideological goals, see Gorlizki (2016: 291–94).

18. On the difficulties of measuring repression, see Alvarez et al. (1996: 11); and Cheibub et al. (2010: 76). An important distinction is that introduced by Poe and Tate (1994) and Poe, Tate, and Keith (1999) between violation of personal integrity rights (including state-sanctioned murders, disappearances, torture, and prolonged incarceration) and the infringement of civil liberties. For an empirical evaluation of repression in these terms in Stalin's dictatorship, see Gorlizki (2016).

19. A partial exception to this is Gregory (2008: chap. 5)

20. On the role of agreements, bargains, credible promises, and the lure of future rewards in structuring dictatorship, see, for example, Bueno de Mesquita et al. (2003: 28–29), Myerson (2008: 127, 125), Desai et al. (2009), and Svolik (2012: 14). This touches on the broader question of how the exercise of political authority—which ultimately rests on compulsion—can be combined with economic models premised on voluntary exchange. Efforts to square this circle in democracies—e.g., Knight (1992: 18, 41–42, 113), Pierson (2004: 31) and Moe (2005: 217, 226–27)—run into particular problems in dictatorships, in part because of the more prominent and explicit role of repression in the latter.

21. Cf. Geddes (1999; 2003: 55–62), Geddes et al. (2014: 319).

22. Svolik (2012: 2, 14, 57).

23. Recent works on electoral, democratic, or competitive authoritarianism include Levitsky and Way (2002, 2010), Brownlee (2007), Morse (2012), Schedler (2013), and Brancati (2014). For a more wide-ranging discussion of elections under dictatorship, see Gandhi and Lust-Okar (2009).

24. Cf. Getty (1991). On industrial democracy, see Goldman (2007). A later important work on Soviet (i.e., state), not party, elections is Zaslavsky and Brym (1978).

25. The formal rule change of 1939 had, in turn, been prompted by Andrei Zhdanov's call at the February–March 1937 plenum for the extension of the new constitutional provision on secret ballots in state elections to party elections, and in particular to the elections of regional party agencies. Getty (1985: 141–43, 153–55), Getty and Naumov (1999: 357–58). Although it had devoted an entire chapter to elections (chap. 11) and an article to the secret ballot (art. 140), the 1936 Constitution had concerned itself entirely with state elections, making no mention of party elections. The first formal amendment to the party rules was at the XVIII Party Congress in 1939. See Triska (1968: 52–53) and Gill (1988: 169). For the fierce opposition of some regional party leaders to the idea of extending

these principles to party elections, see Easter (2000: 60, 151–52). The Instruction of 1941 and its effects are considered at greater length in appendix G.

26. On the electoral revolts of 1948, see chap. 2.

27. This is a theme of Moore (1950: e.g., 118, 234, 274, 276). To the extent that they showed how elements of democracy were incorporated into authoritarianism precisely in order to strengthen it, contemporary authors such as Barrington Moore can be credited with anticipating the thrust of recent writings on "electoral authoritarianism" by over half a century. Moore (1950: 234), for example, wrote of elections as one of the "ways in which the democratic . . . aspects of the present ideology may be used to perform the paradoxical function of supporting the authoritarian regime." Recent works on electoral or democratic authoritarianism include Schedler (2013), Morse (2012), and Brancati (2014). It should be emphasized, however, that Moore was not writing about *competitive* authoritarianism—cf. Levitsky and Way (2002, 2010)—as there was no choice among candidates.

28. Earlier scholars who stressed the slow-moving and incremental nature of institutional change included North (1990: 6, 89) and Knight (1992: 127). For recent examples, see Pierson (2004: 153), Streeck and Thelen (2005), Mahoney and Thelen (2010), and Thelen and Conran (2016: esp. 54–55).

29. Fitzpatrick (1985: 135, 149), Fieseler (2006), Edele (2008: 22, 231 n.6), Fürst (2010: 36–37, 46), Lovell (2010: 113–14), Dale (2015: chap. 2) and Nove (1989: 280–81, 302–3).

30. For the social effects of the amnesty of 1953, see Dobson (2009), Adler (2012), Elie (2013), Barenberg (2014), and Hardy (2016). For a useful survey of the various riots and uprisings, see Kozlov (2002) and Baron (2001).

31. Whereas almost four-fifths of regional first secretaries in Russia and Ukraine in February 1937, at the beginning of the purge, were over thirty-five years old, over three-fifths of the new generation (as of March 1939) were under thirty-six. Khlevniuk (2016a: 48).

32. Ibid., 50.

33. Cohn (2015: 18–21, 25).

34. Clark (2000: 201).

35. Cohn (2015: 38).

36. This is a key theme of Brubaker (1996: 26–29). In addition to the union and autonomous republics there were autonomous oblasts and autonomous districts.

37. In the 1920s the Bolsheviks set up hundreds of ethnic territorial units and inscribed them into the new Soviet federal constitution. As part of the centralizing thrust of the 1930s most of these were dissolved, eventually leaving 31 national republics (15 at the union republic level and 16 autonomous republics), of which 22 (out of the 139 in 1947) are treated as units of analysis in this book. On this, see appendix B.

38. On this, see Suny (1993: 102–6, 110–12), Martin (2001a: 10–12), Martin (2001b: 73–74).

39. With the introduction of internal passports the ascription of nationality was initially a matter of personal choice; later, however, Soviet citizens were compelled to take on the nationality of their parents, the only choice being for those of mixed parentage.

40. Suny and Martin (2001: 16). On the resentment in the 1920s and 1930s of local national administrators toward indigenization, see Martin (2001a: 137–40, 151–52, 398–401).

41. Even then there continued to be exceptions, most notably in Kazakhstan, Moldavia, and, to an extent, Ukraine, where, although after the appointment of Kirichenko all the leaders were technically Ukrainian, not all were or were thought of as needing to be proficient in Ukrainian.

42. Second secretaries tended to manage the party organs department, which was in charge of cadres, and the administrative organs department, which oversaw the work of the state security service. Miller (1977: 7–8, 19), Grybkauskas (2013: 343).

43. Hirsch (2005).

44. Examples included the local blocking of Filip Kashnikov as candidate for second secretary in Latvia in 1956, the rejection of Tikhon Kiselev as Moscow's candidate for first secretary in Belorussia in 1965, and, in a proxy election, the rejection of Juozas Maniušis as first secretary in Lithuania in 1974. See Prigge (2015: 82–83), Loader (2016: 152–56), Grybkauskas (2013: 352, 357–58).

45. Following Magaloni and Kricheli (2010), we treat one-party regimes as an overarching category that includes single-party regimes such as the Soviet Union, where only one party is permitted, and dominant party regimes, where although other parties may be tolerated, the ruling party maintains a continuous supermajority in the parliament. Magaloni and Kricheli (2010: 123–24) report that one-party regimes accounted for 56 percent of all authoritarian regimes from 1950 to 2006.

46. On this, see Geddes (1999: 135; 2003: 69, 78, 82), Smith (2005), Magaloni (2008), Blaydes (2010), Magaloni and Kricheli (2010: 124), Reuter and Gandhi (2010), Svolik (2012), Geddes et al. (2014: 318–19), and Levitsky and Way (2012; 2015; 2016). The terms "longevity," "stability," and "durability" have different meanings. Longevity refers to the tenure of the dictator or the duration of a countrywide regime; stability to the likelihood that a leader will be removed by a coup or a revolt; and durability to the ability of the regime to withstand major, systemic crises. Levitsky and Way (2012: 870, 880).

47. Gandhi (2008), Magaloni (2008), Blaydes (2010), Svolik (2012).

48. Svolik (2012: 184–92).

49. Gandhi (2008: 20, 29–31). For a somewhat different reading, one which emphasizes the role of procedures as publicly observable signals of the leader's commitment to sharing power, see Boix and Svolik (2013: 309, 311).

50. Svolik (2012: chap. 6); for a different reading, see Gandhi (2008: 76–82, 100).

51. Adherents of this position include Smith (2005), Brownlee (2007), Slater (2010, 2010a), and Levitsky and Way (2012, 2015, 2016). These arguments derive from the earlier work of Huntington (1968: 418, 424–25; 1970: 14). This is slightly confusing in that Huntington (e.g., 1968: 336–43, 400) is normally credited with stressing the institutional role of the party in communist state building. Part of this confusion stems from the fact that Huntington considered the party notionally (i.e., on the basis of programmatic statements) rather than empirically, as do current institutional theorists.

52. Levitsky and Way (2012: 870–71; 2015: 102).

53. For examples of this vagueness, see Levitsky and Way (2012: 872, 880).

54. On this, see Wintrobe (1998: 219).

55. There was, in fact, one final mass purge after 1939, that of 150,000 Communists who had either spent time as German prisoners of war or lived in Nazi-occupied territory, most of whom were expelled from 1944 to 1949. On this, see Cohn (2015: chap. 2) and Voisin (2011).

56. On this in the Roman Empire, see Saller (1982: 38, 67–68, 130, 153–54).

57. Of the 59 obkoms in the Russian Federation and the Ukraine, between December 1936 and December 1938 112 first secretaries were sacked, of whom 79 were arrested. In some regions up to 4 first secretaries were eliminated. Khlevniuk (2016a: 46–47).

58. Hardin (2002: 98). For other historical examples, see Hardin (2002: 96–100, 103–5).

59. Following standard definitions—e.g., Hardin (2002), Cook, Hardin, and Levi (2005), and Cook, Levi, and Hardin (2009)—we take "trust" to mean that one person trusts another if the truster expects the trusted to cooperate on a specific matter in circumstances that they cannot anticipate. For trust to be relevant there needs to be some divergence of interests between the two actors; if their interests are perfectly aligned, cooperation requires not trust but coordination. Trust enters the picture only when the raw payoff from defection may be higher than from cooperation but, for some reason, usually because of an ongoing personal relationship, the trusted may choose to cooperate. From this it follows that trust and, in particular, acting on trust involves genuine risk to the truster. A low-trust environment is one in which levels of risk—be it, as in this case, because of the presence of spies, informers, or a recent epidemic of betrayals—are unusually high. For a helpful exploration of these issues, see Bacharach and Gambetta (2001).

60. For historical examples from a variety of contexts of people of low social origin, foreigners, former slaves, eunuchs, and people of limited education or even competence being elevated to positions of influence so that "their loyalty could be trusted," see Rosenberg (1958: 65 [quote], 67–68, 88–89), Saller (1982: 112, 140), Gambetta (2009: 42–45), and Egorov and Sonin (2011: 904–8).

61. On the various types of card catalogues held by the police and the party through which kompromat could be obtained, see Shearer (2009: chap. 5) and Shearer and Khaustov (2015: 153–56). On materials held in archives, see the articles by Korneev and Kopylova (1992) and Weiner and Rahi-Tamm (2012: 16–19, 23–34). For a general discussion, see Gambetta (2009: chap. 3).

62. In this vein, Rigby (1984: 40) wrote of the "shared complicity for actions which violate official policies or norms." Also see Fairbanks (1983: 350–51, 354).

63. For excellent treatments of these themes for the prerevolutionary period, see Hosking (2000) and Ledeneva (2004). Our archive-based approach is quite different from Kharkhordin's discursive analysis, which, working from published manuals, pamphlets, booklets, lexicological commentaries, and philosophical tracts, tends to emphasize what he sees as "mutual horizontal surveillance among peers." Kharkhordin 1999: 110–11, 122, 355 (quote). Unlike Kharkhordin, we see the processes of informal exclusion in the Soviet era as fundamentally hierarchical, not horizontal.

64. See, for example, Fainsod (1958), Getty (1983, 2016), Harris (1999), and Easter (2000). For a collection of essays on Soviet regional history across the Stalin era, see Raleigh (2001).

65. E.g., Fairbanks (1983: 342), Getty (1985: 145; 2016: 77–78), Harris (1999: 187), Easter (2000: 104, 150–51), Alexopoulos (2008: 107–8).

66. As with much else, the one real exception to this general tendency was the Great Purges of 1937–38. For a detailed discussion of the specific circumstances of that purge, see Khlevniuk (2016a: 43–44, 50–51). For a good example of Stalin's double-talk on this issue, consider the behavior of Stalin's agent in the Mingrelian Affair, Mgeladze, who, at the same time he launched a bitter attack on patronage in Georgia, proceeded to recruit a large group of his own clients when taking over as first secretary of the Georgian central committee. Fairbanks (1983: 342–43, 355).

67. Asking why Stalin did not simply sack one of his own lieutenants, namely, Beria, in the Mingrelian Affair, instead of using the "very strange Stalinist technique" of the gradual purge, Fairbanks (1983: 361–62) suggests that Beria's own clientelist network was "such an important mechanism for the coordination of government" that to have removed Beria directly would have "produced widespread disorganization." As Fairbanks puts it, "There can be no doubt that Stalin's most important lieutenants were [themselves] major patrons."

68. Khlevniuk (2016a: 47–49).

69. Armstrong (1959), Stewart (1968), and Hill (1977).

70. Blackwell (1972a, 1972b, 1973, 1979), Blackwell and Hulbary (1973), Moses (1974, 1976, 1981, 1985, 2008), Miller (1977).

71. Rigby (1983, 1984), Fairbanks (1983), Urban (1989), Willerton (1992).

72. Hough (1969), Rutland (1992).

73. Examples in Hough (1969) include an acute reading of the role of the closed ballot in party elections (161–63), the emergence, from the late 1940s, of soft rotation of regional party secretaries (278), an understanding of the low status of obkom industrial secretaries in relation to some factory directors and ministerial officials (69, 204–5), and a grasp of how hard it was for officials in Moscow to appraise candidates in the provinces, as a result of which this task was often delegated to regional and republican organizations (169).

74. Ibid., 146–47, 177, 276–77.

75. Citing a Soviet source, he writes (ibid., 249), "It is not the party obkom which makes demands on the oblast organizations but the leaders of these organizations which present their endless demands to the obkom."

76. Armstrong (1959), Rigby (1959, 1983, 1984), Fairbanks (1983), Urban (1988), and Willerton (1992).

77. Note that patron–client ties were by their nature asymmetric and in this sense differed from "family circles" and "friendship circles" of the kind described in detail by Fainsod (e.g., 1958: 48–49, 85–86, 270–72), which tended to consist of equals. On the difference between the two, see Fairbanks (1983: 348).

78. As Rigby (1983: 6) put it, "Surely the most valuable resource—subject to administrative decision and, therefore, forming part of the 'stock' of reciprocal favour is position itself."

79. On this, see, for example, Rigby (1983: 6–7) and Jozsa (1983: 144). On the unique network opportunities of party positions, see Willerton (1992: 50–51);

Urban (1989: 88); Jozsa (1983: 144); and Fairbanks (1983: 365). For the notion that client network size reflected a patron's power and prestige, see Willerton (1992: 52). For more on the relationship between patron–client relations and networks, see appendix D

80. From 1941 to 1956 the USSR had a sixteenth union republic, the Karelian-Finnish SSR. For more on these republics and their subdivisions, see appendix B.

81. According to the democracy and dictatorship dataset, how incumbents are removed from office is the only effective criterion for classifying statewide regimes; see, for example, Cheibub et al. (2010: 67, 84). Here, we point not to how substate leaders were removed—they were invariably removed from above, by the Central Committee—but to the *grounds* on which they were removed.

82. Svolik (2012: 55–56). One implication of this argument is that the established dictator is, in some respects, too powerful for his own good, as, even if he wants to, he is too powerful to "credibly commit" to sharing power. His only way out of the conundrum is to give up power or, in the language of this book, to delegate it. On this, see Svolik (2012: 99).

83. For a consideration of such effects on the structure of Russian regional elites in the post-Soviet era, see Gelman et al. (2003: 33, 48–49, 60–61, 251–52).

84. There are two main exceptions. One is the Smolensk archives, captured by the Germans at the beginning of the Second World War, on which Fainsod's classic monograph *Smolensk under Soviet Rule* (1958) is based. For our purposes, however, the relevance of Fainsod's book is limited by its prewar timescale and by the fact that, although he addresses the question of "family circles" and *krugovaia poruka,* a shortcoming of his treatment of this topic is that he tended to recycle the bureaucratic categories used in official documents but did little to peer into the networks they describe or to understand how they formed. With the exception of the infamous Smolensk Scandal of 1928, he is also primarily interested in family circles at the local raion level (1958: 111, 121, 149–51, 270–71). The other exception is the large interview projects with émigrés carried out in the 1950s (i.e., the Harvard Project) and the 1970s (i.e., the Soviet Interview Project). Given that neither of the projects included politicians of any seniority, their findings tended to be limited to observations about economic enterprises, the operation of low-level bureaucracies, public opinion, and the struggles of everyday life. For summaries of their findings, see Bauer et al. (1956) and Millar (1992).

85. Consider the following example: participants at the Moscow gorkom plenum of June 1967 that removed the first secretary Nikolai Egorychev concur that the atmosphere at the meeting was subdued and that the speeches were greeted by an eerie silence, with no debates, questions, or applause. Yet the transcripts in the party archive, which appear to have been amended by the Central Committee's general department, indicate that there was prolonged applause, so as to give the impression that Egorychev's unpopular sacking did in fact have the active backing of the entire membership of the committee. Hence arguably the most significant feature of this meeting has been subsequently edited out. N.G. *Egorychev* (2006: 333).

86. Many party meetings of the aktiv, in particular, were convened for show and for propaganda, so that the records of these meeting reflect only an imaginary reality that local party leaders wanted to project. A nice fictional example comes from

Aleksandr Iashin's celebrated short story *Rychagi* of 1954, in which the moment the meeting began, having cavilled in private against virtually every aspect of village life, "suddenly the participants stop criticizing party policies in the countryside and start speaking in dull, official cliché-ridden language [and] even imitate the district party secretary, who only seconds before was the object of their ridicule" Cited in Brudny (1998: 49).

87. As a partial exception, see Darden (2001).

CHAPTER 1. SUBSTATE DICTATORS

1. RGASPI f.17 op.122 d.131 ll.209–12. Referring to a regional first secretary as a dictator was not uncommon in this period. The first secretary in Riazan, for example, A.I. Marfin, under whom "there was, in effect, no obkom buro," whose "rudeness reached impossible heights," and who was known to "hysterically smash his fists on the table swearing to all and sundry," was told by the raikom secretary, Isaev, in April 1948 that "we need an obkom secretary, not a dictator." *TsK VKP(b)* (2004: 175–78)

2. It is testimony to the hypercentralization of the late Stalinist era that the Central Committee nomenklatura penetrated the very depths of the regional power structure, down to the raikom first secretary. In reality, however, overloaded Central Committee cadre departments usually ceded the initiative on such low-level appointments to regional party leaders. "More often than not the Central Committee instructor rubber stamps the recommendation of the obkom, as he just does not know the nominees well enough," observed one review of Central Committee practices in April 1949. "That is why it is so rare for a nomination to be declined." By contrast, appointments at the obkom level tended to be taken more seriously. RGASPI f.17 op.131 d.45 ll.46–47; and f.17 op.127 d.1334 ll.3, 43–44, 47.

3. This is explored at greater length in chapter 6.

4. Such tactics were later made famous in Ovechkin's 1952 sketch "raionnye budni," where the district party secretary, Borzov, "oppressed kulaks by Stalinist reflex" and sent "thunderbolt telegrams to every farm and MTS: 'fulfill, finish, hurry,' all of them spiced with threats of court action." Dunham (1976: 232–33). For real historical examples in Kaluga and Kostroma, see RGASPI f.17 op.131 d.1 l.8.

5. *Tsk VKP(b)* (2004: 179, 387).

6. RGASPI f.17 op.127 d.1343 ll.106–7.

7. Although there was a small handful of Old Bolsheviks who became territorial first secretaries after the purges, the only territorial first secretaries to survive the Terror in post were Bagirov, Khrushchev, and Zhdanov. See Khlevniuk (2016: 47–48) and, for an older source, Avtorkhanov (1966: 154).

8. Whereas 87.4 percent of territorial first secretaries in February 1937, on the eve of the Great Purges, had joined the party before 1924, 75.7 percent of territorial first secretaries in March 1939, after the purges, had joined from 1924 to 1931. Over three-fifths (61.6 percent) of first secretaries in March 1939 were thirty-five years old or under. Khlevniuk (2016: 39, 48).

9. For a broader discussion, see Tucker (1990: 526–30, 545–50), Mawdsley and White (108–13).

10. Letter from the chair of the Khabarovsk radio committee, V.V. Pavlova to G.M. Malenkov of 16 July 1945. RGASPI f.17 op.127 d.733 l.156. On the coercive culture of regional party leaders during the war, also see Kaplan (1985:168).

11. *TsK VKP(b)* (2004: 176).

12. RGASPI f.17 op.122 d.130 l.81.

13. RGASPI f.17 op.127 d.733 ll.3, 9.

14. Turnover figures for raikom secretaries across the USSR are unavailable, so we compiled data on a region-by-region basis. The lowest figures we found were in Ukraine, where turnover figures for raikom secretaries in 1945–46 were 26.8 percent per year. Elsewhere turnover rates for raikom secretaries of 47 percent per year were recorded in the twelve Belorussian regions in 1945–46, 39.9 percent per year in Kostroma in 1944–47, 50 percent in Kaluga in 1946–47, 44.0 percent in Tambov in 1947, and 36.1 percent of all rural raikom first secretaries in 1950. RGASPI f.17 op.131 d.1 ll.9–10; f.17 op.122 d.137 l.24; f.17 op.127 d.1700 l.76; f.17 op.127 d.1344 l.140; f.17 op.127 d.1335 l.56; f.17 op.131 d.284 ll.155–56. Admittedly, a share of this turnover was taken up by promotions (e.g., 11.8 percent in Tambov). We cannot discount the possibility that some of this turnover was due to resignations and voluntary migration. Certainly, the early postwar years were a period of high labor mobility, as some cadres abandoned their posts to rejoin their families and return to their home region. Raikom secretaryships were also clearly less alluring than more senior positions in the Central Committee nomenklatura. However, abandoning a raikom secretaryship without permission came at considerable cost, as it involved violating party discipline and potentially jeopardizing one's whole career. One measure of the punitive nature of these high levels of turnover was the high incidence of party punishments that accompanied cadre replacements. Thus, for example, approximately a third of the replacements in Ukraine and a half in Kaluga were associated with party penalties, while over a third of rural raikom first secretaries replaced in 1950 were removed for incompetence or for having compromised themselves. RGASPI f.17 op.122 d.137 l.24; f.17 op.127 d.1335 l.56; f.17 op.131 d.284 ll.155–56.

15. RGASPI f.17 op.131 d.1 l.8.

16. High-profile figures such as the first secretary, the chair of the regional executive committee, or the second secretary might miss over half of scheduled buro meetings. Of the 104 meetings in Odessa, the first secretary, Kirichenko, was absent from 50, the chair of the regional executive committee from 56, the head of the MGB from 50, the second secretary from 72, and the second secretary of the Odessa gorkom from 91. RGASPI f.17 op.131 d.4 ll.22–23. From January to August 1948 the buro of the Vinnitsa obkom met 44 times, but only on three occasions with the full complement of seven members. The first secretary Stakhurskii attended only 21 meetings, the chair of the regional executive committee 17, and the head of the MVD 11. DAVO f.P-136 op.29 d.176 ll.2–3.

17. *TsK VKP(b)* (2004: 174–75).

18. For examples in Kaluga in 1945 and Astrakhan in 1946, see RGASPI f.17 op.127 d.1335 l.57, d.1344 ll.16–17.

19. For an example in Kostroma in 1946, see RGASPI f.17 op.131 d.136 ll.79–85, 117.

20. Appointed to strategically important structures in the republic, these individuals were resented by local officials, who, following Gusarov's dismissal in 1950, openly referred to them as his personal agents and informers. RGASPI f.17 op.131 d.115 ll.14–15.

21. There was never a set rule as such on this, only a norm. This was reflected in an apologetic note that the new first secretary in Riazan sent to Malenkov in November 1948, after he had proposed bringing with him cadres from the Central Committee, where he had previously worked, to shore up the local obkom: "Please know that none of these comrades is or has ever been a friend or a close acquaintance of mine." RGASPI f.17 op.131 d.148 ll.183–84.

22. One reason for this may have been Bagirov's role, strongly backed by Stalin, in creating a pro-Soviet autonomous territory in the ethnically Azerbaijani northern region of Iran in the immediate aftermath of the war. On this, see Swietochowski (1995: chap. 6), Hasanli (2006). Bagirov's autonomy is discussed at greater length at the end of this chapter.

23. From 1951 to 1952 in only twenty districts Bagirov had sacked, and in most cases convicted on criminal charges, 134 raikom secretaries and raiispolkom chairs, while across the republic 874 heads of cattle farms were arrested. RGASPI f.82, op. 2, d.148, ll.14–17.

24. RGASPI f.17 op.53 d.7 l.130. Another source suggests that by the late 1940s Emel'ianov had been admitted into Bagirov's close circle. Ismailov (2003: 149).

25. There may also have been other factors which commended Emel'ianov to Bagirov. He was, for example, a Russian, which may have pleased Moscow, but, having operated in low-key posts, he was not known in Moscow and appears to have had no connections there. Born to a peasant family in Tataria, Emel'ianov had come to Azerbaijan while serving in the army. For more on Emel'ianov's past, see *Kto rukovodil NKVD* (1999: 186–87).

26. Ismailov (2003: 134–36, 198–99).

27. RGASPI f.82, op.2, d.148, l.9. The author, I.K. Efendiev, an operative of the Azeri secret service of thirty years' standing, certainly had an animus against Bagirov, having been imprisoned by him the previous year. Nonetheless, most of the evidence presented by Efendiev in his letter of 5 October 1953 was later corroborated, on the basis of a separate investigation, in a Central Committee report of 15 December. Ibid., l.14. The Efendiev letter is in ibid., ll.1–13.

28. Examples included the second secretary of the republic, Samedov, the secretary of the Baku gorkom, Gezalov, the department head at the gorkom, Abramova-Skirskaia, a department head at the Kirovobad gorkom, and others. Ibid., ll.16–18.

29. Following Schelling's (1960: 43–44) example of a kidnap where both the captor and a prisoner want the prisoner released, but the kidnapper needs reassurance that once released the prisoner will not inform on him, Gambetta (2009: 59) goes a step further by conceiving the notion of "self-inflicted blackmail." Here we may have an interest in *"volunteering* negative information about ourselves." "Being bad," Gambetta writes, "and displaying credible evidence of it can make our promises credible." In some environments—late 1940s Azerbaijan appears to be a striking example—the potential stock of ambient trust was so low

that "blackmail may have been the only route to cooperation." Also see Gorlizki (2013a: 131–32).

30. Note that what lends Efendiev's letter added credibility is that it was addressed to members of the Presidium and traced the fates of individuals whom, he claimed, members of the Presidium, such as Molotov and Malenkov, "personally knew." Ibid., ll.7–9.

31. Ibid., ll.18–19.

32. As one of the five large union republics, this is the one example in the book where we deviate from the principles for selecting territorial units set out in appendix B. We do this simply because this was the most clear-cut example we could find of this type of network formation in the late Stalin era.

33. RGASPI f.17 op.122 d.321 ll.5–7; op.48 d.1952 ll.79–82.

34. RGASPI f.17 op.48 d.1952 l.71.

35. RGASPI f.17 op.122 d.321 ll.7–8.

36. RGASPI f.17 op.48 d.1952 l.61.

37. RGASPI f.17 op.122 d.321 ll.7–8.

38. RGASPI f.17 op.122 d.321 l.8.

39. Lomakin was also given to understand that were he "not to correct his behavior," he would be sacked for "not fulfilling the trust of the Central Committee." *TsK VKP(b)* (2004:106–8).

40. RGASPI f.17 op.122 d.296 l.4.

41. RGASPI f.17 op.122 d.296 l.6.

42. RGASPI f.17 op.122 d.321 ll.5–7; op.48 d.1952 l.295.

43. RGASPI f.17 op.127 d.1343 l.4.

44. RGASPI f.17 op.127 d.1704 l.33.

45. RGASPI f.17 op.127 d.1343 l.4.

46. Although using different labels, a number of earlier scholars, such as Fairbanks (1983: 368) and Rigby (1984: 56–57), observed this practice.

47. DAVO f.P-136 op.12 d.351 l.24. Kozyr's later career is discussed in chapter five.

48. RGASPI f.17 op.127 d.1704 ll.33–35.

49. RGASPI f.17 op.127 d.1704 l.33.

50. RGASPI f.17 op.131 d.136 l.87.

51. RGASPI f.17 op.131 d.136 l.135.

52. Further, over 30 percent of cadres in Uzbekistan who were on the Central Committee nomenklatura had only a primary education. RGASPI f.17 op.122 d.321 ll.7–8.

53. Cohn (2015: 19, 38–41).

54. This was normally preceded by a hearing and a recommendation from the obkom party collegium. For a helpful outline of the disciplinary process, see Cohn (2015: 43).

55. Cohn (2015: 39–42, 44).

56. Cohn (2015: 35–36, 197 fn.6).

57. Cohn (2015: 121, 132–34).

58. Cohn (2015: 116–28).

59. On this, see Zubkova (2000: 121–22).

60. See points 2 and 3 of the NKVD order approved by the Politburo on 26 December 1938 in *Lubianka* (2003: 600).

61. So, for example, in Penza in 1947 the obkom nomenklatura included fifty-four positions in the regional administration of the MGB, including key figures from its leadership such as heads and deputy heads of the regional departments and the heads of city and district departments. GAPO f.148 op.1 d.1703 l.80.

62. *Obschestvo i vlast'* (2006: t.2, 285–87).

63. For an excellent description of the various schemes surrounding the money reforms, see Zubkova (2000: 81–84).

64. *Obschestvo i vlast'* (2006: t.2, 281–82).

65. Leibovitch (2008: 99–108).

66. RGASPI f.17 op.131 d.59 l.37.

67. OGAChO f.288 op.42 d.47 ll.35–36.

68. For examples in Irkutsk and Penza, see RGASPI f.17 op.48 d.575 ll.51–52 and GAPO f.148 op.1 d.2338 l.60.

69. RGASPI f.17 op.122 d.129 ll.15–18.

70. RGASPI f.17 op.127 d.1345 ll.84–85.

71. RGASPI f.17 op.127 d.1345 l.84.

72. RGASPI f.17 op.88 d.901 l.276.

73. *TsK VKP(b)* (2004: 388, 407).

74. RGASPI f.17 op.127 d.1352 ll.146–49.

75. RGASPI f.17 op.127 d.1352 l.145.

76. The mismatch between the skills of the leader and the demands of running the region was often at its most glaring in large, complex, economically strategic regions. In addition to Aleksandriuk in Rostov, other, slightly later examples include Kireev in Gor'kii (1946–50) and Nedosekin in Sverdlovsk (1946–52).

77. Patolichev (1977: 280).

78. Technically the department was known at the time as the "organization and instruction department," but in essence it was the same as what would later become the party organs department and, for ease of reference, we shall refer to it here as the latter.

79. Patolichev (1977: 281–82).

80. Recent research has shown that during the war regional party organizations in effect usurped powers which by design were supposed to belong to the center. They did so by engaging in, among other things, the unauthorized reallocation of equipment, raw materials, and fuel, in altering state plans at the local level, in allocating products intended for other regions to local uses, and in drawing on central reserves of strategic resources, the most important of which was grain. Khlevniuk (2018: 478–81).

81. RGASPI f.17 op.131 d.45 l.37; f.17 op.122 d.129 ll.101–11.

82. RGASPI f.17 op.122 d.129 ll.98–100. For a good summary of the housing crisis in the early postwar years, see Zubkova (2000: 55).

83. RGASPI f.17 op.122 d.131 ll.158–68.

84. RGASPI f.17 op.127 d.1083 l.139.

85. RGASPI f.17 op.127 d.1335 l.57.

86. RGASPI f.17 op.127 d.1335 ll.50–57.

87. RGASPI f.17 op.127 d.1335 ll.67–68.

88. *TsK VKP(b)* (2004: 163–64). Although expelled from the party, Popov did escape prosecution. From 1948 to 1950 he was the director of a garment factory in Chkalov and from 1950 to 1953 the chair of the Chkalov regional radio broadcasting committee.

89. There are various versions of these events. See, for example, Rubtsov (2002: 158–61); Ismailov (2003: 225–26).

90. Baibakov (1998: 123). An analogous account can be found in a contemporary letter from Azerbaijan sent immediately after Bagirov's removal in 1953. RGASPI f.82 op.2 d.148 l.9. The Politburo resolution of 30 July 1948 on the results of the inquiry also noted that the head of the group of inspectors had discredited himself "through his amoral conduct (his connection with casual and politically dubious women, visits with these women to disreputable flats, and a trip with the same women to Makhachkala)." *TsK VKP(b)* (2004: 114–15).

91. *TsK VKP(b)* (2004: 113–14).

92. The meeting took place in Stalin's office. See *Istoricheskii arkhiv,* nos. 5–6 (1996): 41.

93. *TsK VKP(b)* (2004: 113–20). This was all the more striking given that in 1940 it had been Stalin himself who had pushed for the creation of a commissariat of state control with wide prerogatives. RGASPI f.17 op.3 d.1023 l.2; d.1028 ll.193–94, 213–15, 308–14.

94. RGASPI f.17 op.131 d.4 ll.21–22.

95. On this, see Khlevniuk (2018).

CHAPTER 2. AUTHORITARIAN CHECKS AND BALANCES

1. Rigby (1980: 60).

2. The stories were F. Panfyerov's "Bol'shoe iskusstvo" and V. Popov's "Stal i shlak," both published in 1949, cited in Dunham (1976: 188–89, 163–66).

3. This had been a long-running concern. On the eve of the war, on 21 March 1941, the Orgburo banned economic commissars and enterprise directors from "awarding [party functionaries] prizes, bonuses, or rewards in any form" and it forbade the latter from accepting them. *TsK VKP(b)* (2004: 157–58). Another concern was the proliferation of factory-based full-time party officials (*osvobozhdennye secretary*) whose salaries were paid out of the factory budget and who were therefore, in effect, employees of the factory. Gorlizki (2011: 332–33); and *TsK VKP(b)* (2004: 160–61).

4. The following week Andrianov responded with a list of 113 representatives (mainly obkom first secretaries) from whom he had received assurances on the matter. RGASPI f.17 op.121 d.448 ll.5, 8–11.

5. *TsK VKP(b)* (2004: 156–57).

6. *TsK VKP(b)* (2004: 157–61).

7. RGASPI f.17 op.122 d.137 ll.33–35.

8. RGASPI f.17 op.122 d.325 ll.54–56.

9. GAPO f.P-148 op.1 d.1926 l.25 GAPO f.P-148 op.1 d.1931 l.39.

10. *TsK VKP(b)* (2004: 240–44).

11. For more on this, see Sushkov (2015), Sushkov and Mikailev (2015), and Fedorov (2016a).

12. Kostyrchenko (2001: 616–18).

13. Magnitogorsk a decade earlier, in the 1930s, is the subject of Kotkin's landmark study (1995).

14. Gol'dshtein (1995: 172).

15. In 1941 he was made Hero of Socialist Labor and, in addition to winning the Stalin prize and the orders of Kutuzov, Suvorov, and the Red Star, he was made a general and was elected to the all-union Supreme Soviet.

16. Gol'dshtein (1995). On Zal'tsman's oratory and his ability to persuade a packed, hostile auditorium of the need for evacuated employees—three-quarters of the workforce—to postpone their return home in the summer of 1945, see Zubkova (2000: 43). For more on Zal'tsman, see Samuelson (2011: 148–49, 195, 267–68).

17. OGAChO f.288 op.14 d.2 l.103. Of Nosov, Patolichev later reminisced, "I would have regarded it as a great blessing to have worked with Nosov as a Central Committee party organizer." OGAChO f.288 op.14 d.2 l.77. A Central Committee party organizer was a representative directly appointed by the Central Committee in a factory and was independent of the territorial party structure.

18. OGAChO f.288 op.14 d.2 l.16.

19. OGAChO f.288 op.14 d.2 l.51.

20. OGAChO f.288 op.14 d.2 ll.5, 6.

21. OGAChO f.288 op.14 d.2 l.153. Nosov appears to have been the model for Rotov the factory director in Popov's "Stal i shlak," who is described in nearly identical terms. See Dunham (1976: 163).

22. OGAChO f.288 op.14 d.2 l.24. Again the parallel with Rotov's treatment of the head of the city soviet is unmissable. See Dunham (1976: 163–64).

23. On this, see Fedorov (2016b: 303–5), OGAChO f.288 op.14 d.2 ll.24, 46–50, 76–78, 102–4.

24. OGAChO f.288 op.14 d.2 ll.152–57.

25. After Stalin's death, in 1955 Zal'tsman's membership in the party was restored, and he returned to Leningrad, where he had begun his career and where he would go on to head one of the local factories. He died in 1988 at the age of eighty-three.

26. Note that the examples we came across mostly occurred in the autonomous republics, where the populations were, on the whole, more ethnically divided than they were in the union republics. Most autonomous republics were in the Russian Federation, but there were also autonomous republics in Georgia, Armenia, and Kazakhstan. For more on the regime's wartime policy of ethnic mobilization, see Brandenberger (2002: 129–30, 187–89).

27. RGASPI f.17 op.122 d.129 l.164.

28. RGASPI f.17 op.122 d.129 ll.165–66.

29. RGASPI f.17 op.122 d.89 ll.1–7.

30. RGASPI f.17 op.122 d.129 ll.156–58, 160.

31. RGASPI f.17 op.122 d.129 ll.159–60.

32. RGASPI f.17 op.122 d.129 l.170. On the scandals in the buro of the Chuvash obkom also see the reports from the KPK plenipotentiary for the Chuvash ASSR over the course of December 1946. Ibid., d.130 ll.200–209.

33. RGASPI f.17 op.122 d.129 l.171.

34. RGASPI f.17 op.122 d.129 l.175.

35. The position taken by the second secretary, Akhazov, did him little harm. Taking over from Charykov, he stayed on as first secretary for another seven years, until 1955. Following a short study spell in Moscow, he held the honorary position of chair of the presidium of the Chuvash supreme soviet for another decade.

36. For example, lack of cooperation (*nesrabotannost'*) between first secretaries and chairs of the ispolkom was observed in 1944–48 in Kaluga (RGASPI f.17 op.127 d.1335 l.57), in 1947–48 in L'vov (RGASPI f.17 op.27 d.1343 l.107), in 1948 in Vinnitsa and Khabarovsk (RGASPI f.17 op.127 d.1335 l.57; d.301 ll.21–34), and in 1952 in Kirov (RGASPI f.558 op.11 d.903 ll.27–33).

37. Almakaev (1998: 144–46).

38. Almakaev (1998: 146–47).

39. RGASPI f.17 op.127 d.1702 ll.93–94.

40. On this, see Harrison (2016: 6–7).

41. Harrison (2016: 9–12, 15–17) reports that from 1941 to 1949, all under Goglidze's watch, over 150 victims fell into this hideous trap.

42. RGASPI f.17 op.127 d.1684 l.36.

43. RGASPI f.17 op.122 d.301 l.21.

44. RGASPI f.17 op.122 d.301 l.34.

45. RGASPI f.17 op.122 d.301 l.21.

46. A proposal to send Nazarov to Moscow to continue his studies, so that he could redress the faults in his work and improve on his low level of training, had been first drafted by the cadres administration in December 1947 (RGASPI f.17 op.127 d.1684 l.36).

47. RGASPI f.17 op.3 d.1074 l.44.

48. RGASPI f.17 op.121 d.101 ll.60–65.

49. *TsK VKP(b)* (2004: 87).

50. At the end of June 1953 Goglidze was arrested, and in December 1953 he was executed, along with Beria. Efimov's fate was a happier one. He stayed on as first secretary in Khabarovsk until 1954. He was then transferred to Moscow as first deputy minister of timber industries. He ended his career with a fifteen-year stay in the lucrative position of trade representative of the USSR in Czechoslovakia.

51. See Gill (1988: 175).

52. The party rules of 1939 made it clear that voting lists were forbidden—so that at the discussion stage candidates were considered one by one—and that voting should take place by closed ballot (art. 23). See Gill (1988: 169). In this regard the 1939 rules were much more detailed about the electoral process and in particular the role of the closed ballot than the previous party rules of 1934. The latter had referred to elections only in general terms, and their discussion of "intra-party democracy" emphasized party discipline. See articles 18 and 57–60 in Gill (1988: 153, 162–63). In any case, the 1939 rules were superseded by much more detailed instructions on party elections that were issued in 1941. On this, see appendix G.

53. On the difference between this figure and the number of territorial party committees surveyed in the book, see appendix B.

54. RGASPI f.17 op.122 d.291 l.137.

55. There were no conferences in sixteen organizations in the RSFSR as well as in regions in Belorussia, Uzbekistan, and the autonomous republics of Georgia. RGASPI f.17 op.88 d.901 l.268.

56. RGASPI f.17 op.88 d.901 ll.293–303.

57. RGASPI f.17 op.88 d.901 ll.274–75; op.122 d.245 ll.126–29; d.126 ll.12–13.

58. GAPO f.P-148 op.1 d.2128 l.25.

59. RGASPI f.17 op.88 d.901 ll.63–67.

60. RGASPI f.17 op.127 d.1700 l.73.

61. RGASPI f.17 op.122 d.296 ll.22–23.

62. Despite this, Riabik was nominated as obkom second secretary instead of Ivanov. RGASPI f.17 op.122 d.296 ll.22–23.

63. RGASPI f.17 op.127 d.1704 ll.33–35; f.17 op.127 d.1343 l.4.

64. RGASPI f.17 op.122 d.296 ll.14–15.

65. RGASPI f.17 op.122 d.296 l.14.

66. RGASPI f.17 op.131 d.197 ll.7–9.

67. RGASPI f.17 op.131 d.197 ll.5–6.

68. The purge was so wide-ranging that replacements at a number of levels had to be drafted in from Moscow. *TsK VKP* (2004: 198–208).

69. The crux of the reorganization, based on a decision of the Politburo of 10 July 1948, was the dissolution of the broad overarching administrations of the Central Committee and the creation in their place of specialized branch departments. Preparatory documents spoke scathingly of the "serious failures" of the former cadres administration. *Politbiuro* (2002: 59–62).

70. The connections of Popkov and Kuznetsov with Leningrad were the strongest: Popkov had served in Leningrad from 1925 to 1949 and Kuznetsov from 1937 to 1946. Voznesenskii had been in Leningrad for two years, from 1935 to 1937. Thirty-six leading functionaries from the Leningrad obkom and gorkom were either executed or sentenced to various terms, as were nine district leaders. In total, an estimated 214 people were convicted, 69 as main defendants and 145 associates or relatives. A larger proportion of the region's officials were fired: of 379 leading functionaries in the city in 1949, almost half, 45.9 percent, were replaced. Trials of Leningrad officials continued until the end of 1952. RGANI f.5 op.29 d.13 l.111, *Reabilitatsiia* (1991: 319–20), *Reabilitatsiia* (2000: 74–75), and Tromly (2004: 716, 727 fn. 86).

71. *Kommunisticheskaia partiia* (1985: vol. 8, 189).

72. For discussions of the wider regional fallout from the Leningrad Affair, see *Leningradskoe delo* (1990: 177–262), Tromly (2004: 718–19), Brandenberger (2004: 243), Kelly (2011: 106). On Kupriianov, see his memoirs (1989: 170–78), and on Smirnov, see Semenov (1997: 47–50).

73. RGASPI f.17 op.131 d.130 ll.15, 19–22.

74. RGASPI f.17 op.131 d.148 ll.80–96, 109–16.

75. RGASPI f.17 op.131 d.130 ll.103–4.

76. RGASPI f.17 op.131 d.191 l.49.

77. RGASPI f.17 op.127 d.1334 l.3. This process was reinforced by the fact that many provincial secretaries, such as Larionov himself, had themselves earlier done

stints at the Central Committee apparatus, during which time they had come to know their soon-to-be overseers.

78. A good example relates to the case that was suddenly started against the second secretary of the Cheliabinsk obkom, G.S. Pavlov, whose father was accused of having aided the Nazis during the occupation. In this case Pavlov's immediate boss, the first secretary A.B. Aristov, along with Pavlov's overseers in Moscow, stepped in to protect Pavlov and staunch the damage. See Sushkov, Mikhalev, and Baranov (2013).

79. *TsK VKP(b)* (2004: 135).

80. *TsK VKP(b)* (2004: 389–92).

81. In comparative terms this is known as a particular form of institutional change, conversion, "the changed enactment of institutional rules due to their strategic redeployment." This has been contrasted with drift, "the changed impact of existing rules due to changes in the environment"; layering, "the introduction of new rules on top of existing ones"; and displacement, the "removal of existing rules and the introduction of new ones." On this, see Pierson (2004: 137–38), Streeck and Thelen (2005), and Mahoney and Thelen (2010a: 15–22, quotations at 15–16).

CHAPTER 3. INSIDE THE NOMENKLATURA

1. RGASPI f.17 op.131 d.224 l.192. Glushkov's recommendations were bold. He proposed that officials who were released on grounds of ill health or who had reached the age of fifty and who had served in the party bureaucracy for ten to fifteen years should have their pensions fixed at their current salary.

2. RGASPI f.17 op.131 d.224 ll.193–94.

3. This term, along with the notion of loyalists, is from Belova and Lazarev (2012: 3). The term is also used by Schull (1992: 732; 1993: 8–9) and Kotkin (1995: 228, 593 n.4).

4. Ironically, a significant number may have ended up in the camps. On this, see Adler (2012).

5. To take another example, in April 1948 the party's chief financier, Dmitrii Krupin, in a bid to improve the party's finances, urged local party leaders to take over local publishing businesses, most of which were running at a profit but which were then in the hands of regional government agencies. When asked what they should do in case of opposition, his response was as follows: "If the head of the local government does not like your bossing, let us talk to him at the obkom meeting, and probably he will find the obkom's decision acceptable. . . . Let's drop these niggly details: 'Soviet or not Soviet.' Everyone is Soviet and must understand the meaning of the party's leadership." Belova and Lazarev (2012: 51).

6. For more on Soviet ideology as a discourse or political language rather than as a belief system, see Schull (1992, 1993).

7. On this, see in particular Sheila Fitzpatrick's remarkable essay (1993).

8. For appeals of this kind in the justice system, for example, see Heinzen (2016: 169–71).

9. Cf. Fürst (2010: 3, 201–8).

10. E.g., Saller (1982: 80, 84, 112).

11. Svolik (2012: chap. 6).

12. Khlevniuk (2016: 50).

13. Khlevniuk (2016: 39, 48–49).

14. Average monthly salaries crept up to 550 rubles in 1947, 646 rubles in 1950, and 715 rubles in 1955. *Sovetskaia zhizn'* (2003: 501), Nove (1989: 302–4), Zaleski (1980: 668), Popov (1993: 146), *TsK VKP(b)* (2004: 144).

15. The division of obkoms into four pay categories was introduced in October 1938. See *Regional'naia* (2009: 135 n.1).

16. Fitzpatrick (1992a [1979]: 174–76).

17. In March 1939 only 28.6 percent of territorial first secretaries had a higher education. Khlevniuk (2016: 49).

18. In 1952 68.7 percent of all territorial party secretaries had a higher education, as did 62.8 percent of obkom departmental heads. RGANI. 5. op. 29. d. 15, ll. 65, 68.

19. T.H. Rigby (1968: 275–76), Edele (2006: 118–20).

20. T.H. Rigby (1968: 278), *Kommunisticheskaia partiia* (1986: t.8, 39–48).

21. Mawdsley and White (2000: 116–17). An earlier Higher Party School appears to have existed in 1930s. Easter (2000: 147).

22. Technically, the course was to attract thirty to forty participants a year who were to include leading functionaries from the state sector. In reality, however, the majority of functionaries were obkom first secretaries, and it was often referred to in shorthand as "retraining courses of first secretaries." See points 5, 6, and 8 of the October 25 resolution. *TsK VKP(b)* (2004: 135).

23. On this, see, for example, Kelly (2001: 237–40).

24. *TsK VKP(b)* (2004: 135–36).

25. For a general discussion of the Soviet economy in these terms, see Kornai (1980). For a historically nuanced version of this argument that suggests that one of the main consequences of the system of rationing that emerged in the early 1930s was that the socialist state replaced traditional class hierarchies with its own unique forms of stratification, see Osokina (2001: 69, 78, 81).

26. Osokina (2001: 49, 61–62, 67).

27. Osokina (2001: 164–65, 171–72, 174–77), Hessler (2004: 183–84, 242–43), Gromow (2003: 122–23).

28. *TsK VKP(b)* (2004: 144).

29. Provision of party officials was regulated by a resolution of SNK of 12 July 1943, "*O snabzhenii rukovodiaschchikh rabotnikov partiinykh, komsomolskikh, sovetskikh, khoziaistvennykh i profsoiuznykh organizatsii,*" see *TsK VKP(b)* (2004: 145).

30. For an excellent summary, see Ironside (2018: chap. 1, 1–2).

31. A report from May 1946 showed that only 9 percent of regional officials were entitled to industrial consumer goods vouchers and that, of the three tiers of obkom staff who were allocated food assignments, those in the second tier received assignments that were "insufficient," while assignments for those in the lowest tier were "grossly inadequate." See *TsK VKP(b)* (2004: 145, 147).

32. For a helpful discussion, see Ironside (2018: chap. 1, 6).

33. RGASPI f.17 op.122 d.193 ll.3–4.

34. *TsK VKP(b)* (2004: 146).

35. Tverdiukova (2015: 259–62).

36. Belova and Lazarev (2012: 48–49).

37. Some of the more prominent examples that came to light are from Orel in 1946 (RGASPI f.17 op.121 d.454 ll.71–72), Voronezh in 1946 (RGASPI f.17 op.116 d.286 l.98), Belorussia in 1946–47 (RGASPI f.17 op.122 d.308 ll.244–45), Dagestan in 1948 (RGASPI f.17 op.128 d.81 ll.13–23), Turkmenia in 1948 (RGASPI f.17 op.88 d.902 l.92), and Azerbaijan in 1944 (*TsK VKP(b)* 2004: 117).

38. RGASPI f.17 op.127 d.1353 ll.124–26.

39. RGASPI f.17 op.122 d.308 ll.244–45.

40. RGASPI f.17 op.121 d.463 ll.60–61.

41. Ironside (2018: chap. 1, 12–13). Under the currency reforms which were supposedly intended to wipe out the illicit gains that had been made by "speculative elements," cash holdings were converted at the punitive rate of 10:1, old money for new, while deposits in state savings banks and investments in state bonds were reduced at preferential rates.

42. *TsK VKP(b)* (2004: 153).

43. *TsK VKP(b)* (2004: 154, pt.2).

44. *TsK VKP(b)* (2004: 154, pt.3).

45. See Politburo resolutions of 24 and 29 December in *TsK VKP(b)* (2004: 162–63).

46. Ironside (chap. 1: 16).

47. On these practices after 1935, see Osokina (2000: 153, 164, 171, 174–75).

48. RGASPI f.17 op.127 d.1702 l.19. For a very similar opening in 1948 of a special shop for serving sixteen leaders in the city of Kuznetsk in Penza, see GAPO f.P-148 op.1 d.2128 l.61.

49. GARF f.R-5446 op.75 d.22 ll.47–48.

50. On this, see in particular Fitzpatrick (1992b: 218–19, 224–31), Kelly (2001: 295).

51. The most important of these scandals was that surrounding the construction of a lavish home for A.M. Azizbekov in Azerbaijan in 1944, which was one of the triggers of the Azerbaijan Affair reported in chapter 1. *TsK VKP(b)* (2004: 117). There were also major scandals in Altai and Orel, both in 1946. *TsK VKP(b)* (2004: 161–62); RGASPI f.17 op.121 d.454 ll.71–72.

52. Belova and Lazarev (2012: 73, 77–81, quotations at 73, 78).

53. E.g., Svolik (2012: chap. 6).

54. Belova and Lazarev (2012: 23–4, 41, 50).

55. *TsK VKP(b)* (2004: 144).

56. The precise figure of 735,283 expulsions from the party accounts for 12 percent of the average membership figure across the six years, which grew from 5,510,863 in 1946 to 6,462,975 in 1951. Cohn (2015: 38).

57. Cohn (2015: 40).

58. Dobson (2009: 73–77), Adler (2012).

59. Although we do not have precise figures for the number of reprimands across the Soviet Union in our period, the best estimates suggest that at any one time roughly one in ten party members had a reprimand of one sort or another. Cohn

(2015: 35–36) reports a 1952 KPK survey of thirty-two party organizations with 2.4 million members which found that 254,897 had a reprimand on their record; similarly, a 1950 KPK report from Moldavia found that 11 percent of the republic's communists had some kind of censure.

60. In the 1930s leading KPK officials spoke of supply agents accumulating a dozen or more reprimands on their party cards and seemingly thinking little of it. Belova (2001: 153–55), Belova and Lazarev (2012: 111, 116–17).

61. From 1946 to 1951, 67,713 expulsions, or 9.2 percent of all expulsions, were appealed to the KPK collegium in Moscow, of which 7,322 were successful, leading to pardons. Belova and Lazarev (2012: 178–79).

62. These are covered in Cohn (2015: 122–26). For a broader discussion of the effects of these and other repressive policies of the early postwar Stalin era on the Soviet penal system and, in particular, on the Gulag, see Alexopoulos (2005, 2017), Barenberg (2014), Barnes (2011), and Cadiot and Elie (2017).

63. Cohn (2015: 117); Heinzen (2016: 132). At the height of the campaign these charges accounted for up to a third, and in some regions a half, of all those expelled from the party. *TsK VKP(b)* (2004: 86); Cohn (2015: 118).

64. For a broader discussion of the ideological rationale behind the campaign, see Gorlizki (2016: 290, 296–97).

65. There were two theft decrees, one for theft of socialist property and the other for theft of personal property. Solomon (1996: 410–13), Gorlizki (2016: 301–3), *GULAG* (2000: 433), GARF f.9492 op.6 d.14 ll.14, 18.

66. RGASPI f.17 op.3 d.1004 ll.6, 51; *Arkhiv Presidentskii Rossiiskoi Federatsii* f.3 op.22 d.91 l.173; *Lubianka, 1937–8* (2004: 624–25). In a separate development, the new party rules agreed to in March 1939 set out guidelines on the expulsion of party members, which required confirmation by the corresponding party committee. See article 9 (1939) in Gill (1988: 152, 167–68).

67. From internal correspondence among procurators, Cadiot (2015: 253) suggests that the party secretaries cited the party's disciplinary procedures from the 1939 party statute more often than the rule of 1 December 1938. However, it was the latter rule that was invoked by statewide officials and that would eventually be overturned in December 1962, when Khrushchev sought to strip party members of what for many members had become their immunity from prosecution. *Regional'naia* (2009: 210), Cohn (2013: 1921).

68. Cohn (2013: 1923–26).

69. Cohn (2013: 1913, 1922), Cohn (2015: 131–32, 134, and 120–21, 123).

70. GARF f. R-8131 op.32 d.11 l.36.

71. GARF f. R-8131 op.32 d.11 l.34.

72. Under the law of 4 June seven years was the mandatory minimum sentence for theft of socialist property. First-time offenses had a maximum sentence of ten years; however, so-called qualified cases, such as large-scale thefts, could lead to sentences of ten to twenty-five years.

73. Although we cannot be sure of what happened to him afterward, he had not been found by the time the case file ended, eight months after the trial. RGASPI f.17 op.131 dl.44 ll.14–15, 18–20, 37.

74. RGASPI f.17 op.88 d.900 l.177; *Sovetskaia zhizn'* (2003: 578).

75. They included (as we saw in chapter 1) I.G. Popov, first secretary in Kaluga, the first secretary of the Udmurt obkom, A.P. Chekinov, and N.G. Kuprianov, the first secretary of the Finnish-Karelian republic, who was arrested in early 1950. RGASPI f.17 op.122 d.308 l.180; f.17 op.131 d.44 ll.204–5; *TsK VKP(b)* (2004: 389, 395, 435, 462).

76. RGASPI f.17 op.122 d.308 l.183.

77. *Sovetskaia zhizn'* (2003: 579).

78. Cohn (2013: 1921).

79. For example, deadlines for procuratorial investigations were broken and rules of confidentiality were breached, giving the accused additional time to flee the region, to prepare his defense, to influence witnesses, and to conceal evidence. Cadiot (2013: 263).

80. GARF f. R-8131 op.32 d.11 l.240.

81. Hooper (2006: 156), Cohn (2013: 1919), Cadiot (2013: 261–62).

82. GARF f. R-8131 op.32 d.11 l.233.

83. GARF f.R-8131 op.37 d.4668 l.126. Gorlizki (1997: 259–60), Cadiot (2013: 249).

84. For a recent account, see the excellent article by Juliette Cadiot (2013). For earlier explorations of this theme, see Solomon (1992) and Gorlizki (1997).

85. Belov and Lazarev (2012: 112).

86. Cadiot (2013: 255).

87. Cadiot suggests that there were official circulars of this kind in Kostroma, Voronezh, Molotov, Sverdlovsk, Astrakhan, Irkutsk, Ul'ianovsk, Krasnodar, Stavropol', Circassia, and the Republic of Moldova. (2013: 258, 254–55, 249).

88. Nikonorova (2015: 36).

89. From 1942 to 1952 KPK staff accounted for 8–9 percent of the Central Committee's staff, making it (depending on the period) either the second or third largest department in the Central Committee bureaucracy. Nikonorova (2015: 30).

90. Although Andrei Andreev was the nominal head, Shkiriatov had, in effect, taken over the leadership of the KPK in 1936. Nikonorova (2015: 31). The only leader of a justice agency to make it on to the Central Committee was Minister of Justice Konstantin Gorshenin, who became a candidate member in 1952.

91. Conquest (1961: 118).

92. For an example, see Cadiot (2013: 254–55).

93. Cadiot (2013: 255–56), Cohn (2013: 1920–21).

94. Hooper (2006).

95. In Ul'ianovsk Terent'ev was himself expelled from the party and arrested, while the third secretary was expelled. In all, forty people were arrested after an estimated sixty-five million rubles had been stolen. See *TsK VKP(b)* (2004: 198–201, 408, 458).

96. Cadiot (2013: 260–61, quotation at 260).

97. Cadiot (2013: 266). This also had what we might think of as a regional ideological aspect. In a letter appealing his sentence, one party member questioned whether judicial authorities who were ten thousand kilometers away were entitled to sentence him when the local kraikom knew him and could vouch for his conduct and behavior over his entire adult life. Cadiot (2013: 260–61).

98. See Thelen (2003: 228–30), Pierson (2004: 138), and Mahoney and Thelen (2010: 17–18). Other forms of institutional change include displacement, the replacement of existing rules with new ones, layering, the attachment of new rules to existing ones, and drift, when the impact of rules changes as a result of a shift in the external environment.

CHAPTER 4. MOSCOW, CENTER

1. While the purpose of Khrushchev's actions seems relatively clear (it triggered Bagirov's dismissal later that month as chair of the Azeri council of ministers; he was arrested the following March), the circumstances under which Efendiev composed the letter are not. Not only is the letter very detailed, but also it traces the fates of individuals whom, Efendiev claims, members of the Presidium, such as Molotov and Malenkov, "knew personally," thereby giving it an air of truthfulness. Khrushchev circulated the letter to all members of the Presidium and the secretaries of the Central Committee on 16 November. The Central Committee report of 12 December confirmed that "all [Efendiev's] claims do in fact reflect the true situation in the republic under Bagirov." RGASPI f.82, op.2, d.148 ll.1, 14.

2. RGASPI f.82, op.2, d.148 ll.14, 18–19. For more details, see Gorlizki (2013: 134–36).

3. Following a clash in the early 1930s between the territorial party leadership, supported by the Politburo member Ordzhonikidze, and the Transcaucasian secret police, headed by Beria and Bagirov, it was the latter that had triumphed, leading to a takeover of the party leadership by a "completely formed secret-police based network." Blauvelt (2011: 78–79).

4. Fairbanks (1978: 165) argued that another member of the emerging triumvirate, Georgii Malenkov, had clients among ten of the thirty-eight RSFSR obkom secretaries who were on the Central Committee, but evidence on the nature and strength of these ties or of Malenkov's ability to mobilize them is not presented.

5. Cohen, who also refers to a "cluster of reformist policies" under Khrushchev (1980: 15–17).

6. Examples from a variety of fields include Van Goudoever (1986), Hauslohner (1987), Filtzer (1992), Reid (2002), Bohn (2014), Kibita (2014), and Zezina (2014). For a helpful typology of the different uses of "de-Stalinization," see Merl (2014: 67).

7. Robert Tucker (1971: 182–83), for example, once famously presented Stalin's special sector as a "little gear box through which the massive machinery of Soviet rule over nearly 900 million human beings on about one-third of the earth's surface was operated."

8. Jones (2006: 3), Bittner (2014: 32).

9. The term "cult of personality" was used well before the Secret Speech and appears to have been first introduced at a statewide level—in direct reference to Stalin's violation of the rules of "collective leadership"—in Malenkov's address to the July 1953 plenum (*Lavrentii Beriia* [1999: 350–52]). The two axes of the critique of cult of personality appeared prominently at the very beginning of Khrushchev's Secret Speech—*Doklad* (2002: 57)—as well as in various other interventions, such as the

comment at a meeting of the Presidium of the Central Committee on the eve of the
Congress by the deputy chair of the council of ministers, Mikhail Pervukhin, that
Stalin "usurped power . . . and exterminated cadres" (*Reabilitatsiia* [2000: 350]).

10. For examples of dramatic responses to the Secret Speech at the local level, especially among obkom aktivs, see Jones (2006a: 42–48), Dobson (2009: 88–89).

11. The main exception was in March 1956 in Georgia (see chapter 6). Another,
more limited exception was the autumn of 1956, when, as Hornsby has shown, in
some regions the regime experienced a problem of authoritarian control. On this,
see Hornsby (2013: 58, 111–29; 2014: 98–106).

12. Cohn (2015: 38, 89; 2018: 24–27).

13. One of the first to notice this was Embree (1959: 111), who observed the
"fantastically high" turnover of regional officials from April 1953 to April 1954.
He added, "It would be necessary to go back to the Great Purges of the 1930s to
find a comparable period of such turbulence among top Soviet officials."

14. Two examples from the last phase of Stalin's life were the threat that hung
over the two veteran members of the ruling circle, Molotov and Mikoian, in the
wake of the XIX Party Congress in October 1952 and the campaign against the
"doctor-murderers" in the Kremlin, whose purge could easily have spread to members of Stalin's leadership. See Gorlizki and Khlevniuk (2004: chap. 6), Fitzpatrick
(2015: chap. 8).

15. Beria's emphasis on "socialist legality" was a theme both of his oration
at Stalin's funeral and of the Presidium resolution "approving the measures [of
10 April 1953] carried out by L.P. Beria." Moreover, within a week of Stalin's death
Beria had set up investigative groups to look into the Doctors' and Artillery Officers' Affairs, and by the middle of April he made proposals on the rehabilitation
of those wrongly accused in both. Further, on 4 April he issued an order prohibiting
the "Application of Any Measures of Coercion or Physical Force Against those in
Custody." Then, on 10 April he launched a retrospective investigation into "criminal activities committed over a number of years in the former Ministry of State
Security." *Lavrentii Beriia* (1999: 17, 21–23, 28–29, 41–42, 52–55). More recent
archival collections, while adding new details, have tended to confirm the general
thrust of these earlier revelations. See in particular *Politbiuro i delo Beriia* (2012);
and *Delo Beriia* (2012).

16. See, for example, *Lavrentii Beriia* (1999: 23).

17. A quintessential party apparatchik, Ignat'ev had worked at the Central Committee for various spells in 1935–37, 1946–47, and 1950–51 and as first secretary
of the Buriat-Mongol obkom in 1937–43, of the Bashkir obkom in 1943–46, and
as secretary and then second secretary in Belorussia in 1947–49.

18. *Lavrentii Beriia* (1999: 23, 66, 347–48, 398, 418). This point was originally
made by Barsukov (1991: 16).

19. These points were first made by Fairbanks (1978: 164–65, 169–74, quotation at 170). For more recent discussion, see Smith (2011: 80–81; 2013: 191–93),
and Loader (2016: 1766–68).

20. As noted earlier, the late Stalin-era ministries of state security (MGB, the secret police) and of internal affairs (MVD) had been merged into a single ministry—
the MVD under Beria—in March 1953.

21. In the wake of the Great Terror Beria had appointed his clients to leading positions across the union, including M.M. Gvishiani in the Far East, A.Z. Kobulov in Ukraine, I.F. Nikishov in Khabarovsk, A.N. Sadzhaya in Uzbekistan, L.F. Tsanava in Belorussia, and Goglidze in Leningrad (and later Khabarovsk). See Blauvelt (2011: 86).

22. Fairbanks (1978: 181), Mawdsley and White (2000: 102).

23. Gorlizki (1995: 20).

24. On the transfer of party functionaries to West Ukraine from other regions of the Soviet Union, including East Ukraine, after the war, see *Sovetskaia Natsional'naia* (2013: 489).

25. Mawdsley and White (2000: 101 n.26). Serdiuk's association with Khrushchev may even have gone further, as, before becoming second secretary of the Kiev obkom in 1939, he had worked in Moscow beginning in 1937, also under Khrushchev.

26. *Lavrentii Beriia* (1999: 118–20, 220–22, 369).

27. Strokach was restored to his original position as Ukrainian minister of internal affairs, while Serdiuk was made republican first secretary in Moldavia.

28. *Lavrentii Beriia* (1999: 118).

29. As Serdiuk reportedly said to Mel'nikov, "Were I to get a call from the Central Committee, then I could give you the information within two hours." *Lavrentii Beriia* (1999:118)

30. *Lavrentii Beriia* (1999: 135).

31. From 2,075 expulsions for "political misdeeds" in 1954 the numbers fell to 702 in 1955 and 510 in 1956. See Cohn (2015: 91–92).

32. *Arkhiv Presidentskii Rossiiskoi Federatsii* f.3, op.23, d.153, ll.34–36, 44–48. The changes to how information on cadres was collected would in fact take a long time to unfold. The process had its roots in Zhdanov's assurance at the XVIII Party Congress that the party would no longer take a biological approach to its cadres. Yet these categories were retained, arguably with the support of party principals, who could use them as a form of leverage. They were finally removed from the party's record-keeping procedures at the XXIII Party Congress in 1966 (see chapter 9).

33. Two years later he became the second secretary of the regional party committee

34. RGASPI f.556, op. 14, d.25, l.65.

35. Cited in Leonhard (1962: 29).

36. *Reabilitatsiia* (2000: t.1, 130; and 115–16, 117–29, 134).

37. Shepilov (2007: 153–54).

38. On the Abakumov trial of December 1954 and Malenkov's implied involvement in the Leningrad Affair, see Leonhard (1962: 91).

39. RGASPI f.556, op.14, d.25, ll.65–66.

40. This is discussed at greater length in Gorlizki (2013a: 143–44). For a more general discussion of the role of obkom first secretaries in the defeat of the Anti-Party group, see Tompson (1991: 175–77).

41. Robert Conquest once observed that despite Khrushchev's reputation as an architect of de-Stalinization some of his clients were individuals who, as Stalin's former henchmen, were now particularly vulnerable to attack. Conquest (1961: 190, 209, 225).

42. On this, see, in particular, *Molotov, Malenkov, Kaganovich* (1998), and *Reabilitatsiiia* (2003: t.2, 310–24).

43. Rigby (1959: 149–50, 158).

44. For variants of this argument, see Rigby (1959: 149–50; 1984: 67), Embree (1959: 110), Rush (1958: 24), Ballis (1961: 159), Fainsod (1963: 120–21), Tompson (1991: 70–72, 134–35), and Mitrokhin (2011: 28). From mid-March Khrushchev had been the only Central Committee secretary with a seat on the cabinet, a position of preeminence that was formalized in his election as first secretary at the Central Committee plenum in September. For more on the Stalin precedent, see Daniels (1966).

45. On the high turnover, see Embree (1959: 110), Rigby (1959: 156), Tompson (1991: 134). The most painstaking reconstruction of Khrushchev's clientelist ties with new appointees is Rigby (1984).

46. The notion that "Khrushchev received a more or less free hand within the party apparatus" is from Rigby (1959: 154).

47. Rigby (1959: 156) showed that from September 1953 until the XX Party Congress in February 1956 over half (forty-five of eighty-four) of the first secretaries of territorial party committees directly under the jurisdiction of the Central Committee were replaced. However, this much-cited figure refers to those committees directly under the jurisdiction of the Central Committee (i.e., those whose leaders were directly appointed by the Central Committee, that is, leaders of the regions of the RSFSR and of the central committees of the union republics). But this is different from regional leaders who were themselves on the Central Committee and, in particular, from those who were *voting* members of the Central Committee. The latter point is especially relevant, as only voting members were invited to the plenum that eventually settled the Anti-Party Affair. Just over half of RSFSR first secretaries were voting members of the Central Committee elected in 1952. For comparative figures, see Rigby (1959: 151) and Mawdsley and White (2000: 99).

48. These clients were G.V. Eniutin (Kamensk), A.P. Kirilenko (Sverdlovsk), V.S. Markov (Orel), D.S. Polianskii (Orenburg), S.O. Postovalov (Kaluga), M.M. Stakhurskii (Khabarovsk), and A.I. Struev (Perm). Khrushchev's limited success in appointing clients was noted by Conquest (1961: 264, 284–85), who added laconically, "Khrushchev had to rely, therefore, on manoeuvre."

49. This attempted concentration of power in the hands of centrally mandated regional officials is why alternative terms such as "territorial forms of administration" (Swearer 1962: 24), "territorialisation of administration" (Tompson 2000: 143), and the "deconcentration of public administration" (Breslauer 1982: 4 n.5, 44 n.15) are preferred by many commentators to "decentralization."

50. The first reform also saw the introduction of a secondary nomenklatura, the *uchetno-kontrol'naia nomenklatura,* whose positions were confirmed not by the Presidium or by the Secretariat but by the departments of the Central Committee. This accounted for 11,400 of the 25,300 positions, leaving a primary nomenklatura of only 13,900 posts. These decisions reduced the load on the Politburo and the Secretariat but were also more realistic in that many positions on the previous nomenklatura had been confirmed post hoc, and some had never been confirmed at all. *Arkhiv Presidentskii Rossiiskoi Federatsii* f.3 op.22 d.151 ll.13–115. Under

the second reform, that of 1956, the new nomenklatura was to be divided into a primary list of 9,400 positions and a secondary one of 3,200. Of the positions on the primary nomenklatura, 1,152 went to the Presidium, 5,671 to the Secretariat, and 2,580 to the RSFSR buro. See RGANI f.5 op.31 d.41 l.17.

51. Bahry (1987: 44, 47).

52. Bahry (1987: 26), Rigby (1984: 57–58). Whereas all-union ministries had administrative headquarters only in Moscow, union-republic ministries had joint all-union and republican administrations.

53. See *Kommunisticheskaia partiia* (1985: t.8 303–45), Kassof (1964: 566), Miller (1984: 120), Smith (1987: 100).

54. Rigby (1984: 58).

55. *Prezidium* (2006: 525–27).

56. Tompson (1991: 178–79), Vasiliev (2011: 120), Kibita (2013: 46–48), *Regional'naia* (2009: 169–78), Mertsalov (2015: 146).

57. Swearer (1962: 24, 34), Ballis (1961, 162), Tompson (1991: 184–85, 229), Markevich and Zhuravskaya (2011: 1552).

58. On Khrushchev's campaign against bureaucracy, see Gorlizki (1996: 1291–94), *Regional'naia* (2009: 92–122). On the territorialization of administration in the party apparatus, see Titov (2011: 44–46).

59. There were sixty-eight sovnarkhozy and seventy regions in the Russian Federation. Only in the Leningrad, Pskov, and Novgorod regions was a single sovnarkhoz shared among three oblasts. Markevich and Zhuravskaya (2011: 1552).

60. On this, see Ballis (1961: 162), Markevich and Zhuravskaya (2011).

61. For the best summary of this issue in the Soviet economy, see Gregory (1990: 15–24).

62. Gorlizki and Khlevniuk (2004: 82–88), Belova and Lazarev (2012: chap. 6).

63. Kibita (2011: 100–103), Tompson (1991: 180). These problems were especially acute in the RSFSR, where, as a result of successful lobbying by obkom leaders during the debates over the sovnarkhoz reforms in the spring of 1957, seventy regional councils were established, just short of the number of territorial units in the republic. By contrast, in Ukraine most of the eleven councils had large, multi-oblast jurisdictions. Of the other republics, there were a further nine in Kazakhstan, four in Uzbekistan, and one each in the other republics. Tompson (1991: 157–67).

64. Although this formulation had been used in the late Stalin period, it was adopted rarely and usually took a qualified or amended form. Thus G.M. Popov had been removed from Moscow on 12 December 1949 "for mistakes and shortcomings in his leadership"; V.A. Sharapov had been removed from the Kurgan obkom on 16 July 1947 "for his failure of leadership and compromised behavior at home"; G.M. Kapranov had been released from Ivanovo on 28 January 1947 "for failure of leadership over the economy and party political work"; and A.L. Orlov had been dismissed from Stavropol' on 20 November 1946 for "his inability to carry out the party line and to secure the interests of the state in grain procurements." The only case that approximated the post-Stalin formulations was the dismissal of Gryza for his "failure of leadership of the party organization" in Kiev on 22 December 1952.

65. On this, see Gorlizki (1995: 3–4, 10–11).

66. *Pravda*, September 15 1953; *Kommunisticheskaia partiia* (1985: t.8, 343).

67. *Regional'naia* (2009: 61–62, 100–101); RGASPI f.82 op.2 d.149 ll.6, 129–30, 172; d.152 l.202.

68. *Regional'naia* (2009: 566–67, 576, 582, 585, 588). Khrushchev clearly coordinated this campaign, insisting that reports on the errant regional leaderships be passed on to all the members of the Presidium. RGASPI f.82 op.2. d.149 ll.1, 6, 130, 170, 202. Viktor Churaev, an old associate from Ukraine, was also the cadres official in charge of staging these party conferences.

69. *Regional'naia* (2009: 52–53, 59–60).

70. RGASPI f.82 op.2 d.149, Astrakhan (ll.3–4), Briansk (l.8), Kalinin (l.129), Crimea (l.170), Iaroslavl' (d.153 l.202).

71. These were either Central Committee inspectors (e.g., Pezavich) or senior officials from the cadres department, such as Afanas'ev, Storozhev, Alonov, and Churaev; RGASPI f.82 op.2 d.149 ll.4, 9, 134, 147, 172, and d.153 l.204.

72. *Regional'naia* (2009: 65, 69); RGASPI f.82 op.2 d.149 ll.1, 4, 5, 7, 169.

73. In all, there were thirty-one second secretary replacements within a ten-week phase from 18 March to 3 June 1954. These occurred in Moscow, Leningrad, Rostov, Gor'kii, Krasnodar, Cheliabinsk, Krasnoiarsk, Novosibirsk, and Kalinin in the RSFSR and in Dnepropetrovsk and Odessa in Ukraine. On criticisms of agricultural secretaries, see *Kommunisticheskaia partiia* (1986: t.8 359–91).

74. Gorlizki (1995).

CHAPTER 5. THE NEW ART OF SURVIVAL

1. Cohn (2015: 38, 89, 93; 2018: 24–5).

2. Prior to the Secret Speech the number of expulsions from the party for "violations of socialist legality" was small and mostly related to very senior figures from the Military Collegium of the Supreme Court. *Reabilitatsiia* (2000: 239–46). After 1956 the numbers grew, but expellees were confined to regional functionaries of the security police. At the XXII Congress in 1961 it was reported that 347 party members had been expelled for violations of socialist legality, nearly all of whom were former employees of the NKVD or MGB. *Reabilitatsiia* (2003: 360–61; also see 261–65), Dobson (2009: 93).

3. RGASPI f.17 op.56 d.2082 l.13.

4. RGASPI f.17 op.56 d.1739 l.433.

5. RGASPI f.556 op.14 d.79 l.75.

6. Zhegalin would remain as first secretary in Stalingrad for another four years, Kannunikov for another five, and Organov for another two before his appointment as deputy chair of the RSFSR council of ministers.

7. This was the first position noted in the one-paragraph summary of his career sent to Stalin in March 1952, confirming his appointment.

8. One of Pcheliakov's first moves had been to reassure the aktiv: "Some of you may think that the change in leadership at the obkom and oblispolkom will herald the removal of other regional cadres. But you are wrong. Our cadres are good, and there is no need for a change of guard. All comrades should be at their ease and work in a calm and directed way." As one observer noted, "This statement by

comrade Pcheliakov became widely known across the whole aktiv." RGASPI f.558 op.11 d.903 l.27.

9. RGASPI f.558 op.11 d.903 ll.27–33.

10. RGASPI f.558 op.11 d.903 l.33.

11. RGANI f.5 op.32 d.5 ll.76, 78.

12. RGANI f.5 op.32 d.5 l.76 ob.

13. RGANI f.5 op.32 d.5 ll.76 ob, 77.

14. RGANI f.5 op.32 d.5 ll.75, 78ob.

15. RGANI f.5 op.32 d.5 ll.76b, 78.

16. RGANI f.5 op.32 d.5 l.77.

17. RGASPI f.556 op.14 d.57 ll.178–79. Thus in the view of the Central Committee official Putintsev, the party secretary of the Soviet district, was "issued a reprimand by the obkom not for his failure to fulfill the grain procurement plan, but for honorably pressing questions about the poor grain harvest in his district." RGASPI f.556 op.14 d.57 ll.179–80.

18. RGASPI f.82 op.2 d.149 ll.144–47.

19. RGASPI f.17 op.56 d.1675 ll.252–53. Until 1959 there were forty-two districts in the region, but as part of the administrative reorganization of 1960 the number was reduced to twenty-eight.

20. RGASPI f.17 op.56 d.1676 l.34.

21. RGASPI f.17 op.89 d.1751 l.113.

22. RGASPI f.17 op.57 d.1743 l.46.

23. RGASPI f.17 op.58 d.1797 l.44.

24. RGASPI f.17 op.3 d.1096 l.56.

25. RGASPI f.556 op.14 d.24 ll.22–24.

26. RGASPI f.17 op.56 d.1675 ll.237–39.

27. RGASPI f.17 op.56 d.1675 ll.247, 252–53.

28. RGASPI f.556 op.14 d.57 ll.43–44.

29. RGASPI f.17 op.56 d.1675 ll.53–57. Despite all this, Pcheliakov continued to ensure high turnover at the obkom buro. At the beginning of 1957 he engineered the transfer out of the region of his most implacable foe, Sanin. RGASPI f.17 op.57 d.1743 l.46. In June 1957 the obkom secretary, Moshchakov, was replaced. RGASPI f.17 op.57 d.1747 l.2. Through a combination of these tactics, Pcheliakov was eventually able to effect the dismissal of Safronov as chair of the regional executive committee. I.P. Safronov was moved out of the obkom buro on 28 April 1958. RGASPI f.17 op.58 d.1797 l.52; d.1798 ll.2–3.

30. From 1953 to 1957 Kirov's milk yields went up by 139 percent and its meat production by 70 percent. *Stroitel'stvo* (1963: t.3, 370, 375).

31. Ibid., l.39 (RGASPI f.556 op.14 d.57.) On 7 March 1956 Churaev informed Shepilov that Pcheliakov had been called in for a chat at the department of party organs and that his shortcomings had been pointed out. "With that I think we can bring the matter to a close." Ibid., l.52.

32. Ignatov was a veteran substate dictator who had served as regional first secretary in Kuybishev (1938–40) and Orel (1943–48) before taking over in Krasnodar in 1949.

33. RGASPI f.17 op.57 d.1797 l.70.

34. RGASPI f.17 op.57 d.1797 ll.71–72.

35. The urban–rural divide in Sverdlovsk was 77:23 in 1961, by comparison with 40:60 in Krasnodar. See appendix C.

36. *TsK VKP(b)* (2004: 399).

37. Later Andrianov famously went on to become city first secretary in Leningrad, where he played a key role in overseeing the Leningrad Affair.

38. RGASPI f.556 op.14 d.58 l.36.

39. Kutyrev had to miss the first owing to illness. One factor which may have played a part in weakening Kutyrev's position was his poor state of health. This, however, could be interpreted in one of two ways. It may be that his illness weakened his position; alternatively, it may be that he fell ill precisely because he was harassed and unable to cope with the pressures on him.

40. RGASPI f.556 op.14 d.58 ll.28–29, 32–33, 35.

41. Sushkov (2003: 12–13).

42. The documentation suggests that this decision had been taken earlier but that the Central Committee had bided its time while it waited on Kutyrev's successor. Sevast'ianov likely had a prepared report at the ready since early summer, in anticipation of a prompt from the Presidium, as his report was based entirely on documents from the April and June meetings and contained no new materials. RGASPI f.556 op.14 d.58 ll.19–24.

43. Sushkov and Raznikov (2003: 46–47).

44. Konovalov (2004: 164–65).

45. Konovalov (2004: 181, 194).

46. RGASPI f.556 op.14 d.142 ll.17–18.

47. *TsK VKP (b)* (2004: 283–318).

48. RGASPI f.556 op.14 d.83 l.101.

49. RGASPI f.556 op.14 d.83 l.102; f.17 op.57 d.2564 l.27; op.58 d.2649 ll.85–88. Only forty-four years old in January 1958, Skulkov was given a second chance. After a year in a largely honorary position at the Committee of Soviet Control he went on to become first secretary in Udmurtiia from 1959 to 1964 before proceeding to head the party organization in Kostroma from 1965 to 1971.

50. The *Pravda* correspondent in 1943 observed the following: "In [Moskvin's] Stalino gorkom they meet for hours, but there is no collective leadership or collective discussion of pressing issues. Comrade Moskvin follows the example set by comrade Kulagin in carrying out cross examinations [*doprosy*] of those present." RGASPI f.17 op.88 d.644 l.23.

51. RGASPI f.556 op.14 d.110 ll.72–77.

52. RGASPI f.556 op.14 d.110 ll.86–91.

53. This section draws on the excellent paper by Roman Podkur (2008).

54. Podkur (2008: 6–7, 10, 13).

55. Podkur (2008: 11–12, 14).

56. Podkur (2008: 5–6).

57. Note that Perm was known from 1940 to 1957 as Molotov but reverted to its original name in the wake of the Anti-Party Affair. For ease of reference we refer to it throughout as Perm.

58. His tenure as first secretary in Stalinsk in Ukraine had coincided with the latter phase of Khrushchev's leadership of the republic, and Struev himself liked to refer to the special relationship he enjoyed with the new party leader. RGASPI

f.17 op.54 d.2686 ll.180–81. On Struev as a Khrushchev acolyte, see Rigby (1984: 80).

59. Although no direct statistics are available comparing industry with agriculture, we can use as a rough proxy the urban–rural divide, which was 61:39 in Perm in 1961 by comparison with 41:59 in Kirov. See appendix C. In addition, Perm had three obkom branch departments for industry, including defense, timber and paper, and transportation. RGASPI f.17 op.56 d.2041 l.35; op.58 d.2247 l.33.

60. RGASPI f.17 op.56 d.2041 l.4.

61. RGASPI f.17 op.57 d.2161 ll.27–28, 195–98, 202, 204.

62. RGASPI f.17 op.56 d.2040 ll.104, 139.

63. RGASPI f.17 op.56 op.2041 l.7.

64. RGASPI f.17 op.56 d.2040 l.105.

65. RGASPI f.17 op.56 d.2040 l.138.

66. RGASPI f.17 op.56 d.2040 ll.137–39.

67. RGASPI f.17 op.56 d.2040 l.335. For Struev's support of Malkov, see ibid., ll.105, 137–38, 291.

68. Another case of overpromotion concerns the veteran substate dictator in Krasnoiarsk, N.N. Organov. Organov put his weight behind the recently promoted agriculture secretary T.V. Tiurikov, who, having fallen foul of the aktiv, registered 69 votes against (out of 644) at the kraikom elections of January 1956. Brushing aside this opposition, Organov stood by his man and insisted that Tiurikov be reelected as secretary. RGASPI f.17 op.56 d.1739 ll.408, 430–34.

69. RGASPI f.17 op. 57 d.2161 ll.30–32. A year later he reported that the obkom had sent out 450 "30,000ers" (urban communists assigned to work in the countryside, the latter-day equivalent of the "25,000ers" of the early 1930), yet 24.6 percent of these had been removed for incompetence. RGASPI f.17 op.58 d.2246 l.240; d.2249 l.99.

70. RGASPI f.17 op.56 d.2040 l.294.

71. RGASPI f.17 op.58 d.2246 l.258.

72. Exactly half of the main officeholders on the obkom (i.e., those who did not occupy purely symbolic roles) when Struev arrived in January 1954 were still in place four years later, in January 1958. RGASPI f.17 op.54 d.2685 ll.253–57; op.58 d.2246 ll.270–73.

73. Thus in place of the obkom second secretary M.A. Ponomarev, who was transferred to the Central Committee apparat, Struev promoted a person who had occupied the same position under Prass, K.I. Galanshin, while another member of the original leadership group, I.Ia. Kirienko, was also made an obkom secretary.

74. RGASPI f.17 op.57 d.2161 l.312. When a vacancy to lead the department of party, trade union, and komsomol agencies arose, the position was given to the next candidate "in line," the secretary of the Krasnokamskii city party committee, A.V. Pervov. Moreover, Struev made much play of the fact that the new head of the department of agriculture was a local person who had studied and worked in the region since 1938. RGAPSI f.17 op.57 d.2161 l.244.

75. RGASPI f.17 op.56 d.2040 l.104.

76. RGASPI f.17 op.56 d.2040 l.293.

77. RGASPI f.17 op.56 d.2040 ll.334–37; op.17 f.58 d.2246 ll.307–11.

78. The figure of 18 percent per year was low for a leader sent in to "knock heads together." Figures are calculated from RGASPI f.17 op.54 d.2232 ll.154–57; and op.56 d.1703 ll.204–5.

79. Thus, for example, though the former second secretary suffered a demotion, he was allowed to retain his seat on the regional executive, the obkom buro; and although the former head of the regional executive committee lost his seat on the buro, he was given the lucrative post of chair of the regional council of consumer associations and retained his seat on the obkom.

80. Thus Sumtsov awarded the post of head of the obkom department of propaganda and agitation to the chair of the regional komsomol organization, while the former head of the administrative department was moved to the honorary position of chair of the regional council of trade unions, and the previous head of the department of propaganda and agitation took over as editor of the regional paper. RGASPI f.17 op.54 d.2232 ll.154–57; d.2233 l.2, 102–5; op.56 d.1703 ll.103, 204–5.

81. RGASPI f.17 op.56 d.1703 ll.136–38, 172; d.1704 ll.27, 33–34.

82. RGASPI f.17 op.56 d.1703 ll.219–20.

CHAPTER 6. SUBSTATE NATIONALISM

1. From a vast literature, see in particular Gellner (2006), Anderson (1991), and Smith (1986). For a valuable summary, from which we have drawn here, see Suny (1993: 12–14).

2. The most consistent in this approach is John Breuilly (1983).

3. See in particular the works of Hroch (1985) and Billig (1995).

4. Political demands of this kind include Abkhaz calls to be transferred out of the Georgian republic and into the RSFSR, Georgian demands to have ethnic Georgians reinstated to the Politburo, or to have a change in the republican leadership. See Kemoklidze (2016: 132), Avalishvili (2016: 40, 43).

5. The four resolutions, of 26 May and 12 June, were on western Ukraine, Lithuania, Belorussia, and Latvia and were drawn up in response to Beria's notes of 8 and 16 May. Although ostensibly relating to the republic as a whole, the resolution on Belorussia dwelt specifically with how to address problems in western Belorussia, which is to say, in those areas gained from Poland as a result of the Molotov-Ribbentrop accords. *Lavrentii Beriia* (1999: 62, 400 n.28)

6. Although copies of Beria's notes—of 8 and 16 May—have not been recovered, there are references to them in the Presidium resolutions. See, for example, *Lavrentii Beriia* (1999: 49, 52, 400 n.28).

7. *Lavrentii Beriia* (1999: 47, 51).

8. Brandenberger (2001: 281, 283–85; 2002: 187–89), *Sovetskaia natsional'naia* (2013: 213, 216, 234–36, 309). One measure of this aspect of late Stalin-era policy was that at the XIX Party Congress in October 1952 twenty-three speakers condemned "bourgeois nationalism," but none attacked the twin evil of "Great Russian Chauvinism." See Simon (1991: 230).

9. *Lavrentii Beriia* (1999: 46–47, 50).

10. *Lavrentii Beriia* (1999: 46, 48, 50–51, 62). Similarly, in the oblasts of West Belorussia the low proportion of "local Belorussians, that is, of natives of these

oblasts" (*ugrozhentsy etikh oblastei*) in senior positions was presented in the Presidium resolution as a "gross violation of Soviet nationalities policy." *Lavrentii Beriia* (1999: 62).

11. *Lavrentii Beriia* (1999: 51–52).

12. Structural impediments to cadre indigenization did not always take this form. In Central Asia the glaring underrepresentation of natives in elite positions in Kirgizia, Tajikistan, Uzbekistan, and Turkmenistan was more closely tied to the low literacy and educational level of party members from the titular national groups. *Sovetskaia natsional'naia* (2013: 499, 535, 539, 546, 548, 554).

13. *Lavrentii Beriia* (1999: 47).

14. Blitstein (2001: 256–57, 265–66), Martin (2001b: 80–81).

15. *Lavrentii Beriia* (1999: 52).

16. The leaders included Khrushchev himself and the Ukrainian first secretary, Kirichenko, in the commission on western Ukraine and Mikoian and the Lithuanian first secretary, Sniečkus, on the Lithuanian commission. Zubkova (2008: 320–23, 336), Loader (2015, 2016).

17. Grybkauskas (2014: 284–85).

18. The systematic appointment of nonnative second secretaries was first observed by Bilinsky (1967) and Miller (1977). The idea that such appointments were part of a more complex institution, one consisting of a number of different elements, has been advanced by Grybkauskas (2014). The four key features of the institution were, first, that the second secretary should be a Slav, normally a Russian but sometimes a Ukrainian or Belorussian; second, that in addition to being a Slav he should have been raised outside of the republic (in the 1940s some Slavic second secretaries had been native Slavs who, it was feared, might identify too closely with local interests); third, that the first secretary should be a member of the titular nationality (the expectation that first secretaries should come from the titular republic became a general pattern only after the Second World War); and, fourth, that the Slavic second be recruited from the party organs department of the Central Committee. Grybkauskas (2014: 270, 282–83). Although it began in Azerbaijan in 1955, in some republics the institution of the second would arrive much later, for example, in 1971 in Estonia, 1975 in Tajikistan, and 1979 in Armenia. (Ibid., 274).

19. Of the eighty-three second secretaries appointed from 1955 to 1991, fifty-eight conformed to Grybkauskas's broader institutional definition, and thirty-eight were specifically from the department of party organs. Grybkauskas (2014: 272–73).

20. Grybkauskas (2014: 275, 285–88).

21. Avalishvili (2016: 33), Blauvelt and Smith (2016: 153).

22. Avalishvili (2016: 41–46, 48), Blauvelt and Smith (2016: 153, 160–61, 164–67).

23. Blauvelt and Smith (2016: 164, 166–67).

24. Blauvelt and Smith (2016: 182–83).

25. As a senior political commissar in Kharkov and then Kiev, Mzhavanadze had entered Khrushchev's political orbit during the latter's stint as first secretary of the Ukraine and would come to be known as Khrushchev's appointee.

26. Khlevniuk (2016: 13–15); Blauvelt (2009).

27. Khlevniuk (2016: 15, 23–27), Kaiser (2016: 106).

28. Avalishvili (2016: 36); Blauvelt and Smith (2016: 163–64, 191).

29. Kaiser (2016: 92, 110 n.3); Blauvelt and Smith (2016: 153).

30. Kaiser (2016: 109).

31. Avalishvili (2016: 40–41); Blauvelt and Smith (2016: 154–56).

32. Blauvelt and Smith (2016a: 5).

33. Cited in Avalishvili (2016: 35).

34. Kaiser (2016: 109–10). This view is quite different from how an earlier generation of scholars, largely informed by Georgian émigrés, viewed the March 1956 events. On this, see Blauvelt and Smith (2016a: 4).

35. This mismatch is true, for example, of the speech by Ruben Kipiani that called for Khrushchev, Mikoian, and Bulganin to be put on trial and for elections for a new union government. Avalishvili (2016: 42–43).

36. Kldiashvili (2016: 81).

37. Kaiser (2016: 96–97).

38. Avalishvili (2016: 46–47), Blauvelt and Smith (2016: 159, 172), Kldiashvili (2016: 82, 84).

39. Kozlov (2002: chap 5), Avalishvili (2016: 46).

40. Jeremy Smith makes the point that the punishments were much less severe than those in Novocherkassk in 1962. Smith (2016: 147). Also see Avalishvili (2016: 48).

41. Avalishvili (2016: 37, 42, 44).

42. Kemoklidze (2016: 132).

43. Loader (2016: 233–36, 315), Hasanli (2015: 376–77).

44. *Regional'naia* (2009: 232). This report, later referred to as a memorandum (*zapiska*), appears to have been read only by Khrushchev himself on the last day of his visit to Riga, 12 June. See *Prezidium* (2003: t.1 371, 378).

45. *Regional'naia* (2009: 224–25, 230–31).

46. *Regional'naia* (2009: 227–29).

47. Loader (2016: 260, 263–64), *Regional'naia* (2016: 231).

48. Hasanli (2015: 388), *Prezidium* (2003: t.1 1058).

49. *Prezidium* (2003: t.1, 355–87). There was a certain asymmetry in the treatment of the two republics. Unlike Latvia, and much to its frustration, the Azerbaijani leadership was informed of the results of the Central Committee commission only at this meeting. After the Presidium meeting Mukhitdinov flew out to Baku to circulate the decisions of the Central Committee at the republican party plenum on 6 July. *Prezidium* (2003: t.1, 382, 387, 1062 n.65).

50. Loader (2016: 254–56); *Prezidium* (2003: t.1, 355); Hasanli (2015: 388).

51. *Prezidium* (2003: t.1, 382; and 377, 380).

52. Thus, for example, at the Presidium session of 2 July the organizers of the forthcoming plenum in Azerbaijan were instructed "not to take the nationalist question (that is, not to accentuate it)." See *Prezidium* (2003: t.1 387); and Loader (2016: 280).

53. *Prezidium* (2003: t.1, 378).

54. *Prezidium* (2003: t.1, 380).

55. *Prezidium* (2003: t.1, 386; and 357, 380). The demonstration effect of the high-profile sackings and the widely publicized republican party plenums which

followed were reinforced by various ideological interventions. In September the party's theoretical journal *Kommunist* printed a scathing made-to-order article titled "On the history of local party organizations." See *Prezidium* (2003: t.1, 1059 n.25); Hasanli (2015: 413–14). Behind the scenes in the summer of 1959 responsibility for combating nationalism was handed over to specialized units in the republican KGBs. Hasanli (2015: 367, 369).

56. Loader (2016: 224–26, 231–32, 238, 312); *Regional'naia* (2009: 225, 227–29); *Prezidium* (2003: t.1, 366–68); Hasanli (2015: 113, 121).

57. Loader (2016: 189, 191–93, 196–99); *Regional'naia* (2009: 226).

58. *Prezidium* (2009: 363–64), Hasanli (2015: 303, 391). The tendency toward localism of economic production was a theme of Khrushchev's address at the June 1959 Central Committee plenum, which immediately preceded the July Presidium meeting. In this speech Khrushchev lambasted the Kazakh and Ukrainian republics for meeting their own meat production quotas while falling significantly short of their quotas for the all-union fund. Simon (1991: 256).

59. Hasanli (2015: 93).

60. Hasanli (2015: 96).

61. In doing so it brought Azeri practice into line with that of the neighboring Caucasian states, Georgia and Armenia, where the indigenous languages had been recognized as "state languages" in the republican 1936 constitutions.

62. Hasanli (2015: 112–13, 135).

63. Loader (2016: 123–27, 311–12).

64. Loader (2016: 170–72, 175, 177, 180, 182), Smith (2013: 209–11), *Regional'naia* (2009: 223).

65. Of the three factors, it was clearly the standoff over Article 19 that was the tipping point. Ever since 1956 Moscow had received a steady flow of complaints about Mustafaev and Berklavs but chose to do little about them other than to warn them to "put their house in order." It was only in March 1959, at the height of the impasse over Khrushchev's Article 19, that Semichastnyi cashed in on these complaints. Loader (2016: 224, 231–34, 312, 315). Also see *Prezidium* (2003: t.1, 364).

66. Recently Altstadt (2016: chap 1) has argued, on the basis of a close reading of native language sources, that there was an "Azerbaijani enlightenment" toward the end of the nineteenth century. It remains unclear, however, how widely shared this emergent Azerbaijani culture was. Certainly the scholars Nikolai Marr and Vasilii Bartol'd, both of whom were proficient in the Turkic vernacular of the east Caucasus as well as in other languages of the region and who were deeply familiar with the local cultures, were of the view that national consciousness in Azerbaijan was far behind that of the Georgians and Armenians. On this, see Tolz (2011: 151–54) and the work of Baberowski (2010), who suggests that for much of the 1920s most inhabitants of Azerbaijan continued to identify predominantly as "Turks," "Moslems," or simply as "peasants."

67. Altstadt (2016: 9, 13, 83). Azerbaijani is a Turkic language with close connections to the Turkic languages of Central Asia, to the languages of the Crimean and Volga Tatars, and to Turkish. In order to distance it from these other languages, a number of orthographic reforms with specific adaptation to Azeri phonemes were instituted, including a transfer from Arabic to Latin script in the early 1920s and

372   Notes to Pages 186–192

its replacement with Cyrillic in the late 1930s. On the orthographic reforms, see Hasanli (2015: 165, 313, 314).

68. For a useful comparison of Azerbaijan and Latvia at the time of the Revolution, see Suny (1993: 38–43, 55–58).

69. On the concept of ethnie, see Smith (1986).

70. Loader (2016: 7, 135, 191, 321).

71. Prigge (2015: 93).

72. Hasanli (2015: 79–81, 318, 337–38, 375–76).

73. Hasanli (2015: 88–89, 107–8).

74. Hasanli (2015: 97–106), Loader (2016: 110, 313–14).

75. Cited in Loader (2016: 113).

76. Cited in Loader (2016: 110).

77. *Prezidium* (2003: 378).

78. Hasanli (2015: 292, 385).

79. Hasanli (2015: 380).

80. Loader (2016: 60).

81. Loader (2016: 47, 105).

82. Loader (2016: 93–94).

83. Loader (2016: 146, 334).

84. Loader (2016: 220, 323).

85. Cited in Loader (2016: 220).

86. Cited in Loader (2016: 219).

87. Quoted in *Prezidium* (2003: t.1 364).

88. This point is emphasized in Hasanli (2015: 1, 3–5).

89. Hasanli (2015: 19).

90. Hasanli (2015: 112–13, 135). Born in south Azerbaijan, Ibrahimov had been appointed in 1945 as the head of a group of political workers to coordinate a separatist movement in south Azerbaijan (i.e., in Iran). After the failed bid to establish a united Azerbaijani state in 1946 Ibrahimov wrote his celebrated novel *The Day Will Come,* which won the Stalin prize in 1950 (ibid., 5–6).

91. For a discussion of the reasons for this kompromat, see chapter 1. In Mustafaev's case a claim dating back to 1937 was that he had been a member of a "counterrevolutionary organization of teachers in Nukha or Agdash in 1928"; in the case of Rahimov there was information on his aunt and her husband's visit to Iran in 1938 as well as his father's pilgrimage to Mecca. Hasanli (2015: 4–5).

92. Hasanli (2015: 34–35, 186). Mustafaev eventually managed to get his way after telling Khrushchev, in person, that he was unable to work with Guskov (ibid., 145)

93. Hasanli (2015: 35).

94. Hasanli (2015: 35–36). Mustafaev, it turned out, may well have had grounds to be suspicious of Rahimov. In a bid to turn the first secretary of the Baku city committee, Tofik Allahverdiev, against Mustafaev, Rakhimov repeatedly told Allahverdiev that Mustafaev had kompromat on him that would be used to prevent Allahverdiev's reelection. Rahimov also became convinced that his own deputy, Ilyas Abdullayev, was operating as a stooge for Mustafaev and did his best to pit officials from the council of ministers, under him, against those from the central committee. Hasanli (2015: 145, 147, 184, 188–89).

95. Hasanli (2015: 183; and 187, 304).

96. Hasanli (2015: 108).

97. Loader (2016: 115–17).

98. Loader (2016: 301), Hasanli (2015: 428). The process of reevaluation had in fact begun a year earlier, in August 1958, when the former first secretary of the Tajikistan central committee, Bobojan Gafurov, had published an influential article in the party's flagship theoretical journal, *Kommunist,* which had condemned local currents of "chauvinism" in certain union republics. Gafurov had also written of a future "merging" of nations, a topic that was returned to at the XXI Party Congress in February 1959. In December 1958 the first secretary of Turkmenistan, Sukhan Babaev, who only a year earlier had proudly reported a marked increase in the share of ethnic Turkmens in the republican party apparatus, was sacked and, along with other colleagues, expelled from the party, for "mechanical" favoritism toward national cadres. Gafurov's article and the new theme of the coming together of nations have often been attributed to Khrushchev's growing displeasure at the slow progress of his 1957 sovnarkhoz reforms, which had decreed a devolution of economic power to regional councils. Khrushchev was aghast that some republics had taken this as a signal that they could pursue their own economic agendas to the detriment of all-union economic goals. The new theme of the merging of nations also tallied with preparations toward the end of 1958 for a hyperambitious seven-year plan which stressed interregional cooperation rather than economic localism. Hodnett (1967: 458–59), Simon (1991: 246, 251–52).

99. Simon (1991: 251–54).

100. Rakowska-Harmstone (1972: 16).

CHAPTER 7. SCANDAL IN RIAZAN

1. Yanov (1984: 73). Others who noted this purge include Fainsod (1963: 226), Tatu (1969: 127), and Breslauer (1982: 99).

2. This is a general theme of Tatu (1969: chap. 1, esp. 135–39).

3. RGASPI f.17 op.56 d.2110 ll.10–11.

4. Taubman (2004: 305); and *Stroitel'stvo* t.3 (1963: 373). The prototype for this commitment was Stalin's promise at the end of 1929 that Soviet industrial production, which then stood at 5 percent of US levels, would outstrip America's by 1940. Davies (1989: 68), as cited in Vasiliev (2011: 130 n.4).

5. Specifically, as Khrushchev announced to the December 1958 Central Committee plenum, the average yearly amount of milk produced per cow in Riazan had risen from 1,129 kg in 1953 to 3,200 kg in 1958, outstripping its rivals in Moscow, Kiev, and Tula. See *Stroitel'stvo* t.3 (1963: 370), Agarev (2005:18, 22–23, 94–95), and RGANI f.13 op.1 d.793 l.48.

6. Agarev (2005: 23–26, 52, 61), Sushkov (2009: 167).

7. *Regional'naia* (2009: 189–90, 193–94). According to a joint resolution of 4 July 1957, obligatory deliveries from private plots were to cease from 1 January 1958. In practice, however, a speech by Khrushchev in December 1957 on how local farmers from his home village of Kalinovka had "voluntarily" sold their cattle to the kolkhoz was taken as a sign by party secretaries that, under the euphemism of purchase, they could expropriate cattle. Although this practice was already

apparent at the beginning of 1958, as a *Pravda* editorial of March 1959 made clear, it appeared to have become commonplace with the onset of the new drive to raise production, with "some kolkhoz leaders forcing kolkhozniks to sell their cattle . . . and local leaders declaring that it is now forbidden for kolkhoz members to have cattle in their personal possession." Wädekin (1973: 277–83, *Pravda* quotation at 283), *Kommunisticheskaia partiia* (1985: t.9, 190–92), Nove (1989: 359), Smith (1987: 109).

8. *Regional'naia* (2009: 195–98).

9. *Regional'naia* (2009: 255).

10. *Stroitel'stvo* t.4 (1963: 167), *Regional'naia* (2009: 260, 264).

11. *Regional'naia* (2009: 272–311).

12. *Plenum 1961 g.* (1961: 589–91), Tatu (1969: 129–30), Breslauer (1982: 98 cf. 45–46).

13. Tatu (1969: 129).

14. RGANI f.13 op.1 d.793 ll.72, 107; also ll.26, 65.

15. *Prezidium* t.1 (2003: 469), Gorlizki (2013b: 249).

16. RGANI f.13 op.1 d.790 l.51.

17. RGASPI f.17 op.91 d.2421 ll.13, 36, 52 (italics added).

18. RGANI f.13 op.1 d.793 ll.11, 14, 21, 27.

19. RGANI f.13 op.1 d.790 l.1.

20. RGASPI f.17 op.91 d.2421 ll.4, 12–13, 18; RGANI f.13 op.1 d.793 ll.1–2, 21, 71–72.

21. RGANI f.13 op.1 d.793 ll.13, 14, 62. They were also sometimes referred to as "imaginary transactions" (*fiktivnye operatsii*). RGASPI f.17 op.91 d.2421 l.5.

22. This is a mixture of the "buy-back" and "carousel" schemes reported by Harrison (2011: 51–52) as it involves fake receipts for meat that was supposed to have been sold on—but never was—to the population.

23. RGANI f.13 op.1 d.793 ll.13, 22–23, 63; RGASPI f.17 op.91 d.2421 l.5, 13–14.

24. RGANI f.13 op.1 d.793 l.13. They were also known as "pure cheating" (*priamye pripiski*) (ibid., l.26) or "pure forgery" (*priamoi podlog*). *Regional'naia* (2009: 345).

25. RGANI f.13 op.1 d.793 ll.23, 26.

26. Also see RGANI f.13 op.1 d.793 ll.36, 99; RGASPI f.17 op.91 d.2421 l.84; Agarev (2005: 78).

27. Kabanov and Zigalenko had been candidate members of the obkom buro since the early 1950s and full members since July 1957; Ponomarev had been elected a candidate member in 1957. For more on their leading roles, see RGASPI f.17 op.56 d.2111 ll.7–8; op.56 d.2112 l.1; op.57 d.2234 ll.1, 183; op.91 d.2421 l.52; RGANI f.13 op.1 d.793 l.98.

28. RGASPI f.17 op.90 d.2434 l.11, 118, Agarev (2005: 184).

29. RGASPI f.17 op.91 d.2421 ll.27–28, 44, Agarev (2005: 149).

30. RGANI f.13 op.1 d.793 l.4, Agarev (2005: 127) (these materials refer to the same source).

31. RGANI f.13 op.1 d.793 ll.5, 18, RGASPI f.17 op.91 d.2421 l.184, Agarev (2005: 130–34).

32. These were leaders whom Larionov had consistently elevated and endorsed over a period of around five years: Ryzhnikov (Rybnovskii district), Tarasov (Shatskii), Protasov (Pronskii), Egorov (Starozhilovskii), Pushkarev (Miloslavskii), Pronin (Erakhturskii), Makeev (Mozharskii), Kagakov (Novoderevenskii), Rogova (Putiatinskii), Susliakov (Mikhailovskii), Taranov (Zheleznodorozhnii), Chumakova (Sovetskii), and Susanov (Oktiabrskii). RGASPI f.17 op.56 d.2110 ll.1–2; d.2111 ll.7, 50, 138; d.2112 l.1 (e); d 2126 l.40; f.17 op.57 d.2234 ll.1, 183; d.2243 l.1.

33. RGASPI f.17 op.90 d.2422 l.1; op.91 d.2421 ll.1, 3, 59.

34. Agarev (2005: 45, 48).

35. Three were members in 1960 and four in 1957.

36. RGANI f.13 op.1 d.793 l.56, Gorlizki (2013a: 258–59).

37. For more details on the use of force in the meat roundups in Riazan, see Gorlizki (2013b: 249–51).

38. Granovetter (1985). For a more extended discussion, see Gorlizki (2013b: 273–74, 276–77).

39. Regional'naia (2009: 251–54). Also see Prezidium t.1 (2003: 443–44); Prezidium t.3 (2008: 132).

40. Regional'naia (2009: 345–49).

41. Gorlizki (2013b: 247–48).

42. Gorlizki (2013b: 258–59); Heinzen (2016: 50).

43. RGASPI f.17 op.89 d.1752 ll.94–95.

44. For more on Pcheliakov's obsession with Riazan, see Gorlizki (2013b: 265–66).

45. RGASPI f.17 op.91 d.1787 ll.72–74, 110.

46. RGASPI f.17 op.91 d.1787 l.110. The RSFSR resolution of 1 November 1960 showed that the perederzhki in regions that were not even among the front-runners of the agricultural competitions of 1959, such as Kurgansk, Voronezh, and Krasnodar, exceeded those in Kirov almost threefold. RGANI f.13 op.1 d.790 ll.1–2. As Pcheliakov would later proclaim, again with a certain ring of truth, "We [did do this] but in other oblasts the perederzhky were far worse." RGASPI f.17 op.91 d.1787 l.111.

47. RGASPI f.17 op.89 d.1751 l.191.

48. RGASPI f.17 op.91 d.1787 l.120.

49. In 1959 40 percent of district first secretaries and second secretaries and half of ispolkom heads in Kirov had been in post for no more than a year. RGASPI f.17 op.91 d.1751 ll.110–11. In addition, owing to what a Central Committee official termed Pcheliakov's "administrative itch," twenty-four first secretaries received party reprimands. RGASPI f.17 op.91 d.1787 l.79.

50. Ibid., l.55. For other examples of caustic attacks on his peers, see ibid., ll.37, 48, 88, 114; 123; f.17 op.89 d.1751 ll.187–89.

51. RGASPI f.17 op.89 d.1751 ll.119–20. For more on this, see Gorlizki (2013b: 268–70).

52. RGASPI f.17 op.91 d.1787 l.122.

53. RGANI f.13 op.1 d.805 ll.6–7.

377 Notes to Pages 210–225

54. RGASPI f.17 op.91 d.1787 ll.22, 37, 122. Bulatov was subsequently transferred by Pcheliakov to the post of first deputy chair of the regional executive committee as part of a bid to unseat the chair, Ob'edkov.

55. Ibid., l.51.

56. *Stroitel'stvo* (1963: t.3, 374).

57. *Regional'naia* (2009: 255–58). These details come from an anonymous letter. An inquiry by the Ukrainian central committee subsequently confirmed the broad outlines of the letter. Ibid., 260–61.

58. *Regional'naia* (2009: 255, 257).

59. *Regional'naia* (2009: 255, 257–58).

60. RGASPI f.17 op.91 d.1787 l.129.

61. *Regional'naia* (2009: 260–61).

62. Harrison (2011: 62).

63. *Stroitel'stvo Kommunizma* (1963: t.4, 264–66, 362–63), *Plenum 1961 g.* (1961: 589–91).

64. *Stroitel'stvo Kommunizma* (1963: t.4, 268–70), *Prezidium* (2003: 1: 443–44).

65. *Regional'naia* (2009: 360).

66. *Regional'naia* (2009: 323).

67. RGANI f.13 op.1 d.793 ll.48, 53, 54, 99.

68. *Regional'naia* (2009: 255–56).

69. See Tatu (1969: 136–39).

70. *Regional'naia* (2009: 334–35, 590).

71. *Regional'naia* (2009: 326–27).

72. *Regional'naia* (2009: 354–57, 360–61, 363).

73. *Regional'naia* (2009: 365, 617–18, 722).

74. For a useful sketch of Voronov, see Tatu (1969: 132–34, quotation on 132).

75. Cited in Yanov (1984: 74).

76. RGASPI f.17 op.91 d. 2421 ll.6–8, 16, 42, 66–67, 182–84.

77. These tended to happen where data fixing was linked to theft and self-enrichment, especially in Tajikistan and Kazakhstan. *Regional'naia* (2009: 325, 365, 616–17).

78. They got off unpunished despite the fact that on 19 May a joint resolution of the Central Committee and the Council of Ministers noted that "certain local party leaders" had "not only failed to react to critical signals but . . . had themselves gone on the path of deceiving the state and of forcing functionaries from the economic, procurement, and statistical agencies into their schemes." *Postanovleniia* (1961: 102). For more on the new legislation and its effects, see *Regional'naia* (2009: 365–68).

79. Stakhurskii was released "in connection with transfer to other work," while Khvorostukhin was removed in connection with his appointment as ambassador to the Mongolian People's Republic.

80. *XXII S'ezd* (1961: t.1, 252–53).

81. See, for example, Linden (1990 [1966]: chap. 6), and Tatu (1969: 41–53).

82. Taubman (2003: 480).

83. Tompson (1991: 245).

84. *Nikita Khrushchev* (2007: 225, 227, 229, 245, 259).

85. *Leonid Brezhnev* (2016: t.1, 39).

CHAPTER 8. ADMINISTRATIVE REVOLUTION

1. Taubman (2003: 587).

2. *Prezidium* (2004: t.1 561)

3. A version of this argument—that in increasing the number of regional first secretaries Khrushchev would be widening the pool of candidates for Central Committee membership—has been advanced by Mikhail Gorbachev. "Even then," recalled Gorbachev, "the niggling thought kept creeping in that Khrushchev's intention was not quite as it seemed. Many obkom first secretaries were members of the Central Committee. The replacement of one with two first secretaries could have paved the way for the complete rejuvenation of the Central Committee." Gorbachev (1995: t.1, 96–97).

4. Some scholars, for example, taking Khrushchev's pronouncements more at face value, have argued that the reforms were the culmination of Khrushchev's desire to strengthen party control of the economy: see Chotiner (1984), Taubman (2003).

5. Taubman (2003: 523–24).

6. *Prezidium* (2004: t.1, 575).

7. *Stroitel'stvo kommunizma* (1963: t.7, 163–77).

8. *Presidium TsK KPSS*, t.1, 576–80.

9. *Regional'naia* (2009: 487–93).

10. *KPSS v rezolutsiiakh* . . . t.7, 200–201.

11. *Prezidium* (2004: t.1 576–77, 580–81, 580–81).

12. Hodnett (1965: 637 n.1).

13. *Prezidium* (2004: t.1 578).

14. On an average day those surveyed consumed half a kilo of bread, 330 grams of potatoes, only 130 grams of meat or sausage, 30 grams of fresh or tinned fish along with meager quantities of sugar, butter, and other products. The report carried out by the state statistical agency does not say how many people were surveyed, only that the survey was carried out across Ukraine, the Urals, the Donbass, Karaganda, the Kuzbass, Baku, Moscow, Leningrad, Gor'kii, Rostov, Novosibirsk, and Ivanovo oblasts, plus Uzbekistan. GARF f R-5446 op.96 d.351 ll.50–52.

15. *Pravda* 1 June 1962.

16. *Istoricheskii arkhiv* (1993: no. 1, 110–36; no. 4, 143–77), *Neizvestnaia Rossiia* (1993: 3:154–76), *Obshchestvo i vlast'* (2006: t.2, 218–22).

17. Kozlov (2002; 2010), Baron (2001), *Prezidium* (2004: t.1 568).

18. The bifurcation of the party apparatus was part of a huge administrative package that also saw the abolition of the rural raikoms, the enlargement and reduction in the number of the sovnarkhozy, and the establishment of a new USSR Sovnarkhoz.

19. *Regional'naia* (2009: 499), Pikhoia (1998: 246–50).

20. *Regional'naia* (2009: 201–2), RGASPI f.556 op.14 d.224 l.6.

21. *Regional'naia* (2009: 204).

22. *Regional'naia* (2009: 209–11).

23. Two key cases of resistance came from Shelest in Ukraine and the Leningrad obkom. *Tsental'nyi Gosudarstvennyi Arkhiv Obshchestvennykh Ob'edinenii Ukrainy* (Ukrainian Central State Archive of Public Associations, TsDAGOU) f.1 op.31 d.1911 ll.1–15, *Politicheskoe rukovodstvo* (2006: 276–80); *Nikita Khrushchev* (2007: 385), RGANI f.13 op.2 d.477 ll.22–23.

24. For a useful discussion, see Hodnett (1965: 638).

25. Although two additional branch buros (for agriculture and industry) were set up in each republic, the existing central committee presidia, the republican party bureaucracies, and the role of a single first secretary were left untouched. It was also on this principle that the buros of those nine autonomous republics in the RSFSR with relatively advanced industrial economies were reorganized. The other seven autonomous republics in the RSFSR, along with the autonomous oblasts, remained unchanged. RGANI f.2 op.18 d.117 ll.10–15. *Regional'naia* (2009: 491–92).

26. *Prezidium* (2006: 580).

27. Other regions which fell into this category included Amur, Arkhangel'sk, Astrakhan, Kaliningrad, Khabarovsk, Murmansk, and Sakhalin in the RSFSR.

28. *Regional'naia* (2009: 487–93), Hodnett (1965: 640).

29. Our categories try to build status into the definition. In this sense we differ from Hodnett, who distinguishes the incumbents (whom he calls the "1962 group") from newly appointed secretaries (whom he calls the "incomers"), and Clark, who distinguishes incumbent first secretaries who stayed on in the region from what he calls the "second" first secretaries. The latter included all "new" first secretaries, including those who were, for one reason or another, more senior (by position within the region or membership of the Central Committee) than the other first secretary. Hodnett (1965), Clark (2013).

30. Clark (2013: 281 n.8).

31. Twenty-two of these twenty-seven were incumbent first secretaries. In two of the remaining five, one of the new first secretaries was, in nomenklatura terms, unmistakably senior, leading to a straightforward positioning of the two within the region. In Gor'kii, the former first secretary, L.N. Efremov, who was promoted to a position in Moscow, was replaced by the former first secretary of the Cheliabinsk obkom, M.T. Efremov. The junior secretary, in the agricultural obkom, was the former chair of the regional executive committee of the regional soviet and was clearly on a far lower level than Efremov in the nomenklatura hierarchy. The changeover in Smolensk also accorded with this pattern. There, the former first secretary, who had been posted as ambassador to East Germany, was replaced as senior secretary (of the agricultural obkom) by the former second secretary of the obkom, while the junior secretary in the industrial obkom was the former deputy chair of the Smolensk sovnarkhoz. The reshuffling in Cheliabinsk, Lipetsk, and Kuibyshev was more complicated, and in this case we cannot speak in clear-cut terms of a senior secretary prior to the appointment, for here there was parity of status among the appointees. In Cheliabinsk the former first secretary, as we have seen, was transferred to Gor'kii. Leadership of the obkoms was shared between the former second secretary and the former head of the regional executive committee, positions of relatively equal status. Here we can only speak of the first secretary of the industrial obkom as being senior after his appointment, on the grounds that the industrial obkom

was far more powerful than the other. In Kuibyshev, another industrial region, the former first secretary had died in the course of the reorganization. Here, the chair of the regional executive committee was appointed to head the industrial obkom and is treated as the senior secretary. In Lipetsk, where the former first secretary had also died in the interim, the weightings were reversed. Here, it was the agricultural obkom, headed by the former chair of the regional executive committee, that was the more powerful, so that he will be treated as the senior secretary, and the former second secretary, who headed the industrial obkom, became the junior secretary. Given that in the last three cases there was relative parity of status among the appointees, it was the asymmetry of the obkoms that settled the status question.

32. In Briansk M.K. Krakhmalev had been a full member of the Central Committee since 1961 and a candidate since 1956; in Kalinin N.G. Karytkov had been a full member since 1961; in Saratov A.I. Shibaev had been a full member since 1961; in Stavropol' F.D. Kulakov had been a full member since 1961; in Volgograd A.M. Shkol'nikov had been a full member since 1956 and a candidate since 1952; and in Voronezh S.D. Khitrov had been a candidate since 1961.

33. This seems to confirm Hodnett's (1965: 640–42, 651) assertion that the majority of incumbent first secretaries were still, in 1962, drawn to agriculture for reasons of education, training, and expertise. Also see Armstrong (1966: 418–19, 422–23).

34. With the exception of Moscow all the senior secretaries were both incumbents and members of the Central Committee. In Chita A.I. Smirnov had been a candidate since 1961; in Irkutsk A.I. Shchetinin had been a full member since 1961; in Krasnoiarsk A.A. Kokarev had been a full member since 1961; in Novosibirsk F.S. Goriachev had been a full member since 1952; in Rostov V.V. Skriabin (appointed on 22 August 1962) had been a full member since 1961; in Tula I.Kh. Iunak had been a full member since 1961; in Ul'ianovsk A.A. Skochilov had been a candidate since 1961; and in Vladimir M.A. Ponomarev had been a candidate since 1961. In Moscow the incumbent had departed and neither of the new officeholders was a Central Committee member. Here, however, we can say that the senior secretary (who went to the agricultural obkom) was the former chair of the regional executive committee while the junior secretary was a former gorkom secretary of one of the towns of Moscow oblast and had only very recently been promoted to obkom secretary.

35. This included ten former obkom second secretaries, eleven rank-and-file secretaries, six chairs and two deputy chairs of the regional executive committees, four sovnarkhoz heads, and three secretaries of the party committees of regional capitals. Clark suggests that the tendency to recruit as junior secretaries subordinate officials from within the region was not restricted to the Russian Republic. According to his findings, 81.1 percent of his category of junior secretaries from across the Soviet Union came from within the oblast, which by definition would have meant the recruiting of officials from within the region who had occupied a position lower than the first secretary. Clark (2013: 288–89). Hodnett (1965: 649) similarly argued that his "newcomers simply tended to come from lower positions than 1962 group members."

36. According to Clark, forty-nine of the fifty-nine incumbent first secretaries in divided regions were either full (twenty-nine) or candidate members (twenty) of the

Central Committee. By contrast, only two of his four "second" first secretaries (out of ninety-five) were either candidates or full members. Clark (2013: 287–88).

37. RGASPI f.556 op.14 d.243 ll.165–66.

38. The authors are grateful to Viktor Kondrashin for providing the information for this section.

39. For a very brief interim, from June to August 1961, Ermin had worked as second secretary of the Penza obkom

40. The other prime candidate, A.F. Eshtokin, the chair of the regional executive committee, was transferred out of the region, first as inspector of the Central Committee, before being made first secretary of the Kemerovo industrial obkom.

41. Sushkov and Raznikov (2003: 59–62).

42. The numbers following senior and junior secretaries, respectively, for Category I obkoms (i.e., where the senior secretary went to the larger obkom by population and party membership size) were 90/70 (Gor'kii, industrial), 82/54 (Sverdlovsk, industrial), 71/50 Stavropol' (agricultural), 55/43 Tiumen' (agricultural), and for Category II obkoms (i.e., where the senior secretary went to the smaller obkom) 82/78 (Rostov, agricultural) and 62/50 (Tula, agricultural). According to the design of the reform, with the exception of administrative organs and higher educational institutions the staffs were supposed to have been divided exactly equally. *Regional'naia* (2009: 473–4); For Gor'kii: RGASPI f.17 op.91 d.1548 ll.263–71; op.93 d.1971 ll. ll.119–23; op.93 d.1980 ll.92–96; for Rostov: RGASPI f.17 op.91 d.2392 ll.73–79; op.92 d.2348 ll.29–32; op.93 d.2911 ll.189–91; for Sverdlovsk: RGASPI f.17 op.91 d.2479 ll.394–406; op.93 d.3013, ll.216–23; op.93 d.3029 ll.184–89; for Stavropol': RGASPI f.17 op.91 d.2540 ll.50–60; op.92 d.2501 ll.14–18; op.92 d.2504 ll.15–20; for Tula: RGASPI f.17 op.91 d.2701 ll.33–43; op.93 d.3215 ll.13–19; op.93 d.3224, ll.18–23; for Tiumen': RGASPI f.17 op.2736 ll.15–25; op.93 d.3235 ll.14–17; op.93 d.3248 ll.12–16.

43. Interview given by A.I. Alekseev to Viktor Kondrashin on 29 March 2007.

44. *Stroitel'stvo* (1963: t.5, 418).

45. RGASPI f.17 op.93 d.3225 ll.185–86.

46. RGASPI f.17 op.93 d.3032 ll.162–67.

47. RGASPI f.556 op.10 d.1331 ll.207–13.

48. RGASPI f.556 op.10 d.1331 l.216.

49. RGASPI f.17 op.93 d.2447 ll.85–87.

50. RGASPI f.17 op.93 d.2452 ll.55–58.

51. RGASPI f.17 op.93 d.2452 l.82.

52. RGASPI f.17 op.93 d.2468 ll.124–29, 137–38. For another example, see the speeches of the obkom secretaries at the meetings of the party aktiv at the Cheliabinsk regional industrial party conference (OGAChO f.1470 op.2 d.126 ll.27, 97, 99, 108).

53. RGASPI f.17 op.94 d.784 ll.87–89.

54. RGASPI f.17 op.94 d.807 l.14.

55. RGASPI f.17 op.94 d.784 ll.87–89.

56. RGASPI f.17 op.94 d.796 l.94.

57. Of the forty-two divided regions in the Russian Federation in only one was the principle of nomenklatura seniority unmistakably broken. Here, the former

first secretary was put in charge of the much weaker obkom in a process that he clearly did not control and that clearly ran against his own interests. In Kemerovo, a heavily industrial region, the former obkom first secretary, L.I. Lubennikov, was made first secretary of the agricultural obkom; meanwhile, an outsider, the former chair of the Sverdlovsk regional executive committee, A.F. Eshtokin, was appointed to the inestimably more powerful position of first secretary of the industrial obkom. This particular case was a clear signal of Moscow's displeasure with Lubennikov, a point highlighted by the fact that, in the short interim before coming to Kemorovo, Eshtokin had held the position of Central Committee inspector, from which vantage point he was expected to bring order to the region. Lubennikov was eventually forced out of the region in 1964.

58. RGASPI f.556 op.10 d.588 ll.40; and 55 (plenum of the Kirov agricultural obkom of 24 April 1964).

59. RGASPI f.556 op.10 d.381 l.16.

60. RGASPI f.17 op.94 d.1532 ll.12, 16.

61. Thus, for example, following a petition from the agricultural kraikom and kraiispolkom, the film and press administrations were taken out of the industrial kraikom and moved over to the agricultural kraikom. RGASPI f.556 op.14 d.224 ll.146–53.

62. RGASPI f.556 op.14 d.224 ll.146–53.

63. Gorbachev (1995: t.1, 96).

64. RGASPI f.556 op.14 d.224 l.154.

65. GAPO f.P-5892 op.1 d.71 l.30.

66. GAPO F.P.5892 op.1 d.71 ll.52–54.

67. The head of the rural ispolkom noted as well that the regional transportation department, which operated under the auspices of the industrial obkom, also completely disregarded the needs and requirements of the rural sector. RGASPI f.556 op.14 d.219 ll.52, 53.

68. OGAChO f.1470 op.2 d.126 ll.26–27.

69. RGASPI f.17 op.94 d.1532 l.12.

70. The proportion of new executive obkom members as a result of the creation of two obkoms was as follows: Gor'kii 34.74 percent, Sverdlovsk 34.23 percent, Stavropol' 33.41 percent, Tiumen' 44.19 percent, Tula 35.7 percent, and Rostov 45.13 percent. See sources for n.42.

71. Wintrobe (1998: chap. 2).

72. Taubman (2003: 524).

73. Consider, for example, the outright rejection of the request by the first secretary of the agricultural obkom in Chita on 27 December 1963 that he follow the example of the neighboring regions of Khabarovsk and Amur and reunify the apparatus. Regional'naia (2009: 519–23).

74. N.S. Khrushchev: 1964 (2007: 378). Speech by N.V. Podgornyi at the Central Committee plenum of 16 November 1964.

75. Taubman (2003: 587).

76. In the other five cases the senior secretaries either received a promotion or were transferred to first secretaryships in other regions. Armstrong (1966: 426) reports that forty-one of the sixty-one 1962 incumbents in the RSFSR and Ukraine

returned to their posts. Clark (2013: 281) writes that forty-three of the fifty-nine prebifucation first secretaries found themselves back in charge of the obkoms in 1965. As Hodnett (1965: 640) suggests, "One of the most striking features of the entire undertaking was the degree to which the original obkom first secretaries managed to retain or better their positions."

77. The exceptions were in Volgograd, where the first secretary of the industrial obkom became an ordinary secretary of the united obkom; in Kemerovo and Rostov, where the first secretaries of the agricultural obkoms did not join the new oblast leadership at all; and in Kostroma, where it was the first secretary of the industrial obkom who was cast aside. Clark (2013: 289) notes that seventy-nine out of ninety of the "second" first secretaries for whom he could locate data stayed within the oblast and over a quarter returned to the posts they had held prior to the bifurcation.

CHAPTER 9. THE NEW COURSE

1. For the Central Committee Presidium resolution of 19 July 1962 and the subsequent KGB order of 28 July titled "On strengthening the struggle with hostile, anti-Soviet elements," see *Lubianka* (2003: 702–10). In the RSFSR corresponding revisions to the criminal code were passed on 25 July. Berman (1966: 60).

2. Pikhoia (1998: 245).

3. The term "party vertical" is used by Pikhoia (1998: 273–74).

4. Gustafson (1981: 25–29, 155); Breslauer (1982: 140–43).

5. Brudny (1998: 60–63, 72–73, 104–7); Mitrokhin (2003: 109–40).

6. In a report from 1963 the head of the KGB, Vladimir Semichastny, noted that forty-six thousand officers had been fired from the security service since 1954, including half since 1959. Pikhoia (1998: 242–43).

7. From 1967 to 1974 the ratio of "especially serious state crimes" treated through prophylaxis rather than through formal prosecutions was approximately 100 to 1. On this, see *Kramola* (2005: 36); Denninghaus and Savin (2014: 128); and Dimitrov (2014: 235–36).

8. Gill (1990: 47), Easter (2000: 45–46, 71). For much the same reasons, tours of duty of regional governors had been a feature of a number of early modern empires. On this, see Ch'ü (1962), cited in Miller (1983: 62, 92 n.1) and Barkey (1994: 36, 65).

9. In the RSFSR the appointment of the senior secretary as the new first secretary occurred in thirty-seven of the forty-two divided obkoms. In the other five cases the senior secretaries either received a promotion or were transferred to first secretaryships in other regions. In only two cases that we know of was this rank order contested by a local leader. In Tiumen' the first secretary of the industrial obkom, Protazanov, who was the junior secretary, decided to take on the senior secretary, B.E. Shcherbina, but was overwhelmingly defeated. *V plameni zhizni* (1990: 70, 147).

10. In the RSFSR junior secretaries who had headed industrial obkoms tended to become second secretaries of the united obkom (twenty-seven cases), while those who had led the rural obkom became chairs of the newly united regional execu-

tive committees (eleven cases). The four exceptions were in Volgograd, Kemerovo, Rostov, and Kostroma.

11. RGASPI f.17 op.94 d.807 l.18.

12. RGASPI f.17 op.94 d.782 ll.79–80.

13. RGASPI f.17 op.94 d.807 l.14.

14. In the RSFSR sudden departures of former junior secretaries, usually on the grounds that they could not get along with the new first secretary, occurred in Krasnoiarsk, Kaluga, Smolensk, Orel, Penza, Cheliabinsk, and Omsk. Lingering tensions between rival industrial and agricultural networks could also surface at obkom elections. In Kuibyshev, a predominantly industrial region, 82 delegates (out of 805) voted against the junior secretary (that is, the first secretary of the rural obkom), I.G. Baliasinskii, while 32 voted against the former second secretary of the rural obkom. Within months Baliasinskii had left for Moscow. Sizov (2000: 2:191); RGASPI f.556 op.10 d. d.751 ll.138–41 d.1046 ll.8–12.

15. In the RSFSR in twenty-five of the forty-two divided regions the senior and junior secretaries continued in the most senior roles in the region for at least a year after the reorganization. Of the other seventeen cases, eight—five of the senior secretaries and three of the junior secretaries—left the region on account of a promotion.

16. Levels of continuity of obkom elites from December 1961 to December 1964 were 59.8 percent in Altai Krai, 59.8 percent in Gor'kii, 62.0 percent in Kalinin, 57.7 percent in Kaluga, 64.8 percent in Rostov, 67.8 percent in Sverdlovsk, 52.8 percent in Stavropol' krai, 55.3 percent in Tula, 52.3 percent in Tiumen', 58.2 percent in Voronezh and 68.0 percent in Ul'ianovsk. The average across all eleven obkoms was 59.8 percent. By "core elite" we mean members and candidates of obkoms and members of obkom auditing committees, excluding all those, such as workers, collective farm laborers, doctors, teachers, who did not hold elite positions. Sources: calculated from the following regions: Altai ([all citations are from RGASPI] f.17 op.91 d.1282 ll.32–44; f.556 op.10 d.25 ll.12–16); Voronezh (f.17 op.91 d.1529 ll.48–58; f.556 op.10 d.300 ll.26–32); Gor'kii (f.17 op.91 d.1548 ll.263–71; f.556 op.10 d.323 ll.130–36); Kalinin (f.17 op.91 d.1674 ll.9–14; f.556 op.10 d.463 ll.16–20); Kaluga (f.17 op.91 d.1707 ll.124–30; f.556 op.10 d.497 ll.56–60); Rostov (f.17 op.91 d.2392 ll.73–79; f.556 op.10 d.1242 ll.27–32); Sverdlovsk (f.17 op.91 d.2479 ll.394–406; f.556 op.10 d.1340 ll.168–75); Stavropol' (f.17 op.91 d.2540 ll.50–60; f.556 op.10 d.1419 ll.15–20); Tula (f.17 op.91 d.2701 ll.33–43; f.556 op.10 d.1522 ll.17–24); Tiumen' (f.17 op.91 d.2736 ll.15–25; f.556 op.10 d.1548 ll.15–21); Ul'ianovsk (f.17 op.91 d.2784 ll.281–92; f.556 op.10 d.1606 ll.102–8).

17. Stewart's study of the Stalingrad obkom (1968: 51) of the late 1950s suggests an annual turnover that was actually higher, 26.9 percent, but that figure included nonelite members of the obkom, who tended to have a higher level of volatility.

18. *Spravochnik* (1967: 324, 326). In its emphasis on personnel, the decree on Estonia differed not only from the Kharkov decree of July 1965 (discussed below), which was devoted to admissions policy and ideological retrenchment, but also from the more recent resolution on the Tula party organization of December 1966, which centered on economic discipline. *Spravochnik* (1967: 311–17, 323–29).

19. Meyerzon (2004: 72–75).

20. *Spravochnik* (1968: 291, 295).

21. Cited in Konovalov (2006: 47).

22. E.g., *Partiinaia zhizn'* (1965: no.17, 7), as cited in Tatu (1969: 434).

23. This was articulated most clearly at the XXIV Party Congress in 1971, when Brezhnev announced that "the Central Committee has pursued a consistent policy of promoting local personnel," for which he received an ovation. *XXIV S'ezd* (1971: 124). This passage is also cited in Moses (1974: 146, 214), Miller (1977: 19), and Rigby (1978: 13–14).

24. Rigby (1978: 13–14), Blackwell (1979: 36), Rutland (1993: 192–93). For discussion of individual cases, see Moses (1974: 69, 147–48).

25. Rigby (1978: 13).

26. Konovalov (2006: 219).

27. This point was first made by Moses (1974: 141–46).

28. The idea that Russian nationalism became the "operative," as opposed to the "official," ideology of the state under Brezhnev comes from Zaslavsky (1982: 81, 84). On the notion of "politics by culture," see Brudny (1998). Note that despite these national accretions to the regime's "operative ideology," in our understanding of ideology as the political language of the elite, the main terms of Marxism-Leninism would continue to hold sway. As *Pravda* opined in February 1976, "Under conditions of developed socialism, when the Communist Party has become the party of all the people, it by no means loses its class character. By its nature, the CPSU has been and remains a party of the working class." Cited in Breslauer (1980: 64).

29. See Donovan (2015: 473–78) and (2019: chap. 2).

30. Tolz (2011: 37–41), Donovan (2015), Kelly (2014).

31. I.e., either the second secretary or the chair of the regional executive committee. Recruitment from these positions accounted for thirty-eight of the seventy-two first secretaries in the RSFSR in 1976, some of whom had been appointed before 1964. Rigby (1978: 13–14). From 1972 to 1974 this was true of all seven new first secretaries in Siberia, six of whom had earlier been the second secretaries in the region. Konovalov (2006: 221). On this tendency in later years, see Rutland (1993: 190–91).

32. This applied to forty-one of the seventy-two obkom first secretaries in the RSFSR in 1976. Rigby (1978: 21). Also see Moses (1974: 218, 220).

33. Rigby (1978: 23).

34. Churbanov (1993), cited in Sokolov (2004: 206). For a more detailed discussion of the contrast between Brezhnev's generally courteous and respectful forms of address and Khrushchev's rude and mocking ones, see Schattenberg (2015: 843–45; 2016: 247, 283).

35. Grybkauskas (2014: 284–85).

36. As Zaslavsky (1982: 111) put it, the center "takes care to place in positions of major responsibility the most Russified elements which, due to the system of internal passports, still belong to the local nationality."

37. Grybkauskas (2013: 344, 353). Kharazov replaced and consulted with two other seconds who had earlier served in Lithuania, Boris Sharkov (1956–61) and Boris Popov (1961–67) (ibid., 353).

38. Maniušis was the preferred choice of Senior Central Committee Secretary Mikhail Suslov; but he also had good contacts at the department of leading party organs. Maniušis's anointment as Moscow's preferred successor was inferred from the fact that he had been appointed to head Snieckus's funeral committee. Grybkauskas (2013: 350, 355).

39. Grybkauskas (2013: 355–57).

40. Grybkauskas (2013: 357). Note that Šumauskas, the chair of the council of ministers, also threatened to "make the plenum fail" (ibid., 364).

41. Grybkauskas (2013: 352, 359–61).

42. For a general discussion of the effects of the Kharkov resolution, see Rigby (1968: 297–306, 316–22).

43. For what remains the best account, see Tatu (1969: 500–502).

44. Tatu (1969: 510); Rigby (1978: 11 n.25).

45. Only four years prior to his appointment Katushev had been a mere party secretary in the Gor'kii automobile works. See Rigby (1978: 11 n.26).

46. Rigby (1978: 11).

47. Blackwell (1979: 34–35); also see Rigby (1978: 12).

48. See Rigby (1970: 179); and Blackwell (1979: 37–38).

49. On this, see Rigby (1978: 23).

50. In September 1976 Brezhnev had prepared for him a list (it turned out to be seventeen pages long) of all territorial party leaders with, against their name, a tally of how many awards each had. Brezhnev made a point of personally telephoning each award holder, thereby setting up another ritual through which he could firm up personal ties. Denninghaus and Savin (2014: 141–43). For more on Brezhnev's phone calls to obkom leaders, see Mawdsley and White (2000: 182) and Schattenberg (2015: 859).

51. Mlechin (2008: 236–37).

52. Ligachev, cited in Mlechin (2008: 236).

53. In his first fifteen months Brezhnev appointed new first secretaries to four of the five largest regions in the RSFSR (Moscow, Rostov, Gor'kii, and Krasnodar) as well as new leaders to some of the most powerful of the other provinces in the republic. New appointments in Moscow (V.I. Konotop), Rostov (M.S. Solomentsev), and Stavropol' (L.N. Efremov) were made on 16 and 18 January 1965, while the new assignments to Cheliabinsk (N.N. Rodionov), Volgograd (L.S. Kulichenko), Gor'kii (K.F. Katushev), and Krasnodar (G.S. Zolotukhin) were made on 16 and 29 November 1965 and 14 and 28 January 1966.

54. Other members of this group included a second Central Committee secretary, Petr Demichev; the head of the committee for radio and television, Nikolai Mesiatsev; the head of TASS, Dmitry Goriunov; and the RSFSR minister for public order, Vadim Tikunov.

55. The partial exception to this was Shelepin, who had become secretary of the party's youth wing, the Komsomol, in 1943 and its first secretary in 1952. On the various hang-ups of Brezhnev's cohort—"one did not have a proper education, another had written denunciations, the third had been a minister under Stalin"— see N.G. Egorychev (2006: 179–80).

56. Mesiatsev was made ambassador to Australia, Romanovskii to Norway, Goriunov to Morocco, Grigorian to Cypress, and Tolstikov to China. Others fared

worse. Vadim Tikunov, the former RSFSR minister for social order, was left in limbo without employment for several months before being offered a low-key position on the apparat. *N.G. Egorychev* (2006: 186, 188), Semichastny (2002: 392).

57. *N.G. Egorychev* (2006: 131, 335).

58. *N.G. Egorychev* (2006: 157–61, 346).

59. *N.G. Egorychev* (2006: 169, 341–42, 369).

60. *N.G. Egorychev* (2006: 342–43; and see 316, 332, 345).

61. *N.G. Egorychev* (2006: 171, 311, 316, 333). In private some members of his inner network at the Moscow gorkom, especially his former aides, former fellow students, and more senior figures such as the head of Gossnab, Veniamin Dymshits, the foreign trade minister, Nikolai Patolichev, and the writer Konstantin Simonov, continued to support and befriend him (ibid., 176).

62. In fact, only in the previous year, at the XXIII Party Congress in April 1966, had the party finally dispensed with "concealing one's social origins" or "violating revolutionary legality" as grounds for expulsion. This is reflected in the amendment to the party's statistical forms, which had included "connection with alien elements" and "concealing one's social origins" in 1966 but not in 1967. Compare RGANI f.77 op.1 d.13 l.90b (1966) with f.77 op.1 d.13 l.102 ob (1966). Soon after, the category of social class origin was also eliminated from passports. Zaslavsky (1982: 103–4).

63. Although the Kharkov decree had led to a brief uptick in expulsions from the party, even at the post-Khrushchev peak of expulsions, in 1966, when 61,981 full members and 53,936 candidates were expelled, they accounted for no more than 0.9 percent of the overall membership that year. RGANI f.77 op.1 d.13 ll.9, 90b.

64. On Andropov's involvement in circulating the idea of a "Komsomol plot," see *N.G. Egorychev* (2006: 180–81, 349, 352), Grishin (1996: 41), Semichastny (2002: 391). Egorychev himself was convinced that his office was bugged—*N.G. Egorychev* (2006: 130, 179)—and that he was followed and his associates checked (ibid., 179, 182).

65. Rigby (1978: 14–15).

66. Senior figures who had, in effect, been demoted by Brezhnev, including Gennady Voronov, Dimitry Poliansky (both closely associated with Khrushchev), and Nikolai Podgorny (i.e., from the Kharkov group), were allowed to keep their Politburo seats until the mid-1970s.

67. *N.G. Egorychev* (2006: 167). Egorychev was eventually removed at the next Party Congress in 1971.

68. On some occasions the disjuncture between an excluded leader's continued membership in the Politburo and his actual portfolio was so great that he was humiliatingly forced to oversee policies he himself had championed dismantled by a successor who was, in status terms, subordinate to him. So, for example, Voronov had to endure seeing the agricultural policy he had pioneered undone and the promotion of opponents, such as L.Ia. Florentiev, first secretary of Kostroma, as minister of agriculture of the RSFSR. Tatu notes (496) that "in some cases the function did not fit the rank."

69. *N.G. Egorychev* (2006: 346).

70. *N.G. Egorychev* (2006: 184). Note that this also happened in the KGB, where Semichastny's deputies were also all removed. Semichastny (2002: 392).

71. N.G. *Egorychev* (2006: 345).

72. Grishin (1996: 333–34).

73. One of the best examples from the Stalin era was Nikolai Voznesenskii. On this, see Gorlizki and Khlevniuk (2004: 82–83).

74. Churbanov (1993) cited in Sokolov (2004: 206).

CHAPTER 10. PARTY GOVERNORS

1. On higher levels of economic and political freedom at the microlevel, see Millar (1985) and Ledeneva (1998). On the launch of the new campaign for trust in cadres in 1966, see Gorlizki (2010: 676) and Breslauer (1982: 154).

2. Following standard definitions—e.g., Hardin (2002), Cook, Hardin, and Levi (2005), and Cook, Levi, and Hardin (2009)—we take "trust" to mean that one person trusts another if the truster expects the trusted to cooperate on a specific matter in circumstances that they cannot anticipate. This is most likely to happen when trust relations are mutual and grounded in an ongoing personal relationship. For an excellent account, see Hardin (2002: chap 1).

3. Republican and regional party secretaries accounted for 36 percent of the Central Committee elected in 1976. The next largest group was government ministers, who made up 24 percent. Rigby (1978: 1); Mawdsley and White (2000: 171, 173). As Mawdsley and White (2000: vii) observe, the Central Committee was not simply "a collection of individuals; it was a collection of people holding the positions that the regime itself defined as the most important." The fact that territorial party secretaries accounted for the largest single group on the Central Committee therefore serves as an indicator of the relative weight attached to this group by the regime. In addition, by the mid-1970s two-thirds of the Politburo, the country's ruling cabinet, had spent long stints as territorial first secretaries before coming to Moscow. Rigby (1972: 18; 1978: 1).

4. Mal'bakhov had followed a classic party career in the republic, climbing up the ranks from raikom secretary in 1946–47 and raikom first secretary in 1947–49, to secretary and then second secretary of the Kabardinian obkom from 1949 to 1952 and chair of the presidium of the republican supreme soviet from 1952 to 1956.

5. Mal'bakhov himself was born in the village of Deiskoe in the Tersk district on 18 November 1917.

6. RGANI f.5 op.61 d.9 l.31.

7. RGANI f.5 op.61 d.9 l.34, Dokshokov (1998: 99), Zumakulov et al. (2000: 30, 350, 352).

8. RGANI f.5 op.61 d.9 l.34.

9. RGANI f.5 op.61 d.9 l.39. For additional evidence, see ibid., l.37; and RGASPI f.17 op.105 d.294 l.4. f.17 op.103 d.282 ll.26–27.

10. RGANI f.5 op.61 d.9 ll.39, 30.

11. RGANI f.5 op.61 d.9 ll.33–34.

12. RGASPI f.17 op.104 d.330 l.23. "The criticisms made by comrades Cheremisin, Mishkov, and Khachetlov have no obvious content," Mal'bakhov concluded. Ibid., l.24.

13. RGASPI f.17 op.104 d.330 l.22. (italics added).

14. RGASPI f.17 op.104 d.330 l.24. Mishkov was not nominated for reelection. See f.17 op.104 d.324 ll.244–51.

15. RGANI f.5 op.61 d.9 ll.37–38.

16. See RGASPI f.17 op.102 d.304 ll.6–7.

17. On this and Bessarabov's poor personal relations with Mal'bakhov, see Dokshokov (1998: 119).

18. Krupin's biography is in RGASPI f.17 op.104 d.330 ll.7–8. Khubaev's reference to the republic as his "second homeland" is in ibid., l.10.

19. Miller (1977: 16, 19).

20. RGASPI f.17 op.104 d.330 l.29.

21. Most of these facts were confirmed at the trial, which was held in November and December 1968. Three defendants were sentenced to death, six to terms of twelve to fifteen years, and a further twenty-four to terms varying from six months to ten years. RGASPI f.17 op.104 d.336 ll.93–94, 105–6; d.337 l.133; and d.338 ll.87, 97–98; also RGANI f.5 op.61 d.9 l.24.

22. RGASPI f.17 op.104 d.336 l.94; RGANI f.5 op.61 d.9 ll.24, 26.

23. Dokshokov (1998: 98); RGANI f.5 op.61 d.9 l.42; Gorlizki (2010: 685).

24. Bilinsky (1967); Miller (1977); Grybkauskas (2014).

25. RGANI f.5 op.61 d.9 l.29.

26. RGASPI f.17 op.104 d.336 ll.115–17; op.105 d.295 l.36.

27. RGANI f.5 op.61 d.9 l.43.

28. RGASPI f.17 op.105 d.295 l.129; op.106 d.306 l.105.

29. RGASPI f.17 op.105 d.295 l.42.

30. Zumakulov et al. (2000: 376) (italics added).

31. Petukhov had studied in Rostov and served for almost a decade in senior party and state positions in Krasnodar and North Ossetia.

32. RGASPI f.556 op.10 d.588 ll.48, 80. In June 1963 Petukhov also organized a highly controversial economic conference which reportedly descended into a celebration of Petukhov's own "teachings" on the economy. See ibid., ll.21–23, 78.

33. RGASPI f.556 op.10 d.588 ll.1–3, 21–22, 78, and RGANI f.5 op.61 d.8 ll.128, 107.

34. RGASPI f.556 op.10 d.588 ll.46–49, 54–55.

35. RGASPI f.556 op.14 d.243 ll.170–71, and RGASPI f.556 op.10 d.596 l.112.

36. RGASPI f.556 op.10 d.596, ll.63–65, 78–79, 93, 97. One of Petukhov's most ardent former supporters, the obkom secretary A.V. Smirnov, switched sides and also began to criticize Petukhov. See ibid., ll.73–75.

37. Those with the highest protest votes (thirty and over) were the senior officials from the former agricultural obkom, V.P. Liamov, E.N. Nekrasov, and E.A. Rodin, who had stood by Petukhov in the debates of 1962 to 1964. See RGASPI f.556 op.10 d.588 ll.23, 80–81, and d.596 ll.24–25, 79, 93; also see Tatu (1969: 436).

38. RGANI f.5 op.61 d.8 l.115.

39. RGANI f.5 op.61 d.8 l.118.

40. RGANI f.5 op.61 d.8 l.120.

41. RGANI f.5 op.61 d.8 ll.123–4.

42. RGANI f.5 op.61 d.8 ll.85, 119.

43. RGANI f.5 op.61 d.8 l.103.

44. RGANI f.5 op.61 d.8 ll.76, 82 (italics added).

45. RGANI f.5 op.61 d.8 ll.82, 94.

46. RGANI f.5 op.61 d.8 ll.84–85.

47. The two main flashpoints were the so-called Nolinskii Affair, after which the former head of the oblispolkom, A.V. Smirnov, was sacked, and a tragedy at the local sports stadium on 25 May 1968, when thirty-nine people were killed. The stadium tragedy forced Petukhov to take action against a number of local officials, including Zaporozhskii, Liamov, and Kolbin, following which the latter two refused even to greet or acknowledge him in public. RGANI f.5 op.61 d.8 ll.81, 86, 97, 100–101, 107, 117, 119.

48. RGANI f.5 op.61 d.8 ll.94–55.

49. RGANI f.5 op.61 d.8 ll.96–99, 106–9, 123–25.

50. RGANI f.5 op.61 d.8 l.96.

51. RGANI f.5 op.61 d.8 l.82.

52. RGANI f.5 op.61 d.8 ll.114–5.

53. RGANI f.5 op.61 d.8 l.86.

54. RGANI f.5 op.61 d.8 l.122.

55. RGANI f.5 op.61 d.8 ll.96–97, 106.

56. RGANI f.5 op.61 d.8 l.129 (italics added).

57. RGANI f.5 op.61 d.8 l.89.

58. RGANI f.5 op.61 d.8 l.113. "Is it really the case that you can keep this post until the end of your days?" the chair of the Iskra kolkhoz asked Chemodanov. "That is not the way of the party." Ibid., l.129.

59. RGANI f.5 op.61 d.8 l.89. The phrase was also used by Petukhov in his letter to the Central Committee of 30 June 1969. RGANI f.5 op.61 d.8 l.68.

60. RGANI f.5 op.61 d.8 l.111.

61. RGANI f.5 op.61 d.8 l.121. Podoplelov had also used the term in the RSFSR soviet controversy, which led to his censure on 31 January 1967, ibid., l.70.

62. Bespalov had risen up the ranks, first serving as first secretary of the Kirov gorkom from 1964 to 1968 and then as obkom second secretary from 1968 to 1971.

63. Petukhov was chided by some local party leaders for his excessive softness and liberalism. RGANI f.5 op.61 d.8 ll.85, 88. It was perhaps a measure of this leniency that Liamov was the only person in Petukhov's eight years as obkom first secretary to receive a formal reprimand (vygovor) from him. Ibid., ll.117, 122.

64. RGANI f.5 op.61 d.8 l.100.

65. On how unusual this conflict was and how it attracted attention on the national stage, see Tatu (1969: 436).

66. RGASPI f.17 op.103 d.469 ll.182–84; Frank (1974: 229).

67. In line with the argument in chapter 9, none of these appointees, including Zolotukhin, had previous close work associations with Brezhnev.

68. As first secretary in Tambov Zolotukhin had emerged as a leading light among a formidable group of agricultural first secretaries in the RSFSR. In Tambov he came to know the then first secretary of the nearby Ivanovo obkom, Ivan

Kapitonov, and it was Kapitonov who, having recently been installed as Central Committee secretary in December 1965, introduced Zolotukhin as the new leader of Krasnodar at a kraikom meeting on 12 January 1966. RGASPI f.17 op.102 d.499 l.57.

69. Gorbachev (1995: 1:140–41); Egorychev (2006: 160).

70. Thus in November 1968 Zolotukhin announced major over-the-plan allocations of tractors, manure, agricultural machinery, and investment in transportation infrastructure. RGASPI f.17 op.104 d.536 ll.272–73.

71. Saloshenko (2002: 399–400).

72. Saloshenko (2002: 374). The Kuban is the historic southern territory along the Kuban river which straddled all of Krasnodar krai and a part of nearby Stavropol' krai.

73. RGASPI f.17 op.103 d.472 ll.54–58.

74. See RGASPI f.17 op.103 d.474 ll.139–44.; d.477 ll.306–9. As a krai, Krasnodar encompassed an obkom-level administrative unit, the Adygei autonomous oblast.

75. This followed a series of carefully orchestrated attacks on Tupitsyn, especially at the kraikom buro on 9 August and at the kraikom plenum on 19 September, which progressively sapped Tupitsyn of his authority. See RGASPI f.17 op.102 d.504 l.125, op.102 d.500 ll.40–41; op. 103 d.474 ll.80, 91.

76. See especially RGASPI f.17 op.105 d.480 l.47, and also op. 103 d.469 l.189, op.104, d.536 l.282.

77. For the Kiriakin affair, see RGASPI f.17 op.102 d.500 l.42; on other "organizational measures," see op.105 d.479, l.192, d.480 l.54; op.103 d.469 ll.190–91, and op.105 d.479 l.192.

78. Gorbachev (1995: 1:139).

79. This applied to Albert Churkin, Sergei Medunov, A.A. Khomiakov, O.S. Nikitiuk, and N.A. Ogurtsov. At the lower levels, too, the seniority principle was closely adhered to. Thus all eight of the new raikom first secretaries appointed in January 1967 climbed up one rung on the nomenklatura hierarchy. RGASPI f.17 op.103 d.472 ll.54–56.

80. Like Brezhnev, he had to wait nearly three years, until February 1969, before he replaced any of his obkom secretaries—in this case one who was in any case due to retire—or tampered with the composition of the obkom buro. RGASPI f.17 op.105 d.478 ll.4–5.

81. RGASPI f.17 op.102 d.500 l.108.

82. RGASPI f.17 op.105 d.480 l.53.

83. RGASPI f.17 op.102 d.500 l.101; and see his speech of December 1967 in ibid., op.103 d.477 l.309.

84. On this, see Grybkauskas (2018: 454–57).

85. On Kharazov's control of the cadres department and of the department for supervising the KGB, see *Lietuviškoi* (2015: 160).

86. Grybkauskas (2013a: 127, 131, 142, 144–45).

87. Indeed, it was those in the first club who were able to successfully organize and intervene to prevent Maniušis from being nominated as Sniečkus's successor. Grybkauskas (2013a: 133, 136, 143).

88. Grybkauskas (2013a: 134).

89. For overviews, see Dallin (1992) and Kotkin (2008).

90. The effect of horizontal networks on vertical controls is a theme of Wintrobe (1998: 225, 229–30).

91. On the origins and effects of the national rebellions, see in particular Beissinger (2002, 2009).

92. Vaksberg (1991: 11, 16–17, 34–35), and for a more detailed description of the so-called Medunov clan, see 52–61. Also see Mlechin (2008: 262–65). For more on the prohibition under Brezhnev on indicting senior party officials for corruption and on how this was lifted under Andropov, see Duhamel (2010: 32–33, 87–90, 110–11).

CONCLUSION

1. Zubkova (2000), Weiner (2001), Bittner (2008), Edele (2008), Jones (2008), Fürst, Jones, and Morrisey (2008), Lovell (2010), Cohn (2015).

2. See Gorlizki (2002); Gorlizki and Khlevniuk (2004).

3. The incentive problem derives from two considerations: the dictator lacks reliable information on the capacities, preferences, and tasks of actors at the local level; and often these actors have objectives which are different from his. See Laffont and Martimort (2002: 2–3).

4. Scholars who use the selectorate theory include Roeder (1993: 24–25, 70–72) and Geddes et al. (2014: 315). Earlier scholars who did not use the term but made much the same point were Rigby (1959) and Pethybridge (1962). Somewhat confusingly, Bueno de Mesquita et al. (2003) use the term "selectorate" in a quite different way, reserving the term "minimum winning coalition" for what Roeder and others refer to as the selectorate.

5. On the general features of this form of institutional change, which is known as conversion, "the changed enactment of institutional rules due to their strategic redeployment," see Pierson (2004: 137–38), Thelen and Streeck (2005), and Mahoney and Thelen (2010: 15–16).

6. Examples of hegemonic or dominant party regimes include Mexico under the Institutional Revolutionary Party (PRI), Egypt under the National Democratic Party (NDP), and Indonesia under Golkar. On these cases and on the use of the terms "hegemonic" or "dominant party" regimes, see Magaloni (2006), Blaydes (2010), Magaloni and Kricheli (2010), Reuter and Gandhi (2010), and Geddes et al. (2014: 318–19). On the longevity of single party and dominant party regimes with strong supermajorities, see Geddes (2003: 69, 78, 82; 1999: 135) and Svolik (2012: 162, 191–92).

7. Gandhi (2008: 76–82, 100).

8. Svolik (2012: 167–84).

9. Smith (2005), Brownlee (2007), Slater (2010, 2010a), and Levitsky and Way (2012, 2015, 2016).

10. Levitsky and Way (2012: 870–71; 2015: 102).

11. This point was first made by Wintrobe (1998: 219). Note that party membership was not merely encouraged, as in dominant party regimes—cf. Svolik (2012: 180–81)—but was *compulsory* for any aspiring member of the elite.

12. The most lucid exposition of Soviet ideology as a discourse or political language rather than as a belief system is Schull (1992, 1993). For a later assessment that treats Soviet ideology in similar terms, see Yurchak (2006: chaps. 1 and 2). On evaluative terms, propositions, and conventions, see Schull (1992: 735; 1993; 12).

13. Schull (1992: 732–3; 1993: 14).

14. Gorlizki (1995).

15. Note the close attention paid to this very point at the beginning of the speech. *Doklad* (2002: 52–53). This was also the theme of a long piece in *Pravda* of 28 March 1956 under the headline, "Why is the cult of personality alien to the spirit of Marxism-Leninism?" as cited in Dobson (2009: 101).

16. Schull (1992: 736).

17. Gel'man et al. (2003), Gel'man (2010: 9).

18. Chebankova (2005, 2009), Gel'man (2010).

19. Gibson (2005, 2013).

20. This was true of the system of city machine politics in the US from the 1870s to the 1920s and subnational authoritarian regimes in Latin America until the 1980s and 1990s. In the first case political machines headed by local bosses were edged out from below, as a result of the political activism of a rising middle class, and from above, as a result of organized political competition at the federal level. The two eventually fused as Theodore Roosevelt established informal alliances with progressive movements in the cities. By contrast, Russia in the 1990s had neither organized political competition at the statewide level nor a civil movement from below. Gel'man (2010: 4, 13).

21. On this point, see Sharafutdinova (2009: 683) (the source of our quotation). Also see Reuter (2010), Reuter and Robertson (2012: 1030), and Gel'man (2010: 6, 10–12).

22. Hale (2006: 166–73), Reuter and Robertson (2012: 1026–27, 1035–36).

23. On this, see the excellent article by Reuter and Robertson (2012).

24. On this, see, in particular, Ledeneva (2006: chap. 3).

APPENDIX A. A NOTE ON DICTATORSHIP

1. On this, see McCormick (2004: 197–98), Nicolet (2004: 263–65), and Gandhi (2008: 3–7).

2. On parallels between Soviet and Nazi understandings of dictatorship and on how both grew out of a modern understanding of "sovereign dictatorship," see McCormick (2002: 199–200, 208–9).

3. A key impetus behind this dichotomous understanding of dictatorship as "nondemocracy" is the "Democracy and Dictatorship (DD)" measure of political regimes introduced by Przeworski and his associates in the mid-1990s: see Alvarez et al. (1996: 6); Gandhi (2008: 7); Cheibub et al. (2010: 71–74). Other, more informal uses of the term in this dichotomous sense include Moore (1967) and Acemoglu and Robinson (2006).

4. Some definitions, such as Gandhi's (2008: 7), that dictatorship is "a regime in which rulers acquire power by means other than competitive elections," hinge on telling us what dictatorship is not.

5. Geddes claims that her categories are underpinned by her theoretical frame-

work. Yet to the extent that her coding rules rest on detailed instructions on picking out a multitude of observable traits from existing regimes, her approach is inductive. Her debt to the earlier inductive work of Huntington and Linz and Stepan is, in this regard, quite telling. Geddes (2003: 71 n.22, 225–27).

6. Although the terms "minimalist" and "procedural" are usually conjoined, they have different meanings. On this, see Cheibub et al. (2010: 74). However, for convenience we will refer to the two jointly as the minimalist approach.

7. Alvarez et al. (1996: 3–4, 18–21); Cheibub et al. (2010: 70–73); Gandhi (2008: 8–9).

8. Alvarez et al. (1996: 21); Cheibub et al. (2010: 71).

9. Although Svolik (2012: 17, 22–23) claims that his approach is procedural and minimalist, he differs from other minimalists in that at the country level he uses four dimensions for categorizing regimes (ibid., 21). His position is that we should explicitly identify the conceptual dimension of authoritarianism that we want to measure (e.g., degree of military involvement in politics or restrictions on political parties) and *then* develop appropriate scales or typologies (21, 28–29). At the same time, to the extent that he is opposed to "classifying dictatorships into ideal types or according to their prominent descriptive characteristics" (ibid., 32), we place him in the minimalist camp. There is, in addition, a third vein of writers on dictatorship—Olson (1993, 2000), Wintrobe (1993, 1998), and Bueno de Mesquita et al. (2003)—whose approach is minimalist but not procedural in that it focuses on a minimal number of variables while having little to say about institutional procedures. Some of these writers (e.g., Wintrobe) have generated their own sui generis categories of dictatorship while others (e.g., Bueno de Mesquita et al.) go so far as to reject the categories of dictatorship and democracy altogether.

10. For criticism of Geddes on these grounds, see Hadenius and Teorell (2007: 145).

11. The category "personalist" is a distillation of earlier Weberian terms such as "patrimonial," "neo-patrimonial" and "sultanistic" used by, among others, Roth (1968), Linz (1975), Chehabi and Linz (1998), and Bratton and Van de Walle (1997: chap. 3). See Geddes (2003: 71 n.22) and Svolik (2012: 56).

12. Svolik (2012: 31).

13. For evidence, see Gorlizki and Khlevniuk (2004).

14. Geddes (2003: 52); and Geddes et al. (2014: 323).

15. Jackson and Rosberg (1982), for example, argue that variants of this concept can be applied to certain states in postcolonial tropical Africa where political institutions were extremely underdeveloped. One should also note that some minimalists, such as Gandhi (2008: 101), who do not recognize the category of personalist dictatorship, do admit the possibility of "pure autocrats without institutions." As against this, Svolik suggests (2012: 30) that the category wrongly presents two traits—concentration of power in the hands of an individual and the personalization of interactions (i.e., the extent to which political interactions are based on personal ties rather than formal rules)—as distinctive to personalist regimes whereas they exist, to a greater or lesser degree, in all dictatorships. Similar misgivings can be found in Brooker (2000: 37) and Hadenius and Teorell (2007: 149).

16. Svolik moves beyond the empirical distinction between autocracy and oligarchy to advance theoretical micro-foundations for what he sees as "two qualitatively

different power-sharing regimes." According to Svolik, the makeup of these different regimes in effect boils down to one question: Are the dictator's allies capable of replacing him? If the dictator is vulnerable to an allied rebellion, the ruling coalition is a contested autocracy and if not, it is an established autocracy. Svolik (2012: 78 (quotation) and 56, 61).

17. Specifically, they characterize such regimes as "civilian (a residual category often characterized by the presence of a political party as the institution capable of determining the fate of existing governments)." Cheibub et al. (2010: 97; also see 89).

18. See, for example, Svolik (2012: 32–43).

19. Although the mechanism for removing substate leaders tells us little, the *grounds* on which leaders are removed can be instructive, for, as we shall see, they changed markedly over time. Indeed, there are interesting parallels with Svolik's categories for removing leaders through constitutional means (natural, term limit, resignation, elections, and consensus). Svolik (2012: 39–40).

APPENDIX B. UNITS OF ANALYSIS

1. A sixteenth union republic, the Karelian-Finnish SSR, set up in 1941 in the wake of the Winter War with Finland, was dissolved in 1956.

2. We do this to simplify what would otherwise have been an impossibly confusing picture. In the mid-1940s administrative designations were remarkably fluid, with, for example, sixteen new regions having been formed in the Russian Federation between 1943 and 1947. From then until early 1954, when six new regions were formed in the Russian Federation, the situation remained relatively stable.

3. By population size, Azerbaijan and Georgia were equivalent to Gor'kii or Sverdlovsk.

4. The Central Asian republics of Kirgizia, Tajikistan, and Turkmenistan all had their own oblasts (six, five, and four, respectively), but the republics themselves were no larger than some Russian regions. The largest by population, Tajikistan, was broadly comparable to the medium-size Russian provinces of Irkutsk or Novosibirsk.

5. I.e., sixty-six in the Russian Federation, twenty-five in Ukraine, twelve in Belorrusia, sixteen in Uzbekistan, and ten in Kazakhstan, along with the ten other union republics. See Shul'gina (2005: 33).

APPENDIX C. SAMPLE

1. Note that this is a different census date from that for calculating our units of analysis (i.e., 1 July 1947, see appendix B). We were unable to obtain data for our sample for the earlier date.

APPENDIX D. POLITICAL NETWORKS

1. Wasserman and Faust (1994), Borgatti, Everett, and Johnson (2013: 1–2).
2. Knoke (1990: 3–4, 11–14).

3. This is what Borgatti, Everett, and Johnson (2013: 6) refer to as basic network analysis; also see Knoke (1990: 9).

4. The idea of networks having their own norms goes back to a series of seminal American studies from the 1930s and 1940s which found evidence of cohesive nonkin subgroups or cliques within larger organizations, with their own norms and values, which often ran counter to the official or formal culture. See Scott (2000: 16, 20, 100).

5. Borgatti, Everett, and Johnson (2013: 4–5) refer to such relations as ones of "relational cognition."

6. Knoke (1990: 142).

7. Earlier works in this tradition on the Soviet Union include Rigby (1979), Bauman (1979), and Rigby and Harasymiw (1983). In Soviet studies one work that stands at the cusp of the clientelist and network approaches is Willerton (1992: esp. 52–71). While making widespread use of the concept of patron–client relations, Willerton also deployed network tools. First, he argued that the size of a client network "roughly parallels the degree of power and authority" that a patron possesses; in other words, one could empirically measure the power of a politician by the size of his or her network (1990: 52, 61). Second, organizations had different network attributes, and in this regard the party stood out: other things being equal, service in the party bureaucracy was likely to generate a larger network than officeholding in any other state or economic organization. Willerton (1992: 50–51); Jozsa (1983: 144). On the merging of patron–client relations with the wider literature on networks, see Knoke (1990: 13–14, 140–42).

8. On this, see Cook, Rice, and Gerbasi (2004: 196) and Knoke (1990: 108). With regard to the Soviet Union, this line of argument can also be found in Bauman (1979) and Willerton (1992: 7, 232).

APPENDIX E. ARCHIVAL SOURCES

1. E.g., Berliner (1957), Millar, ed. (1992), and Ledeneva (1998).

2. Indeed, very often these scandals were characterized by the *absence* of within-region conflict.

APPENDIX F. THE NOMENKLATURA

1. Oliver (1973), Miller (1977, 1983); Moses (1974, 1981, 1985); Blackwell (1979), Rigby (1978).

2. Urban (1989: 114, 132, 138).

3. Willerton (1992: 2–3, 8, 10–11, 15, 235–36).

4. This included 8,761 functionaries who worked at the republican, krai, and oblast level and 10,278 at the town and district tier. RGANI f.5 op.29 d.14 l.47. These figures do not include functionaries from military and military-naval ministries, the agencies of state control, troops in the ministry of internal affairs and the ministry of state security, and the special courts.

5. RGANI f.5 op.29 d.15 ll.60, 63, 72.

APPENDIX G. REGIONAL PARTY ELECTIONS

1. Gill (1988: 174–75, 194–96).

2. Article 23 in Gill (1988: 169).

3. E.g., Stewart (1968: 33–36).

4. RGANI f.3 op.16 d.70 ll.110–18. The main difference between the 1941 and 1962 versions appears to be the inclusion in the latter of three articles (8–10) on the renewal of party agencies in line with article 25 of the new 1961 Party Statute, on which see Gill (1988: 212).

5. In Russian, the more neutral noun *golosovanie*—literally, "a vote"—is used here rather than *vybory* (elections), which has a presumption of choice and which features in the title to the Instructions.

6. Article 15 and 16 of the 1962 Instruction. RGANI f.3 op.16 d.70 ll.114–15.

7. Articles 18, 20, 22–24. RGANI f.3 op.16 d.70 ll.115–17.

8. Articles 20 and 23. RGANI f.3 op.16 d.70 ll.115–16.

9. We still do not know enough about the practical arrangements for voting. We do know, however, that in some regions the issuing of ballot papers and the voting itself took place in the same room. According to officials from the Central Committee, this increased the pressure on delegates to mark the papers and drop them in the ballot box as quickly as possible, lest they stand out as potential troublemakers. RGASPI f.17 op.88 d.901 l.283.

10. Those people regarded as being elected are the ones who have been voted for by more than half the voting delegates of the conference. Article 26. Although no candidates failed to meet this minimum threshold, a heavy protest vote could seriously dent a leading figure's credibility.

11. Article 19. RGASPI f.17 op.88 d.901 l.115.

12. The 1939 and 1952 party rules dictated that the obkom buro should have no more than eleven members. Unlike the 1939 rules, those of 1952 stipulated that three of the eleven "should be party secretaries confirmed by the Central Committee of the Party." Beyond that, however, the first secretary had considerable leeway, depending on the configuration of the regional power structure and their own preferences. Gill (1988: 175, 195).

Bibliography

ARCHIVES

References refer to f., *fond;* op., *opis'* (plural *opisi*), or inventory; d., *delo,* or file; and l., page number.

Central Archives

Russian State Archive of Social and Political History (RGASPI)

Fond 17. Central Committee
Opis' 3. Politburo
Opisi 48, 50. Department of Party Information at the Administration for Checking Party Organs
Opisi 51–54. Sector for Party Information at the Department of Party, Trade Union, and Komsomol Agencies
Opisi 55–58, 89–91, 93, 94. Sector for Organizational Statutory Questions and Information at the Party Organs Department for the Union Republics
Opisi 102–6. Sector for Information at the Department of Party Organs
Opisi 139, 140. Sector for Information at the Department of Organizational Party Work
Opis' 88. Organizational Instruction Department
Opis' 121. Orgburo and Secretariat
Opis' 122. Organizational Instruction Department and the Administration for Checking Party Organs
Opis' 127. Cadres Administration

Opis' 131. Department for Party, Trade Union, and Komsomol Agencies
Fond 82. V.M. Molotov
Fond 556. RSFSR Buro of the Central Committee
Opisi 10, 14. Department of Party Organs
Opis' 17. Department of Heavy Industry, Transport, and Communications
Opis' 18. Department of Machine Building
Opis' 19. Department of Building and Construction
Opis' 20. Department of Light and Food Industries
Opis' 21. Department of Industry and Transport
Opis' 23. Department of Administrative and Trade–Financial Organs
Fond 574. Central Committee Plenipotentiary for Uzbekistan

State Archive of the Russian Federation (GARF)

Fond 5446. USSR Council of Ministers
Opisi 92–104. Administration of Affairs
Fond 8131. USSR Procuracy

Russian State Archive of Contemporary History (RGANI)

Fond 2. Stenographic Reports and Materials of Central Committee Plenums
Fond 3. Politburo and Presidium of the Central Committee
Fond 4. Secretariat of the Central Committee
Fond 5. Apparatus of the Central Committee
Opis' 15. Department of Party, Trade Union, and Komsomol Agencies
Opis' 16. Department of Propaganda and Agitation
Opis' 25. Technical Secretariat of the Orgburo
Opis' 26. Administration of Affairs
Opis' 29. Department for the Selection and Distribution of Cadres in All Party, Public, and State Organs
Opis' 30. General Department
Opis' 31. Departments of Party Organs and of Party Organs for the Union Republics
Opis' 32. Department of Party Organs for the RSFSR
Opis' 55. Ideology Department
Opisi 58–61, 63. Department of Propaganda
Fond 13. RSFSR Buro of the Central Committee

Archive of the President of the Russian Federation

Fond 3
Opisi 22, 23. Politburo files

Ukrainian Central State Archive of Public Associations (TsDAGOU)

Fond 1. Central Committee of the Ukrainian Communist Party
Opis' 31

Regional Archives

State Archive of Vinnitsa Oblast (DAVO)

Fond 136 Obkom
Opis' 12.
Opis' 29.
Opis' 32.

State Archive of Penza Oblast (GAPO)

Fond 148 Obkom
Opis' 1. Plenums and Materials

State Archive of Cheliabinsk Oblast (OGAChO)

Fond 288
Opis' 42. Plenums and Materials

REFERENCES

Acemoglu, Daron, and James A. Robinson. 2006. *Economic Origins of Dictatorship and Democracy.* New York: Cambridge University Press.

Adler, Nanci. 2012. *Keeping Faith with the Party: Communist Believers Return from the Gulag.* Bloomington: Indiana University Press.

Agarev, Aleksandr. 2005. *Tragicheskaia avantiura: Sel'skoe khoziaistvo Riazansoi oblasti 1950–1960 gg. A.N. Larionov, N.S. Khrushchev i drugie.* Riazan: Russkoe slovo.

Alexopoulos, Golfo. 2005. "Amnesty 1945: The Revolving Door of Stalin's Gulag." *Slavic Review* 64 (2): 274–306.

———. 2008. "Stalin and the Politics of Kinship: Practices of Collective Punishment, 1920s–1940s." *Comparative Studies in Society and History* 50 (1): 91–117.

———. 2017. *Illness and Inhumanity in Stalin's Gulag.* New Haven: Yale University Press.

Almakaev, P.A. 1998. *Gody i liudi. Vospominaniia i razmyshleniia.* Ioshkar-Ola.

Altstadt, Audrey L. 2016. *The Politics of Culture in Soviet Azerbaijan, 1920–1940.* London: Routledge.

Alvarez, Michael E., José Antonio Cheibub, Fernando Limongi, and Adam Przeworski. 1996. "Classifying Political Regimes." *Studies in Comparative International Development* 31 (2): 3–36.

Amosova, A.A. 2016. *Predannyi zabveniu: politicheskaia biografiia Petra Popkova, 1937–1950.* Saint Petersburg: Ateleiia.

Anderson, Benedict. 1991. *Imagined Communities: Reflections on the Origin and Spread of Nationalism.* Rev. ed. London: Verso.

Armstrong, John A. 1959. *The Soviet Bureaucratic Elite: A Case Study of the Ukrainian Apparatus.* New York: Praeger.

———. 1966. "Party Bifurcation and Elite Interests." *Soviet Studies* 17 (4): 417–30.

Arrow, Kenneth J. 1974. *The Limits of Organization.* New York: W.W. Norton.

Avalishvili, Levan. 2016. "The March 1956 Events in Georgia: Based on Oral History Interviews and Archival Documents." In Timothy K. Blauvelt and Jeremy Smith, eds., *Georgia after Stalin: Nationalism and Soviet Power,* 32–52. Abingdon: Routledge.

Avtorkhanov, Abdurakhman. 1966. *The Communist Party Apparatus.* Chicago: Henry Regnery.

Baberowski, Jörg. 2010. *Vrag est' vezde: Stalinizm na Kavkaze.* Moscow: Rosspen.

Bacharach, Michael, and Diego Gambetta. 2001. "Trust in Signs." In Karen S. Cook, ed, *Trust in Society,* 148–84. New York: Russell Sage.

Bahry, Donna. 1987. *Outside Moscow: Power, Politics, and Budgetary Policy in the Soviet Republics.* New York: Columbia University Press.

Baibakov, N.K. 1998. *Ot Stalina do El'tsina.* Moscow: GazOil Press.

Ballis, William B. 1961. "Political Implications of Recent Soviet Economic Reorganizations." *Review of Politics* 23 (2): 153–71.

Barenberg, Alan. 2014. *Gulag Town, Company Town: Forced Labor and Its Legacy in Vorkuta.* New Haven: Yale University Press.

Barkey, Karen. 1994. *Bandits and Bureaucrats: The Ottoman Route to State Centralization.* Ithaca: Cornell University Press.

Barnes, Steven A. 2011. *Death and Redemption: The Gulag and the Shaping of Soviet Society.* Princeton: Princeton University Press.

Baron, Samuel. 2001. *Bloody Saturday in the Soviet Union: Novocherkassk, 1962.* Stanford: Stanford University Press.

Barsukov, Nikolai. 1991. *XX S'ezd KPSS i ego istoricheskie real'nosti.* Moscow: Politizdat.

Bauer, Raymond A., Alex Inkeles, and Clyde Kluckhorn. 1956. *How the Soviet System Works: Cultural, Psychological and Social Themes.* New York: Vintage.

Bauman, Zygmunt. 1979. "Comment on Eastern Europe." *Studies in Comparative Communism* 12 (2–3): 184–89.

Beissinger, Mark R. 2002. *Nationalist Mobilization and the Collapse of the Soviet State.* Cambridge: Cambridge University Press.

———. 2009. "Nationalism and the Collapse of Soviet Communism." *Contemporary European History* 18 (3): 331–47.

Belova, Eugenia. 2001. "Economic Crime and Punishment." In Paul R. Gregory, ed., *Behind the Façade of Stalin's Command Economy: Evidence from the Soviet State and Party Archives,* 131–58. Stanford: Hoover Institution Press.

Belova, Eugenia, and Valery Lazarev. 2012. *Funding Loyalty: The Economics of the Communist Party.* New Haven: Yale University Press.

Benton, Allyson Lucinda. 2012. "Bottom-Up Challenges to National Democracy: Mexico's (Legal) Subnational Authoritarian Enclaves." *Comparative Politics* 44 (3): 253–71.

Berliner, Joseph S. 1957. *Factory and Manager in the USSR.* Cambridge: Harvard University Press.

Berman, Harold J. 1966. *Soviet Criminal Law and Procedure. The RSFSR Codes.* Translated by H.J. Berman and James W. Spindler. Cambridge: Harvard University Press.

Biddulph, Howard. 1983. "Local Interest Articulation at CPSU Congresses." *World Politics* 36 (1): 28–52.

Bilinsky, Yaroslav. 1967. "The Ruler and the Ruled." *Problems of Communism* 16 (5): 16–26.

Billig, Michael. 1995. *Banal Nationalism.* London: Sage.

Bittner, Stephen V. 2008. *The Many Lives of Khrushchev's Thaw: Experience and Memory in Moscow's Arbat.* Ithaca: Cornell University Press.

———. 2014. "What's in a Name? De-Stalinization and the End of the Soviet Union." In Thomas M. Bohn, Rayk Einax, and Michel Abesser, eds., *De-Stalinization Reconsidered: Persistence and Change in the Soviet Union,* 31–42. Frankfurt: Campus Verlag.

Blackwell, Robert E. 1972a. "Elite Recruitment and Functional Change: An Analysis of the Soviet Obkom Elite 1950–1968." *Journal of Politics* 34 (1): 124–52.

———. 1972b. "Career Development in the Soviet Obkom Elite." *Soviet Studies* 24(1): 24–40.

———. 1973. "The Soviet Political Elite: Alternative Recruitment Policies at the Obkom Elite." *Comparative Politics* 6 (1): 99–121.

———. 1979. "Cadres Policy in the Brezhnev Era." *Problems of Communism* 28 (2): 29–42.

Blackwell, Robert E., and William E. Hulbary. 1973. "Political Mobility among Soviet Obkom Elites: The Effects of Regime, Social Background and Career Development." *American Journal of Political Science* 17 (4): 721–43.

Blauvelt, Timothy K. 2009. "Status Shift and Ethnic Mobilisation in the March 1956 Events in Georgia." *Europe-Asia Studies* 61 (4): 651–68.

———. 2011. "March of the Chekists: Beria's Secret Police Patronage Network and Soviet Crypto-Politics." *Communist and Post-Communist Studies* 44 (1): 73–88.

Blauvelt, Timothy K., and Jeremy Smith, eds. 2016. *Georgia after Stalin: Nationalism and Soviet Power*. Abingdon: Routledge.

———. 2016a. "Introduction." In Timothy K. Blauvelt and Jeremy Smith, eds., *Georgia after Stalin: Nationalism and Soviet Power*, 1–12. Abingdon: Routledge.

Blaydes, Lisa. 2010. *Elections and Distributive Politics in Mubarak's Egypt*. New York: Cambridge University Press.

Blitstein, Peter A. 2001. "Nation-Building or Russification? Obligatory Russian Instruction in the Soviet Non-Russian School, 1938–1953." In Ronald Grigor Suny and Terry Martin, eds., *A State of Nations: Empire and Nation-Making in the Age of Lenin and Stalin*, 253–74. New York: Oxford University Press.

Bohn, Thomas M. 2014. "'Closed Cities' versus 'Open Society'? The Interaction of De-Stalinization and Urbanization." In Thomas M. Bohn, Rayk Einax, and Michel Abesser, eds., *De-Stalinization Reconsidered: Persistence and Change in the Soviet Union*, 115–31. Frankfurt: Campus Verlag.

Boix, Carles, and Milan W. Svolik. 2013. "The Foundations of Limited Authoritarian Government: Institutions, Commitment, and Power-Sharing in Dictatorships." *Journal of Politics* 75 (2): 300–16.

Borgatti, Stephen P., Martin G. Everett, and Jeffrey C. Johnson. 2013. *Analysing Social Networks*. Thousand Oaks, CA.: Sage.

Borisov, S.Z. 2000. *Almazy i vozhdi*. Moscow: Aiyna.

Brancati, Dawn. 2014. "Democratic Authoritarianism: Origins and Effects." *Annual Review of Political Science* 17: 313–26.

Brandenberger, David. 2001. "'. . . It is Imperative to Advance Russian Nationalism as the First Priority': Debates within the Stalinist Ideological Establishment, 1941–1945." In Ronald Grigor Suny and Terry Martin, eds., *A State of Nations: Empire and Nation-Making in the Age of Lenin and Stalin*, 275–99. New York: Oxford University Press.

———. 2002. *National Bolshevism: Stalinist Mass Culture and the Formation of Modern Russian National Identity, 1931–1956*. Cambridge: Harvard University Press.

Bratton, Michael, and Nicolas Van de Walle. 1997. *Democratic Experiments in Africa: Regime Transitions in Comparative Perspective*. New York: Cambridge University Press.

Breslauer, George W. 1977. "The Twenty-Fifth Congress: Domestic Issues." In Alexander Dallin, ed., *The Twenty-Fifth Congress of the CPSU: Assessment and Context*, 7–25. Stanford: Stanford University Press.

————. 1980. "Khrushchev Reconsidered." In Stephen F. Cohen, Alexander Rabinowitch, and Robert Sharlet, eds., *The Soviet Union since Stalin*, 50–70. Bloomington: Indiana University Press.

————. 1982. *Khrushchev and Brezhnev as Leaders: Building Authority in Soviet Politics*. Hemel Hempstead: George Allen and Unwin.

————. 1986. "Provincial Party Leaders' Demand Articulation and the Nature of Centre-Periphery Relations in the USSR." *Slavic Review* 45 (4): 650–72.

Breuilly, John. 1985. *Nationalism and the State*. Manchester: Manchester University Press.

Brooker, Paul. 2000. *Non-Democratic Regimes*. Basingstoke: Palgrave Macmillan.

Brownlee, Jason. 2007. *Authoritarianism in an Age of Democratization*. New York: Cambridge University Press.

Brubaker, Rogers. 1996. *Nationalism Reframed: Nationhood and the National Question in the New Europe*. New York: Cambridge University Press.

Brudny, Yitzhak M. 1998. *Reinventing Russia: Russian Nationalism and the Soviet State, 1953–1991*. Cambridge: Harvard University Press.

Bueno de Mesquita, Bruce, Alastair Smith, Randolph M. Siverson, and James D. Morrow. 2003. *The Logic of Political Survival*. Cambridge: MIT Press.

Cadiot, Juliette. 2013. "Equal Before the Law? Soviet Justice, Criminal Proceedings against Communist Party Members, and the Legal Landscape of the USSR from 1945 to 1953." *Jahrbücher für Geschichte Osteuropas* 61 (2): 249–69.

Cadiot, Juliette, and Marc Elie. 2017. *Histoire du Goulag*. Paris: La Découverte.

Chebankova, Elena A. 2005. "The Limitations of Central Authority in the Regions and the Implications for the Evolution of Russia's Federal System." *Europe-Asia Studies* 57 (7): 933–49.

————. 2009. *Russia's Federal Relations, Putin's Reforms and Management of the Regions*. Abingdon: Routledge.

Chehabi, H.E., and Juan J. Linz, eds. 1998. *Sultanistic Regimes*. Baltimore: Johns Hopkins University Press.

Cheibub, José Antonio, Jennifer Gandhi, and James Raymond Vreeland. 2010. "Democracy and Dictatorship Revisited." *Public Choice* 143: 67–101.

Chotiner, Barbara A. 1984. *Khrushchev's Party Reform: Coalition Building and Institutional Innovation*. Westport, CT.: Greenwood.

Ch'ü, T'ung-Tsu. 1962. *Local Government in China under the Ch'ing*. Cambridge: Harvard University Press.

Chuianov, A.S. 1977. *Na stremnine veka: zapiski sekretaria obkoma*. Moscow: Politizdat.

Churbanov, Iurii. 1993. *Ia raskazhu vse kak bylo . . .* 2nd rev. ed. Moscow: Nezavisimaia gazeta.

Clark, Katerina. 2000. *The Soviet Novel: History as Ritual.* 3rd ed. Bloomington: Indiana University Press.

Clark, William A. 2013. "Khrushchev's 'Second' First Secretaries: Career Trajectories and Unification of Oblast Party Organizations." *Kritika* 14 (3): 279–312.

Cleary, J.W. 1974. "Elite Career Patterns in a Soviet Republic." *British Journal of Political Science* 4 (3): 323–44.

Cohen, Stephen F. 1980. "The Friends and Foes of Change: Reformism and Conservatism in the Soviet Union." In Stephen F. Cohen, Alexander Rabinowitch, and Robert Sharlet, eds., *The Soviet Union since Stalin,* 11–31. Bloomington: Indiana University Press.

Cohn, Edward. 2013. "Policing the Party: Conflicts between Local Prosecutors and Party Leaders under Late Stalinism." *Europe-Asia Studies* 65 (10): 1912–30.

———. 2015. *The High Title of a Communist: Postwar Party Discipline and the Values of the Soviet Regime.* Dekalb: Northern Illinois University Press.

———. 2018. "The Paradox of Party Discipline in the Khrushchev-Era Communist Party." In Rüdiger Bergien and Jens Gieseke, eds., *Communist Parties Revisited: Socio-Cultural Approaches to the Party in the Soviet Bloc, 1956–1961,* 23–45. Oxford: Berghahn.

Conquest, Robert. 1961. *Power and Policy in the USSR: The Study of Soviet Dynastics.* London: Macmillan.

Cook, Karen S., Russell Hardin, and Margaret Levi. 2005. *Cooperation without Trust.* New York: Russell Sage.

Cook, Karen S., Eric R.W. Rice, and Alexandra Gerbasi. 2004. "The Emergence of Trust Networks under Uncertainty." In Janos Kornai, Bo Rothstein, and Susan Rose-Ackerman, eds., *Creating Social Trust in Post-Socialist Transition,* 193–212. New York: Palgrave.

Cook, Karen S., Margaret Levi, and Russell Hardin, eds. 2009. *Whom Can We Trust? How Groups, Networks, and Institutions Make Trust Possible.* New York: Russell Sage.

Dale, Robert. 2015. *Demobilized Veterans in Late Stalinist Leningrad: Soldiers to Civilians.* London: Bloomsbury Academic.

Dallin, Alexander. 1992. "Causes of the Collapse of the USSR." *Post-Soviet Affairs* 8 (2): 279–302.

Daniels, Robert V. 1966. "Stalin's Rise to Dictatorship." In Alexander Dallin and Daniel F. Westin, eds., *Politics in the Soviet Union: Seven Cases,* 1–38. New York: Harcourt, Brace and World.

Danilov, A.A., and A.V. Pyzhikov. 2001. *Rozhdenie sverkhderzhavy. SSSR v pervye poslevoennye gody.* Moscow: Rosspen.

Darden, Keith. 2001. "Blackmail as a Tool of State Domination: Ukraine under Kuchma." *East European Constitutional Review* 10 (2): 67–71.

Davenport, Christian. 2007. "State Repression and the Tyrannical Peace." *Journal of Peace Research* 44 (4): 485–504.

Davies, R.W. 1989. *The Soviet Economy in Turmoil, 1929–1930.* Cambridge: Harvard University Press.

Delo Beriia. Prigovor obzhalovaniiu ne podlezhit. 2012. Compiled and edited by V.N. Khaustov. Moscow: MFD.

Denningaus, Viktor, and Andrei Savin. 2014. " 'Smotrish, i Mane, i Tane kakoi-to 'Znak Pocheta' popadet.' Brezhnevskaia 'industriia' nagrazhdenii i sovetskoe obshchestvo." *Rossiiskaia Istoriia* 2: 127–49.

Desai, Raj M., Anders Olofsgård, and Tarik M. Yousef. 2009. "The Logic of Authoritarian Bargains." *Economics and Politics* 21 (1): 93–125.

Diekmann, Andreas, Ben Jann, Wojtek Przepiorka, and Stefan Wehrli. 2014. "Reputation Formation and the Evolution of Cooperation in Anonymous Online Markets." *American Sociological Review* 79 (1): 65–85.

Dimitrov, Martin K. 2014. "Tracking Public Opinion under Authoritarianism: The Case of the Soviet Union during the Brezhnev Era." *Russian History* 41: 329–53.

Dobson, Miriam. 2009. *Khrushchev's Cold Summer: Gulag Returnees, Crime, and the Fate of Reform after Stalin.* Ithaca: Cornell University Press.

Doklad N.S. Khrushcheva o kul'te lichnosti Stalina na XX s'ezde KPSS. Dokumenty. 2002. Edited by K. Aimermakher. Moscow: Rosspen.

Dokshokov, M.I. 1998. *Glavnaia privilegiia—otvetstvennost' za drugikh.* Nal'chik: El'-FA.

Donovan, Victoria S. 2015. "How Well Do You Know Your Krai? The Kraevedenie Revival and Patriotic Politics in Late Khrushchev-Era Russia." *Slavic Review* 74 (3): 464–83.

———. 2019. *Chronicles in Stone: Preservation, Patriotism, and Identity in Northwest Russia.* DeKalb: Northern Illinois University Press.

Duhamel, Luc. 2010. *The KGB Campaign against Corruption in Moscow, 1982–1987.* Pittsburgh: University of Pittsburgh Press.

Dunham, Vera S. 1976. *In Stalin's Time: Middleclass Values in Soviet Fiction.* New York: Cambridge University Press.

Easter, Gerald. 2000. *Reconstructing the State: Personal Networks and Elite Identity.* New York: Cambridge University Press.

Edele, Mark. 2006. "Soviet Veterans as an Entitlement Group, 1945–1955." *Slavic Review* 65 (1): 111–37.

———. 2008. *Soviet Veterans of the Second World War: A Popular Movement in an Authoritarian Society, 1941–1991.* Oxford: Oxford University Press.

Eggertsson, Thráinn. 1990. *Economic Behaviour and Institutions.* Cambridge: Cambridge University Press.

Egorov, Georgy, and Konstantin Sonin. 2011. "Dictators and Their Viziers: Endogenizing the Loyalty–Competence Trade-off." *Journal of the European Economic Association* 9 (5): 903–30.

Elie, Marc. 2013. "Khrushchev's Gulag: The Soviet Penitentiary System after Stalin's Death, 1953–1964." In Denis Kozlov and Eleonory Gilburd, eds., *The Thaw: Soviet Society and Culture during the 1950s and 1960s,* 109–42. Toronto: University of Toronto Press.

Embree, G.D. 1959. *The Soviet Union between the 19th and 20th Party Congresses, 1952–1956.* The Hague: Martinus Nijhoff.

Escribà-Folch, Abel. 2013. "Repression, Political Threats, and Survival under Autocracy." *International Political Science Review* 34 (5): 543–60.

Fainsod, Merle. 1958. *Smolensk under Soviet Rule.* Cambridge: Harvard University Press.

———. 1963. *How Russia Is Ruled.* 2nd ed. Cambridge: Harvard University Press.

Fairbanks, Charles H. 1978. "National Cadres as a Force in the Soviet System: The Evidence of Beria's Career, 1949–1953." In Jeremy Azrael, ed., *Soviet Nationality Policies and Practice,* 144–86. New York: Praeger.

———. 1983. "Clientelism and Higher Politics in Georgia, 1949–1953." In Ronald Suny, ed., *Transcaucasia: Nationalism and Social Change,* 339–68. Ann Arbor: University of Michigan Press.

Fedorov, A.N. 2016a. "I.M. Zal'tsman i cheliabinskii obkom BKP(b): vzaimootnosheniia mestnykh partiinykh i khoziaistvennykh organov v pervye poslevoennye gody." *Vestnik Tomskogo gosudarstvennogo universiteta. Istoriia* 3 (41): 65–73.

———. 2016b. "'Magnitogorskoe delo' 1949 g.: deiatel'nost' mestnykh partiinykh organov v usloviiakh poslevoennogo vremeni." *Problemy istorii, filosofii, kul'tury.* (2): 302–14.

Fieseler, Beate. 2006. "The Bitter Legacy of the 'Great Patriotic War': Red Army Disabled Soldiers under Late Stalinism." In Juliane Fürst, ed., *Late Stalinist Russia: Society between Reconstruction and Reinvention,* 46–61. Abingdon: Routledge.

Filtzer, Donald. 1992. *Soviet Workers and De-Stalinization: The Consolidation of the Modern System of Soviet Production Relations, 1953–1964.* Cambridge: Cambridge University Press.

———. 2002. *Soviet Workers and Late Stalinism: Labour and the Restoration of the Stalinist System after World War II.* Cambridge: Cambridge University Press.

FirstBook of Demographics for the Republics of the Former Soviet Union, 1951–1990. 1992. Shady Side, MD: New World Demographics, L.C.

Fitzpatrick, Sheila. 1985. "Postwar Soviet Society: The 'Return to Normalcy,' 1945–1953." In Susan J. Linz, ed., *The Impact of World War II on the Soviet Union,* 129–56. Totowa, NJ: Rowman and Allanhead.

———. 1992a [1979]. "Stalin and the Making of a New Elite, 1928–1939." *Slavic Review* 38: 377–402. Reprinted in Sheila Fitzpatrick, *The Cultural Front: Power and Culture in Revolutionary Russia,* 149–82. Ithaca: Cornell University Press.

———. 1992b [1988]. "Becoming Cultured: Socialist Realism and the Representation of Privilege and Taste." Reprinted in Sheila Fitzpatrick, *The Cultural Front: Power and Culture in Revolutionary Russia,* 216–37. Ithaca: Cornell University Press.

———. 1993. "Ascribing Class: The Construction of Social Identity in Soviet Russia." *Journal of Modern History* 65 (4): 745–70.

———. 2015. *On Stalin's Team: The Years of Living Dangerously in Soviet Politics.* Princeton: Princeton University Press.

Frank, Peter. 1971. "The CPSU Obkom First Secretary: A Profile." *British Journal of Political Science* 1 (1): 173–90.

———. 1974. "Constructing a Classified Ranking of CPSU Provincial Committees." *British Journal of Political Science* 4 (2): 217–30.

Friedrich, Carl J., and Zbigniew K. Brzezinski. 1956. *Totalitarian Dictatorship and Autocracy.* Cambridge: Harvard University Press.

Fürst, Juliane. 2010. *Stalin's Last Generation: Post-War Youth and the Emergence of Mature Socialism.* Oxford: Oxford University Press.

Fürst, Juliane, Polly Jones, and Susan Morrisey, eds. 2008. "The Relaunch of the Soviet Project, 1945–1964." *Slavonic and East European Review* 86 (2): 201–394.

Gambetta, Diego. 2009. *Codes of the Underworld: How Criminals Communicate.* Princeton: Princeton University Press.

Gandhi, Jennifer. 2008. *Political Institutions under Dictatorship.* New York: Cambridge University Press.

Gandhi, Jennifer, and Ellen Lust-Okar. 2009. "Elections under Authoritarianism." *Annual Review of Political Science* 12: 403–22.

Geddes, Barbara. 1999. "What Do We Know about Democratization after Twenty Years?" *Annual Review of Political Science* 2: 115–44.

———. 2003. *Paradigms and Sand Castles: Theory Building and Research Design in Comparative Politics.* Ann Arbor: University of Michigan Press.

Geddes, Barbara, Joseph Wright, and Erica Frantz. 2014. "Autocratic Breakdown and Regime Transitions: A New Data Set." *Perspectives on Politics* 12 (2): 313–31.

Gellner, Ernest. 2006. *Nations and Nationalism.* 2nd ed. with an introduction by John Breuilly. Oxford: Blackwell.

Gel'man, Vladimir. 2010. "The Dynamics of Sub-National Authoritarianism: Russia in Comparative Perspective." In Vladimir Gel'man and Cameron Ross, eds., *The Politics of Sub-National Authoritarianism in Russia,* 1–19. Surrey: Ashgate.

Gel'man, Vladimir, Sergei Ryzhenkov, and Michael Brie. 2003. *Making and Breaking Democratic Transitions: The Comparative Politics of Russia's Regions.* Lanham, MD: Rowman and Littlefield.

General'nyi sekretar' L.I. Brezhnev 1964–1982. 2006. Edited by Sergei Kudriashov. Moscow: Rodina.

Gervasoni, Carlos. 2010. "A Rentier Theory of Subnational Regimes: Fiscal Federalism, Democracy, and Authoritarianism in the Argentine Provinces." *World Politics* 62 (2): 302–40.

Getty, J. Arch. 1985. *Origins of the Great Purges: The Soviet Communist Party Reconsidered, 1933–1938.* Cambridge: Cambridge University Press.

———. 1991. "State and Society under Stalin: Constitutions and Elections in the 1930s." *Slavic Review* 50 (1): 18–35.

———. 2016. "The Rise and Fall of a Party First Secretary: Vainov of Iaroslavl'." In James Harris, ed., *The Anatomy of Terror: Political Violence under Stalin,* 66–84. Oxford: Oxford University Press.

Getty, J. Arch, and Oleg V. Naumov. 1999. *The Road to Terror: Stalin and the Self-Destruction of the Bolsheviks, 1932–1939.* New Haven: Yale University Press.

Gibson, Edward L. 2005. "Boundary Control: Subnational Authoritarianism in Democratic Countries." *World Politics* 58 (1): 101–32.

———. 2013. *Boundary Control: Subnational Authoritarianism in Federal Democracies.* New York: Cambridge University Press.

Gill, Graeme. 1988. *The Rules of the Communist Party of the Soviet Union.* Houndmills, Basingstoke: Macmillan.

———. 1990. *The Origins of the Stalinist Political System.* Cambridge: Cambridge University Press.

Giraudy, Augustina. 2015. *Democrats and Autocrats: Pathways of Subnational Undemocratic Regime Continuity within Democratic Countries.* New York: Oxford University Press.

Goldman, Wendy Z. 2007. *Terror and Democracy in the Age of Stalin: The Social Dynamics of Repression.* Cambridge: Cambridge University Press.

Gol'dshtein, Ia. E. 1995. *Otkrovenno govoria. Vospominaniia, razmyshleniia.* Cheliabinsk: Rifei.

Gorbachev, Mikhail. 1995. *Zhizn' i reformy.* 2 vols. Moscow: Novosti.

Gorlizki, Yoram. 1995. "Party Revivalism and the Death of Stalin." *Slavic Review* 54 (1): 1–22.

———. 1996. "Anti-Ministerialism and the USSR Ministry of Justice, 1953–56: A Study in Organizational Decline." *Europe-Asia Studies* 48 (8): 1279–1318.

———. 1997. "Political Reform and Local Party Interventions under Khrushchev." In Peter Solomon, ed., *Reforming Justice in Russia, 1864–1994: Power, Culture and the Limits of Legal Order*, 258–82. New York: M.E. Sharpe.

———. 2002. "Ordinary Stalinism: The Council of Ministers and the Soviet Neo-Patrimonial State, 1945–1953." *Journal of Modern History* 74 (4): 699–736.

———. 2010. "Too Much Trust: Regional Party Leaders and Local Political Networks under Brezhnev." *Slavic Review* 69 (3): 676–700.

———. 2011. "Governing the Interior: Extraordinary Forms of Rule and the Regional Party Apparatus in the Second World War." *Cahiers du Monde Russe* 52 (2–3): 321–40.

———. 2013a. "Structures of Trust after Stalin." *Slavonic and East European Review* 91 (1): 119–46.

———. 2013b. "Scandal in Riazan: Networks of Trust and the Social Dynamics of Deception." *Kritika* 14 (2): 243–78.

———. 2016. "Theft under Stalin: A Property Rights Analysis." *Economic History Review* 69 (1): 288–313.

Gorlizki, Yoram, and Oleg Khlevniuk. 2004. *Cold Peace: Stalin and the Ruling Circle, 1945–1953*. New York: Oxford University Press.

Goudoever, Albert P. van. 1986. *The Limits of Destalinization in the Soviet Union: Political Rehabilitations in the Soviet Union since Stalin*. Translated by Frans Hijkoop. London: Croom Helm.

Granovetter, Mark. 1985. "Economic Action and Social Structure: The Problem of Embeddedness." *American Journal of Sociology* 91 (3): 481–510.

Gregory, Paul R. 1990. *Restructuring the Soviet Economic Bureaucracy*. Cambridge: Cambridge University Press.

———. 2008. *Terror by Quota: State Security from Lenin to Stalin (An Archival Study)*. New Haven: Yale University Press.

Gregory, Paul R., and Mark Harrison. 2005. "Allocation under Dictatorship: Research in Stalin's Archives." *Journal of Economic Literature* 43 (3): 721–61.

Greif, Avner. 1993. "Contract Enforceability and Economic Institutions in Early Trade: The Maghribi Traders' Coalition." *American Economic Review* 83 (3): 525–48.

Grishin, V.V. 1996. *Ot Khrushcheva do Gorbacheva: Politicheskie portrety piati gensekov i A.N. Kosygina*. Edited and compiled by Iu. Iziumov. Moscow: Aspol.

Gromow, Jukka. 2003. *Caviar with Champagne: Common Luxury and the Ideals of the Good Life in Stalin's Russia*. Oxford: Berg.

Grybkauskas, Saulius. 2013. "The Role of the Second Party Secretary in the 'Election of the First': The Political Mechanism for the Appointment of the Head of Lithuania in 1974." *Kritika* 14 (2): 343–66.

———. 2013a. "The Hunting Club of Petras Griškevičius and the Consolidation of the Lithuanian Nomenklatura." *Lithuanian Historical Studies* 18: 123–45.

———. 2014. "Imperializing the Soviet Federation? The Institution of the Second Secretary in the Soviet Republics." *Ab Imperio* no. 3: 267–92.

———. 2018. "Anti-Soviet Protests and the Localism of the Baltic Republics' *Nomenklatura*: Explaining the Interaction." *Journal of Baltic Studies* 49 (4): 447–62.

GULAG 1918–1960. 2000. Compiled by A.I. Kokurin and N.V. Petrov. Moscow: Materik.

Gustafson, Thane. 1981. *Reform in Soviet Politics: Lessons of Recent Policies on Land and Water*. Cambridge: Cambridge University Press.

Hadenius, Axel, and Jan Teorell. 2007. "Pathways from Authoritarianism." *Journal of Democracy* 18 (1): 143–56.

Hale, Henry E. 2006. *Why Not Parties in Russia? Democracy, Federalism, and the State*. New York: Cambridge University Press.

Hammer, Darrel P. 1970. "The Dilemma of Party Growth." *Problems of Communism* 20 (4): 16–21.

Hardin, Russell. 2002. *Trust and Trustworthiness*. New York: Russell Sage.

Hardy, Jeffrey S. 2016. *The Gulag after Stalin: Redefining Punishment in Khrushchev's Soviet Union, 1953–1964*. Ithaca: Cornell University Press.

Harris, James R. 1999. *The Great Urals: Regionalism and the Evolution of the Soviet System*. Ithaca: Cornell University Press.

Harrison, Mark. 2011. "Forging Success: Soviet Managers and Accounting Fraud, 1943–1962." *Journal of Comparative Economics* 39 (1): 43–64.

———. 2016. *One Day We Will Live without Fear: Everyday Lives under the Soviet Police State*. Stanford: Hoover Institution Press.

Hasanli, Jamil. 2006. *At the Dawn of the Cold War: The Soviet–American Crisis over Iranian Azerbaijan, 1941–1946*. Lanham, MD: Rowman and Littlefield.

———. 2015. *Khrushchev's Thaw and National Identity in Soviet Azerbaijan, 1954–1959*. Lanham, MD: Rowman and Littlefield.

Hauslohner, Peter. 1980. "Prefects as Senators: Soviet Regional Politicians Look to Foreign Policy." *World Politics* 33 (1): 197–233.

———. 1987. "Politics before Gorbachev: De-Stalinization and the Roots of Reform." In Seweryn Bialer, ed., *Politics, Society and Nationality inside Gorbachev's Russia*, 41–90. Boulder: Westview.

Heinzen, James. 2006. "A 'Campaign Spasm': Graft and the Limits of the 'Campaign' against Bribery after the Great Patriotic War." In Juliane Fürst, ed., *Late Stalinist Russia: Society between Reconstruction and Reinvention*, 123–41. Abingdon: Routledge.

———. 2016. *The Art of the Bribe: Corruption under Stalin, 1943–1953*. New Haven: Yale University Press.

Hessler, Julie. 2004. *A Social History of Soviet Trade*. Princeton: Princeton University Press.

Hill, Ronald J. 1977. *Soviet Political Elites: The Case of Tiraspol*. London: Martin Robertson.

Hirsch, Francine. 2005. *Empire of Nations: Ethnographic Knowledge and the Making of the Soviet Union*. Ithaca: Cornell University Press

Hodnett, Grey. 1965. "The Obkom First Secretaries." *Slavic Review* 24 (4): 636–52.

———. 1967. "The Debate over Soviet Federalism." *Soviet Studies* 18 (4): 458–81.

———. 1978. *Leadership in the Soviet Republics: A Quantitative Study of Recruitment Policy*. Oakville, Ontario: Mosaic Press.

Hodnett, Grey, and Val Ogareff. 1973. *Leaders of the Soviet Republics 1955–1972: A Guide to Posts and Occupants*. Canberra: Australian National University.

Hooper, Cynthia. 2006. "A Darker 'Big Deal': Concealing Party Crimes in the post–Second World War Era." In Juliane Fürst, ed., *Late Stalinist Russia: Society between Reconstruction and Reinvention*, 142–63. Abingdon: Routledge.

Hornsby, Robert. 2013. *Protest, Reform and Repression in Khrushchev's Soviet Union*. Cambridge: Cambridge University Press.

———. 2014. "A 'Merciless Struggle': De-Stalinization and the 1957 Clampdown on Dissent." In Thomas M. Bohn, Rayk Einax, Michel Abesser, eds., *De-Stalinization Reconsidered: Persistence and Change in the Soviet Union*, 93–112. Frankfurt: Campus Verlag.

Hosking, Geoffrey. 1991. *The Awakening of the Soviet Union*. Rev. ed. London: Mandarin.

———. 2000. "Patronage and the Russian State." *Slavonic and East European Review*, 78 (2): 301–20.

Hough, Jerry F. 1969. *The Soviet Prefects: The Local Party Organs in Industrial Decision-Making*. Cambridge: Harvard University Press.

Hroch, Miroslav. 1985. *Social Preconditions of National Revival in Europe: A Comparative Analysis of the Social Composition of Patriotic Groups among the Smaller European Nations.* Translated by Ben Fowkes. Cambridge: Cambridge University Press.

Hughes, James, and Peter John. 2003. "Local Elites in Russia's Transition: Generation Effects on Adaptation and Competition." In Anton Steen and Vladimir Gelman, eds., *Elites and Democratic Development in Russia,* 124–47. London: Routledge.

Huntington, Samuel P. 1968. *Political Order in Changing Societies.* New Haven: Yale University Press.

———. 1970. "Social and Institutional Dynamics of One-Party Systems." In Samuel Huntington and Clement Moore, eds., *Authoritarian Politics in Modern Society: The Dynamics of Established One-Party Systems,* 3–47. New York: Basic Books.

———. 1993. *The Third Wave: Democratization in the Late Twentieth Century.* Norman: University of Oklahoma Press.

Ironside, Kristy. 2018. "Money and the Pursuit of Communist Prosperity in the Postwar Soviet Union, 1945–1964." Manuscript.

Ismailov, El'dar. 2003. *Vlast' i narod. Poslevoennyi Stalinism v Azerbaidzhane, 1945–1953.* Baku: "Adil'ogly."

Ivanova, G.V., ed. 1990. *Ot ottepeli do zastoia.* Moscow: Sovetskaia rossiia.

Jackson, Robert H., and Carl G. Rosberg. 1982. *Personal Rule in Black Africa: Prince, Autocrat, Prophet, Tyrant.* Berkeley: University of California Press.

Jensen, Michael C., and William H. Meckling. 1976. "Theory of the Firm: Managerial Behavior, Agency Costs and Ownership Structure." *Journal of Financial Economics* 3 (4): 305–60.

Jones, Jeffrey W. 2008. *Everyday Life and the "Reconstruction" of Soviet Russia during and after the Great Patriotic War, 1943–1948.* Bloomington, IN: Slavica.

Jones, Polly. 2006. "Introduction: The Dilemmas of De-Stalinization." In Polly Jones, ed., *The Dilemmas of De-Stalinization: Negotiating Cultural and Social Change in the Khrushchev Era,* 1–18. Abingdon: Routledge.

———. 2006a. "From the Secret Speech to the Burial of Stalin: Real and Ideal Responses to De-Stalinization." In Polly Jones, ed., *The Dilemmas of De-Stalinization: Negotiating Cultural and Social Change in the Khrushchev Era,* 41–63. Abingdon: Routledge.

Jozsa, Gyula. 1983. "Political *Seilschaften* in the USSR." In T.H. Rigby and B. Harasymiw, *Leadership Selection and Patron–Client Relations in the USSR and Yugoslavia,* 139–73. Hemel Hempstead: Allen and Unwin.

Kaiser, Claire P. 2016. "'A Kind of Silent Protest'? Deciphering Georgia's 1956." In Timothy K. Blauvelt and Jeremy Smith, eds., *Georgia after Stalin: Nationalism and Soviet Power,* 92–115. Abingdon: Routledge.

Kaplan, Cynthia S. 1985. "The Impact of World War II on the Party." In Susan Linz, ed., *The Impact of World War II on the Soviet Union*, 157–87. Totowa, NJ: Rowman and Allanheld.

Kassof, Allen. 1964. "The Administered Society: Totalitarianism without Terror." *World Politics* 16 (4): 558–75.

Kelly, Catriona. 2001. *Refining Russia: Advice Literature, Polite Culture, and Gender from Catherine to Yeltsin.* Oxford: Oxford University Press.

———. 2011. "'The Leningrad Affair': Remembering the 'Communist Alternative' in the Second Capital." *Slavonica* 17 (2): 103–22.

———. 2014. *St. Petersburg: Shadows of the Past.* New Haven: Yale University Press.

Kemoklidze, Nino. 2016. "Georgian–Abkhaz Relations in the post-Stalin Era." In Timothy K. Blauvelt and Jeremy Smith, eds., *Georgia after Stalin: Nationalism and Soviet Power*, 129–45. Abingdon: Routledge.

Kharkhordin, Oleg. 1999. *The Collective and the Individual in Russia: A Study in Practices.* Berkeley: University of California Press.

Khlevniuk, Oleg. 2003. "Sistema tsentr-regiony v 1930–1950-e gody. Predposylki politizatsii 'nomenklatury.'" *Cahiers du Monde Russe* 44 (2–3): 253–68.

———. 2007. "Regional'naia vlast' v SSSR v 1953-kontse 1950-kh godov. Ustoichivost' i konflikty." *Otechestvennaia Istoriia* no.3: 31–49.

———. 2011. "The Economy of Illusions: The Phenomenon of Data-Inflation in the Khrushchev Era." In Jeremy Smith and Melanie Ilic, eds., *Khrushchev in the Kremlin: Policy and Government in the Soviet Union, 1953–1964*, 171–89. Abingdon: Routledge.

———. 2012. "Rokovaia reforma N. S. Khrushcheva: razdelenie partiinogo apparata i ego posledstviia. 1962–1964 gody." *Rossiiskaia Istoriia* 4: 164–79.

———. 2016. "Kremlin—Tbilisi: Purges, Control and Georgian Nationalism in the First Half of the 1950s." In Timothy K. Blauvelt and Jeremy Smith, eds., *Georgia after Stalin: Nationalism and Soviet Power*, 13–31. Abingdon: Routledge.

———. 2016a. "Nomenklaturnaia revolutsiia: regional'nye rukovoditeli v SSSR v 1936–1939 gg." *Rossiiskaia Istoriia* 5: 36–52.

———. 2018. "Decentralizing Dictatorship: Soviet Local Governance during World War II." *Russian Review* 77 (2): 470–84.

Kibita, Nataliya. 2011. "Moscow–Kiev Relations and the *Sovnarkhoz* Reform." In Jeremy Smith and Melanie Ilic, eds., *Khrushchev in the Kremlin: Policy and Government in the Soviet Union, 1953–1964*, 94–111. Abingdon: Routledge.

———. 2013. *Soviet Economic Management under Khrushchev. The Sovnarkhoz Reform*. Abingdon: Routledge.

———. 2014. "De-Stalinizing Economic Administration: The Alternative Version in Ukraine (1953–1965)." In Thomas M. Bohn, Rayk Einax, and Michel Abesser, eds., *De-Stalinization Reconsidered: Persistence and Change in the Soviet Union*, 161–73. Frankfurt: Campus Verlag.

Kldiashvili, Giorgi. 2016. "Nationalism after the March 1956 Events and the Origins of the National-Independence Movement in Georgia." In Timothy K. Blauvelt and Jeremy Smith, eds., *Georgia after Stalin: Nationalism and Soviet Power*, 77–91. Abingdon: Routledge.

Klimenko, I. Ie. 2000. *Dumy o bylom*. Smolensk: Soiuz zhurnalistov Smolenskoi oblasti.

Knight, Jack. 1992. *Institutions and Social Conflict*. Cambridge: Cambridge University Press.

Knoke, David. 1990. *Political Networks: The Structural Perspective*. New York: Cambridge University Press.

Kommunisticheskaia partiia Sovetskogo Soiuza v rezoliutsiiakh i resheniiakh s"ezdov, konferentsii i plenumov TsK (1898–1986). 1983–1987. 9th ed. 13 vols. Edited by A.G. Egorov and K.M. Bogoliubov. Moscow: Politizdat.

Konovalov, A.B. 2004. *Istoriia Kemerovskoi oblasti v biografiiakh partiinykh rukovoditelei (1943–1991)*. Kemerovo: Kuzbassvuzidat.

———. 2006. *Partiinaia nomenklatura Sibiri v sisteme regional'noi vlasti (1945–1991)*. Kemerovo: Kuzbassvuzidat.

Kornai, Janos. 1980. *The Economics of Shortage*. Amsterdam: North Holland.

———. 1992. *The Socialist System: The Political Economy of Communism*. Princeton: Princeton University Press.

Korneev, V.E., and O.N. Kopylova. 1992. "Arkhivy na sluzhbe totalitarnogo gosudarstva (1918—nachalo 1940-hk gg.). *Otechestvennye arkhivy* 2: 13–24.

Kostyrchenko, G.V. 2001. *Tainaia politika Stalina. Vlast' i antisemitizm*. Moscow: Mezhdunarodnye otnosheniia.

Kotkin, Stephen. 1995. *Magnetic Mountain: Stalinism as a Civilization*. Berkeley: University of California Press.

———. 2008. *Armageddon Averted: The Soviet Collapse 1970–2000*. New York: Oxford University Press.

Kozlov, Vladimir A. 2002. *Mass Uprisings in the USSR: Protest and Rebellion in the Post-Stalin Years*. Translated and edited by E.M. Mackinnon. New York: M.E. Sharpe.

———. 2010. *Massovye besporiadki v SSSR pri Khrushcheve i Brezhneve. 1953—nachalo 1980-kh gg.* Moscow: Rosspen.

Kramola. Inakomyslie v SSSR pri Khrushcheve i Brezhneve 1953–1982 gg. Rassekrechennye dokumenty Verkhognogo suda in Prokuratury SSSR. 2005. Edited by V.A. Kozlov and S.V. Mironenko and compiled by O.V. Edel'man. Moscow: Materik.

Kto rukovodil NKVD. 1934–1941. Spravochnik. 1999. Compiled and edited by N.V. Petrov and K.V. Skorkin. Moscow: Zven'ia.

Kunaev, D.A. 1992. *O moem vremeni: vospominaniia.* Alma-Ata: Yntymak.

Kupriianov, G.N. 1989. "Svidetel'stvuiu." *Zvezda* (3): 170–78.

Laffont, Jean-Jacques, and David Martimort. 2002. *The Theory of Incentives: The Principal-Agent Model.* Princeton: Princeton University Press.

Lavrentii Beriia, 1953. Stenogramma iul'skogo plenuma Tsk KPSS i drugie dokumenty. 1999. Compiled by V. Naumov and Iu. Sigachev. Moscow: MFD.

Ledeneva, Alena V. 1998. *Russia's Economy of Favours: Blat, Networking and Informal Exchange.* Cambridge: Cambridge University Press.

———. 2004. "The Genealogy of *Krugovaia Poruka:* Forced Trust as a Feature of Russian Political Culture." In Ivana Markova, ed., *Trust and Democratic Transition in Post-Communist Europe,* 85–108. Oxford: Oxford University Press.

———. 2006. *How Russia Really Works: The Informal Practices that Shaped Post-Soviet Politics and Business.* Ithaca: Cornell University Press.

Leibovich, Oleg. 2008. *V gorode M. Ocherki sotsial'noi povsednevnosti sovetskoi provintsii.* Moscow: Rosspen.

Leningradskoe Delo. 1990. Compiled by V.I. Demidov and V. A. Kutuzov. Leningrad: Lenizdat.

Leonhard, Wolfgang. 1962. *The Kremlin since Stalin.* Oxford: Oxford University Press.

Leonid Brezhnev. Rabochie i dnevnikovye zapisi: v 3-kh tomakh. 2016. Compiled by A.S. Stepanov and A.V. Korotkov. Moscow: Istlit.

Levitsky, Steven R., and Lucan A. Way. 2002. "The Rise of Competitive Authoritarianism." *Journal of Democracy* 13 (2): 51–65.

———. 2010. *Competitive Authoritarianism: Hybrid Regimes after the Cold War.* Cambridge: Cambridge University Press.

———. 2012. "Beyond Patronage: Violent Struggle, Ruling Party Cohesion, and Authoritarian Durability." *Perspectives on Politics* 10 (4): 869–89.

———. 2015. "Not Just What, But When (and How): Comparative-Historical Approaches to Authoritarian Durability." In James Mahoney and Kathleen Thelen, eds., *Advances in Comparative-Historical Analysis,* 97–120. New York: Cambridge University Press.

———. 2016. "Durable Authoritarianism." In Orfeo Fioretos, Tulia G. Falleti, and Adam Sheingate, eds., *The Oxford Handbook of Comparative Institutionalism,* 208–22. Oxford: Oxford University Press.

Lewin, Moshe. 2003. "Rebuilding the Soviet Nomenklatura, 1945–1948." *Cahiers du Monde Russe* 44 (2–3): 219–52.

Liashko, A.P. 1997. *Gruz pamiati: Trilogiia. Vospominaniia.* 3 vols. Kiev: Delovaia Ukraina.

Lichnost' gosudarstvennogo masshtaba. Afanasii Fedorovich Eshtokin. 2000. Edited and compiled by G.V. Kornitskii and P.M. Dorofeev. Kemerovo. Sibirskii pisatel'.

Lietuviškoji nomenklatura 1956–1990 metais: tarp sovietinės sistemos ir neformalių praktikų. 2015. Compiled and edited by Saulius Grybkauskas. Vilnius: Aukso žuvys.

Linden, Carl A. 1990 [1966]. *Khrushchev and the Soviet Leadership: With an Epilogue on Gorbachev.* Baltimore: Johns Hopkins University Press.

Linz, Juan J. 2000 [1975]. *Totalitarian and Authoritarian Regimes.* Rev. ed. Boulder: Lynne Rienner.

Loader, Michael. 2015. "Khrushchev's Thaw in Soviet Latvia: National Politics 1953–1961." Ph.D. diss., King's College, London.

———. 2016. "Beria and Khrushchev: The Power Struggle over Nationality Policy and the Case of Latvia." *Europe-Asia Studies* 68 (10): 1759–92.

Lovell, Stephen. 2010. *The Shadow of War: Russia and the USSR, 1941 to the Present.* Chichester: Wiley Blackwell.

Lubianka: Organy VChK—OGPU—NKVD—NKGB—MGB—MVD—KGB 1917–1991. Spravochnik. 2003. Compiled by A.I. Kokurin and N.V. Petrov. Moscow: Materik.

Lubianka: Stalin i glavnoe upravlenie gosbezopasnosti NKVD 1937–1938. 2004. Compiled by V.N. Khaustov, V.P. Naumov, and N.S. Plotnikov. Moscow: Materik.

Luhmann, Niklas. 1988. "Familiarity, Confidence, Trust: Problems and Alternatives." In Diego Gambetta, ed., *Trust: Making and Breaking Cooperative Relations,* 94–107. Oxford: Basil Blackwell.

Magaloni, Beatriz. 2006. *Voting for Autocracy: Hegemonic Party Survival and Its Demise in Mexico.* New York: Cambridge University Press.

———. 2008. "Credible Power-Sharing and the Longevity of Authoritarian Rule." *Comparative Political Studies* 41 (4–5): 715–41.

Magaloni, Beatriz, and Ruth Kricheli. 2010. "Political Order and One-Party Rule." *Annual Review of Political Science* 13: 123–43.

Mahoney, James, and Kathleen Thelen, eds. 2010. *Explaining Institutional Change: Ambiguity, Agency, and Power.* New York: Cambridge University Press.

———. 2010a. "A Theory of Gradual Institutional Change." In James Mahoney and Kathleen Thelen, eds., *Explaining Institutional Change:*

Ambiguity, Agency, and Power, 1–37. New York: Cambridge University Press.

Markevich, Andrei, and Ekaternia Zhuravskaya. 2011. "M-form Hierarchy with Poorly-Diversified Divisions: The Case of Khrushchev's Reform in Soviet Russia." *Journal of Public Economics* 95 (11–12): 1550–60.

Martin, Terry. 2001a. *The Affirmative Action Empire: Nations and Nationalism in the Soviet Union, 1923–1939*. Ithaca: Cornell University Press.

———. 2001b. "The Affirmative Action Empire: The Soviet Union as the Highest Form of Imperialism." In Ronald Grigor Suny and Terry Martin, eds., *A State of Nations: Empire and Nation-Making in the Age of Lenin and Stalin*, 67–90. New York: Oxford University Press.

Matsuzato, K., and A.B. Shatilova, eds. 1997. *Regiony Rossii: khronika i rukovoditeli*, vols. 1–6. Sapporo, Japan: Slavic Center, Hokkaido University.

Mawdsley, Evan, and Stephen White. 2000. *The Soviet Elite from Lenin to Gorbachev: The Central Committee and Its Members, 1917–1991*. Oxford: Oxford University Press.

McAuley, Mary. 1974. "Hunting the Hierarchy: RSFSR Obkom Secretaries and the Central Committee." *Soviet Studies* 26 (4): 473–501.

McCormick, John P. 2004. "From Constitutional Technique to Caesarist Ploy: Carl Schmitt on Dictatorship, Liberalism, and Emergency Powers." In Peter Baehr and Melvin Richter, eds., *Dictatorship in History and Theory: Bonapartism, Caesarism, and Totalitarianism*, 197–219. Cambridge: Cambridge University Press.

Merl, Stephan. 2014. "Political Communication under Khrushchev: Did the Basic Modes Really Change after Stalin's Death?" In Thomas M. Bohn, Rayk Einax, and Michel Abesser, eds., *De-Stalinization Reconsidered: Persistence and Change in the Soviet Union*, 65–82. Frankfurt: Campus Verlag.

Mertsalov, V.I. 2015. *Proiskhozhdenie i evolutsiia reform upravleniia promyshlennost'iu i stroitel'stvom 1957–1965 gg*. Chita: Zabaikal'skii gosardsvennyi universitet.

Meyerzon, Svetlana. 2004. "The Center versus Its Periphery: Nikita Khrushchev, Dinmukhamed Kunaev, and the Emergence of the Kazakh Political Elite, 1953–1971." MA thesis, Harvard University.

Mgnoveniia zhizni. Anatolii Semenovich Drygin v vospominaniiakh sovremennikov. 2006. Edited and compiled by V.E. Pozgalev. Vologda: Vologodskaia nedelia.

Millar, James R. 1985. "The Little Deal: Brezhnev's Contribution to Acquisitive Socialism." *Slavic Review* 44 (4): 694–706.

———, ed. 1992. *Cracks in the Monolith: Party Power in the Brezhnev Era*. Armonk, NY: M.E. Sharpe.

Miller, John, H. 1977. "Cadres Policy in Nationality Areas: Recruitment of CPSU First and Second Secretaries in Non-Russian Republics of the USSR." *Soviet Studies* 29 (1): 3–36.

———. 1983. "Nomenklatura: A Check on Localism?" In T.H. Rigby and B. Harasymiv, eds., *Leadership Selection and Patron–Client Relations in the USSR and Yugoslavia*, 15–61. London: George Allen.

Miller, Robert F. 1984. "Khrushchev and the Soviet Economy: Management by Re-Organization." In R.F. Miller and F. Féhér, eds., *Khrushchev and the Communist World*, 108–38. London: Croom Helm.

Mirrlees, James A. 1976. "The Optimal Structure of Incentives and Authority within an Organization." *Bell Journal of Economics* 7 (1): 105–31.

Mitrokhin, Nikolai. 2003. *Russkaia partiia: Dvizhenie russkikh natsionalistov v SSSR 1953–1985*. Moscow: Novoe literaturnoe obozrenie.

———. 2009. "'Zakrytye' sovetskie obshestva." *Novoe Literaturnoe obozrenie* (6): 607–30.

———. 2011. "The Rise of Political Clans in the Era of Nikita Khrushchev: The First Phase, 1953–1959." In Jeremy Smith and Melanie Ilic, eds., *Khrushchev in the Kremlin: Policy and Government in the Soviet Union, 1953–1964*, 26–40. Abingdon: Routledge.

Mlechin, Leonid. 2005. *Brezhnev*. Moscow: Prospekt.

Moe, Terry. 1984. "The New Economics of Organization." *American Journal of Political Science* 28 (4): 739–77.

———. 2005. "Power and Political Institutions." *Perspectives on Politics* 3 (2): 215–33.

Molotov, Malenkov, Kaganovich. 1957. Stenogramma iun'skogo plenuma TsK KPSS i drugie dokumenty. 1998. Compiled by N. Kovaleva, A. Korotkov, S. Mel'chin, Iu. Sigachev, and A. Stepanov. Moscow: MFD.

Moore, Barrington. 1950. *Soviet Politics—The Dilemma of Power*. Cambridge: Harvard University Press.

———. 1954. *Terror and Progress—USSR: Some Sources of Change and Stability in the Soviet Dictatorship*. Cambridge: Harvard University Press.

———. 1967. *Social Origins of Dictatorship and Democracy: Lord and Peasant in the Modern World*. London: Allen Lane.

Morgun, F.T. 1975. *Khleb i liudi*. 2nd ed. Moscow: Politizdat.

Morse, Yonatan L. 2012. "The Era of Electoral Authoritarianism." *World Politics* 64 (1): 161–98.

Moses, Joel C. 1974. *Regional Party Leadership and Policy-Making in the USSR*. New York: Praeger.

———. 1976. "Regional Cohorts and Political Mobility in the USSR: The Case of Dnepropetrovsk." *Soviet Union* 3 (1): 63–91.

———. 1981. "The Impact of Nomenklatura in Soviet Regional Recruitment." *Soviet Union* 8 (1): 62–102.

———. 1985. "Regionalism in Soviet Politics: Continuity as a Source of Change, 1953–1982." *Soviet Studies* 37 (2): 184–211.

———. 2008. "Who Has Led Russia? Russian Regional Political Elites, 1954–2006." *Europe-Asia Studies* 60 (1): 1–24.

Mukhitdinov, N. 1994. *Gody, provedennye v Kremle.* Tashkent: Izdatel'stvo narodnogo naslediia im. A. Kadyri.

Myerson, Roger B. 2008. "The Autocrat's Credibility Problem and Foundations of the Constitutional State." *American Political Science Review* 102 (1): 125–39.

Neizvestnaia Rossiia. XX vek. 1992–94. Compiled by V. A. Kozlov and S.M. Zav'ialov. 4 vols. Moscow: Istoricheskoe nasledie.

N.G. Egorychev—Politik i Diplomat. 2006. Compiled and edited by G.A. Iudinkova and N.N. Egoricheva. Moscow: Kniga i biznes.

Nicolet, Claude. 2004. "Dictatorship in Rome." In Peter Baehr and Melvin Richter, eds., *Dictatorship in History and Theory: Bonapartism, Caesarism, and Totalitarianism,* 263–78. Cambridge: Cambridge University Press.

Nikita Khrushchev: 1964, Dokumenty. 2007. Compiled by A.N. Artizov, V.P. Naumov, M.Iu. Prozumenshchikov, Iu.V. Sigachev, N.G. Tomilina, and I.N. Shevchuk. Moscow: Materik.

Nikonorova, Tat'iana. 2015. "Komissiia partiinogo kontrolia pri TsK VKP(b) (1934–1952)." *Rossiikaia istoriia* 6: 26–40.

North, Douglass C. 1990. *Institutions, Institutional Change and Economic Performance.* New York: Cambridge University Press.

North, Douglass C., and Barry Weingast. "Constitutions and Commitment: The Evolution of Institutions Governing Public Choice in Seventeenth-Century England." *Journal of Economic History* 49 (9): 803–32.

Nove, Alec. 1989. *An Economic History of the USSR.* 2nd ed. Reading, Berks.: Pelican.

Nuriev, Z.N. 2000. *Ot aula do Kremlia.* Ufa: Kitap.

Obshchestvo i vlast.' Rossiiskaia provintsiia. 1917–1985. Dokumenty i materialy. Cheliabinskaia oblast.' 2006. 2 vols. Cheliabinsk: Institut istorii i arkheologii Ural'skogo otdeleniia RAN.

Oliver, James H. 1973. "Turnover and Family Circles in Soviet Administration." *Slavic Review* 32 (3): 527–45.

Olson, Mancur. 1993. "Dictatorship, Democracy, and Development." *American Political Science Review* 87 (3): 567–76.

———. 2000. *Power and Prosperity: Outgrowing Communist and Capitalist Dictatorships.* New York: Basic Books.

Osokina, Elena. 2001. *Our Daily Bread: Socialist Distribution and the Art of Survival in Russia, 1927–1941.* Edited and translated by Kate Transchel. Armonk, NY: M.E. Sharpe.

Patolichev, N.S. 1977. *Ispitanie na zrelost'.* Moscow: Politizdat.

Pethybridge, Roger W. 1962. *A Key to Soviet Politics: The Crisis of the "Anti-Party" Group*. London: George Allen and Unwin.

Pierson, Paul. 2004. *Politics in Time: History, Institutions, and Social Analysis*. Princeton: Princeton University Press.

Pikhoia, Rudolf G. 1998. *Sovetskii Soiuz. Istoriia vlasti. 1945–1991*. Moscow: Izdatel'stvo RAGS.

Plenum Tsentral'nogo komiteta kommunisticheskoi partii sovetskogo soiuza 10–18 ianvaria 1961 g. 1961. Moscow: Politizdat.

Podkur, Roman. 2008. "Pervyi sekretar' Vinnitskogo obkoma partii P.P. Kozyr' v formirovanii i funktsionirovanii oblastnoi uprvalencheskoi seti." Unpublished paper at http://personalpages.manchester.ac.uk/staff/yoram.gorlizki/sovietprovinces/documents/Romanpaper.pdf.

Poe, Steven C., and C. Neal Tate. 1994. "Repression of Human Rights to Personal Integrity in the 1980s: A Global Analysis." *American Political Science Review* 88 (4): 853–72.

Poe, Steven C., C. Neal Tate, and Linda Camp Keith. 1999. "Repression of the Human Right to Personal Integrity Revisited: A Global Cross-National Study Covering the Years 1976–1993." *International Studies Quarterly* 43 (2): 291–313.

Pogrebniak, Ia. 1999. *Ne predam zabveniu: Zapiski professional'nogo partiinogo rabotnika*. Kiev: IPTs "Letopis'—XX."

Politbiuro i delo Beriia. Sbornik dokumentov. 2012. Compiled and edited by O.B. Mazokhin. Moscow: Kuchkogo pole.

Politbiuro Tsk VKP(b) i Sovet Ministrov SSSR 1945–1953. 2002. Compiled by O.V. Khlevniuk, I. Gorlitskii (Y. Gorlizki), L.P. Kosheleva, A.I. Miniuk, M.Iu. Prozumenshchikov, L.A. Rogovaia, and S.V. Somonova. Moscow: Rosspen.

Politicheskoe rukovodstvo Ukrainy 1938–1989. 2006. Compiled by V.Iu. Vasil'ev, R.Iu. Podkur, Kh. Kuromiia [Hiroaki Kuromiya], Iu.I. Shapoval, and A. Vainer [Amir Weiner]. Moscow: Rosspen.

Popov, V.P. 1993. *Rossiiskaia derevnia posle voiny (iun' 1945—mart 1953): Sbornik dokumentov*. Moscow: "Prometei."

Postanovleniia Sovet Ministrov. 1961. GARF.

Prezidium Tsk KPSS 1954–1964. Chernovye protokol'nye zapisi zasedanii: Stenogrammy. Postanonvleniia. 3 vols. [2003, 2006, 2008]. Edited by A.A. Fursenko. Moscow: Rosspen.

Prigge, William D. 2015. *Bearslayers: The Rise and Fall of the Latvian National Communists*. New York: Peter Lang.

Przeworski, Adam, Michael E. Alvarez, José Antonio Cheibub, and Fernando Limongi. 2000. *Democracy and Development: Political Institutions and Well-Being in the World, 1950–1990*. New York: Cambridge University Press.

Rakowska-Harmstone, Teresa. 1972. "The Dialectics of Nationalism in the USSR." *Problems of Communism* 23 (3): 1–22.

Raleigh, Donald J., ed. 2001. *Provincial Landscapes: Local Dimensions of Soviet Power, 1917–1953.* Pittsburgh: University of Pittsburgh Press.

Rauch, James. 2001. "Business and Social Networks in International Trade." *Journal of Economic Literature* 39 (4): 1177–1203.

Reabilitatsiia. Politicheskie protsessy 30–50-kh godov. 1991. Compiled by I.V. Kurilov, N.N. Mikhailov, and V.P. Naumov. Moscow: Politizdat.

Reabilitatsiia: kak eto bylo. Dokumenty Prezidiuma TsK KPSS i drugie materialy. Mart 1953-fevral' 1956. 2 vols [2000, 2003]. Compiled by A. Artizov, Iu. Sigachev, I. Shevchuk, and V. Khlopov. Moscow: MFD.

Regional'naia politika N.S. Khrushcheva: TsK KPSS i mestnye partiinye komitety 1953–1964 gg. 2009. Compiled by O.V. Khlevniuk, M.Iu. Prozumenshchikov, V.Iu. Vasil'ev, I. Gorlitski [Y. Gorlizki], T.Iu. Zhukova, V.V. Kondrashin, L.P. Kosheleva, R.A. Podkur, and E.V. Sheveleva. Moscow: Rosspen.

Reid, Susan. 2002. "Cold War in the Kitchen: Gender and the De-Stalinization of Consumer Taste in the Soviet Union under Khrushchev." *Slavic Review* 61 (2): 211–52.

Reisinger, William M., and John P. Willerton Jr. 1988. "Elite Mobility in the Locales: Towards a Modified Patronage Model." In David Lane, ed., *Elites and Political Power in the USSR,* 99–126. Aldershot: Edward Elgar.

Reuter, Ora John, and Jennifer Gandhi. 2010. "Economic Performance and Elite Defection from Hegemonic Parties." *British Journal of Political Science* 41 (1): 83–110.

Reuter, Ora John, and Graeme B. Robertson. 2012. "Subnational Appointments in Authoritarian Regimes: Evidence from Russian Gubernatorial Appointments." *Journal of Politics* 74 (6): 1023–37.

Rigby, T.H. 1954. "The Selection of Leading Personnel in the Soviet State and Communist Party." Ph.D. diss., University of London. (Chapters 7 and 8 reproduced as "The Nomenklatura and Patronage under Stalin," in Rigby [1990], *Political Elites,* 94–126.)

———. 1959. "Khrushchev and the Resuscitation of the Central Committee." *Australian Outlook* 13 (1): 165–80. (Reproduced in T.H. Rigby [1990], *Political Elites,* 147–64.)

———. 1968. *Communist Party Membership in the USSR.* Princeton: Princeton University Press.

———. 1970. "The Soviet Leadership: Towards a Self-Stabilizing Oligarchy?" *Soviet Studies* 22 (2): 167–91.

———. 1972. "The Soviet Politburo: A Comparative Profile, 1951–1971." *Soviet Studies* 24 (1): 3–23.

————. 1976. "Soviet Communist Party Membership under Brezhnev." *Soviet Studies* 28 (3): 317–37.

————. 1978. "The Soviet Regional Leadership: The Brezhnev Generation." *Slavic Review* 37 (1): 1–24.

————. 1979. "The Need for Comparative Research on Clientelism: Concluding Comments." *Studies in Comparative Communism* 12 (2–3): 204–11.

————. 1980. "How the Obkom Secretary Was Tempered," *Problems of Communism* 29 (3): 57–63.

————. 1981. "Early Provincial Cliques and the Rise of Stalin." *Soviet Studies* 33 (1): 3–28.

————. 1983. "Introduction." In Rigby and B. Harasymiw, eds, *Leadership Selection and Patron–Client Relations in the USSR and Yugoslavia*, 1–11. London: George Allen.

————. 1984. "Khrushchev and the Rules of the Game." In R.F. Miller and F. Feher, eds., *Khrushchev and the Communist World*, 39–81. London: Croom Helm.

————. 1990. *Political Elites in the USSR: Central Leaders and Local Cadres from Lenin to Gorbachev.* Aldershot: Edward Elgar.

Rigby, T.H., and B. Harasymiw, eds. 1983. *Leadership Selection and Patron–Client Relations in the USSR and Yugoslavia*. London: George Allen.

Roeder, Philip G. 1993. *Red Sunset: The Failure of Soviet Politics.* Princeton: Princeton University Press.

Rosenberg, Hans. 1958. *Bureaucracy, Aristocracy, and Autocracy: The Prussian Experience 1660–1815.* Boston: Beacon Press.

Ross, Stephen A. 1973. "The Economic Theory of Agency: The Principal's Problem." *American Economic Review* 63 (2): 134–39.

Roth, Guenther. 1968. "Personal Rulership, Patrimonialism, and Empire-Building in the New States." *World Politics* 20 (2): 194–206.

Rubtsov, Iu.V. 2002. "Reviziia Mingoskontrolia SSSR 1948 goda v Azerbaidzhane: revansh praviashchei elity." *Otechestvennaia istoriia*, no. 2 (2002): 158–61.

Rush, Myron. 1958. *The Rise of Khrushchev.* Washington, DC: Public Affairs Press.

Rutland, Peter. 1993. *The Politics of Economic Stagnation in the Soviet Union: The Role of Local Party Organs in Economic Management.* Cambridge: Cambridge University Press.

Saller, Richard P. 1982. *Personal Patronage under the Early Empire.* Cambridge: Cambridge University Press.

Saloshenko, Viktor. 2002. *Predsedateli i gubernatory: Vzaimosviaz' vremen.* Krasnodar: Severnii kavkaz.

Samuelson, Lennart. 2011. *Tankograd, The Formation of a Soviet Company Town: Cheliabinsk, 1900s–1950s*. Basingstoke: Palgrave Macmillan.

Schattenberg, Susanne. 2015. "Trust, Care, and Familiarity in the Politburo: Brezhnev's Scenario of Power." *Kritika* 16 (4): 835–58.

———. 2018. *Leonid Brezhnev: Velichie i tragediia cheloveka i strany*. Moscow: Rosspen.

Schedler, Andreas. 2013. *The Politics of Uncertainty: Sustaining and Subverting Electoral Authoritarianism*. Oxford: Oxford University Press.

Schelling, Thomas C. 1960. *The Strategy of Conflict*. Cambridge: Harvard University Press.

Schull, Joseph. 1992. "What Is Ideology? Theoretical Problems and Lessons from Soviet-Type Societies." *Political Studies* 40 (4): 728–41.

———. 1993. "The Self-Destruction of Soviet Ideology." In Susan Solomon, ed., *Beyond Sovietology: Essays in Politics and History*, 8–22. Armonk, NY: M.E. Sharpe.

Scott, John. 2000. *Social Network Analysis*. 2nd ed. Thousand Oaks, CA: Sage.

Semenov V.B. 1997. "'Leningradskoe delo' v Penze." *Kraevedenie* [Penza]: 47–50.

Semichastny, Vladimir. 2002. *Bespokoinoe serdtse*. Moscow: Vagrius.

Sharafutdinova, Gulnaz. 2009. "Subnational Governance in Russia: How Putin Changed the Contract with His Agents and the Problems It Created for Medvedev." *Publius: The Journal of Federalism* 40 (4): 672–96.

Shearer, David R. 2009. *Policing Stalin's Socialism: Repression and Social Order in the Soviet Union, 1924–1953*. New Haven: Yale University Press.

Shearer, David R., and Vladimir Khaustov. 2015. *Stalin and the Lubianka: A Documentary History of the Political Police and the Security Organs in the Soviet Union, 1922–1953*. New Haven: Yale University Press.

Shelest, P.E. 1995. *"Da sudimy budete." Dnevnikovye zapisi, vospominaniia chlena Politbiuro TsK KPSS*. Moscow: Edition q.

Shepilov, Dmitrii. 2007. *The Kremlin's Scholar: A Memoir of Soviet Politics under Stalin and Khrushchev*. New Haven: Yale University Press.

Shevchenko, V.S. 2005. *Moi lita, moe bagatstvo: Spogadi, rozdumy, vypovydi*. Kiev: Prosvita.

Shul'gina, O.V. 2005. "Administrativno-territorial'noe delenie Rossii v XX veke." *Voprosy istorii*, no. 4: 23–38.

Simon, Gerhard. 1991. *Nationalism and Policy Toward the Nationalities in the Soviet Union: From Totalitarian Dictatorship to Post-Stalinist Society*. Translated by Karen Forster and Oswald Forster. Boulder: Westview.

Sizov, L.G. 2000. *Vse ostaietsia liudiam*. 2 vols. Krasnoiarsk: Platina.

Slater, Dan. 2010. *Ordering Power: Contentious Politics and Authoritarian Leviathans in Southeast Asia*. New York: Cambridge University Press.

———. 2010a. "Altering Authoritarianism: Institutional Complexity and Autocratic Agency in Indonesia." In James Mahoney and Kathleen Thelen, eds., *Explaining Institutional Change: Ambiguity, Agency, and Power*, 132–67. New York: Cambridge University Press.

Smeliakov, N.N. 1975. *S chego nachinaetsia Rodina: Vospominaniia i razdum'ia*. Moscow: Politizdat.

Smirnov, N.G. 2005. *Na virazhakh vremeni*. Iuzhno-Sakhalinsk: "Lukomor'e."

Smith, Anthony E. 1986. *The Ethnic Origins of Nations*. Oxford: Basil Blackwell.

Smith, Benjamin. 2005. "Life of the Party: The Origins of Regime Breakdown and Persistence under Single-Party Rule." *World Politics* 57 (3): 421–51.

Smith, G.A.E. 1987. "Agriculture." In Martin McAuley, ed., *Khrushchev and Khrushchevism*, 95–117. Bloomington: Indiana University Press.

Smith, Jeremy. 2013. *Red Nations: The Nationalities Experience in and after the USSR*. Cambridge: Cambridge University Press.

———. 2016. "Conclusion: Georgian Nationalism after 1956." In Timothy K. Blauvelt and Jeremy Smith, eds., *Georgia after Stalin: Nationalism and Soviet Power*, 146–51. Abingdon: Routledge.

Smith, Kathleen E. 2017. *Moscow 1956: The Silenced Spring*. Cambridge: Harvard University Press.

Smith, Mark B. 2010. *Property of Communists: The Urban Housing Program from Stalin to Khrushchev*. Dekalb: Northern Illinois University Press.

Sokolov, B.V. 2004. *Leonid Brezhnev. Zolotaia epokha*. Moscow: AST-Press.

Solomon, Peter H., Jr. 1992. "Soviet Politicians and Criminal Prosecutions: The Logic of Party Intervention." In James R. Millar, ed., *Cracks in the Monolith: Party Power in the Brezhnev Era*, 3–32. Armonk, NY: M.E. Sharpe.

———. 1996. *Soviet Criminal Justice under Stalin*. Cambridge: Cambridge University Press.

Sovetskaia zhizn' 1945–1953. 2003. Compiled by E.Iu. Zubkova, L.P. Kosheleva, G.A. Kuznetsova, A.I. Miniuk, and L.A. Rogovaia. Moscow: Rosspen.

Sovetskaia natsional'naia politika: ideologiia i praktiki 1945–1953. 2013. Compiled by L.P. Kosheleva, O.V. Khlevniuk, V. Denningkhaus (Victor Denninghaus), Dj. Kadio (Juliette Cadiot), M.Iu. Prozumenshchikov, L.A. Rogovaia, A.E. Svennitskaia, Dj. Smit (Jeremy Smith), and E.V. Sheveleva. Moscow: Rosspen.

Spravochnik Partiinogo rabotnika. 1967, 1968. 7th and 8th eds. Moscow: Politizdat.

Statiev, Alexander. 2010. *The Soviet Counterinsurgency in the Western Borderlands.* Cambridge: Cambridge University Press.

Stewart, Philip D. 1968. *Political Power in the Soviet Union: A Study of Decision-Making in Stalingrad.* Indianapolis: Bobbs Merrill.

Stewart, Philip D., et al. 1972. "Political Mobility and the Soviet Political Process: A Partial Test of Two Models." *American Political Science Review* 66 (4): 1269–94.

Stiglitz, Joseph E. 1989. "Principal and Agent." In John Eatwell, Murray Milgate, and Peter Newman, eds., *The New Palgrave: Allocation, Information, and Markets,* 241–53. New York: W.W. Norton.

Stoner-Weiss, Kathryn. 1997. *Local Heroes: The Political Economy of Russian Regional Governance.* Princeton: Princeton University Press.

Streeck, Wolfgang, and Kathleen Thelen, eds. 2005. *Beyond Continuity: Institutional Change in Advanced Political Economies.* Oxford: Oxford University Press.

Stroitel'stvo kommunizma v SSSR i razvitie sel'ksogo khoziaistva. 1962–64. Speeches and writings of N.S. Khrushchev. 8 vols. Moscow: Politizdat.

Suny, Ronald Grigor. 1993. *The Revenge of the Past: Nationalism, Revolution, and the Collapse of the Soviet Union.* Stanford: Stanford University Press.

Suny, Ronald Grigor, and Terry Martin. 2001. "Introduction." In Ronald Grigor Suny and Terry Martin, eds., *A State of Nations: Empire and Nation-Making in the Age of Lenin and Stalin,* 3–20. New York: Oxford University Press.

Sushkov, A.V. 2003. *Rukovoditeli Sverdlovskoi oblastnoi organizatsii VLKSM-LKSM RSFSR 1934–1992.* Ekaterinburg: Bank kul'turnoi informatsii.

———. 2009. *Prezidium TsK KPSS v 1957–1964 gg: lichnosti i vlast'.* Ekaterinburg: UrO RAN.

———. 2011. "Vlast' i korruptsiia: rukovodstvo Krasnoiarskogo kraia i delo o khischeniiakh produktsii na krasnoiarskom zavode plodovoiagodnykh vin (1949 g.)." *Ural'skii istoricheskii vestnik* 32 (3): 89–95.

———. 2015. " 'I boiatsia . . . kak by Zal'tsman ne ster v poroshok.' I. M. Zal'tsman i Cheliabinskaia partnomenklatura v seredine 1940-kh godov." *Vestnik Cheliabinskaia gosudarstennogo universiteta* 24 (379) [History series, 66]: 91–109.

Sushkov, A.V., N.A. Mikhalev, and E.Iu. Baranov. 2013. "Rasplata za sotsproiskhozhdenie: 'Delo' vtorogo sekretaria cheliabinskogo obkoma VKP (b) G.S. Pavlova 1950–1951 gody." *Vestnik Cheliabinskogo gosudartvennogo universiteta* 6 (297) [History series, 54]: 57–71.

Sushkov, A.V., and N.A. Mikhalev. 2015. "'Ia schitaiu dlia sebia pozorom sostoiat' chlenom takogo raikoma!' I. M. Zal'tsman i Cheliabinskaia partnomenklatura v seredine 1940-kh godov." *Vestnik Cheliabinskaia gosudarstennogo universiteta,* 14 (369) [History series, 64]: 94–108.

Sushkov, A.V., and S.L. Raznikov. 2003. *Rukovoditeli Sverdlovskoi oblasti: Pervye sekretari obkoma VKP(b)—KPSS i predsedetali oblispolkoma 1934–1991.* Ekaterinburg: Bank kul'turnoi informatsii.

Svolik, Milan W. 2012. *The Politics of Authoritarian Rule.* New York: Cambridge University Press.

Swearer, Howard R. 1962. "Changing Roles of the CPSU under First Secretary Khrushchev." *World Politics* 15 (1): 20–43.

Swietochowski, Tadeusz. 1995. *Russia and Azerbaijan: A Borderland in Transition.* New York: Columbia University Press.

Taranov, I.G. 1995. *Gody, liudi, vstrechi.* Stavropol': Knizhnoe izdatel'stvo.

Tatu, Michel. 1969. *Power in the Kremlin: From Khrushchev's Decline to Collective Leadership.* Translated by Helen Katel. London: Collins.

Taubman, William. 2003. *Khrushchev. The Man and His Era.* London: Free Press.

Thelen, Kathleen. 2003. "How Institutions Evolve: Insights from Comparative Historical Analysis." In James Mahoney and Dietrich Rueschemeyer, eds., *Comparative Historical Analysis in the Social Sciences,* 305–36. Cambridge: Cambridge University Press.

Thelen, Kathleen, and James Conran. 2016. "Institutional Change." In Orfeo Fioretos, Tulia G. Falleti, and Adam Sheingate, eds., *The Oxford Handbook of Historical Institutionalism,* 51–70. New York: Oxford University Press.

Tilly, Charles. 2005. *Trust and Rule.* New York: Cambridge University Press.

Titov, Alexander. 2011. "The Central Committee Apparatus under Khrushchev." In Jeremy Smith and Melanie Ilic, eds., *Khrushchev in the Kremlin: Policy and Government in the Soviet Union, 1953–1964,* 41–60. Abingdon: Routledge.

Tolz, Vera. 2011. *Russia's Own Orient. The Politics of Identity and Oriental Studies in the Late Imperial and Early Soviet Periods.* Oxford: Oxford University Press.

Tompson, William James. 1991. "Nikita Khrushchev and the Territorial Apparatus, 1953–1964." D.Phil. thesis, University of Oxford.

———. 2000. "Industrial Management and Economic Reform under Khrushchev." In William Taubman, Sergei Khrushchev, and Abbott Gleason, eds., *Nikita Khrushchev,* 138–59. New Haven: Yale University Press.

Triska, Jan F. 1968. *Constitutions of the Communist Party-States.* Stanford: Hoover Institution Press.

Trivellato, Francesca. 2009. *The Familiarity of Strangers: The Sephardic Diaspora, Livorno, and Cross-Cultural Trade in the Early Modern Period*. New Haven: Yale University Press.

Tromly, Benjamin. 2004. "The Leningrad Affair and Soviet Patronage Politics, 1949–1950." *Europe-Asia Studies* 56 (5): 707–29.

TsK VKP(b) i regional'nye partiinye komitety 1945–1953. 2004. Compiled by V.V. Denisov, A.V. Kvashonkin, L.N. Malashenko, A.I. Miniuk, M.Iu. Prozumenshchikov, and O.V. Klevniuk. Moscow: Rosspen.

Tucker, Robert C. 1971. "The Politics of Soviet De-Stalinization." In Robert C. Tucker, *The Soviet Political Mind: Stalinism and Post-Stalin Change*, 173–202. New York: Norton.

———. 1990. *Stalin in Power, 1928–1941: The Revolution from Above*. New York: W.W. Norton.

Tverdiukova, E.D. 2015. "Nemedlenno otmenit' vse nezakonnye formy snabzheniia": obespechenie sovetskoi regional'noi nomenklatury tovaramy shirokogo potrebleniia (1943–1947 gg.). *Trudy istoricheskogo fakul'teta Sankt-Peterburgskogo universiteta* (21): 254–71.

Urban, Michael E. 1989. *An Algebra of Soviet Power: Elite Circulation in the Belorussian Republic, 1966–1986*. Cambridge: Cambridge University Press.

V plameni zhizni: Kniga vospominanii o B.E. Shcherbine. 1990. Tiumen': Izdatel'stvo Iu. Mandriki.

Vaksberg, Arkady. 1991. *The Soviet Mafia*. London: Weidenfeld and Nicolson.

Vasiliev, Valery. 2011. "Failings of the Sovnarkhoz Reform: The Ukrainian Experience." In Jeremy Smith and Melanie Ilic, eds., *Khrushchev in the Kremlin: Policy and Government in the Soviet Union, 1953–1964*, 112–32. Abingdon: Routledge.

Voisin, Vanessa. 2011. "Caught between War Repressions and Party Purge: The Loyalty of Kalinin Party Members Put to the Test of the Second World War." *Cahiers du monde Russe* 52 (2–3): 341–72.

Vorotnikov, V.I. 2003. A bylo eto tak . . . Iz dnevnikov chlena Politbiuro TsK KPSS. 2nd ed. Moscow: Kniga i bizness.

Vrublevskii, V.K. 1993. *Vladimir Shcherbitskii: pravda i vymysli. Zapiski pomoshchnika: Vospominaniia, dokumenty, slukhi, legendy, fakty*. Kiev: Dovira.

Wädekin, Karl-Eugen. 1973. *The Private Sector in Soviet Agriculture*. Edited by George Karcz. Translated by Keith Bush. Berkeley: University of California Press.

Wasserman, Stanley, and Katherine Faust. 1994. *Social Networks Analysis: Methods and Applications*. Cambridge: Cambridge University Press.

Weiner, Amir. 2001. *Making Sense of War: The Second World War and the Fate of the Bolshevik Revolution*. Princeton: Princeton University Press.

Weiner, Amir, and Aigi Rahi-Tamm. 2012. "Getting to Know You: The Soviet Surveillance System, 1939–57." *Kritika* 13 (1): 5–45.

Willerton, John P. 1992. *Patronage and Politics in the USSR*. Cambridge: Cambridge University Press.

Wintrobe, Ronald. 1990. "The Tinpot and the Totalitarian: An Economic Theory of Dictatorship." *American Political Science Review* 84 (3): 849–72.

———. 1998. *The Political Economy of Dictatorship*. Cambridge: Cambridge University Press.

XXII S'ezd Kommunisticheskoi partii Sovetskogo Soiuza, 17–31 oktiabria 1961 goda. Stenograficheskii otchet. 1961. Moscow: Politizdat.

XXIV S'ezd Kommunisticheskoi partii Sovetskogo Soiuza, 30 marta–9 aprelia 1971 goda. Stenograficheskii otchet. 1971. Moscow: Politizdat.

XXV S'ezd Kommunisticheskoi partii Sovetskogo Soiuza, 25 fevralia–5 marta 1976 goda. Stenograficheskii otchet. 1976. Moscow: Politizdat.

Yanov, Alexander. 1984. *The Drama of the Soviet 1960s: A Lost Reform*. Berkeley: Institute of International Studies.

Yurchak, Aleksei. 2006. *Everything Was Forever, Until It Was No More: The Last Soviet Generation*. Princeton: Princeton University Press.

Zaleski, Eugene. 1980. *Stalinist Planning for Economic Growth, 1933–1952*. Translated and edited by Marie-Christine MacAndrew and John H. Moore. Chapel Hill: University of North Carolina Press.

Zaslavsky, Victor. 1982. *The Neo-Stalinist State: Class, Ethnicity, and Consensus in Soviet Society*. Armonk, NY: M.E. Sharpe.

Zaslavsky, Victor, and Robert J. Brym. 1978. "The Functions of Elections in the USSR." *Soviet Studies* 30 (2): 362–71.

Zezina, Maria. 2014. "De-Stalinization and Socialist Realism. The Union of Soviet Writers in the Period of the Thaw." In Thomas M. Bohn, Rayk Einax, and Michel Abesser, eds., *De-Stalinization Reconsidered: Persistence and Change in the Soviet Union*, 193–207. Frankfurt: Campus Verlag.

Zubkova, Elena. 1999a. "Kadrovaia politika i chistki v KPSS." *Svobodnaia mysl'* 3: 117–27.

———. 1999b. "Kadrovaia politika i chistki v KPSS." *Svobodnaia mysl'* 4: 96–110.

———. 1999c. "Kadrovaia politika i chistki v KPSS." *Svobodnaia mysl'* 5: 112–20.

———. 2000. *Poslevoennoe sovetskoe obshchestvo: Politika i povsednevnost'*. Moscow: Rosspen.

———. 2008. *Pribaltika i Kreml'. 1940–1953*. Moscow: Rosspen.

Zumakulov, B.M, S.N. Beituganov, and V.Zh. Kudaev. 2000. *Govoril tikho, slyshali vse*. Nal'chik: El'brus.

Acknowledgments

The publication of this book gives us a welcome opportunity to thank the friends, colleagues, and institutions who have helped to bring it into being. The original research project on which it is based was made possible by a large grant from the United Kingdom Economic and Social Research Council (ESRC), by ancillary awards from the British Academy and the Basic Research Program of the National Research University Higher School of Economics, and by periods of research leave from the University of Manchester.

We offer our warm thanks to Valery Vasil'ev, Viktor Kondrashin, and Roman Podkur for their invaluable research assistance on the project and to Liudmila Kosheleva, Galina Gorskaia, Mikhail Prozumenshchikov, and Tatiana Zhukova for guiding it so skillfully through the archives. For perceptive comments on draft chapters of the book our thanks go to Don Filtzer, Vladimir Gel'man, Mark Harrison, Rob Hornsby, Stephen Lovell, Peter Rutland, Vera Tolz, and Lynne Viola. Mark Harrison deserves special mention for his unfailing generosity over the years, and for giving us the initial germ of an idea about "networks and hierarchies" from which our application to the ESRC eventually grew. The editors of The Yale-Hoover Series on Authoritarian Regimes, Paul Gregory and Norman Naimark, were kind enough to show their support for an early version of the manuscript and to recommend it to the Yale University Press.

In Larry Kenney we have had a wonderfully exacting and supportive copy editor and in Mary Pasti a thorough and enthusiastic production editor, while Jaya Chatterjee and Ewa Skewes deserve praise for allowing us to adapt the format of the book to its interdisciplinary content. Full marks, too, to the press for finding two unusually congenial anonymous reviewers, one of whom, in seven pages of single-spaced text, provided a fund of ideas and suggestions which we have happily plundered in revising the manuscript.

For coding data and preparing the diagrams we are grateful to our able research assistant Darya Vanchugova, while for their help in tracing obscure and elusive volumes we take our hats off to the excellent Inter-Library Loans team at the University of Manchester Library: Claire Hordern, Shirley Haigh, Vicky Flood, and Vikki Garlick. Others who have helped with acts of kindness great and small are John Barber, Karel Berkhoff, V.W. Buskens, Nick Crossley, Rob Dale, Evgenii Dobrenko, Miriam Dobson, Victoria Donovan, Martin Everett, Sheila Fitzpatrick, Diego Gambetta, Jennifer Gandhi, Peter Gatrell, Klaus Gestwa, Sarah Green, Chris Gregory, Avner Greif, Saulius Grybkauskas, Jim Heinzen, Geoffrey Hosking, Catriona Kelly, Steve Kotkin, Alena Ledeneva, Mike Loader, Terry Martin, Evan Mawdsley, Alexei Miller, the late Mick Moran, Ben Nathans, Yaacov Ro'i, David Shearer, Jeremy Smith, Ron Suny, Bill Tompson, and Elisabeth Teague. For more reasons than we can easily say the book is dedicated, with love, to Vera, the wife and life companion of one of the authors and a dear friend of the other's.

Y.G. and O.Kh.
Manchester and Moscow

Index

Figures and tables are indicated by *f* and *t,* respectively, endnotes by *n,* and photographs by italicized page numbers.

Mel'nik, Andrei, 284–85
Mel'nikov, L.G., 124, 361*n*29
Merzlyi, Aleksandr, 302
Meshik, P.Ia., 124–25
methodology of study, 19–23; coding rules, 331; conflict-prone vs. calm regions, inclusion in study, 20–21; constraints, 23; contested autocrat model, 21–22, 338*n*11; first secretaries, uncovering support networks of, 23, 322–23; oblast (regional) focus and units of study, 21, 315–16; party governors and, 22–23; selection of case studies, 21, 317–18, 319–21*t*; units of analysis, 17–19
MGB (security police), 47–49, 73–78, 173, 349*n*61, 360*n*20, 364*n*2
Miasnikov, G.V., 238
migration, 9; rural areas, mobilization of specialists in, 245; Slavic migration to Latvia, 187
Mikoian, Anastas, 179, 230, 360*n*14, 369*n*16, 370*n*35
Military Collegium of the Supreme Court, 364*n*2
Mil'shtein, S., 124
Mingrelian Affair, 114, 122, 343*nn*66–67
Ministry of Internal Affairs (MVD), 120–26, 138
Minsk's Pukhovichskii district, 102
Mishkov, N.F., 284, 387*n*12, 388*n*14
Moldavia, 193, 357*n*59
Molotov, V.M., 131, 359*n*1, 360*n*14
Molotov region, 35, 48, 62, 101, 138, 366*n*57. *See also* Perm'
Molotov-Ribbentrop pact, 173, 368*n*5
Monashev, L.G., 242–43, 260
money reforms, 85, 103, 106, 356*n*41; expulsion due to subversion of, 47, 48, 349*n*63; protection from prosecution in, 110–12
Moore, Barrington, 340*n*27
Morozov (Alferov's obkom secretary), 87–88
Moscow, 269, 271–77, 274, 379*n*34, 385*n*53, 386*n*61
Moskvin, V.A., 160, 366*n*50
Mukhitdinov, Nuritdin, 182, 193
multiethnic state, 11–13; ethnic quotas for training and promotion purposes, 12; formation of national republics and, 11, 340*n*37; internal passports based

on ethnic descent, 12, 340*n*39. *See also* second secretaries: Slavic; substate nationalism
Murmansk, 87, 109, 378*n*27
Mustafaev, Imam, 182, 189, 191–92, 371*n*65, 372*nn*91–92, 372*n*94
MVD (Ministry of Internal Affairs), 120–26, 138, 360*n*20
Mzhavanadze, Vasily, 178, 180, 369*n*25

Nagorno-Karabagh, 187
Nakhichevan ASSR, 187
Nal'chik demonstration-cum-riot (1968), 285
nationalism. *See* Russian nationalism; substate nationalism
nationality, defined, 171
Nazarov, R.K., 32, 74–75, 79, 352*n*46
Nedosekin, V.I., 138, 156, 157
nepotism, 17, 49, 58, 62, 98, 114, 277, 289, 344*n*84
networks: ethnic, 12; narrow and asymmetric (under Stalin), 11, 19, 93, 169, 280, 304; network analysis, 395*nn*3–4; oligarchical networks in the regions, 154–55, 159, 323; party, 19, 395*n*7; political, 322–23; resilience of regional networks under Khrushchev, 227–28, 251; social, 322; Stalin and regional, 17–18, 86, 113–14, 277, 304; strategies of network formation, 3–4, 176, 280, 304; trust, 3, 17, 20, 215, 323; wide and shallow (under Brezhnev) 20, 277, 295, 301, 305
Nikitiuk, O.S., 390*n*79
Nikolaev, K.K., 238, 241–42
NKVD (People's Commissariat of Internal Affairs), 31, 36, 364*n*2
Nolinskii Affair, 389*n*47
nomenklatura, 3, 326–27, 335; Beria and, 123; Brezhnev and, 269; Central Committee, 30, 33, 133, 167, 329–30, 345*n*2, 346*n*14, 348*n*52; co-optation and, 99–105, 114, 276; disciplinary steps and, 46; home building for regional elites, 101–2, 356*n*51; institutional change under Khrushchev and, 230; in interregnum, 362*n*50; norms, 35, 49, 164, 240, 249; obkom, 47, 162, 168, 349*n*61; patronage system and, 19; promotion contract model, 105–6;